INTERNATIONAL RELATIONS

With my best
regards!

Andy

INTERNATIONAL RELATIONS

From the Cold War
to the Globalized World

Andreas Wenger
Doron Zimmermann

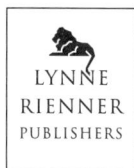

LYNNE
RIENNER
PUBLISHERS

BOULDER
LONDON

Published in the United States of America in 2003 by
Lynne Rienner Publishers, Inc.
1800 30th Street, Boulder, Colorado 80301
www.rienner.com

and in the United Kingdom by
Lynne Rienner Publishers, Inc.
3 Henrietta Street, Covent Garden, London WC2E 8LU

Library of Congress Cataloging-in-Publication Data
Wenger, Andreas.
    International relations : from the Cold War to the globalized world / Andreas Wenger
and Doron Zimmermann.
       p. cm.
    Includes bibliographical references and index.
    ISBN 1-58826-098-4 (hc : alk. paper)
    ISBN 1-58826-074-7 (pb : alk. paper)
       1. World politics—1945–   2. International relations.   3. Globalization.   4. Cold War.
    5. Post-communism.   6. Terrorism.   I. Zimmermann, Doron, 1970–   II. Title.
    D840.W14 2003
    909.82'5—dc21

                                                                                          2002030690

British Cataloguing in Publication Data
A Cataloguing in Publication record for this book
is available from the British Library.

Printed and bound in the United States of America

The paper used in this publication meets the requirements
of the American National Standard for Permanence of
Paper for Printed Library Materials Z39.48-1984.

   5   4   3   2   1

This book is dedicated to our wives

CONTENTS

PREFACE

THE COMMENTS OF MANY PUNDITS NOTWITHSTANDING, THE WORLD DID NOT undergo a fundamental change on 11 September 2001. Rather, the terrorist attacks on the World Trade Center and the Pentagon demonstrated just how complex international relations have become in the past decade. We have come a long way since World War II culminated in the de facto division of Europe in 1945. Since that time, we have, indeed, moved through the Cold War and forward, into the globalized world of the early twenty-first century.

Our book explores the political history of international relations from the end of World War II to the present. Distinctive to our approach is the application of an expanded conception of security policy; as we understand it, security studies embraces aspects of international relations well beyond the purely military perspective, ranging from economic and political issues to social and cultural concerns.

We have sought to provide a balanced account that reflects the shift away from the classical bipolar perspective of the Cold War. We incorporate the view from the "other"—the Soviet—side of the Cold War, as well as events in Asia, Africa, Latin America, and the Middle East, and our research has drawn on a broad, representative archival base. Issues concerning the third world are not confined to a single chapter, but pervade the entire text.

An assumption underlying our interpretation of more than fifty years of international relations is that events, ideas, and developments can be understood only within the context of their particular times. Thus, we have organized the text around several distinct epochs, identifying the specific characteristics and internal dynamics of each. In addition, we have integrated the history of political ideas within the narrative of each chapter and included brief, concise summaries of the key theories, concepts, and terms relevant to the discussion. (Key terms are also included in the comprehensive glossary, which begins on page 343.)

For students interested in further research, the selected bibliography offers an extensive listing of both print and electronic resources.

We hope that you will enjoy reading the book and that it will help, in at least some measure, to explain the complexities both of the recent past and the present.

* * *

In the course of writing this book, we have drawn on the time, knowledge, and critical faculties of our friends and colleagues at the Center for Security Studies—and beyond. Accordingly, we would like to express our sincere gratitude to several individuals. Luzius Mayer-Kurmann and Ulrich Gysel were there at the beginning and proved instrumental in the conceptual phase of the project. We would like to thank Christian Nünlist and Anna Locher of the Parallel History Project (www.isn.ethz.ch/php) for their critical feedback on issues concerning Soviet foreign policy, the Warsaw Pact, and more generally, Eastern Europe under Soviet rule. We were indeed fortunate to have an expert on the Soviet Union and the Russian Federation close at hand: Jeronim Perovic time and again agreed to scrutinize our drafts and share his insights with us. Christof Münger and Christian Nünlist read our entire manuscript and provided much appreciated criticism and recommendations for improvement; Christof Münger also helped choose many of the titles recommended in our bibliography. Two highly competent historians, Thomas Holderegger and Reto Wollenmann, provided us with invaluable advice on the NATO reform process in the late 1960s, for which we owe them our gratitude. Cornelius Friesendorf showed considerable patience in reviewing the "history of ideas" sections of the book and provided us with requisite critical feedback. Finally, Simon Ingold contributed the Internet links list.

INTERNATIONAL
RELATIONS

INTRODUCTION

ARGUABLY, THE ATTACKS AGAINST THE UNITED STATES ON 11 SEPTEMBER 2001 brought an unexpected close to the transitional phase that followed the end of the **Cold War**.* But if the destruction of the Twin Towers in lower Manhattan and the near simultaneous attack on the Pentagon acted as a defining moment in our understanding of recent history, then what period came to a close on that particular day? Were the events of September 11 indeed the ultimate expression of fundamental change in the **international system**? In light of the cultural origins and religio-political motives of the suspected culprits, did the tragedies consequently act as a harbinger of a return to the "clash of civilizations," enunciated by the political scientist Samuel P. Huntington in 1993, with its concomitant religious and ethnic determinants? Or were the attacks not so much connected to the resurgence of old civilizational fault lines and their underlying antagonisms in the absence of **bipolar** ideological conflict but rather the consequence of a pal-pable U.S. **unilateralism** and, by extension, Western military and political preponderance in the decade after the Cold War?

Aside from the simple truth that watersheds in history constitute conceptual devices informed by individual preferences, the above questions cannot be conclusively answered at this stage, if only because historical analysis is predicated on an ex post facto assessment of events. Moreover, there is invariably no silver bullet, no single explanatory model that might provide a definitive answer to the occurrence of violent conflict of any kind at any stage in history. What is clear, however, is that after September 11 the time-honored myth of an invulnerable U.S. **hegemon**, secure between two oceans, has been debunked. Furthermore, the hopes of the early 1990s that growing international economic interdependence would provide the

---

*Boldfaced terms are defined in the Glossary, which begins on page 343.

1

basis for a peaceful world order have not come to fruition. Instead, international politics has become highly complex and is marked by continuous change and a pervading sense of insecurity.

As the dissolution of the Soviet Union sent shockwave after shockwave through the regional as well as international environments, the forces of contending **ideologies** that had taken center stage for half a century gave way to a new, nascent international system. The United States had seemingly arrived at the apex of its global power: U.S. values, such as liberalism and democracy, spread around the globe; U.S. corporations were in the vanguard of building a new global economy; and U.S. military forces were in the forefront of international efforts to provide global stability. The irony was the fact that power had become more diffuse, and thus the U.S. ability to shape the global agenda had actually decreased. In the absence of a compelling nuclear logic of **mutually assured destruction (MAD)** inherent in the dualistic world of the Cold War, U.S. and, by implication, Western **hegemony** in international politics and economics would come under increasing pressure. Various events taking place during the decade after the end of the Cold War are suggestive of widespread skepticism, even hostility, toward the only **superpower** in the world.

In 1991, the U.S.-led Coalition of Western powers was gearing up for military operations in the Persian Gulf region. Aside from the moral rationale for the Gulf War—wanting to protect tiny Kuwait from Iraqi military aggression—a vital interest of the West was at stake: A significant amount of the crude oil that lubricated the world's economic engine was produced in the fields of Kuwait. Western intervention and the stationing of multinational and, in particular, U.S. troops under the auspices of the Western powers in Saudi Arabia elicited widespread indignation among devout Muslims around the world. Simultaneously, and against the backdrop of an unprecedented economic boom, Asian states proved increasingly assertive and resilient vis-à-vis Western influence. Beyond their rising self-confidence, Asian states' policies in relation to China appear highly suggestive of a realignment of power in the region. As China is readying resources to substantiate its aspirations toward regional hegemony, most states of Southeast Asia are directing their attention toward Beijing. Will China—hailed as the greatest potential single market by economists—also supplant the Western powers in the global pecking order in the near future?

Also during the 1990s, Europe achieved unprecedented successes in its economic and political integration, going along with intensified Euroatlantic cooperation. The **European Union (EU)** introduced the single market and a single currency and became the largest trading bloc in the world. Yet at the same time, Europe witnessed ethnic conflicts at its doorstep, resulting from the fragmentation of the Balkans and the circumstance that Africa had long existed on the sidelines of global political concerns. The fact that a series of wars was, for all intents and purposes, fought in Europe's backyard is remarkable in and of itself—or so it appeared to many Europeans, who had not witnessed armed conflict in generations. The Balkans—the historic powder keg of Europe—once again erupted into political violence. In the wider context of the decline of the Yugoslav Federation, war was visited upon Bosnia (1992–1995), Croatia (1991–1995), and later Kosovo (1999). In Africa, tribal rivalries witnessed a bloody comeback, for example, in the genocidal war fought between the Hutu and Tutsi factions in Rwanda and Burundi in the early and mid-1990s. Two attributes stand out in these wars: First, they were fought along ethnic lines within a state; second, multinational peacekeeping forces were deployed. In retrospect, two trends typical of the 1990s—the sharp increase of **intrastate conflicts** (as opposed to **interstate conflicts**) and the challenge to the sanctity of national **sovereignty** by the international community—constitute developments that have had, and continue to exert, significant influence on the conduct, nature, and understanding of international relations in the post–Cold War world.

Paradoxically, while patterns of conflict were reverting from ideological competition to ethnic and religious fault lines, the process of **globalization** gave a new impetus to the neoliberal economic order that placed considerable power in the hands of multinational corporations and consequently further undermined the **nation-state** as unchallenged incumbent key actor in international relations. The world also became smaller due to increased connectivity and a concomitant interdependency, which in turn was caused by a revolution in information technology (IT). Put simply, however, the problem with globalization today is its uneven distribution: Whereas the full impact of the IT revolution was by and large a pervasive phenomenon in the West, many states of the former Soviet bloc in Eastern Europe were struggling to digest the shock of transitioning from a command economy to a free-market economy; for countries in the **third world** of Africa, Asia, and Latin America, the ostensible boon of globalization was anything but. Instead, globalization more often than not proved to be exacerbating the division between the haves and the have-nots of this world. Overall, the period between 1991 and today has brought much change to the international political and economic orders and can therefore appropriately be referred to as a "formative decade" during which we have witnessed the transition from the Cold War world into the globalized world of the early twenty-first century. But what did the international system of the Cold War look like in the time before 1991?

Between 1947 and 1991, the world witnessed a struggle between two fundamentally opposed value and social **systems**: socialist communism and liberal democracy. The two protagonists of this struggle, which in time would engulf the entire globe, were the Soviet Union and the United States.

By the end of World War II, each power had eclipsed the former Great Powers of Europe. The latter had dominated international politics for the greater part of the early modern period (roughly after 1500) but had been superseded by the two flanking powers of the pre–World War II era—the Soviet Union and the United States—among other reasons because their material bases were ravaged and their military power was depleted by 1945. By then, the former flanking powers were in the process of becoming superpowers, that is, political entities endowed with the capability of projecting their power globally. The end of World War II thus acted as the critical watershed between the prevailing modus operandi ante bellum in the international system and the new order of an incipient Cold War.

The old **balance of power** between the Great Powers of Europe had crumbled in the face of rampant nationalism and expansionism; the logic of the Cold War gave birth to the bipolar world, an international system in which the new superpowers maintained a precarious nuclear balance. In the immediate aftermath of World War II, the Cold War was at first centered in Europe. In only one decade, however, the Cold War became the defining feature of the international system. The conflict's second decade (roughly 1955–1965) brought the world to the brink of total destruction, but a significant step toward the relaxation of relations between the superpowers was achieved thereafter. After 1975 the world witnessed the coming of the **Second Cold War**, as well as a fundamental change in the international system, transforming it into a **multipolar** system as economic forces increasingly interlocked with political factors in shaping history. Finally, economic forces, as much as politics, determined the outcome of the Cold War: the Soviet Union ultimately paid a high price for communism and the concomitant command economy it had installed, whereas democracy and capitalism proved more durable in the West.

Aside from the two principal parties to the Cold War, there were those who gained and even more who lost. More often than not, for those caught between the rivals there was no recourse. They became the victims of the Cold War. It was no coincidence that the hot spots of the Cold War were located in the third world, where millions yearned for national independence only to struggle with massive impoverishment and political instability once they achieved it. To the superpowers, Europe as the terminus a quo (point of origin) of the Cold War did not present itself as a practicable battlefield for an important reason: the risk of escalation—conventional and nuclear—was too high. Whereas most battles of the Cold War were fought in Asia, the Middle East, and Africa, in Europe the Cold War evolved into a **long peace**. As of the late 1950s, the superpowers wooed developing countries with every intention of turning them into auxiliaries, thereby spreading and perpetuating the dynamic of the Cold War beyond its erstwhile limits.

The principal difference between previous wars, even global wars, and the Cold War was that the earlier wars (with the exception of the U.S. bombings of Hiroshima and Nagasaki in August 1945) had all been fought with conventional weapons, whereas the antagonists of the Cold War had nuclear arsenals at their fingertips. The destructiveness of nuclear weapons, to state the obvious, far exceeded that of any conventional weapon. If the equilibrium of the Cold War had ever been seriously disturbed—say, in the late 1970s—this subsequent attempt at composing a history of international relations would, in all probability, never have been written. More generally, the stakes and risks of the Cold War while it lasted were higher still than those for which World War II had been fought. Figuratively speaking, if the Cold War had ever turned hot, it literally would have been the war to end all wars, plunging the world into a nuclear holocaust of unprecedented levels. It is to the beginning of this story and its history that we now turn.

International Systems in Historical Perspective

AFTER WORLD WAR II, THE STRUGGLE BETWEEN THE SUPERPOWERS—THE SOVIET Union and the United States—would endure for almost half a century. How, and especially why, did the Cold War come about? What forces shaped the bipolar world, and what processes culminated in its establishment? In order to understand the origins of the Cold War, we need to delve into the past. What kind of international system was prevalent before the war? Notably, experts in the field of international relations, as well as practitioners of history, do not agree on the number or nature of prewar international systems; this lack of consensus does not so much denote controversy as it emphasizes a variety of perspectives enriching both academic disciplines.

The French Universal Monarchy, the League of Augsburg, and the Anglo-French Rivalry, 1660–1774

European history had a defining influence on the development of the international system. It is thus that we turn to Europe's past. Following the turmoil of dynastic and religious war during the Middle Ages and the later sixteenth century, in the early seventeenth century the nation-state emerged as the key actor in European relations. With the Hapsburg Empire waning, a new power rose to prominence in the West: France. The drive to expand France's boundaries to its "Natural Frontiers" under Louis XIV (1638–1715) threatened to culminate in a French position of preponderance. French expansionism and the threat of French hegemony united a number of lesser powers under the auspices of the Dutch Stadholder, William of Orange, who forged the League of Augsburg (1686) to halt the French advance.

The act of drawing together disparate potentates in order to contain French expansionism in the mid–seventeenth century exemplified a new type of conflict: **coalition war**. As in the case of the League of Augsburg, the purpose of coalitions was to act as a balancing force by denying any one state a position of predominance. In a loose sense, the period of French expansionism ushered in a new European system that gradually developed and, during the period of European colonial expansion in the age of the nation-state, grew to become an early international system. This new system was designed toward the end of maintaining the balance of power.

In 1713, the Treaty of Utrecht concluded the War of Spanish Succession (1702–1713, alternatively dated as 1701–1714). By and large, the period following the Utrecht Treaty can be understood as an affirmation of the balance-of-power system. Fleeting alliances among various European powers served to achieve limited objectives. The early eighteenth century witnessed the rise to power of Russia and Prussia at the expense of Sweden. Russo-Prussian rivalry coincided with the prolonged disputes between France and Hapsburg Austria. Thus, Russia and Austria allied themselves against France and Prussia, the latter of which was joined by the balancing power of Britain. The **Diplomatic Revolution** of 1756 changed the face of the European **alliance system**: as Prussia drew into the British orbit, Austria, Russia, and France acted together in an effort to curb British overseas expansion in the Seven Years War (1756–1763). During the U.S. Revolutionary War (1775–1783), Anglo-French rivalry came to a new head, with Russia and Prussia remaining neutral. Toward the end of the eighteenth century, the rise of Napoleon again raised the specter of French universal monarchy. Under British leadership, Europe again united to thwart French ambitions.

The Age of Napoleonic Wars and the End of the Concert of Europe, 1798–1848

Following Napoleon's defeat at Waterloo, the European powers met at Vienna in 1815 to deliberate a new settlement. The old system of transitory coalitions was ended. The architects of the new system at the Congress of Vienna sought to construct a lasting and stable peace. Despite underlying differences between the leading liberal states, Britain and France, and the forces of conservatism headed by Prince Klemens Metternich and a group consisting of Russia, Prussia, and Austria, the new settlement achieved its principle objective of stability by preventing the rise of another hegemon for a staggering half-century. The new system was sustained by the **Concert of Europe**, that is, the implementation of conservative, antihegemonic policy on the part of the major European powers.

Metternich's system was undermined when, in 1848, revolution struck conservative European governments. As new leaders rose to power, the international system as constituted and upheld by the Concert of Europe quickly fell into desuetude. Russian intervention in the Crimean Peninsula provoked the decisive response of the liberal Western states. The former allies—Britain, France, and Russia—fought each other in the Crimean War and thus ended the second international system.

From the Rise of the Second German Reich to the Entanglement of Alliances, 1860–1914

A significant difference of this age was the full impact of the Industrial Revolution on military technology, which served as an accessory to political change by accelerating the disintegration of the balance of power. Recent advances in the construction of arms had led to an increasingly destructive power and were widely and ruthlessly instrumentalized in the service of European powers. In terms of strategy, the principle of balance of power was challenged by younger, ascendant powers. Thus, the period before World War I was marked by the increasing disintegration of international stability, as each state vied for power in Europe and the continental powers began to stake out territorial claims in the colonies.

While incumbent colonial powers such as the British Empire sought to maintain the status quo, more recently formed states sought to enter the race for overseas territory. Germany especially sought for itself a place in the sun. A swift victory during the Franco-Prussian War of 1870–1871 had allowed Chancellor Otto von Bismarck to found the Second Reich, a power soon to be reckoned with. The creation of a united Germany under Prussian leadership severely upset the informally maintained balance of power. With Bismarck at the helm, Germany aptly maneuvered the complex system of alliances that divided its neighbors. However, after Bismarck's dismissal by Kaiser Wilhelm II in 1890, Germany pursued an active, even aggressive foreign policy that once more threatened Europe with hegemony.

Consequently, a dualistic alliance system manifested itself in the shape of the **Triple Entente**, led by France and Britain, and the **Central Powers** headed by Germany and allied with Austria-Hungary. The threat of German hegemony was at the hub of the nascent international system. Thus, German expansionism in Europe and abroad prompted the traditional colonial powers of the West—France and Britain—to curb further German advances. Conversely, the **entanglement of alliances** paved the road to war; according to the treaties concluded on the eve of World War I, mobilization and war plans were designed to come into force on the basis of third-party intervention. In other words, the foreign policies of the European powers led them into a costly contest of arms.

The Interwar System, 1919–1939

Subsequent to their victory in World War I, the Western allies attempted to counteract the reinstitution of an international system based on the precepts of **realpolitik**, that is, a definition of policy based on the ruthless pursuit of power and national self-interest. They sought to effect such a change by instituting a formalized version of the accords reached pursuant to the nineteenth-century model (i.e., the Concert of Europe). As in that system, individual states were to provide for **collective security** by rendering legal and necessary mutual action against any aggressor. The underlying tendency to collectively achieve stability was rooted in **idealist** thought, made manifest in U.S. President **Woodrow Wilson's Fourteen Point Program** (1918–1919). Wilson's program envisaged the foundation of statehood being rooted in the idea of **national self-determination**.

In the event, the Western allies based the Paris and Versailles Treaties on the prewar usage of rigid formal alliances, even though the situation required that they accommodate dynamic changes. Predictably, the experiment failed. Equally, the **League of Nations**, the organization that would implement collective security, failed to rise to the occasion. Effectively, the league's dismal failure was due to the absence of the United States, the Soviet Union, and, until 1926, Germany among its ranks. Moreover, the impact of the **Great Depression** compounded by the rise of **totalitarian regimes** undermined the very foundation of the League of Nations. The rise of the Third Reich yet again threatened Europe and the world with the prospect of German preponderance. Thus did the **interwar international system** come to a dramatic closure as the Wehrmacht crossed into Poland in late 1939.

The Alliance-Axis System, 1939–1945

World War II forced yet another change on the international system. This system was dualistic in nature and highly polarized. On the one hand, the totalitarian regimes (Germany, Italy, and Japan) converged to form the **Axis**; on the other hand, the Allies—liberal European democracies, the United States, and others—wedded themselves to the Soviet **regime** after 1941 in a desperate attempt to defeat the Axis. Thus, the **alliance-Axis system** was the defining feature of World War II and, ironically, served as a harbinger of developments in the near future. The Allies' victory in 1945 put an end to the operating international system in place since 1939.

The conclusions of the victors were similar to those of their predecessors acting in 1918: the war had been a direct consequence of unchecked national expansionism, aggrandizement, and the acquisition of economic resources. Adolf Hitler's rise to power and German claims to European hegemony had unsettled the interwar international system as designed by the signatories of the Versailles Treaty. The postwar international system would have to be built on the lessons of history. Under Western political thought, the solution to the problem of constructing a durable international order could not be exclusively steeped in idealist tenets or a product of political **realism**. In fact, it would have to accommodate both. President Franklin Roosevelt, who had led the United States into the war, displayed a clear understanding of both intellectual traditions. His contribution to the postwar world order was to bridge the gap between **idealism** and realism in U.S. foreign policy; he proved at least partially successful.

Consequences of World War II for the International System

This brings us to the immediate postwar period. In 1945, the Allies faced a completely new set of circumstances shaped by the course of the war. Similarly, the period after 1945 was influenced by the consequences of the war; several of them helped define international relations in the postwar world.

- The era of European preponderance in world politics drew to a close, as European nations were overshadowed by the flanking powers—the United States and the Soviet Union. In the course of the war, this pair had outmatched their European counterparts militarily as well as economically. The Axis onslaught had taxed the last of the Great Powers of Europe— namely, the British Empire and France—to the limits. The victors filled the position of vanquished Germany, the third Great Power of Europe, on the stage of world politics.
- As a former flanking power acting on the European periphery, the United States emerged as the true victor of the war, having sustained no significant damage to its infrastructure. Economically, the United States had done well. Militarily, U.S. forces had prevailed over the armies of the Axis in Europe, Africa, and Asia. In the process, the United States obliterated two Japanese cities with a new weapon of enormous destructive potential: the atomic bomb. Self-confident yet reluctant, the United States abandoned its former **isolationist** reticence to assume the leading role in shaping the **new world order**.
- Having changed alliances during the war, the Soviet Union was on the winning side in 1945. Although the Soviet Union had sustained unimaginable losses—by all accounts, some 20 million casualties—it had contributed to the destruction of the Axis. The Soviets pitted their own power against that of the Third Reich and won; they wanted to consolidate their **sphere of influence** and become a player in the new international arena. At the same time, however, the Soviet Union had to contend with the destruction of a significant percentage of its material basis, which severely hampered its ability to pursue such plans.
- Nearing the close of World War II, the Allies met at the Yalta

Conference in February 1945. Diverging interests over the shaping of the postwar European order, as expressed by Soviet dictator Joseph Stalin and U.S. President Roosevelt, initiated a growing divide that in turn set the stage for the Cold War and the bipolar international system.

• The nuclear age began when the United States dropped the first atomic bombs on Japan in August 1945. The failure of U.S.-Soviet cooperation subsequent to the war, and the resulting distrust between the two superpowers, created the basis for the **arms race**.

• In addition, the weakening of the Great Powers that resulted from the war allowed nationalist movements in the colonies to challenge their masters. Independence movements were rife throughout Asia, the Middle East, and later Africa.

• Finally, the destruction wrought by German hegemonic aspirations during the war resulted in Allied consensus to forestall the possibility of repetition. Built on the foundations of the League of Nations, Allied hopes to institute collective security were placed with the **United Nations (UN)**, which was created soon after the war ended.

The Onset of
the Cold War, 1945–1955

FOLLOWING THE END OF WORLD WAR II HOPES ABOUNDED THAT THE FUTURE world order would be informed by the vision of "one world" and that law and order would replace the anarchy of international relations. Instead, the antagonism between East and West, between communism and liberal democracy, between a socioeconomic command economy and capitalism—in short, between two fundamentally divergent social and value systems (ideologies)—largely determined international politics. The postwar world was organized into two distinct blocs, with the United States and the Soviet Union at the two centers. The process leading up to the bipolar international system of the Cold War, spanning almost a decade, was one of mutual miscommunication based on a distorted perception of each side's fears and reactions.

Although elements of cooperation between the emerging superpowers after World War II can be identified, a rift over the postwar order was growing. After a phase of ossification (May 1945–early 1947), the Cold War began in earnest. At its center was the creation of a European postwar order. Between 1947 and 1949, Europe was increasingly organized along ideological fault lines. The phase of the formation of blocs in Europe commenced in the political and economic spheres but soon became a military issue as well. And though the division of the world began in Europe, Asia soon took center stage. The phase of globalization (mid-1949–late 1954) resulted in continuous ideologization and militarization between East and West.

The Ossification Phase, 1945–1947

The Cold War was not inevitable, and the superpower conflict did not take effect immediately after the conclusion of World War II. With Germany's surrender in May 1945 peace came to Europe; Japan capitulated following

13

the bombing of Hiroshima and Nagasaki. The Axis was destroyed. Now that the common enemy had been vanquished, the Western alliance turned toward designing the postwar international order and security system. Although preparations for this began early during World War II, a divergence of interests among the Allies surfaced in the first two years after the war. It is in the nature of the Western alliance that the seeds of dissent can be found.

The confrontation with Nazi Germany had overtaxed the Western democracies of Europe. After France had been invaded, Britain bore the brunt of the war in Europe; U.S. entry into the war in 1941 and Hitler's ill-advised invasion of the Soviet Union, which opened a second front (the Eastern Front), thwarted Germany's bid for hegemony. Nazi Germany's aggression was responsible for the eventual formation of an alliance (referred to here as the Western alliance; British leader Winston Churchill called it the Grand Alliance); the Western democracies, including the United States, were thus led into a marriage of convenience with the embattled Soviet Union. In facing an overwhelming threat, the conflicting value systems and diverging political and social perspectives of the wartime Allies were shelved for the duration of the war. As the war drew to a conclusion, fundamental disagreements resurfaced. The increasing conflict between the new superpowers posed insurmountable problems in constructing a viable postwar security system. A number of contentious issues soon crystallized; they emphasized and accelerated the widening rift between the superpowers.

The Bone of Contention: The Atomic Bomb

The sudden detonation of two atomic bombs over Japan by the United States in August 1945 raised Soviet suspicions. The United States had not shared its secret of the new weapon, and the U.S.-British nuclear **monopoly** eroded whatever goodwill there had been. Advisers to U.S. President Harry Truman believed that the Soviet Union was a decade away from constructing its own atomic bomb, and some recommended that the United States use its atomic arsenal to check Soviet aggression. Members of the Manhattan Project, the clandestine U.S. nuclear program that had developed the bombs deployed in Japan, disagreed. It was J. Robert Oppenheimer's opinion that the Soviets would end the U.S. nuclear monopoly in only four years. In the event, Oppenheimer, the leading scientist in the creation of the atomic bomb, was proved right.

After much deliberation, the Truman administration entered a scheme for international nuclear control in June 1946: the Baruch Plan. Essentially, the problem with the Baruch Plan—as well as its precursors and predecessors—was the U.S. demand that both superpowers delegate the pertinent decisions to a supranational body, the UN International Atomic Development Authority. The Soviets rejected this U.S. initiative on the grounds that it perpetuated the U.S. nuclear monopoly. Soviet counterproposals to ban all nuclear weapons were rejected out of hand. In this situation, Soviet efforts were geared toward the closure of the nuclear gap. In the meantime, the U.S. nuclear monopoly was maintained. From the end of the war to 1948, superpower negotiations on the issue of nuclear energy bore no fruit; the impasse became obsolete when the Soviets detonated their first nuclear weapon in 1949. The U.S. refusal to cooperate with the Soviets on the issue of nuclear power, and instead make use of their position of strength underlined by holding the **nuclear edge**, hardened Soviet attitudes.

The Big Three and the Postwar Order in Eastern Europe: Poland

When the Big Three leaders—Winston Churchill, Joseph Stalin, and Franklin Roosevelt—met at Yalta in the Crimean Peninsula in February 1945, diverging wartime experiences served to highlight political, ideological, and social differences. Occurring shortly before the end of the war, Yalta was intended to achieve consensus on the general outlines of the postwar international security system. More specifically, the impending confrontation over Eastern Europe within the Western alliance had to be averted, for in the course of the Soviets' pursuit of the retreating Germans, many of the states on the Soviet border, and much of Central Europe, had been occupied by the Red Army. If the nuclear monopoly would come to serve as the U.S. trump in the relations with the Soviet Union after August 1945, the fait accompli of a strong Soviet troop presence in Eastern Europe would equally leave its imprint on the course of Yalta and, later, at Potsdam.

The Soviet position can be better appreciated if the scope of its sacrifice for the Western alliance during the war is fully understood. The German invasion in 1941 wrought destruction on a staggering scale: nearly 2,000 cities, 70,000 villages, 70 percent of its industries, and 60 percent of its railway and road systems had fallen prey to the ravages of the German military. Worse still, the Soviets had sustained 20–30 million casualties. The United States did support the Soviets by entering into a **lend/lease agreement** and thereby granted a certain measure of material support. Yet the Soviet struggle against the Nazis had been a lonely one and took its toll on the Soviets' centralized economy, which had plummeted to approximately 60 percent of prewar levels. By contrast, the war had boosted the U.S. free-market economy to such a degree that its industrial output had more than doubled; U.S. casualties numbered some 330,000. The sense of vulnerability exhibited by the Soviets after the war must be understood in light of their experience during World War II.

The focus of dissent in Eastern Europe centered on Poland. The Allies had a special interest in maintaining the liberties of Poland, for in 1939 France and Britain had declared war on Germany when Hitler's troops crossed the Polish border. For the Soviets, Poland constituted a historic enemy, Polish lands being the traditional gateway for invasion from the west. In 1921, the Polish army had annexed a sizeable portion of an incipient Soviet state weakened by internal turmoil and legitimized the Polish occupation in the Treaty of Riga. Moreover, Poland's legitimate prewar government had been virulently anticommunist. Based in London, the exiled Polish government awaited the moment of its return and actively lobbied the Allies to ensure its reinstatement. Ultimately, Stalin wanted to prevent the establishment of a Polish state not headed by a pro-Soviet government.

Roosevelt's call for free elections in Poland, seconded by Churchill, gradually subsided after the Soviets' stall tactics. Despite all Western efforts, Stalin was adamant. At last, Stalin's narrow definition of free elections eliminated the possibility of a pluralistic and democratic government for Poland; only a governing body subservient to Stalin's interest would satisfy Soviet security concerns. In the West, the Anglo-U.S. concession over Poland raised the specter of prewar Munich and the attendant policy of **appeasement**.

Soviet-Polish enmity also manifested in the redrawing of borders. British Foreign Secretary Lord George Curzon in 1921 had suggested that the Poles move the new boundary 125 miles westward in aid of resolving the issue. At the time, the victorious Poles would not hear of it. In a secret clause of the **Nazi-Soviet Non-Aggression Pact** of 23 August 1939, eastern Poland, Finland, Estonia, Latvia, and Bessarabia were acknowledged to lie within the Soviet sphere of influence. The secret clause is suggestive of Stalin's desire to retrieve the territory formerly annexed by the Poles. At Yalta, Stalin's wish came true, for the victors of World War II pushed the eastern Polish frontier back to the Curzon Line but compensated Poland by moving its western border some 75 miles into German territory, to the Oder and Neisse Rivers. Obviously, Stalin hoped to gain by intensifying Polish-German hostilities even further. East Prussia was also partitioned by the Soviet Union, with one portion going to Poland. The Baltic states had been under Soviet rule since 1940.

At Yalta it soon became clear that the Soviets wanted to bring Eastern Europe into their own sphere of influence, thereby creating a cordon of states around Soviet territory that would act as a buffer in the event of attack. Western objectives were diametrically opposed, yet the United States required the support of the Soviet Union in order to conclude the war in the Pacific against Japan and to constitute and bring legitimacy to the emerging idea of the United Nations. Concerning Eastern Europe,

Roosevelt's hands were tied; if only for this reason, the United States would resist further Soviet expansion into Central and Eastern Europe. The incremental consolidation of Soviet power in Eastern Europe between the Yalta Conference and early 1947 did much to contribute to superpower estrangement. In the course of this development, the Soviets brought Poland, Hungary, Romania, and Bulgaria under their suzerainty. Churchill's poignant formulation of this state of affairs was that an **Iron Curtain** had descended over Europe.

The Big Three and the Postwar Order in Central Europe: Germany

Concerning Germany, the Allies were unable to resolve the key elements of their conflict. They had instituted a mutual administration in occupied Germany, dividing the country into four zones: Soviet, U.S., British, and French. Conversely, the Allies were not clear on critical issues, such as whether Germany should be disarmed, demilitarized, and partitioned. To what degree could the Allies permit the reconstruction of German industry? And what should the future German society look like? The Soviet agenda was clear: a pauperized, weakened Germany would no longer be able to threaten Soviet interests. In pursuing such a plan, Stalin ultimately intended to diminish Germany's potential for military expansion toward the east. In order to do so, the German economy had to be crippled and the constitution of an independent state on the ashes of the Third Reich prevented.

At the end of 1944, it appeared that the United States was prepared to pursue comparable interests. A plan considered at that time and named after U.S. Secretary of the Treasury Henry Morgenthau envisioned the demilitarization, territorial reduction, and partitioning of Germany, as well as the dismantling of German industrial installations. According to the Morgenthau Plan, Germany was to be reduced to the status of an agrarian society. Even though President Roosevelt had approved the plan for the time being, he soon withdrew his support for its implementation. Gradually, a different perspective took hold in Washington. The reconstruction of the German economy was a critical step toward the reestablishment of a functioning and healthy European economy, which in turn constituted the key to the political stabilization of Europe. Increasingly, the Soviet demand of some U.S.\$20 billion in reparation fees from Germany became the greatest stumbling block to such an objective. The payment of such a lump sum was hardly realistic, as Germany was in shambles. If the Soviets removed the remaining intact industrial infrastructure from Germany as part of the reparation dues, German reconstruction would be possible only in the long run. U.S. funds and matériel pouring into Germany, however, would immediately be seized by the Soviets as part of Germany's debt.

Such a future did not appeal to the Western Allies. The U.S. response

to Soviet recalcitrance was swift and simple: the Soviets were to be excluded from the Western part of occupied Germany and, beyond the Elbe, from
governance in the Western zones of Berlin. Soviet demands would have to
be satisfied by whatever could be impounded within the zone under their
control. As a consequence, Soviet-controlled Germany was stripped of
valuables of any kind. Conversely, the Truman administration was planning
to furnish material aid in an effort to reconstruct the German economy. This
aid was not entirely altruistic in character, for the United States had a keen
interest in finding new markets to sell the enormous overproduction of the
U.S. wartime economy. Finally, the ongoing bickering between the nearly
autonomous military commanders of the occupational zones, among whom
the political and strategic divergences of the Allies were made manifest on
an operational level, went a long way toward showing that there would be
no unitary policy for Germany under Allied rule.

Conflict Issues Beyond Europe:
Iran, Turkey, Greece, and the Truman Doctrine

If both the Polish and German questions were at the center of Allied
geostrategic concerns, incidents on the periphery reinforced superpower
division. The crisis in Iran came to a head when Russian troops failed to
withdraw by March 1946 despite earlier promises to the contrary. Albeit
remote and at best on the fringes of the war, Iran had constituted the main
thoroughfare for Western aid to the Soviet Union during the war.
Furthermore, Iran was rich in oil and thus a prize coveted by the belligerents. The shah's proclivity for the Axis, as well as his refusal to expel all
German citizens, prompted the Soviets and the British to intervene militarily. Joint Allied forces occupied Iran, and the shah was coerced to abdicate
in favor of his son, Mohammed Reza Pahlavi, with whom the Allies agreed
to withdraw their troops subsequent to the war.

In Soviet-occupied Iran, the Soviets encouraged local independence
movements. The shah's authority was further undermined by repeated
Soviet refusals to allow Iranian troops into Soviet-held territory. When the
Soviets added insult to injury by demanding privileged access to Iranian
oil, U.S. pressure in the **United Nations Security Council** mounted.
Determined U.S. support for Iran was rooted in the belief, following Yalta
and Potsdam, that further Soviet expansion had to be prevented at almost
any cost. In May 1946, Russian troops finally quit Iran.

But crises also shook Turkey and Greece. In Turkey, Soviet demands
for the internationalization of the Bosporus Strait, which had been under
Turkish control since 1936, were very much in keeping with prerevolutionary Russian foreign policy. But whereas Churchill had consented to back
the Soviet claim during the war, by 1946 superpower division had funda-

mentally changed the situation. Following the Soviet bid in Iran, the Allies perceived a coordinated effort to expand the Soviet sphere of influence, which had to be resisted. Having met with Western resistance, Stalin retracted his claims on the strait.

While the war was raging across Europe, the Greeks had been actively resisting Nazi occupation. In 1940, Italian forces invaded Greece. In their wake, German troops moved into the Hellenic Peninsula and effectively held the Aegean region while hostilities lasted. By 1944, two partisan groups spearheaded the resistance against the Nazi occupiers. On the one hand, Marxist Ethnikos Laikos Apeleftherotikos Stratos (ELAS), the guerrilla force directed by the Greek government-in-exile, led partisan attacks against Italian and German troops; on the other hand, conservative forces converged around Ethnikos Demokratikos Ellenikos Syndesmos (EDES), the republican resistance, which coordinated its activities with regular government troops. By the time the Germans withdrew, the two factions were gearing up for civil war.

Britain, the traditional arbiter of the region, managed to avert an escalation by including ELAS and EDES supporters in a truce in early 1945. In due course, the communist partisans undermined the decommissioning of arms under British auspices. Skirmishes and open confrontations with Western-backed government troops soon spilled into the areas bordering Yugoslavia, Bulgaria, and Albania. Weakened by war, Britain proved unable to control the situation and reneged upon its commitment in Greece in early 1947. Greek conservative forces called upon the United States for support against the growing threat of communist guerrilla attack. Although the Soviets did not furnish arms for their communist partisans, the newly constituted successor to the ELAS, Dimokratikos Stratos tis Elladas (DSE), acted with at least the connivance of Moscow. Soviet diplomatic support for DSE compounded the situation.

Truman responded by approving legislation passed in Congress that permitted the president to send aid and military advisers to Greece. Considering the prewar history of the United States, with its avoidance of foreign entanglements, this sudden shift in foreign policy was remarkable. In fact, Truman's address to Congress in March 1947 had a significant impact on the future of superpower relations. Truman told Congress: "I believe it must be the policy of the United States to support free peoples who are resisting attempted subjugation by armed minorities or by outside pressure. I believe that we must assist free peoples to work out their own destinies in their own way."[1] The **Truman Doctrine** thus constituted a call to resist outside forces and was clearly directed against international communism and, by implication, the Soviet Union. Congressional compliance with Truman's proposal for an **interventionist** foreign policy can be understood as a renunciation of **isolationism** and the actual prelude to the Cold

War, as well as a sanction for U.S. leadership of the West. Truman's determined stance, however, was no coincidence but rather the result of an emerging new paradigm in U.S. foreign policy.

The Formation of Blocs, 1947–1949

The first two years following World War II witnessed growing estrangement between the two principal contenders, the Soviet Union and the United States. Soon enough tensions rose, and events came to a head in the spring of 1947. The Cold War had begun. The consolidation of Soviet power in Eastern Europe, coupled with the recent memory of Stalin's forays into the Western geostrategic sphere of influence in Iran and Turkey, defined the context in which the United States and its allies perceived Soviet support of the Greek communist guerrillas. The forward character of Stalin's foreign policy since the conclusion of the war, and the tensions it created among the erstwhile allies, sparked a strategic debate in the United States that culminated in the formulation of a new U.S. foreign policy.

George F. Kennan and the Strategy of Containment

A young diplomat at the U.S. embassy in Moscow, George F. Kennan influenced the discourse on security policy with the so-called Long Telegram of 22 February 1946 and his publication of an anonymous article (signed "X.") in the July 1947 issue of *Foreign Affairs*. Kennan emphasized the fundamental difference between capitalism and communism. He maintained that Soviet policy was the product of both communist ideology and traditional prerevolutionary Russian insecurity. Based on this analysis, Kennan reasoned that long-term Soviet policy was geared toward world domination. Thus, it followed that U.S. policy had to assume a long-term perspective. In Kennan's words: "Any United States policy toward the Soviet Union must be that of a long-term, patient, but firm and vigilant containment of Russian expansive tendencies."[2] The **strategy of containment** was born.

The principal weaknesses of Western Europe were its economic frailty and the potential for political destabilization by outside forces. Notably, Kennan argued that no imminent military threat emanated from the East. To Kennan, the appropriate response to such a perceived threat was a focusing of energies in the long term and the economic and political stabilization of Europe in the near term. Kennan's analysis emphasized the need for the long-term ideological containment of communism as opposed to the military encirclement of the Soviet Union. In this sense, Kennan never gave his support to the comprehensive character of the Truman Doctrine, as he believed that it should only be applied differentially.

With the opening of the Soviet archives Western historians have begun to understand that U.S. and British strategic conceptions of the early phase of the Cold War were discolored, for they misperceived Soviet security concerns. The European theater moved to the center of mutual superpower fears. On the Soviet side, apprehensions as to the rapid expansion of capitalism into Western Europe were coupled with fears of anti-Soviet tendencies of national governments in the adjoining East European states. Ironically, U.S. fears of Soviet expansion reinforced Soviet apprehensions of Western encirclement, and vice versa. This vicious circle underpinned the dynamic of the Cold War.

Saving Western Europe from Communism: The Marshall Plan

As we have seen, Soviet control of Eastern Europe to the banks of the Elbe was reinforced by the presence of the Red Army. This circumstance meant that keeping Western Europe free of Soviet influence was critical to the United States. The European security issue was accentuated by the rise of communism in some Western democracies (especially France and Italy) as a result of food shortages during the harsh winter of 1946–1947. The war-torn societies of Europe had hoped for a palpable improvement of their lot. Instead, the European national economies and industries were not recovering but instead continued to struggle. By way of comparison to the production levels of 1938, Belgium achieved an economic output of 77 percent nine years later; Denmark and Norway 93 percent; Finland 65 percent; France 75 percent; Germany only 22 percent; Greece 44 percent; Italy 54 percent; and the Netherlands 62 percent. Only Britain and Sweden expanded by a full 1 percent in 1947.

At the same time, Communists in Europe garnered unusual support. In Belgium, the Communist Party had numbered some 9,000 members in 1939; by November 1945 it had expanded tenfold. In Greece, the party went from 17,000 members in 1935 to no less than 70,000 in 1945; in Italy from a mere 5,000 in 1943 to 1.7 million in September 1945; and in Hungary from a few hundred in 1942 to some 100,000 in December 1945. In France, Italy, and Finland the communist vote reached unprecedented levels (in excess of 20 percent of the popular mandate). In Belgium, Denmark, Norway, the Netherlands, and Sweden the Communists were able to mobilize an average of 10 percent of the vote.

During a trip to Europe U.S. Secretary of State George Marshall witnessed firsthand the economic crises and the many obstacles to resuscitating the European national economies, as well as the consequential threat of communist subversion; he convinced the U.S. government that adequate steps had to be undertaken in support of the security and stability of Europe. As a response to the prevailing situation in Europe, Secretary of

State Marshall put on the table a plan for European economic reconstruction (5 June 1947). The **Marshall Plan** envisaged the transfer of significant funds to Europe. On the strategic level, the underlying assumption of the plan was that only a massive monetary infusion would allow Europe to recuperate from the ravages of war and thus stabilize its material condition and political climate. And only a stable Europe would be able to resist the indigenous and exogenous communist challenges. Financial aid provided for Europe by the United States between 1948 and 1952 added up to almost U.S.$13 billion. Thus, the Truman Doctrine can be understood to have been the program relative to the Marshall Plan, which provided for its implementation.

By extending offers for participation in the scheme to East European states in the Soviet orbit, the Truman administration carried the threat of nascent capitalism to Stalin's doorstep. From the outset, the U.S. government did not expect the Soviet Union to agree to a participation of the East European states, then occupied by the Red Army, in the reconstruction of Europe under the aegis of the Marshall Plan. At the same time, the U.S. government banked on Stalin's refusal to support the Marshall Plan: such a reaction would make it clear to all that the Soviet Union was to blame for a divided Europe. Almost predictably, East European states in the Soviet sphere of influence, such as Czechoslovakia, indicating their interest to participate in, and benefit from, the Marshall Plan, were ruthlessly reminded by Moscow that such decisions were not in the scope of their competence. Economically speaking, then, Marshall's intentions for Western Europe were not entirely altruistic but conveniently coincided with U.S. industrial needs to seek markets abroad; functioning European markets could partially accommodate U.S. overproduction resulting from the wartime boom in the economy. U.S. investment in the future of European economies thus also constituted a self-saving measure.

Western action in Europe was observed with some suspicion by the Soviets. The two-pronged approach to secure Europe from economic collapse and communist control, manifested in the Marshall Plan and the Truman Doctrine, prompted a Soviet response. The foundation of **COMINFORM** in September 1947 to bring communist governments in the Soviet sphere of influence into line with Moscow's policy dictates pointed toward an attempt to further consolidate Soviet power in Eastern Europe. But the Soviet leadership was concerned with more than the pressure being exerted by the Western Allies. Although the arrival of the Red Army in Nazi-occupied territory in 1945 was enthusiastically greeted by the populace of Eastern Europe, by 1948 the strictures of Soviet rule caused a resurgence of nationalist tendencies. In Poland, Wladyslaw Gomulka resisted the collectivization of farms as part of his country's socialist program. Gomulka's government was toppled less than a year later. Conversely, Joseph Tito's government successfully seceded from Moscow's party line, as it would not brook any violation of national sovereignty.

The Overthrow of Democracy in
Czechoslovakia and the Pact of Brussels

In February 1948, Western leaders at a conference in London concluded that the stalemate over Germany had to be ended by managing the U.S., British, and French zones unilaterally, even if it led to an open rift with the Soviets. Moreover, the eventual Soviet rejection of the Marshall Plan lent credence to a decisive course of action by the Western alliance. Notably, the rejection of the Marshall Plan by Stalin was further compounded by the overt feasibility of its implementation in the zones controlled by the Western allies. Meanwhile, in non–Soviet dominated Europe, the success of the Marshall Plan in the West hinged on the sustainable growth of political and institutional structures. As tensions between East and West were running higher, it became apparent to all parties involved that a partitioning of Germany was in the offing.

While the Western leaders met, events in Eastern Europe were coming to a head, for the communist coup directed against the National Front government in Czechoslovakia headed by President Eduard Benes occurred toward the end of February 1948. Growing tensions in the Czechoslovak government culminated in, and escalated due to, a standoff between the communist Ministry of Interior and the cabinet, whereupon twelve non-communist ministers chose to tender resignations. At this stage, supporters of the communist prime minister, Clement Gottwald, would have had to admit other non-Communists into the government or take their chances in a general election scheduled for that summer. But President Benes feared a potential civil war following a campaign of intimidation masterminded by Gottwald and his supporters and thus saw himself forced to give in to communist demands. Gottwald's accession to power and the consequent establishment of a communist government monopoly marked the end of democratic Czechoslovakia. The possible murder (or suicide) in March of Jan Masaryk, a vestige of the former democratic coalition government in the new Communist-dominated cabinet, drove home to the West Stalin's determination to bring Eastern Europe into the Soviet fold.

The main consequence of the Prague coup for the Soviet Union was an end to Western patience in resolving the German question. Against express Soviet wishes, there now would be a separate West German state. More generally, communist aggression in Czechoslovakia brought into focus the need for a comprehensive defense strategy for Western Europe. Nazi Germany had been crushed; according to British Foreign Secretary Ernest Bevin, the new threat emanated from the East. The fall of Czechoslovakia raised apprehensions in Western Europe of a possible military escalation of tensions with the Soviet Union.

Czechoslovakia's absorption into an expanding Soviet sphere forced many Western leaders to reflect upon the demerits of appeasement. Although the Marshall Plan bore the expected fruits of stabilizing the Western European economy and thus bolstered its governments' resistance to communist takeovers, the West still lacked a comprehensive security structure. As a first step, European leaders spearheaded an attempt to fuse the old Continent by concluding a West European Union. After the fall of Czechoslovakia, Bevin met with his French and Belgian colleagues to conclude the **Pact of Brussels** (17 March 1948). In the time-honored tradition of prewar Europe, the Brussels Pact was formulated as a mutual defense treaty. The pact directed the signatories to extend military assistance to any member state in case of attack by Germany or any third party in Europe. A closer look at this remarkable document, specifically Article IV, reveals that the defensive alliance was indeed aimed at the Soviet Union, not Germany. The United States, in turn, remained aloof of a European defensive alliance; it was loath to become entangled in the very kind of politico-military arrangement that had plunged Europe into war twice during the twentieth century. More specifically, George Kennan, as we have seen, had argued that the European fears of Soviet military aggression were exaggerated. The blockade of Berlin did, however, change the U.S. perspective on the Soviet threat for Western Europe.

The Berlin Blockade

On 20 March 1948, in protest of the Brussels Pact, Soviet representatives withdrew from the Allied Control Council, the governing body of occupied Germany. The decision on the establishment of a West German state was taken in early June 1948. Soon a separate currency, the deutsche mark, was introduced in the French, U.S., and British zones. And it was in this set of circumstances that the Soviets exerted massive pressure on the Western allies over Berlin. More and more, allied transports were harassed by the Red Army as they tried to cross into their respective sectors in the capital; railways and road links were blocked under often spurious excuses. Toward the end of the month, Russian troops had cordoned off all land routes to Berlin: the city was under a blockade. In light of stiff Western protests, the Soviets were quick to point out that it was the allies who had rendered accommodation over Germany nearly impossible by their decision to back a West German state. Stalin hoped that the allies would be forced to renege upon their promises for an independent German state, for otherwise they would have to foot the bill for their retentiveness in the shape of West Berlin—the only Western outpost deep within the Soviet-occupied zone.

U.S. General Lucius Clay urged immediate action by, if necessary, direct military confrontation. Truman and Bevin, who stood behind the determined allied effort to establish a West German state given French fears and a Soviet blockade, sought and found a solution to resolve the Berlin crisis in their favor and without provoking a military escalation with the Soviets. Thus far, the Red Army had not contested access to Berlin by air. The Berlin airlift filled the skies over the city with aircraft transporting some 2.3 million tons of supplies. A counterblockade badly hurt Soviet supply lines, too. Both sides wanted to avoid military conflict at all costs, and thus the Soviets refrained from interrupting the airlift by force. In May 1949, when Konrad Adenauer became the first chancellor of West Germany (officially: the Federal Republic of Germany), and following covert negotiations with the West, Stalin pronounced the Berlin blockade at an end. The first confrontation of the Cold War came dangerously close to a hostile exchange between the superpowers. It would not be the last time.

The Soviets' attempt to force the West's hand proved to be a desperate and, diplomatically speaking, costly gamble. To the Soviets, the blockade around Berlin had amounted to a defensive act; it had been a last, desperate attempt to thwart the constitution of a separate West German state, which followed as the logical next step in the implementation of the Marshall Plan. Instead, the Soviet pressure during the Berlin crisis provided a decisive impetus for the progressing formation of the **Western bloc**. The charged atmosphere surrounding the Soviet blockade of Berlin contributed to the erosion of U.S. resistance toward the development of a transatlantic alliance. The French, in turn, had apprehended the recrudescence of German militarism within the new alliance. In light of the Soviet attempts to consolidate power in Eastern Europe and Berlin, however, the French became increasingly conscious of the necessity for including the military and economic potential of West Germany.

The developments in the period 1945–1948 hardened the resolve of both superpowers to maintain a gradually emerging status quo, which had as its immediate consequence the partitioning of the European continent. After the showdown over Berlin, the Western response to Soviet expansion into Eastern Europe was to go through a final phase. The Pact of Brussels had set the stage. Its critical weakness was the U.S. refusal to participate in a peacetime defensive alliance. Historically, successive U.S. governments had heeded George Washington's dictum that they were not to entangle themselves in foreign alliances. Furthermore, the ingrained U.S. antipathy toward standing armies was a legacy of the colonists of the seventeenth century, who had fled Britain due to just such an instrument of arbitrary government.

The Creation of the North Atlantic Treaty Organization

Truman's momentous decision to forge a military alliance bridging the Atlantic Ocean was certainly outside the pale of traditional U.S. foreign policy. The days in which the **Monroe Doctrine** (1823) had divided the world into two hemispheres—one relevant to U.S. security concerns and the other not—were numbered. The articles of the **North Atlantic Treaty Organization (NATO)** were cautiously formulated, as the United States was reluctant to affirm an automatic mutual defense treaty obligation. In George Kennan's perspective, which was seconded by many other senior U.S. government officials, NATO, at that point in time, primarily served the purpose of politically and psychologically containing fears of renewed war in Europe. Article V of the NATO Treaty is the central proviso, stating that an attack on any member NATO would be considered as an act of aggression against all others. However, every member state had the right to decide on the kind of support it wanted to offer toward mutual defense pursuant to the UN Charter:

> The Parties agree that an armed attack against one or more of them in Europe or North America shall be considered an attack against them all and consequently they agree that, if such an armed attack occurs, each of them, in exercise of the right of individual or collective self-defence [would then] assist the Party or Parties so attacked by taking forthwith, individually and in concert with the other Parties, such action as it deems necessary, including the use of armed force, to restore and maintain the security of the North Atlantic area.[3]

Yet the NATO Treaty provided only for limited commitment and obligations, as well as an undefined organizational structure.

However carefully the terms of the treaty were phrased, the United States had thereby committed itself to military engagement in Europe. In political terms, the signing of the NATO Treaty on 4 April 1949, and its subsequent ratification by the U.S. Congress, marked the beginning of a new, tougher Western policy toward the Soviet Union. Set in a broader perspective, NATO served to complement the Marshall Plan and, simultaneously, constituted the security policy corroboration of both the strategy of containment and the Truman Doctrine. The immediate effect of NATO was the concentration of European defensive resources under U.S. guidance. The Allies had come a long way since their victory 1945. The enemy who had tied the emerging superpowers to each other was no more; and with the defeat of Nazi Germany the single most important reason for superpower cooperation had evaporated. By 1949, two antagonistic power blocs, each marshaling its strength for the decisive conflict, were suspiciously facing each other over a deepening fault line in Europe. For the next four decades, the bipolar nature of the postwar international system became the defining characteristic of global superpower competition.

The Globalization of the Cold War, 1949–1955

While in Europe the process of bloc formation proceeded apace with the establishment of NATO, East-West tensions escalated in Asia. Three events allowed the Cold War to spill over into regions beyond Europe and become the defining feature of the postwar international system:

- The communist takeover of China (the so-called fall of China in 1949)
- The detonation of the first Soviet atomic bomb (August 1949)
- The Korean War (1950–1953)

The so-called fall of China occurred in the aftermath of a hard-fought civil war, during which communist forces under Mao Tse-tung recovered after having suffered near defeat at the hands of the Nationalist (Kuomintang) forces under General Chiang Kai-shek and decided the contest in their own favor. As a consequence of Mao's victory, the United States came to see China as a part of an ascendant monolithic communist bloc. This vision of communism as an expansive global phenomenon deeply influenced U.S. foreign policy for the next decade. At the heart of such a clear-cut bipolar perception was that the tensions between East and West received a powerful impetus with the infusion of a strong ideological component. Diametrically opposed social and value systems created an unbridgeable gulf between the contending superpowers and among their allies to a degree as well.

The detonation of the first Soviet nuclear device in August 1949 ended the U.S. nuclear monopoly and undermined Western confidence in U.S. and, by extension, Western military strength. As a consequence, forces in the Western alliance that advocated a commitment to the expansion of military capabilities gained ground. Subsequently, NATO was transformed into an integrated defensive alliance. Essentially, the cumulative effects of developments described were largely responsible for the accelerated militarization of the Cold War after 1949.

Events in the fall of 1949 and their international perception amply demonstrated that the two blocs had become the quintessential hallmark of global politics. And the outbreak of the Korean War in June 1950 confirmed the global nature of the Cold War and further strengthened a general preference toward military solutions. In the West, North Korean aggression was perceived as the final proof of communist plans for expansion.

Increasingly, the challenges of the Cold War seemed to move away from a political dispute and shifted into open military confrontation.

The U.S. Occupation of Japan and the Chinese Civil War

As the principal expansionist power in Asia, Japan had been the most dangerous U.S. adversary during World War II. Accordingly, the starting point for postwar settlement in Asia had been the pacification of the Japanese islands and the liberation of territories controlled by the Imperial Japanese Army. Following the detonation of two atomic bombs over Nagasaki and Hiroshima and the subsequent Japanese capitulation in August 1945, the Allied commander in the Pacific, General Douglas MacArthur, set in motion a program that would leave Japan demilitarized and democratized. The Japanese constitution was redrafted to outlaw war; the powerful conglomerates (the Zaibatsu, the mainstay of Japanese militarism during the war), were neutralized as a political force; the emperor was demoted to the position of figurehead without political power; and a U.S. occupational army enforced Japanese compliance from 1945 to May 1952. The more the Cold War became a reality, the more Japan was groomed to become a close U.S. ally. Thus, the Americans transformed the former Axis empire into a valued Western outpost in the Pacific region.

A further consequence of Japan's defeat in the war was the withdrawal of imperial troops stationed in various Asian nations. In fact, the repatriation of Japanese military personnel went ahead smoothly. The real problem lay in filling the power vacuum left behind by Japanese troops. This also applied to China and, especially, to Manchuria. The Chinese civil war between the U.S.-backed Kuomintang and Mao's communist forces was interrupted in 1937, when the Japanese invaded in force. For the duration of World War II, Chiang Kai-shek and Mao abandoned the civil war to form the United Front against the Japanese aggressors. And whereas Mao's partisans had faced defeat at the hands of the Kuomintang shortly before the Japanese invasion, by 1945 their ranks swelled to approximately 900,000. In addition, they had done more to oust the enemy than Chiang, who had knowingly withheld his elite regiments in order to deploy them against the Communists following an eventual Japanese defeat. Corruption was rife in the Kuomintang officers corps, and numerous counts of peasant abuse militated against popular support in the struggle to come.

Subsequent to the expulsion of the Japanese from the Chinese mainland, the United States sought to prevent a resuscitation of the civil war. By 1947, U.S. mediation had foundered due to Chiang's intransigence and, more generally, the Kuomintang's political ineptitude. Due to widespread support among Chinese peasants, Mao's victory over the armies of the Kuomintang was swift and decisive: if the people provided a metaphorical sea, the Chinese communist forces constituted the fish. Without that sea, the fish would die. In this sense, then, Maoism differed from the tenets of Marxism-Leninism in that it emphasized peasants' support in the countryside over workers' class struggle in urban areas. Mao's strategy has also been referred to as the "Sinification" of Marxism. And so on 1 October 1949, Mao proclaimed the People's Republic of China (PRC). Chiang and his adherents fled to the nearby island of Formosa, where they founded the state of Taiwan and claimed to represent the only legitimate government of China. Until 1971, Taiwan (officially the Republic of China) held the UN seat for China.

The prewar precedent of U.S. military and financial support for the Chinese Nationalist movement had imbued Mao's Communists with distrust. Worse, the landing of more than 50,000 U.S. Marines to hold the coastal towns for the advancing Kuomintang troops in the wake of the Japanese pullout from Manchuria was perceived by the Communists to be a blatant declaration of U.S. pro-Nationalist bias. In 1950, Truman's naval intervention in the Taiwan Strait effectively forced the communist forces to accept their coast as the limit of power and consequently raised the United States to a high place in Chinese communist demonology. The Chinese Communists' experience of unequivocal U.S. support on behalf of their nemesis was to dominate the PRC's foreign political commitments in the decades to come.

According to the germinating bipolar perspective of the United States, the fall of China to Communists was a severe setback to the cause of the West. First, Mao's victory undermined the U.S. postwar security conception for Asia as envisioned by Franklin Roosevelt, according to which a pro-Western Chinese state would have acted as a balancing power vis-à-vis Japan. Second, in the context of Soviet gains in Eastern Europe, the loss of the most populous state to communism created an image of a vast, monolithic, and antagonistic communist bloc united by international socialist solidarity. The U.S. understanding of postwar developments in Europe was to influence the decision to take a firm stand on the issue of communist expansion in Asia. The quintessential consequence of the communist victory in China was the emphasis on ideology in the context of East-West tensions. Increasingly, the underlying problem was vested in the dichotomous relationship between diametrically opposed social and value systems. If not applied globally, the strategy of containment would be deprived of any meaning.

The End of the Western Nuclear Monopoly, NSC-68, and the Militarization of Containment

U.S. fears of a united communist bloc were exacerbated when, true to Oppenheimer's prediction, the Soviets detonated an atomic bomb in August

1949. The Soviet success put an abrupt end to the nuclear monopoly of the West; but it could not offset the nuclear edge that the United States continued to retain. Although the United States would maintain a numerical superiority in terms of a nuclear strike capability, Soviet possession of atomic weapons altered worldwide political perceptions of the strategic balance of power in the Cold War. Contrary to the fundamental assumptions made by George Kennan's strategy of containment, emphasizing the political nature of the Eastern threat, Soviet advances in nuclear weapons development lent hawkish forces in the West, who believed that the Soviets were likely to expand their dominion by taking recourse to their superior conventional military resources, a new impetus and thus also lent credence to such groups' demands for increased and accelerated armament within the U.S. government.

U.S. security policy duly underwent a process of adjustment to the changing strategic perception, which was aptly expressed in a joint working paper released by the defense and state secretaries' offices in February 1950. The basis of the updated security policy was the belief in the Soviet Union's objective to subvert and forcefully destroy all non-Soviet governments and societies and to replace them with regimes subservient to Moscow. Moreover, the authors believed that Soviet foreign policy was then focused on domination of the Eurasian continent. U.S. experts in the State Department no longer judged Soviet conduct according to the effective implementation of Soviet foreign policy; neither were existing divisions between the various communist governments accounted for. Instead, Secretary of State Dean Acheson endeavored to align U.S. foreign policy with the *perceived* threat of communist world domination. The resulting policy formulae were enshrined in a framework document labeled **NSC-68.**

One of the principal figures behind NSC-68 was Paul Nitze. As a personality, he can best be described as George Kennan's antipode. After Kennan left the policy planning staff in 1949, Nitze's perspective had a decisive impact on the formulation of U.S. foreign policy. A hard-nosed pragmatist, Nitze believed in the axiom of safeguarding the **national interest** by military force: "In NSC 68 the need for and use of power—military power in particular—are of fundamental importance to the successful pursuit of foreign policy objectives and the protection of national interest."[4] On the one hand, the recommendations put forward in NSC-68 envisioned the maintenance of economic aid to the free world, that is, the noncommunist states; and, on the other hand, proposed a massive increase in defense expenditures. According to the architects of NSC-68, defense spending was to double if not triple in the near future.

The rationale behind such a course of action was the perceived necessity of a rapid political consolidation of power at home and abroad, as well as an unparalleled buildup of peacetime economic capacity and military capabilities. Structurally, the most significant innovation was the emphasis on directing economic means toward the augmentation of military potential for the containment of communism. The precepts of NSC-68 constituted a blueprint of the Truman administration's overall policy between 1950 and 1953. The immediate impact of NSC-68 could be seen in Truman's sudden support for the proponents of the controversial hydrogen bomb. Furthermore, the president sought to encourage NATO members to intensify their activities in the context of the common transatlantic security policy—especially in relation to the augmentation of conventional military forces.

The Korean War: The Cold War Turns Hot

If the advocates of NSC-68 had been decried as hawks, the sudden North Korean invasion of the (noncommunist) South on 25 June 1950 vindicated their arguments for an abandonment of peacetime **fiscal conservatism**. The fact that communist military aggression in Asia had taken shape shortly after the fall of China prompted Truman's determined intervention in Korea. Washington considered the parallel connection between a partitioned Korea and a divided Germany to be significant: what had become a reality in Asia, it was argued, could also occur in Europe at any time.

The legacy of World War II.   Historically, Korea had existed within the Chinese, Japanese, and Russian spheres of influence and thus time and again suffered invasion and foreign occupation. In the recent past, Japan had repeatedly sought to bring Korea under its rule. In 1910, the Japanese Empire annexed Korea and held on to the country until the Imperial Japanese Army suffered defeat at the hands of the Allies in 1945. The origins of the unfolding conflict in Korea must be sought in the Russo-U.S. Potsdam accord dividing the peninsula along the **38th parallel**. Centered in Japan, U.S. forces held South Korea while Soviet troops occupied North Korea.

The arrangement was intended to be provisional only. Initially, it was intended to accommodate the surrender of imperial forces. The superpowers brokered a deal designed to eventually render Korea a unified state under a single government. The original plan for the administration of Korea proposed joint Allied control vested in a commission. But when Korean Communists, exiled prior to the Japanese surrender, flocked to North Korea and seized the reigns of government, the United States backed the ultranationalist and virulently anticommunist Syngman Rhee in his bid for power in South Korea. Mutual recriminations followed. The Soviets accused the United States of having installed an authoritarian regime in South Korea, whereas the United States blamed the Soviets for conniving at communist one-party rule in North Korea.

In late 1947, the Soviets tabled the Korean question at the United Nations, and achieved a partial success, when the United Nations took the decision to establish a commission in order to supervise free elections. A prior proposition on the part of the Soviets for a simultaneous withdrawal of Russian and U.S. troops from the peninsula had been vetoed by the United States, as the North Korean state was well established while the South Korean nationalists were in utter disarray. Ironically, Soviet advances at the United Nations worked against the proponents of free elections in that the North Korean government refused to admit UN personnel onto its territory during the National Assembly elections in May 1948. In South Korea, Rhee's party decided the elections in its favor and proceeded to proclaim the Korean Republic. In North Korea, Kim Il Sung, the leader of the North Korean Communists, followed suit in September of the same year.

UN intervention in the Korean War.   The stage was thus set for a major confrontation. When the superpowers retreated from Korea, skirmishes along the 38th parallel furnished Kim Il Sung with the pretext required for his next move. As mentioned earlier, North Korean troops invaded South Korea on 25 June 1950, after Stalin signaled his concurrence. Two days later, the United Nations condemned the attack as an act of outright aggression and sanctioned an initiative supported by the United States to intervene on behalf of South Korea. The UN decision in support of U.S. intervention in Korea was largely due to a Soviet blunder. When the United Nations decided to install Chiang Kai-shek's Taiwanese regime as the legitimate Chinese member on the UN Security Council instead of Mao's communist government prior to the debate on Korea, the Soviets responded by summarily boycotting the Security Council sessions. Thus, in the absence of Soviet representation, anticommunist forces were able to successfully garner support for the Korean intercession. General MacArthur was put in charge of the U.S.-led UN operations in Korea. By June 29, North Korean troops had pushed far beyond the 38th parallel and conquered the South Korean capital of Seoul. South Korean troops lacked tanks and heavy artillery and were consequently forced to retreat into the southeastern part of the peninsula. Barely in time, they were relieved by lightly equipped U.S. troops, soon to be followed by mechanized divisions.

U.S. troops had launched a counterattack from Japan before the UN resolution had been taken. In this sense, the UN mandate must be understood as a retroactive legitimization of U.S. military action against the Korean Communists. Although the United States and South Korea were in the vanguard of the military effort to oppose the North Korean invasion, other nations had joined the conflict under the banner of the United Nations. Britain, France, Australia, Turkey, Greece, and the Netherlands sent contingents to Korea. Most of the UN troops were thus drawn from the

Western democracies or states closely tied to them. On the other side of the divide, substantial Soviet support for Kim's regime based in Pyongyang fueled U.S. fears of another communist bid to expand into Asia. Thus, the escalation of superpower tensions over Asia meant that Korea became the first true battlefield of the Cold War; the belligerents not only fought a civil war but also came to be an integral part of a proxy war in the larger context of superpower hostilities.

Centered in the town of Pusan, UN troops retained a foothold in Korea. The reversal of the campaign was effected by MacArthur's bold flanking maneuver: in September, UN and U.S. troops landed in significant numbers behind enemy lines at the port of Inchon on the western coast. Seoul was quickly seized, and within a month the invaders were pushed back across the 38th parallel. At this stage, Rhee and MacArthur intended to carry the war into North Korea. U.S. naval and airborne units harried the North Korean army and pursued it far into its own territory. By 20 October, UN troops had taken Pyongyang and advanced on the Yalu River, dividing Korea from Manchuria. Meanwhile, Rhee's troops began to reaffirm government authority in the townships of South Korea. They made use of their allies' recent successes to destroy North Korean partisan units roaming the area and, in an ugly interlude to the war, to liquidate well-known critics of Rhee's rule.

Chinese intervention in the Korean War.   Washington expressed grave concern over MacArthur's rapid advance into enemy territory. U.S. government exponents feared that UN troops approaching the Yalu would provoke a Chinese intervention. The general tried to alleviate Truman's apprehensions, telling the president that the Chinese could not deploy more than 50,000 troops across the Yalu on short notice. The absence of proper diplomatic channels between the U.S. government and Chinese leaders contributed to a fateful misunderstanding and the ensuing consequences. Zhou Enlai, the Chinese prime minister, warned the Truman administration that any violation of Chinese sovereignty, or even a threat to its borders, would have severe consequences. Because this message was transmitted through the Indian ambassador, U.S. officials did not take it seriously. Despite repeated assurances on the part of the United Nations that its troops did not constitute a threat to Chinese security concerns, a massive offensive involving some 200,000 soldiers of the Chinese People's Army crossed the Yalu on 26 November. Officially, the Chinese government announced that only volunteers were involved, thereby upholding plausible deniability in case of a negative outcome in the campaign along its borders.

In ideological terms, Chinese intervention was understood by the West as a further step in a combined communist effort to decide the war in Korea for the East. Policy interpretations of this type did much to underpin the so-called zero-sum perspective. In a **zero-sum game**, there can be only one winner and one loser. Any setback for one side is perceived as an absolute gain by the other. If, however, a perspective of national interest had been applied to a situation involving the immediate proximity of UN troops to the Chinese border (the frontier to recently occupied Manchuria), then the likely possibility of a Chinese counteroffensive would have become apparent to outside observers.

In the event, the infusion of significant numbers of Chinese troops gave Kim a strategic advantage and brought about the second great reversal of the Korean War. Pyongyang and Seoul changed hands again as the combined communist army forced the UN troops back across the 38th parallel. Following this setback, Western leaders were giving serious thought to drastic measures. MacArthur was a vocal advocate of the immediate use of nuclear devices against China. But the Chinese, whose confidence had grown due to the significant successes against a coalition of its former colonizers and their abettors, remained undeterred. By February 1951, UN troops had again rolled back the combined Chinese and North Korean troops to the 38th parallel, retaken Seoul, and successfully established a stable perimeter along the line dividing the Koreas, barring all further enemy advances into South Korea. In a position of relative security, MacArthur proceeded to offer a truce but actually threatened the use of the atomic bomb should the Chinese not agree to his terms. The Chinese response—that all UN troops from Korea and all U.S. military personnel in Taiwan be immediately withdrawn—provoked MacArthur into staging yet another attack across the 38th parallel. At this stage, Truman relieved MacArthur of his command, as the general had clearly overstepped his authority. General Matthew Ridgeway was appointed the new supreme commander of the UN forces in Korea.

The division of Korea. The final offensive occurred in April 1951, when North Korean troops attacked South Korea. In a concerted effort, U.S. troops under General Ridgeway made short work of the latest communist attempt to decide the war. The war of attrition that ensued lasted another two years. From the summer of 1951 to 17 July 1953, the desultory exchanges between North Korean and UN plenipotentiaries dragged on with no tangible agreement being reached until the very last phase of the negotiations. A line of demarcation was henceforth to divide the parties to the conflict, leaving North Korea in the undisputed possession of Kim Il Sung, South Korea under Rhee's rule. The Korean War had not changed the initial allied division of the peninsula but instead had cost the United Nations at least 27,000 casualties, the Chinese approximately 900,000 fatalities, and uncounted dead among civilians estimated to be in the range of just less than 2 million. Cities in North Korea had been leveled in a series of UN bombardments, and South Korea had experienced substantial destruction in war. The first battle of the Cold War had ended in a stalemate that would endure into the present day.

The Impact of the Korean War on Europe and the Establishment of the Cold War System

The conduct of superpower competition had become subject to highly ideologized perceptions of threat in the early 1950s. U.S. decisionmakers had come to believe that the Soviet Union wanted no less than to dominate the entire Eurasian landmass. Meanwhile, the Soviets were convinced that the West sought to isolate and encircle them by a ring of military bases situated around the Soviet Union. The globalization and militarization of the Cold War was vindicated by the outbreak of the Korean War. The consequences of this military confrontation for events in Europe were palpable.

The militarization of NATO.   As a consequence of the developments between 1949 and 1953, U.S. resistance to a less restrictive engagement in Europe was swept away. NATO's purpose shifted from that of a politico-psychological protection of U.S. financial aid for Europe to that of a military guarantee for European security. In the years following the outbreak of the Korean War, the structure of NATO, as well as its sophistication, more adequately reflected the Western alliance's new purpose and the seriousness of the West's perception of the East's aggressive tendencies. In due course, Congress authorized the permanent deployment of four U.S. divisions for duty in Europe. NATO was subdivided into three commands: the Allied Command Europe, the Allied Command Atlantic, and the Allied Command Channel. The command structures were in turn subject to the NATO's defense commission. NATO also created the post of secretary-general for its principal political officer. The rapid development of NATO's structure between 1950 and 1952 exemplifies the transition from the loose defensive framework it had been in 1949 to an integrated defensive organization only a few years later. At a NATO ministerial meeting at Lisbon in February 1952, the ministers decided to increase the conventional force of NATO. But of the originally projected ninety-six divisions, only eighteen were in place by 1953.

The touchy issue of German rearmament.   The key question of NATO's plans for augmenting the alliance's troop strength concerned German rearmament. Resistance to German rearmament was considerable, as many of Germany's neighbors feared a return to the dark days of the Third Reich. Yet NATO's planning objective of assembling ninety-six divisions was doomed to failure unless the Germans were allowed to participate in the scheme. More generally, the United States advocated German participation and rearmament because U.S. political leaders were convinced that the inclusion of German military and economic potential was essential to the containment of Soviet expansion. Without the considerable German potential, the European economic recovery since the end of World War II would likely be reversed and thereby endanger the very political stability that the Marshall Plan had been attempting to maintain since its inception. Moreover, significant U.S. military resources were then committed in Korea. Accordingly, U.S. Secretary of State Dean Acheson exerted pressure on the West European allies. He offered to guarantee the permanent presence of U.S. troops in Europe, to increase military aid, and to assume the supreme command in an integrated NATO general staff. The U.S. offer, however, was dependent upon British and French consent for the embodiment and integration of ten divisions of West German troops.

A European defense community?   Whereas the British would have acquiesced in the U.S. demand for German inclusion, France had a different position. The French government went out of its way to delay any decision being taken on the issue. In October 1950, the French tabled a proposal for a supranational European defense community. The so-called **Pleven Plan** envisioned the integration of West German forces at the level of battalions and regiments, which would allow for easier control of its troops. Furthermore, Germany was to be denied any voice in the supreme command of the European forces. Predictably, the Germans refused to contemplate the proposal. Protected by Western alliance troops since the end of the war, Germany did not require its own soldiers as badly as did NATO. Under mounting U.S. pressure, France was forced to concede the issue. Finally, the French added their signature to the founding document of the **European Defense Community (EDC)** in May 1952. In contrast to the Pleven Plan, the EDC extended equal rights to West Germany in exchange for its full support. Although representatives of Germany, France, Italy, Belgium, Luxembourg, and the Netherlands signed the EDC founding document, the French parliament refused to ratify the treaty in August 1954. What had happened?

First, the Soviets reacted by attempting to calm East-West relations, which raised West European expectations for a relaxation of tensions. Stalin now seemed to offer the Germans improved terms for reunification. Second, U.S. relations with its European allies deteriorated over the hawkish rhetoric of **rollback** emanating from Dwight Eisenhower's incoming administration. To the Europeans, the road to better relations with the Soviets had become tangible, but the United States knew no better than to threaten Stalin. Eisenhower's insistence that the EDC Treaty be ratified soon also contributed to a downturn in U.S.-European relations. U.S. interest in rendering the EDC operational generated European fears of U.S. intentions to withdraw its military presence from the Continent. Third, French fears of a potential German preponderance within the EDC undermined the project from the very outset. For the time being, any thoughts of a supranational political European community were shelved.

NATO's double-containment. At this stage, the failure of the EDC allowed exponents of a transatlantic alliance to cogently voice their arguments: An exclusively European framework would prove too weak to contain a prospering Germany; equally, a European alliance could never act as a deterrent to Soviet expansion. What was required was a regional security political structure that would act as a viable safety anchor within the Western bloc by providing a framework for so-called double-containment. The gist of the transatlantic solution was that the United States would neutralize Germany as a potential hegemon while effectively combining German forces with those of the Europeans to contain the spread of Soviet communism on the Continent. The only conceivable vessel for German rearmament, the argument ran, was NATO.

The threat of revived German militarism was countered by dredging up the Brussels Pact concluded in 1948. At the Paris Conference of 1954, the Brussels Pact was expanded by the inclusion of West Germany and Italy; it became the West European Union, which was intended to extend collective European control over German naval and aerial armament. At the same time, West Germany agreed not to produce any nuclear or chemical weapons within its own borders. In exchange for this commitment, NATO admitted West Germany as an equal member. The way to German rearmament within NATO had thus been cleared.

The formation of the two blocs had come to a temporary conclusion. The Soviet Union, too, organized its sphere of influence in the shape of a military alliance. The **Warsaw Pact** was concluded on 14 May 1955. On both sides, the formation of blocs had moved from economic coordination to political mergers and culminated in the collective organization of defense. By the mid-1950s, both sides had staked out and secured their turf and also established that they would not countenance any interference by the other side in their own sphere of influence.

Decolonization in Asia, 1945–1955

The expansion of the Cold War beyond Europe coincided with the long-term process of **decolonization** in Asia. Where the paths of the two historical phenomena intersected, they did reinforce one another in general. The Cold War lines of division drawn in Europe and in Asia superimposed themselves over a deeper level of conflictive potential, the causes of which were a consequence of World War II. When the Axis powers threatened to overwhelm the European allies before the United States had entered the war, the colonial dominions were given a taste of their respective masters' weakness. Such a display of human frailty was not lost on the colonized: World War II and the concurrent decline of the Great Powers accelerated a process of emancipation mainly because the colonizers were no longer able to furnish the vast resources required to run their empires in Asia and elsewhere.

The experience of World War II catalyzed the colonial elites' will to act and enlarged its room for maneuver. Colonial troops had actively participated in the struggle against the Axis. The experience of war had raised their self-confidence, which led many a colony to issue demands for independence after the war in exchange for their support while it had lasted. Taking their demands still further, a few colonies during the war threatened defection should their demands not meet with the desired results. Charismatic personalities, who had been educated at Western academic institutions, frequently presented colonial demands. After spells of internment or terms of incarceration as political prisoners in colonial prisons, such figures were to grow into leaders heading successful independence movements.

The colonial powers' reaction to such emancipation efforts was diverse. Whereas the British realized that the only sensible recourse was incremental withdrawal, the French and Dutch resisted decolonization at every turn. The British Empire sustained only minimal damage. France and the Netherlands, by contrast, paid a huge price for their recalcitrance: the initial exorbitant cost of maintaining offshore army establishments and administrations was not offset by the income derived from the exploitation of colonial natural resources and was only slightly less damaging than the final humiliation of military defeat. Gradually, the United States also was confronted with the conundrum of having to chose between containing communism and respecting the right to self-government as enshrined in the articles of the Atlantic Charter of 1941.

Allies at Odds: Churchill, Roosevelt, and the Atlantic Charter

The colonial powers of the West, notably Britain and France, came under increased pressure among their own ranks over the issue of **colonialism**. By 1941, the entry of the United States into the war had become a vital concern for Britain. In their opposition to Nazi hegemony, the Anglo-Saxon powers were united; not so on the issue of the colonies. It must be remembered that the United States had itself evolved from a bloody struggle against the British motherland during the Revolutionary War. In other words, U.S. interest was certainly not geared toward the maintenance of any colonial empire.

Yet the British Empire still contained many Asian, Southeast Asian, and African dependencies within its bounds. The French were also not inclined to let go of their colonial possessions in North Africa, central Africa, and Indochina. U.S. anticolonialism was made manifest in a joint Anglo-U.S. declaration of intent in which British colonial interests were subordinated to the wartime priority of U.S. support in the war. Nevertheless, the Atlantic Charter of 14 August 1941 aptly expressed Roosevelt's moral victory over Churchill's attempts to protect British colonial interests:

> First, [the signatories'] countries seek no aggrandizement, territorial or other; second, they desire to see no territorial changes that do not accord with the freely expressed wishes of the peoples concerned; third, they respect the right of all peoples to choose the form of government under which they will live; and they wish to see sovereign rights and self-government restored to those who have been forcibly deprived of them.[5]

Although Churchill, by including a special proviso in the charter designed to protect British shipping and trade with its Commonwealth associates, was able to alleviate the extent of the concession his government was compelled to make, the tenor of U.S. idealism remained dominant and the anticolonialist connotation of its policy obvious. Significantly, Roosevelt's demand that British and French colonies be turned over to the United Nations after the war were met with consternation and outright skepticism. Also, Allied differences over strategic priorities during the war surfaced when Churchill stated his preference that resources be used to maintain British interests in North Africa, the Balkans, and the Middle East rather than to open a Western Front.

As the Imperial Japanese Army was gradually being pushed out of India, Southeast Asia, and the greater Pacific region, the forces of indigenous independence movements asserted themselves. For the most part, national independence movements in the Asian colonies were Marxist-inspired and thus anathema to many Allied leaders. As in the emerging Cold War divisions, much of the ensuing conflict between the Western colonial powers and the national liberation movements was of a perceptive nature. Marginalized by the rise of the superpowers, the Great Powers of Europe had gone through a demotion during World War II and ended up as second-rate powers. Their colonies were objects of political prestige; colonial losses would make the former Great Powers painfully aware of their decline. For this reason, among others, the European colonial powers were determined to reoccupy territories previously lost to the Japanese in Asia. National liberation movements, however, flocked to the banner of Marxism and, by extension, communism because its ideology was inherently anti-imperialist and because such an alignment would add the benefit of support from the Soviet Union. In summary, the more the global bipolar dynamic gathered momentum, the more the United States was compelled to formulate its foreign policy in accordance with Cold War dictates and hence to make allowances for European colonial interests. Thus, in spite of its earlier overt opposition to colonialism, the United States was forced to grant its European Allies substantial aid in order to retain their overseas possessions.

The Philippines and the U.S. Foreign Policy Dilemma

Since the late nineteenth century, the United States maintained quasicolonial rule in the Philippines, which to Americans felt more like a glaring contradiction in terms of their otherwise resolute anticolonialism. The reluctant island nation had been groomed for independence as early as the 1930s. After World War II the situation had completely changed. By then, Filipino nationalism had received a new impetus. Following the Japanese occupation, the postwar conservative government was soon at loggerheads with the socialist guerrillas known as the Hukbalahap (or Huk, as they were commonly known). During the war, the Huk had supported U.S. operations against the Japanese invaders. By 1946, when the U.S. government granted independence, the newly constituted Philippine government faced a full-scale peasant uprising because it denied legitimately elected Communists the exercise of their offices. By 1949, the Huk had joined the Communists. Until 1954, when government forces suppressed resistance from the left, the Philippines remained in a state of virtual civil war.

The U.S. experience in the Philippines exemplifies the dilemma that was to bedevil decades of U.S. foreign policy: the objectives of the strategy of containment could not be reconciled with U.S. anticolonialist tenets as stated in the Atlantic Charter. Ultimately, the resolution of this question came down to the postwar U.S. perception of the immediate threat. The containment of communism took precedence over idealist principles derived from the U.S. historical experience. Thus, the United States was more often than not forced to keep in power corrupt and dictatorial regimes bent on exploiting the populace, which in turn gave rise to various types of socialist resistance movements. The dilemma of irreconcilable U.S. foreign policy objectives was also a self-perpetuating vicious circle that fed off of the Cold War bipolar logic and reinforced its dynamic. The Philippine example was never only that; instead, it was a precedent to be repeated across Asia.

Great Britain in Malaya: Peaceful Withdrawal

A scenario similar to that of the postwar Philippines confronted Great Britain upon its return to Malaya in 1945. The mainstay of resistance to Japanese occupation in Malaya had been the communist Chinese guerrillas who had enjoyed Allied support (ethnic Malays and a significant number of Indian immigrants had chosen to collaborate with the Japanese forces). The reconstituted British administration wanted to expand equal rights to all of the three ethnic groups but soon met with stiff resistance from the Malay majority. Moreover, the Malay Peninsula was to be unified, whereas Singapore, with a Chinese majority, was to become a separate colony. This time, British intentions were opposed by not only the Malays but also the Chinese minority. Malayan leaders feared that the other ethnic groups would stand to gain at their expense, and Malayan Chinese were loath to be cut off from their brethren in Singapore. Nationalist leaders also came to realize that the British, though guided by considerations of fair play, were not intending to depart in the near future. Indeed, the rationale behind the British presence in Malaya was economic, for the exploitation of natural resources in the colonies had taken on a new importance in light of Britain's depleted Exchequer and a largely crippled economy at home. In particular, rubber and tin exports necessitated the maintenance of British control of Malaya.

Although the communist guerrillas had abandoned their guns for the ballot box following the resumption of British colonial rule, to which the Malays followed suit, in 1946 they took to organizing strikes and infiltrating unions after their calls for a prompt British withdrawal went unheard. By 1948, the Malayan Chinese Communists completely abandoned the pursuit of national independence by constitutional means and disappeared into the countryside, where they hoped to resuscitate the struggle against the foreign occupiers. Moving back into the underground effectively isolated the Chinese Communists, whose protracted struggle endured until 1952; it also paved the way for the establishment of the Alliance Party, consisting of anticommunist ethnic Chinese nationalists and the Malay majority.

The struggle against the communist guerrillas was fought with determination, uniting the British, the noncommunist Chinese, and the Malays. Following this round of domestic hostilities, the country settled back into constitutional politics. The Alliance Party enjoyed significant popular support and in due course negotiated an end to British rule in Malaya. For their own part, the British in Malaya yielded gracefully in 1957. A careful balance of British determination and insight had deprived communism of popular support in Malaya. Elsewhere, Britain's colonial administrators displayed less sense and, fatefully, more brawn.

Britain and the Indian Subcontinent: Religious and Ethnic Tensions
The largest and most significant colony of the British Empire was situated on the Indian subcontinent. There, English adventurers of the East India

Company had made inroads in the seventeenth century and consolidated their rule by constructing an extensive system of alliances with indigenous potentates. This ultimately allowed them to play the ruling Maharajas against each other. By 1757, the British had ousted their French competitors. Following the Sepoy Revolt in 1857, the British government exercised direct rule in India. Henceforth, a viceroy was to implement British policy. India has always been a patchwork of cultures, languages, religions, and ethnicities. It was this diversity that was responsible for lasting internal division and that had allowed foreign powers to establish a foothold in the first place. Successive British viceroys attempted to impose at least a semblance of unity upon the heterogeneous colony. One of the consequences of integrating Indian natives into the colonial administration was the creation of a highly educated elite.

By the 1930s, segments of the Indian administrative elite had evolved into vocal nationalist movements. On the one hand, the Congress Party headed by Mohandas Karamchand Gandhi struggled for an independent and united India; on the other, Muhammad Ali Jinnah's Muslim League lobbied the British for a solution involving a separate state for the Muslim minority. When World War II broke out in 1939, nationalist leaders were confronted with the fait accompli of having automatically entered the war alongside the motherland. The Hindu nationalist leaders reacted with a halt to any collaboration with the viceroy, which in turn forced the British to rescind their plans for devolved government. Simultaneously, Indian troops fought faithfully alongside Britain in most theaters of the war. By early 1942, a British initiative represented by Sir Stafford Cripps offered the nationalists independence after the conclusion of the war. The Hindu leaders—Gandhi and Jawaharlal Nehru—rebuffed Cripps's overtures, as it appeared to them that Britain was primarily interested in retaining Muslim goodwill. With no other option left to the viceroy, the Congress Party was suppressed. Meanwhile, Jinnah's Muslim League gained ground. An eventual partitioning could no longer be prevented.

As a consequence of the British elections in 1945, Churchill and his wartime cabinet were replaced at the helm by a Labor government under Clement Attlee. In contrast to the conservative Churchill, Attlee knew no scruples when it came to abandoning the British imperial legacy. Even so, the Labor government struggled to manage an increasingly hopeless situation in deeply divided India. Several rounds of tripartite negotiations did not bring those concerned closer to a feasible solution. Complicating the talks was the apparent necessity of dividing two key areas: the Punjab in the north, and Bengal in the east. Louis St. Viscount Mountbatten, the British delegate, forced a decision on the nationalist leaders: Britain intended to transfer authority six months earlier—on 15 August 1947—than previously announced. Mountbatten's ultimatum left Gandhi and Jinnah with little space to maneuver.

After the partitioning of the subcontinent and the subsequent proclamations of the Pakistani and Indian states, a veritable mass migration set in. Hindus left Pakistan, and Muslims fled India. An estimated 10 million fell prey to the ensuing religious strife as **refugees**, casualties, or fatalities. In the border country, the battle for the Kashmir and Jammu flared up with uncustomary violence. There the Sikh minority fought both Muslims and Hindus in a bloody conflict for supremacy. To this day, India and Pakistan continue to struggle over Kashmir. Moreover, clashes along the Sino-Indian border transformed the area into a veritable powder keg. The volatile situation in the Kashmir and Punjab districts were to remain a lasting legacy of postimperial rule.

Britain's path to decolonization in India was rocky. Unlike in Malaya, where ethnic divisions were ably bridged, in India the British were hard-pressed to find a satisfactory settlement for the successor states. Nonetheless, with the release of Pakistan and India into independence, the dismantling of the British Empire had moved a significant step forward. In geostrategic terms, the Cold War left the Indian subcontinent largely untouched during the 1940s and 1950s. This would change in the 1960s. Though communism as an issue was relegated to the sidelines of this conflict, Pakistan, seeking protection from its powerful Indian neighbor, was drawn into the Western orbit by becoming a member of the **Southeast Asia Treaty Organization (SEATO)**. India, for its part, eventually joined the **Non-Aligned Movement (NAM)**, which set itself up as an alternative to East and West. Nevertheless, India's ties with the Soviet Union would have unnerved the Western bloc still more had there not been the saving grace of China's lasting enmity.

The Dutch in Indonesia: Repression, Exploitation, and Defeat

In Asia, Britain acted with foresight and applied a realistic perspective to the necessity of abandoning its historical role of arbiter and colonizer. There were problems enough at home. In the end, Britain's quest for accommodation and settlement given rising nationalist movements in Asia made possible the relatively dignified retreat that began soon after the war. Conversely, the British military, freed from costly engagements in Europe and the Middle East, could have held on to the remnants of empire had it needed to. This did not apply to another colonial power present in the area: the Dutch. In 1942, the conquering Imperial Japanese Army drove the Dutch out of Indonesia. As the Dutch became increasingly unpopular with the indigenous peoples, the Japanese were welcomed as liberators.

The Japanese, however, soon began to prove themselves to be even harsher masters. Nationalism was neither encouraged nor actively suppressed. In fact, the occupiers sought to use nationalism in their own interest. The leading figures of the Indonesian nationalist movement, Mohammed Hatta and Achmed Sukarno, had no compunctions about collaborating with the Japanese, whose main interest was a concerted effort at exploiting Indonesia's natural resources. Sukarno and Hatta were willing to work with any one foreign power as long as they achieved their objective of independence. By the time Japanese rule collapsed in the face of Allied victories in Asia, Indonesian nationalism faced an indigenous and an exogenous threat: First, the Communists, fiercely suppressed by the Dutch, had recuperated and were again a force to be reckoned with; second, Viscount Mountbatten had landed Indian troops in order to accept the Japanese surrender in September 1945—but also to ensure the transfer of authority to the Dutch colonial masters.

The proclamation of an Indonesian republic a month prior to the Allied landing did little to facilitate the situation. Under the tutelage of the Japanese, an armed and trained Indonesian militia had been established during the war. Sukarno decided that resistance would be futile. Accordingly, Allied troops seized control of Java, the main island of the Indonesian archipelago. Resistance to the British occupation of Indonesia did, however, assert itself in the course of the next few weeks—as it was, without the sanction of either Sukarno or that of Hatta. The commanding Allied officer was assassinated in November. Retribution was swift: at the Battle of Surabaya, some 15,000 Indonesian resistance fighters were killed. Soon thereafter, Dutch troops poured into Indonesia. But taking control of the cities was one thing; suppressing Indonesian nationalists in the remote rural areas was quite another. Despite growing international and British pressure to abandon Indonesia, the Dutch stubbornly fought on. As in Malaya, economic interests dictated Dutch policy considerations. Indonesia offered a wealth of natural resources.

Put simply, Dutch chances of maintaining colonial rule in Indonesia were at best slim. When the troops that had landed under the Allies pulled out following a truce with the Indonesian nationalist resistance in November 1946, the escalating situation called for increased Dutch revenues in order to maintain a semblance of order. Between 1947 and 1948, the Dutch stepped up their campaign against the nationalists. On the political level, the Indonesians boycotted any and all Dutch initiatives that did not involve complete Dutch withdrawal. Although the nationalist side also was beset by internecine strife—Communists had attempted to overthrow the nationalist leadership in September 1948—some 145,000 Dutch troops proved unable to contain Indonesian guerrilla forces in the far-flung archipelago. Overtaxed by the financial burdens of a continuing military commitment, the Netherlands finally conceded defeat. Toward the end of 1949, some 85,000 members of the Dutch armed forces and colonial administration left for good. As we will see, the Indonesian state was finally constituted in 1960.

The French in Indochina: Colonialism Revisited

The Dutch experience of decolonization highlights the lessons learned by the British. The economic exploitation of a colony could be considered profitable only if there was no indigenous political force opposing foreign domination. In the case of the French colonial empire in Indochina, questions over prestige and power came to augment economic considerations. During the war, Washington had pressured Britain to dissolve its empire, and Britain complied. Equally, France was made to feel U.S. displeasure regarding its colonies, but it would not hear of dissolving its Indochinese possessions. Had not the U.S. apprehension of Soviet expansionism taken on a defining quality in relation to U.S. foreign policy in the years after 1945, it is likely that France would have been subjected to still more pressure to abandon its colonies. Thus the example of Indochina is likely the most instructive in relation to the U.S. foreign policy dilemma: the development of U.S. support for the French was diametrically opposed to the professed principle of anticolonialism. How did this turnabout in U.S. foreign policy affect Indochina?

During the latter half of the nineteenth century, modern Laos, Cambodia, and Vietnam came under French rule. The Japanese occupied the French colonies, known as French Indochina, in the early stages of World War II. While the Japanese were in control from 1940 to 1945, the Communists formed a resistance movement called the **Vietminh**; they received substantial support from the United States in their war against the Japanese Empire. The Vietminh's base of operations lay in northern Vietnam, close to the Chinese border. As early as 1941, communist leader Ho Chi Minh proclaimed the Democratic Republic of Vietnam at Hanoi (this would come to be known as North Vietnam).

In the wake of the Japanese withdrawal from French Indochina, a series of advances by foreign powers came to affect Vietnam between the summer of 1945 and the spring of 1946. The first to intervene in August 1945 were Chiang Kai-shek's republican Chinese forces, who were then battling Mao's Communists in the Chinese civil war. The Kuomintang troops managed to dislodge the Japanese in northeastern Vietnam. In September, British troops landed in the southern part of the country. In January and March 1946, the old colonial masters, the French, returned in force, staging invasions in the north and south. After disarming the former Japanese occupiers, the British and Kuomintang troops relinquished power over the territory held by them to the French.

Tensions between the French colonial administration and the communist national liberation movement quickly escalated and in due course found an outlet in increasingly direct military confrontations. Thus, in 1946 the First Indochina War began and would lead to the disestablishment of the French colonial empire in that region eight years later. The war was not going well for France. The longer it raged, the more the Vietminh attracted followers. In addition, the Vietminh was legitimized in January 1950 by the diplomatic recognitions of the Soviet Union and the recently victorious communist regime in China. In the early 1950s, communist influence spread from Vietnam to adjacent Laos and Cambodia. By 1954, the Vietminh controlled large tracts of North Vietnam and made its influence felt in the southern part of the country. The movement soon extended its control into the Laotian marches and into western Cambodia.

Indochina: The Domino Theory and the
Genesis of U.S. Intervention in Southeast Asia

The United States looked on in a state of increasing anxiety. As early as Truman's tenure in office, the United States tried to support the French endeavor economically and militarily. This track in U.S. foreign policy witnessed a surge following Eisenhower's inauguration. In 1950, U.S. aid had covered some 15 percent of French campaign expenses; only four years later, Eisenhower's administration provided for some 80 percent of the cost. Even so, U.S. troops had not set foot on Vietnamese soil. At the same time, the French could not have held Indochina without U.S. financial support.

In Washington, U.S. aid to the French was legitimized on the grounds that the situation in Vietnam constituted an extension of the Cold War. According to the view held by U.S. policymakers, the principal issue in Vietnam was defending the southern frontier as envisioned in the strategy of containment against the violent expansions of international communism. In a press conference given in early 1954, President Eisenhower elaborated on his apprehensions regarding the situation in Vietnam by putting forward his **Domino Theory**. "You have a row of dominoes set, you knock over the first one, and what will happen to the last one is the certainty that it will go over very quickly. So you could have a beginning of a disintegration that would have the most profound influences."[6] In other words, if Communists were permitted to conquer Vietnam, the Western world was facing the probability of a chain reaction, "knocking over" one Southeast Asian state after another. In the 1960s, the Domino Theory would lead the United States into the debacle of the Second Indochina War, known in the United States as the Vietnam War.

Soon enough, the question that U.S. decisionmakers had to decide was whether the United States ought to commit troops in Indochina. In the spring of 1954, an advance detachment of French troops was cut off and encircled by the enemy at **Dien Bien Phu**. In light of the deteriorating situation, France called on the United States to relieve its embattled army. At the Pentagon, various voices rose to demand a preventive strike against communist China, for Mao's regime was perceived as the mainstay of power underpinning communist efforts in Vietnam. Eisenhower, however, decided against U.S. intervention in Indochina, British and world opinion being pointedly opposed to such a course of action. Lacking U.S. reinforcements, the French were compelled to capitulate on 7 May 1954.

On the following day, the Indochina Conference convened at Geneva. At that conference, the fate of the disputed region was to be decided. Apart from France, Britain, the United States, and the Soviet Union, China set a precedent by participating in an international conference. The result of the long-winded deliberations was the recognition of Laotian and Cambodian independence. In contrast, Vietnam was partitioned along the 17th parallel, dividing the country into Communist-dominated North Vietnam and South Vietnam, where the French installed an authoritarian regime under the Annamese emperor, Bao Dai. Bao Dai's government enjoyed little support from the people it ruled and soon faced growing opposition from South Vietnamese communist guerrillas. The prospects of Bao Dai remaining in power without U.S. support quickly dwindled.

U.S. intervention in Vietnam thus took its fateful turn. In the course of the Vietnam War, Cambodia and Laos became embroiled in the hostilities. For decades, the former French colonial possession fell into the turmoil and chaos of a conflict largely defined by the laws of the Cold War.

Thus the unfolding story of the Vietnam War exemplifies the transition from a struggle for national liberation led by suppressed indigenous peoples against their colonial masters to a confrontation shaped in the process of ossifying Eastern and Western fronts. The Cold War had become a global reality.

IR Theory and Key Concepts

The First International Relations Debate:
Idealism Versus Realism
The first international relations debate centered around two conflicting views of international politics during the interwar period

(1919–1939). The key text for this period, written by E. H. Carr, is entitled *The Twenty Years' Crisis*. In the aftermath of World War I, liberal internationalists (the later idealists) argued that there was an authentic and widespread popular conviction that peace provided the only viable objective in international politics and that democratic governments by and large were supportive of this conception. The liberal internationalist optimism suffered a serious setback in the face of the ascendant fascist and, later, other totalitarian regimes of the 1930s and 1940s. By contrast, E. H. Carr postulated that the fundamental conflict in international relations was not between contending theories, such as the liberal doctrine of the harmony of interests—a widely held tenet of idealism—but between the haves and have-nots. The non-Marxist component of Carr's critique of the idealist position was that politics have to be based on a proper understanding of this basic truth. Idealism, according to Carr, is utopian in that it supposed that the have-nots could be brought to accept legal and moral codes of conduct. Carr's outlook is grounded in early realist thought. The realist-idealist divergence was made manifest in the first international relations debate and can be summarized in the following words: realists claim to work with international relations as they really are, whereas idealists are regarded (especially by realists) as presenting the world as they wish it to be.

The Realist Paradigm

Realism is a theory of international relations that emphasizes the state as unitary and rational actor and focuses on the actions and interactions of states. For the most part, realists study patterns of conflict and cooperation in the context of an anarchical international system. Usually, security issues dominate the realist agenda at the expense of other concerns. National interests or objectives, power, and the balance of power are key concepts for a majority of realists.

The Idealist Paradigm

Idealism contrasts from the above definition of realism in important ways. Following World War I, representatives of the idealist school of thought advocated supranational cooperation and, most of all, national self-determination. Idealist precepts were made manifest in U.S. President Woodrow Wilson's Fourteen Points Program, which was presented at the Paris Conference in 1919. Within the context of international relations studies, idealism emphasizes the importance of justice and a desire for global peace as human preferences and their potential in surmounting obstacles to their realization. Idealists have frequently been criticized for their apparent lack of understanding political, as well as other, "realities" that apparently constrain choice among actors in international relations. In summary, many idealists consider ideas as having significant causal effects, whereas others emphasize power and/or material factors as constituting key determinants in the arena of international politics and relations.

Ideology in the East: Marxism, Leninism, and Stalinism

Inspired by the German Karl Marx, Marxism postulates the dialectical unfolding of historical stages. Moreover, Marxism stresses the significance of economic and material forces and of class analysis. Marxist analysis arrives at the conclusion that contradiction inherent in each historical epoch eventually culminates in the ascendancy of a new dominant class. According to Marx, the rule of the proletariat—the working class—through a revolution will replace the era of capitalism, dominated by the bourgeois class. This first stage in the revolutionary process will be followed by an era of socialism, during which the proletariat will own the means of production. Finally, the socialist society will be eclipsed by the advent of a classless, or communist, society. As a consequence, the state—historically a tool of the dominant class—will wither away. Leninism's main contribution to Marxist thought rests with its introduction of the concept of **imperialism** (based on John Hobson's notions of overproduction and consequent capitalist expansion) as the highest stage of capitalism. Stalinism describes the Soviet strategy of exporting the revolution and its values. Moreover, Stalinism also refers to the forced collectivization of farms, the regimentation of the economy (i.e., the **Five Year Plan**), and, lastly, totalitarian rule.

Communism

In the context of Marxist thought, communism refers to a mode of production. Its achievement is intended to occur after the decline of capitalism and following a socialist transition period. As such, communism is a classless society. In a communist society, everybody produces according to his or her ability, and everyone consumes and receives in accordance with his or her needs. Given the absence of classes, the state (in Marxist thought) as an instrument of class domination ceases to exist.

Key Terms

- Great Powers: The historic European nation-states that grew to prominence, even preponderance, in early modern Europe. In the twentieth century, Germany, France, and Britain are accorded the status of Great Power.
- balance of power: A key concept among realists that refers to a condition of equilibrium among states. Realists disagree on whether the equilibrium among states is (1) decisively influenced by key decisionmakers; or (2) occurs independently from the will of statesmen as an inherent characteristic of international politics. Decisionmakers may use balance-of-power considerations as justification for any given foreign policy. Detractors and critics alike have pointed out that the multiplicity of definitions and their meanings has rendered the concept of balance of power diffuse and, consequently, of only limited value in international relations theory.
- superpowers: In the wake of World War II, the flanking powers of the Western alliance—the United States and the Soviet Union—emerged as the most powerful state actors in the international system. The two superpowers dominated international relations for the next half-century. Compared to the Great Powers of Europe, the superpowers assumed their status by developing increased military (conventional and nuclear) and economic power, that is, **relative power**, which by far outweighed those of their predecessors. A distinct attribute of a superpower is that it is able to project its power forcefully around the world.
- bipolarity: The condition of having two opposing poles in the international system. Many theorists of international relations consider the Cold War international political system to have had a bipolar structure. Bipolarity is introduced as a concept based on the ideological, social, and political antagonism of East and West, as two social systems facing each other across the divide of the Iron Curtain.
- containment and the Domino Theory: George F. Kennan conceived the strategy of containment. It emphasized the need to check the political and economic spread of communism; the application of containment in U.S. foreign policy led to a military emphasis. President Eisenhower's Domino Theory expressed the fear that if a noncommunist state in an unstable region fell under Soviet suzerainty, then other states in that area would inevitably follow.

Confrontation and Fragmentation, 1955–1963

It is conceivable that a world of this kind [of mutual atomic plenty] may enjoy a strange stability arising from a general understanding that it would be suicidal to "throw the switch." On the other hand it also seems possible that a world so dangerous may not be very calm, and to maintain peace it will be necessary for statesmen to decide against rash action not just once, but every time. In particular, since the coming of such a world will be gradual and since its coming may or may not be correctly estimated in all countries, there is a possibility that one nation or another may be tempted to launch a preventive war "before its too late," only to find out that the time for such a blow has already passed.

—J. Robert Oppenheimer, chairman,
Panel on Armaments and U.S. Policy, January 1953[1]

In the perception of many during the early 1950s, the Cold War appeared to be building toward its climax. A chasm divided Europe less than ten years after the conclusion of World War II. At that time, Asian states also had been involved in the confrontation between East and West. Events in Europe were once again shaped by military alliances, and in Asia the Cold War was escalating into a hot war on the Korean Peninsula.

Nevertheless, in the mid-1950s a first, if precarious, balance between the two blocs was in place—at least in Europe. Each superpower made clear that it would not countenance any interference in its sphere of influence by the other. With the rapid, costly expansion of the superpowers' nuclear threat potentials—the new hydrogen bomb was a thousand times more powerful than the bombs dropped on Hiroshima and Nagasaki—as well as the incremental emergence of the age of nuclear plenty, some signs pointed toward a relaxation of tensions between the two blocs.

The Panel on Armaments and U.S. Policy, the study group cited at the beginning of this chapter, was commissioned by the U.S. State Department and as early as 1953 depicted a world in which the superpowers would continuously expand their respective nuclear arsenals. On the one hand, farsighted individuals were capable of imagining the establishment of a strange stability side by side with a balance of terror in the long term. Conversely, nobody could anticipate what would happen on the long road ahead, that is, whether the superpower conflict would eventually escalate into a nuclear confrontation. The advantages of a nuclear **first-strike capability** gave rise to apprehensions because so-called first strikes (whereby one superpower devastated the other before any response could be mounted by the target country) were at times understood to be decisive in a potential nuclear war. In the event of a protracted crisis, two scorpions equipped with deadly weapons, which would strike at the first sign of enemy attack, would therefore face each other across an unbridgeable gap.

The reduction of Cold War tensions, however, would prove a very difficult and time-consuming process, one that was constantly threatened by setbacks. The Berlin crisis and the Cuban missile crisis of the early 1960s brought the world to the brink of a nuclear exchange. Yet President John F. Kennedy, who succeeded Dwight Eisenhower in the White House, and Soviet leader Nikita Khrushchev, who had emerged after a power struggle within the Kremlin, introduced a brief period of relaxed relations between the two superpowers. The two statesmen realized that security and stability for Europe could be sustained only if the two principals of the Cold War would be willing to respect the territorial and nuclear status quo.

The superpowers had a long way to travel on this road. In the 1950s, Washington and Moscow continued to eye each other with suspicion and perceive the enemy mostly in global and ideological terms. Events in Europe seemed to be linked directly with developments in Asia and vice versa. Viewed from the Western perspective, Soviet world domination encouraged by communist ideologues constituted a serious threat to the free world. Conversely, looking at the world from Moscow, the encirclement of the Soviet Union by military alliances of countries in the periphery with the capitalist leadership was instigated and orchestrated by the Western powers. A retreat by a superpower on one front line would, according to this logic, only prompt the other to fill the power vacuum. Pushed along by the security dilemma inherent in the zero-sum game, the Cold War developed its own dynamic, one characterized by the incremental growth of tensions in Asia, the Middle East, and Latin America.

Other factors affected the arduous path to a relaxed climate. Within the two blocs, tensions between the hegemons and their allies were on the rise and hastened a phase of internal polarization. A precarious balance between Soviet control and local autonomy by and large defined tensions in the Eastern bloc. In the event of an overt challenge against Soviet hegemonic claims, as was the case in Poland and Hungary during the 1956 uprisings, Soviet and other Eastern bloc forces acted as an effective instrument of repression. Soviet relations with China were anything but cordial: the decline of Sino-Soviet relations was a creeping process that also acted as a harbinger of the end of international socialist solidarity.

The dynamics within the Western bloc proved more complex. Tense relations in the Western alliance reflected national interests, especially among West European states, and impacted the issues of transatlantic solidarity and European autonomy. The necessity of considering allied interests was at that time understood to be a handicap by Washington (especially when compared to the iron-fisted policy of Moscow toward its clients in the Soviet sphere of influence) and was ultimately to prove the very strength of Western leadership in the sense that over time it created a salutary system of checks and balances that was to stabilize and sustain the Western alliance. For the time being, however, internal bloc tensions were largely responsible for the superpowers' drift toward the two most dangerous instances of the entire Cold War: the Berlin crisis and the Cuban missile crisis.

Fragmentation in the Blocs: Europe and the East

The prelude to the Berlin crisis and the Cuban missile crisis is connected to the prior fragmentation of the blocs and the tensions thereby created. By the mid-1950s, the Soviet Union found itself on the defensive in the Cold War, especially concerning European security. Growing unrest in East European communist countries and the Maoist challenge to Soviet supremacy were real enough problems, but their forceful resolutions only masked the two difficulties that the Soviet Union faced in relation to the West: economic retardation and military inferiority.

Soviet disadvantages were highlighted by the unresolved issue of the division of Germany. Although Stalin had succeeded in isolating the Eastern European dependencies by cordoning them behind the Iron Curtain, he failed to prevent the constitution of a West German state. Worse still, communist-inspired North Korean aggression in 1950 prompted the Western bloc to rearm West Germany less than a decade after the fall of the Third Reich. As a consequence, West Germany became a full member of NATO with its own conventionally armed force (but had to forgo the right to develop its own nuclear arsenal).

Given U.S. nuclear superiority, the Soviet Union found itself in no position to challenge West German rearmament and its integration into the West European strategic framework. The U.S. nuclear edge was in nuclear warheads, delivery systems, and the plethora of qualitative indicators. And into the mid-1950s, the Soviets especially lacked strategic bombers; by 1956, the Soviets could field some sixty of them. Conversely, the U.S. arsenal comprised in excess of 500 strategic aircraft and 4,000 nuclear warheads as opposed to a few hundred on the Soviet side. With little or no choice left, the Soviet Union's response was to reorganize and institutional-ize its sphere of influence in Eastern Europe along the lines of the West. East Germany (the German Democratic Republic) was accordingly given license to rearm under Soviet auspices; much like its Western counterpart, it was also tied into the Warsaw Pact, the military alliance founded in May 1955.

The Soviet Policy of Relaxation in Europe

The Soviet policy of relaxation in Europe developed along a parallel course to a hardening Western position. Against the backdrop of the establishment of a European Defense Community in 1952, a relaxation in the Soviet poli-cy toward Europe could be discerned during Stalin's last years; the so-called Stalin Note of March 1952, however, constituted a diplomatic propa-ganda maneuver, a Soviet attempt to counteract the successful achievement of a consensus by the Western bloc in relation to the question of German rearmament.

With Stalin's death in March 1953, chances for a policy of genuine relaxation rose, albeit briefly. First, however, priority was given to the con-solidation of the superpowers' spheres of influence. This was amply demonstrated by the uprising of workers in East Berlin in June 1953 in response to government demands for higher production quotas. The upris-ing illustrates that the Soviet position in East Germany was anything but firm. In the West, the uprising was viewed as an expression of widespread dissatisfaction with the socialist regime under Soviet suzerainty and a vin-dication of West German calls for reunification. On 17 and 18 June, Soviet and East German troops crushed the protest-turned-revolt. Shocked, the West looked on while hundreds died and many more were interned.

Soviet policy toward Europe worsened over the next two years. On the one hand, the struggle for power in the Kremlin impaired the Soviet leader-ship's ability to formulate policy. On the other hand, Maoist China and the Soviet Union were commencing a phase of estrangement that deflated and debunked the notion of a monolithic communist bloc facing a fragmented West. Finally, and most important, the West successfully resolved the ques-tion of German rearmament toward the end of 1954: West Germany became a member of NATO, and a self-confident Konrad Adenauer visited Moscow the next year.

Out of this combination of adverse developments for the Soviet Union and the resulting sense of inferiority, the new leader, Nikita Khrushchev, formulated a forward-looking policy of relaxation in spring 1955. The most visible sign of the more relaxed climate was the occupying powers' politi-cal agreement on the status of Austria. In May 1955, Austria was released into independence as a neutral state, without becoming a member of either alliance system. Moreover, Khrushchev wanted to approach the reality of a partitioned Germany with a policy of "two Germanies." At the same time, the Warsaw Pact was established (Khrushchev's intention at that time was to balance NATO with a diplomatic counterpart). Intricately linked with this perspective was the hope of creating a pan-European security system in the context of a negotiated solution, with the simultaneous dissolution of NATO and the Warsaw Pact.

The Western perception of the Soviet policy of relaxation was one of skepticism. Accordingly, Khrushchev was disappointed by the reception of his policy in the West. Inside Washington and elsewhere, suspicions were that the Soviet offer was geared toward an attenuation of NATO's cohesion while the Warsaw Pact was to be consolidated into a powerful military instrument. Such an assessment of Soviet policy was corroborated when the Soviets tabled their project for a pan-European security system. The principal reason for Western distrust was the fact that this precursor to the Conference on Security and Cooperation in Europe (CSCE) would have limited the role of the United States to that of observer.

Following the evident failure of Khrushchev's forward policy of relaxation of early 1955, the priorities of the overall Soviet policy toward Europe shifted yet again. First, Moscow moved toward anchoring East Germany in the structures of the Warsaw Pact. Increasingly, the Soviets sought to achieve the diplomatic recognition of East Germany and the maintenance of the status quo in Europe. Moscow believed that only if the West sanctioned the official partitioning of Germany and the Oder-Neisse Line could the Soviet Union remain safe from a resuscitation of anti-Soviet German militancy. Second, Soviet interest in Western Europe was geared toward the neutralization of the conventional and nuclear military capabilities of the Great Powers. Nothing would frighten the Soviets more than nuclear arms at the disposal of West Germany. Third, U.S. influence and the presence of its troops in Europe were to be minimized. The combination of the security policy objectives as established above is what Khrushchev meant by the phrase *peaceful coexistence*. In this instance, it is important to bear in mind that coexistence, however peaceful, did not amount to cooperation. The cooperation of the superpowers at that time would have presupposed a minimum of mutual trust and an understanding that the national interests of the Soviet Union and the United States in Europe did in fact converge on a number of issues.

Stalin's Death and the Power Struggle in the Kremlin

Stalin, who had ruled the Soviet Union with an iron fist since 1924, had established a totalitarian regime maintained by frequent purges of the Communist Party and protected by the secret police. His sudden demise gave the Communist Party the long-awaited opportunity to shift the political climate in its own favor. Stalin's heir apparent, Georgi Malenkov, was neutralized by the party as a political force when he was denied the possibility of assuming two important offices simultaneously. Malenkov's decision to remain prime minister allowed a junior Politburo functionary to rise to the post of first secretary of the party. This man was Nikita Khrushchev. The party's experience under Stalinist rule also prompted it to divide effective power in the communist state. Thus, while Malenkov was prime minister, Stalin's old comrades Vyacheslav Molotov and Lavrentii Beria held the positions of foreign minister and head of secret police, respectively. The party also sought to recapture a measure of political freedom denied it by the secret police under Stalin's aegis. Beria's downfall occurred in the summer of 1953.

Following a three-year struggle between conservative and progressive forces within the Politburo, Khrushchev prevailed. Khrushchev wanted to introduce a turnabout in Soviet policy. Before he could initiate reforms, though, Khrushchev had to address the Stalinist past. At the Twentieth Congress of the Communist Party in February 1956, Khrushchev launched a bristling attack on Stalin and his confederates. The speech was not intended to be publicized beyond the confines of the Congress or to encourage political leaders in the East European dependencies. Khrushchev criticized Beria and Stalin for their crimes against the party, not their excess against the proletariat. The so-called Secret Speech was, however, leaked to Western agents by the Poles; this initiated a wide-ranging strategic debate that reached into the Soviet satellites of Eastern Europe. In the Eastern bloc, the principal question raised after Stalin's death and the announcement of Khrushchev's reformist policy was whether a road to socialism not dictated by Moscow had become feasible. The base for a potential fragmentation in the Eastern bloc had just been created at its very center.

The Precedent: Titoism in Yugoslavia

The precedent for a national communist development had occurred earlier in Yugoslavia after World War II. During the war, Joseph Tito successfully challenged the Nazi occupation in a protracted and hard-fought guerrilla war. Tito, who had always been counted on as a loyal Stalinist, had thus won a measure of independence from Moscow. When Stalin isolated Eastern Europe in an attempt to strengthen the Soviet sphere of influence, Tito quarreled with his former master. The first rupture in the emerging Eastern bloc had occurred. In Soviet-occupied Eastern Europe, Stalin cracked down on any communist leader showing the slightest inclination to pursue a policy not subservient to Moscow's dictates. The term *Titoism* thus came to have a meaning that was synonymous to *deviation*. Stalin's purges in the Eastern bloc were thorough, for until Khrushchev rose to power—

and with the sole exception of Tito—not a single Soviet satellite dared to oppose the official party doctrine from Moscow. Only in 1955 did Khrushchev travel to Belgrade in an effort to see what he could salvage for future Soviet-Yugoslav relations and, implicitly, the integrity of the Eastern bloc. Tito patched up his prior differences with Moscow but remained committed to the pursuit of an independent communist system.

Gomulka and the Polish Reforms

Stalin, based on a suspicion that Wladyslaw Gomulka was a nationalist deviant, imprisoned the leading Polish communist reformer in 1948. The Polish Communist Party set out to reclaim a small measure of its country's political independence when Gomulka was set free in 1954 and rejoined the Soviet party two years later. Khrushchev's Secret Speech came as a godsend and furnished the Poles with the pretext to introduce a national element into communist rule. In the reformist climate of 1956, Polish workers rose in protest against the vestiges of Stalinist repression. To counter a potential catastrophe, the Polish Communists installed Gomulka as their first secretary. Gomulka announced that Stalinist measures, such as the collectivization of farms, were to be abolished. What finally scared Khrushchev was Gomulka's rhetoric of independence and sovereignty. In the fall of 1956, Khrushchev and functionaries from the Soviet party paid Gomulka an unannounced visit at the Polish party summit in Warsaw. The Polish delegates professed loyalty to the Warsaw Pact—established in the preceding year—but would not submit to further dictates from Moscow. Placated, the Soviet leaders returned home, knowing that for the sake of cohesion they had had to make concessions to the Poles. Accordingly, Gomulka introduced a number of moderate reforms designed to improve the lives of Polish workers and peasant.

The Hungarian Rising and the Rhetoric of Rollback

Encouraged by Gomulka's partial retrieval of national independence, the Hungarians also sought to stamp out the Stalinist legacy at home. The culmination of high-level discussions was the ascendancy of Imre Nagy. Nagy, not unlike Gomulka, was a Communist of moderate persuasion with a nationalist slant. Whereas in Poland a gradual change had sufficed to calm the masses, in Hungary the resentment against Soviet repression and communism rose to a fever pitch. It was against a backdrop of rebellion in Budapest that Nagy's statement of Hungarian independence was received in Moscow in early November. Evidently, the Soviets were facing an entirely different situation in Hungary than in Poland. The lynching of some members of the secret police as well as certain proponents of communism soon developed into a full-scale uprising against Soviet hegemony.

The rising could have remained an internal bloc affair had not U.S. Secretary of State John Foster Dulles adopted the aggressive rhetoric of rollback, that is, "rolling back" communism. Even though concepts such as rollback and liberation derived from the rhetoric used in the U.S. elections of 1952, they were only scarcely represented in U.S. strategy under President Eisenhower. Still, Khrushchev could not but feel threatened in his own backyard. The threat of Dulles's rollback was compounded by the circumstance that the U.S. **Central Intelligence Agency (CIA)** was using Radio Free Europe to actively encourage a Hungarian rebellion against Soviet rule.

Khrushchev's room for maneuver was limited. According to the Cold War's bipolar logic, he could not very well let the Hungarians proceed in their demolition of Soviet power. In such an event, Hungary would become the West's bridgehead to the East, which could only have severe consequences for the cohesion of the Eastern bloc. Only days after Nagy's declaration of independence, Soviet tanks entered Budapest. The Soviet suppression of the Hungarian uprising was attended by widespread bloodshed. Approximately 25,000 insurgents and innocent citizens were killed in the fighting that gripped Budapest for a week. Outraged protests around the world followed, to no avail. Dulles's rhetoric of not only containing Soviet expansionism but also pushing back the communist tide rang hollow as thousands of Hungarian resistance fighters lost their lives. Although the CIA had made some ambivalent statements about assisting the revolt, no U.S. guns were forthcoming. President Eisenhower knew full well that U.S. intervention beyond the Iron Curtain would furnish the Soviets with a casus belli. The prospect of World War III forced Eisenhower to watch the destruction of the Hungarian uprising and to silence Dulles's belligerence.

The melancholy postscript to the Hungarian uprising of 1956 was the mass flight of some 200,000 Magyars. In terms of the continuing Cold War, the outcome of the Hungarian uprising reinforced the territorial lines of division established after 1945. Khrushchev had proven that Moscow was prepared, in the event of a threat to the Soviet sphere of influence, to incur the risk of direct superpower confrontation: the cohesion of the Eastern bloc would be guaranteed by whatever means necessary.

The End of International Socialist Solidarity

Disquiet among its Eastern European satellites was not the only concern of the Soviet Union. As opposed to the Western perspective after the fall of China in 1949, which depicted the Soviet Union and China as a single front bound by international socialist solidarity, we know today that Sino-Soviet relations became tense beginning in the mid-1950s. The safety of Soviet preponderance within the communist bloc was threatened not only by internal revolt but also by a straightforward Chinese challenge.

The roots of the Sino-Soviet split are to be found in the years following the Chinese civil war. A fellow communist country, backward China had been treated more like a Soviet dependency. Stalin had extended minimal development loans for which the Chinese were made to pay exorbitant interest. Moreover, the Soviets coerced the Chinese to concede rights over the use of transportation facilities in Manchuria. The slow pace of China's industrial and economic development rendered the continued receipt of Soviet support important enough for Mao to acquiesce to Soviet dominance. This situation held until 1956, when Khrushchev delivered his Secret Speech in which Stalin's cult of personality was criticized and the necessity of peaceful coexistence with the West was introduced as the new Soviet strategy. Khrushchev's attack on Stalin implicitly attacked Mao's style of leadership; peaceful coexistence symbolized an ideological turnabout not only in Soviet foreign policy but also in the strategy of the communist bloc.

China challenged the Soviet leadership's decision to change the shape of communist relations with the West. The rupture between Mao and Khrushchev deepened when the latter repudiated China's confrontational policy toward the West at a 1957 meeting held in Moscow. When the Soviet Union refused to back China against the United States in the Taiwan crisis of 1958, and even denounced China's offensive strategy against India following a border dispute in 1962, the rift between the two major communist powers became obvious. Khrushchev's ridicule of the Great Leap Forward—the Chinese equivalent of the Soviets' Five Year Plan—did little to assuage the growing hostilities. Finally, the 1963 Soviet-U.S. Limited Test Ban Treaty isolated China strategically. But the detonation of the first Chinese nuclear device in October 1964 heralded the end of the Soviet hold on communist China. Mao struck back by charging the Soviet leadership with the betrayal of Marxist-Leninist ideals and collaboration with the capitalist world. China's refusal to cooperate with the Soviets during the Vietnam War therefore did not come as a surprise.

Fragmentation in the Blocs: Europe and the West

In the 1950s, the U.S. government, represented by President Dwight Eisenhower and Secretary of State John Foster Dulles, generally received Soviet offers of **détente** with skepticism. Conversely, West European states elicited interest in reaching an accommodation with Moscow. Tensions between two opposing ideas—European autonomy and transatlantic solidarity—became more pronounced against the backdrop of economic as well as security developments. As European national economies recuperated from World War II, the desire for more independence in international relations grew commensurately. As of the early 1950s, European capitals were exposed to the threat of nuclear annihilation by a Soviet first strike, whereas U.S. cities continued to exist in the relative safety afforded by the limited range of Soviet nuclear capability and the Atlantic Ocean. Thus, in Europe the call for a deflation of international tensions did not fall on deaf ears.

In stark contrast, John Foster Dulles rhetorically championed rollback, a concept that was more aggressive than containment, and the official security policy of the Eisenhower administration promulgated the strategy of massive retaliation, that is, disproportionate U.S. nuclear retaliation against the Soviet Union and the Eastern bloc for any military aggression by a communist power. Understandably, such saber-rattling unsettled the Europeans, who at that stage, and against the backdrop of increasing tensions between the United States and China, believed that the probability of the Cold War turning hot in Asia had increased.

What many Europeans feared was U.S. overreaction and overconfidence (especially in Indochina and the Taiwan Strait) grounded in the arguably erroneous belief that a preemptive strike could eliminate the Chinese communist threat once and for all. Proponents of this hard line argued that if such a strategy were to be implemented, it had do be done while the United States still retained its nuclear edge. Opposing voices in the United States retorted that an advantageous accommodation with the Soviet Union should be sought as long as the West could negotiate from a position of strength. The divergent positions in the West engendered an awareness of dissent in the corridors of power, which did not immediately manifest itself in an attempt to establish a unanimous position toward the East. Obtaining an internal consensus of opinion in an evidently charged atmosphere was not only difficult but also an intrinsically unsavory task.

Thus, the West came to practice a policy of unyielding determination based on U.S. nuclear superiority. In the first half of the 1950s, Western leaders embraced this hard-line policy. But they had little choice, for financial and strategic pressures compelled European members of the Western alliance to rely on the powerful nuclear arsenal of the United States. Dulles was hoping to confound Soviet attempts to consolidate rule in Eastern Europe and to amplify Sino-Soviet tensions by promoting a tough wedge-through-pressure strategy. West German Chancellor Konrad Adenauer was ill-disposed toward a policy of relaxation concerning the Soviet Union that would risk a rupture with the West. Furthermore, Adenauer's position had considerable weight in Washington, for in light of the emancipatory tendencies exhibited by Britain and France, the Germans were increasingly viewed as the most reliable U.S. partner in Europe.

Arguably, the Suez crisis of 1956 was only a sideshow for tensions within the Western alliance—especially those pertaining to the debilitation of European confidence in committed U.S. support. Yet Suez illustrated the escalation of those self-same tensions along the periphery of the Cold War. The Israeli campaign (executed with Britain and France) against Egypt in response to the nationalization of the Suez Canal culminated in a complete political, if not military, fiasco for the European powers involved. To begin with, the Anglo-French attempt at securing their interests within a colonialist agenda met with stiff resistance from the Soviet Union in the shape of undisguised support for Colonel Gamal Abdul Nasser and a threat to deploy nuclear weapons, if required. To add insult to injury, Eisenhower's demand that Britain and France retire from the conflict—a demand with an especially biting edge because the United States had not been involved in the preliminary plans of the Suez intervention—forced London and Paris to draw at least one significant conclusion: their principal ally was unwilling to extend his protection unconditionally. An extension of the Anglo-French deduction was that Europe, without a full U.S. nuclear commitment, would be completely defenseless given Soviet attempts at coercion. The manifestation of internal Western dissent on the periphery thus led to an increased tendency to practice nationalist policies. The three principal exponents were Germany, Britain, and France, whose respective visions of Europe differed considerably.

European Politics: Germany, Britain, and France

Two German states emerged from the immediate postwar period as a result of superpower intervention. East Germany constituted a truncated vestige of the occupation and partitioning of the Nazi state by the wartime Allies. Lying within the territory occupied by the Red Army, East Germany was controlled from Moscow and came into being only as a direct reaction to the proclamation of the pro–Western alliance West Germany in 1949. In 1955, East Germany joined the Warsaw Pact. Under the aegis of West German Chancellor Konrad Adenauer, East Germany was not given any diplomatic recognition, being decried as an illegitimate Soviet puppet state. According to Adenauer, only West Germany could rightfully represent all Germans. In 1955, his position was expanded, corroborated, and transformed into national policy by the **Hallstein Doctrine**. This doctrine stated that West Germany would not pursue or maintain relations of any kind with any other state that had extended diplomatic recognition to East Germany. But the Hallstein Doctrine did not apply to the Soviet Union.

West Germany: Sovereignty and Western Integration

Adenauer, who dominated German politics between 1949 and 1963, pursued a conservative and stringently anticommunist policy and was adamant about the terms under which Germany would again be unified. To be certain, Germany would not fall under communist rule. In order to better understand Adenauer's policy toward the Eastern bloc, we need to explore the temporal and political context of his tenure. When Adenauer was elected chancellor, he faced multiple problems. To the World War II Allies, Germany was first and foremost the vanquished enemy—an occupied country and a potential perpetrator. The heavily industrialized Ruhr and Saar areas were under the control of the Western Allies, who proceeded to dismantle German production installations. West Germany was not yet invested with sovereignty, as the Allied High Commissioners retained final authority by virtue of the Occupation Statute of 10 April 1949. Adenauer understood well the importance of cooperating with the Western powers. The East could not offer any promise beyond the political stillbirth of union under communist rule.

Adenauer skillfully used the situation of the Western bloc, requiring a reconstituted and recuperated Germany in order to strengthen the West, to his best advantage. The chancellor managed to persuade the Western alliance that the appropriation of German industry would cripple the country's capacity for contributing to European defense in any meaningful way. When the French proposed the **European Coal and Steel Community (ECSC)** in 1950, Adenauer seized the chance to improve Franco-German relations. But most of all, Germany's participation in the French joint venture allowed it to take partial repossession of the hitherto internationalized Ruhr industry. Moreover, Germany became a full-fledged member of the Council of Europe in the same year.

Probably Adenauer's greatest feat in purely political terms was the series of negotiations with the occupying powers toward German sovereignty. In the eyes of the U.S. government, Adenauer's anticommunist course, and his unequivocal commitment to the cause of the West, which he had practiced since 1949, helped him establish the image of a political leader whose loyalty was beyond doubt. Therefore, the rejection of, and complete noncooperation with, East Germany constituted the main pillar of Adenauer's political program toward the attainment of German sovereignty. Progress toward full German independence so few years after the end of Hitler's rule would not have been possible without a leader whose anti-Nazi credentials stood up to Western scrutiny.

The chancellor was aware of the U.S. need for German resources in the reconstruction and rearmament of Europe; he understood that his country was indispensable to Western efforts to implement a viable and enduring security architecture on the Continent. When representatives of France, Britain, and the United States approached Germany over raising troops for the European Defense Community and, later, for NATO, Adenauer adeptly introduced the notion that any German contribution was inextricably linked to the question of national sovereignty and, thus, full independence and an end to occupation. In May 1952, the Western alliance and Adenauer's government concluded a treaty designed to reconstitute German sovereignty; but another three years (spanning the rise and fall of the European Defense Community) passed before the promises came true.

In the end, Germany was admitted to NATO and the West European Union in late 1954. With the exception of specific limitations on German rearmament, as well as a prohibition on the development and possession of nuclear weapons, Germany had become an equal member of the Western bloc. Adenauer's achievement was rooted in his conviction that there was no alternative for Germany than to establish the closest possible bonds with the West and to reject the East.

Britain Between Commonwealth, Europe, and the Special Relationship

Unlike France, Britain had not come under Nazi occupation during World War II. This accounted for Britain's drive to maintain its independence from the integrationist ventures on the Continent. While France aspired to assume the position of primus inter pares among the nations of postwar Europe, Britain still had at its disposal a far-flung empire and an imperial common market—the Commonwealth. What Britain did have in common with France, however, was an amassed war debt. Its insolvency in light of direly needed financial aid from the United States was responsible for the future development of, or rather disengagement from, the empire. The empty coffers of the Exchequer forced the British government to continue rationing in the immediate years following the conclusion of the war. Despite the influx of funds provided by the Marshall Plan, Britain was compelled to devalue the pound sterling against the dollar.

Although Britain was hard-pressed to set its affairs in order at home, it still perceived itself as the most powerful nation after the superpowers. Fully comprehending the necessity of strengthening its transatlantic ties, Britain nonetheless sought to prevent a dependency on the United States, which would cripple its independence. Although U.S. support in the maintenance of Western European security was of critical importance, Britain elected to defend its own interests as best it could. Accordingly, the decolonization of the British Empire moved at a pace largely dictated by London but, more often than not, influenced by indigenous aspirations of independence in its colonial possessions.

Concern for the British in Britain led to the election of a Labor government headed by Clement Attlee that steered the country toward a more equitable social policy. The National Health Service, providing free medical care for British subjects, was the penultimate manifestation of Labor's ascendancy in those years. The vicissitudes of war had fused Britons into a comprehensive unit upon which successive Labor governments could install the trappings of a modern welfare state. As a consequence, the harsh division of British society into classes was mitigated, and some measure of social justice was introduced. Under the sage guidance of Sir Stafford Cripps, who became the Labor chancellor of the Exchequer, Britain commenced its economic recovery.

The elections of 1950 brought back Winston Churchill and a Conservative government a year later. The new government set a precedent in the annals of Tory rule, maintaining the majority of the social legislation enacted under the Labor ascendancy. With domestic support ensured, Churchill's government proceeded to formulate its policy goals. In summary, successive conservative governments to 1964 pledged support to strengthening the "special relationship" with the United States; worked toward the attainment of nuclear capability; sought to protect vital British interests in their spheres of influence—especially the Mediterranean, the Middle East, and Asia; fostered improved relations among the nations of the Commonwealth; and cooperated in the defense policy for continental Europe.

The rationale behind Churchill's foreign policy was based on pragmatic observations. The U.S. alliance served to arrest, or at least postpone, the decline of British power. It was hoped that the close association with the actual victor of World War II would secure Britain's position on the world stage. But British Conservatives were disabused of any such aspirations when the United States opposed Anglo-French intervention during the Suez crisis. In fact, the special relationship had ceased to be a reliable pillar of British foreign policy in the 1950s. Britain, like France, had deluded itself into believing that it could retain its former position as a Great Power. Significantly, Britain successfully used the special relationship to obtain admission into the nuclear club. The United States could not afford to discount closer cooperation with Britain, as it had been a major contributor to the success of the U.S. nuclear arms program during World War II. Thus, Britain's national nuclear development program met with success as early as the 1950s: in 1952, Britain detonated its first atomic bomb, followed by the successful explosion of a hydrogen bomb in 1957.

Anglo-U.S. rapprochement was achieved under the aegis of Harold Macmillan, one of Churchill's ablest apprentices of British politics. Macmillan pursued a two-pronged course, attempting to restore the special relationship with the United States while retaining the freedom to shape British foreign policy. He succeeded admirably at both, when Kennedy agreed to furnish Britain with delivery systems for nuclear weapons in the Nassau Accords of 1962. Macmillan's diplomatic successes did not go unobserved by France. French leader Charles de Gaulle interpreted improved Anglo-U.S. relations as a clear sign of Britain's preference for the United States over Europe and an attempt to banish France to the back benches of West European politics. De Gaulle's revenge came in the shape of his blockage of British applications for membership in the **European Economic Community (EEC)** in 1963 and, a second time, in the late 1960s.

The main obstacle to the attainment of French objectives was the special relationship tying Britain to the United States. When Britain opted out of the process of European economic integration due to its vested interests in the Commonwealth and in order to protect its political and military proximity to the United States, de Gaulle realized that France could indeed become the dominant power on the Continent. With Britain not a part of the integration process, and with Germany at pains to keep a low profile, France was presented with the opportunity to grasp the lead role. De Gaulle carefully cultivated his relationship with Adenauer while seeking British and U.S. approval in his attempts at ensconcing French leadership in Western Europe. They turned him down.

Thus, when European countries began to doubt the U.S. ability to guarantee their safety in light of the growing Soviet nuclear strength, France was in the forefront of the skeptics. In 1958, de Gaulle demanded that a tripartite directorate, consisting of France, Britain, and the United States, would act as the principal decisionmaking body of NATO, but the French proposal found no support from the United States and Britain. They regarded de Gaulle's idea as an attempt to accord France Great Power status by setting it on a par with themselves. Moreover, de Gaulle used the European vote of no confidence in the United States in order to introduce the topic of building up a French nuclear force, which had already been initiated by his predecessor, to the public and thereby accelerate the program. U.S. nuclear devices were moved from bases in France, and in 1960 the first French atomic bomb was detonated, closely followed by the successful testing of a hydrogen bomb. By developing its own nuclear capability France expressed its newfound self-confidence to the remainder of the world. At the close of the 1950s the Western alliance was evidently beset by a deep crisis. How had this situation come about?

U.S. Credibility and the Transatlantic Defense of Europe

In the course of the 1950s, the realization that the military and political context of the Western alliance had fundamentally changed, especially as to NATO, dawned upon Western leaders. As realization consolidated into comprehension, the acknowledgement of altered circumstances, and their consequences for the West, effected a reappraisal of Western strategy toward the East. At the very center of this process was the erosion of credibility toward a U.S. nuclear guarantee for Europe due to recent Soviet advances in nuclear weapons technology.

At its meeting in Lisbon in 1952, NATO agreed on expanding its conventional forces. The target was a full ninety-six divisions by 1954. By the end of 1953, the United States and its European allies realized that they could not accomplish such a gargantuan task. Financial as well as strategic considerations moved the Western alliance to rely on the superior nuclear arsenal of the United States. The recovering national economies of Europe would not be able to maintain a military establishment on such a scale.

Europeans came to regard the U.S. nuclear option as the only viable guarantee of their security. During the first half of the 1950s, the Western strategy of **deterrence** relied heavily on the nuclear weapons potential of the U.S. Strategic Air Command (SAC), which was decisively superior to the limited strategic potential then available to the Soviet Union. But Soviet strategic nuclear capability grew during the second half of the 1950s, and so Western strategists shifted their attention to the integration of tactical nuclear weapons (with a smaller payload and a shorter range) into NATO forces stationed in Europe. As only the United States had a significant number of theater-range missiles at their disposal, this change in Western strategic planning was commonly attributed to the theory that the introduction of tactical nuclear weapons would offset the conventional inferiority of Western troops in Europe compared to Soviet forces. In the short term, the presence of tactical nuclear weapons satisfied European requirements. But it also raised certain doubts and fears, as European governments were concerned that the infusion of tactical nuclear devices would turn the Continent into a wasteland in the event of war.

Sputnik shock and the missile gap.   In 1957, just as a sense of calm settled in among the members of NATO, the **Sputnik shock** exacerbated European apprehensions. For the first time in the history of humankind, the Soviets successfully launched a satellite into Earth orbit. It followed that a rocket capable of transporting a satellite into space could also carry a nuclear warhead to the United States within minutes. The age of U.S. invulnerability was clearly drawing to a close. The United States had come within range of Soviet nuclear missiles. In this altered situation, European political leaders came to ask the question of whether the U.S. president would sacrifice New York if he could thereby save Paris.

The myth of the **missile gap** only served to compound a dawning crisis of confidence in the Western camp. In the 1950s, the principal delivery system for nuclear weapons was the strategic bomber; the Soviets, who had fewer aircraft, first understood the significance of developing alternative delivery systems. In 1957, the Soviet Union introduced the **intercontinental ballistic missile (ICBM)**. Exaggerated by Soviet propaganda as a significant leap forward, the testing of ICBMs alarmed the United States. In truth, the development of Soviet ICBMs was not yet concluded; neither was the missile operational. The next blow to U.S. confidence in its own scientific and military superiority followed when the Soviets launched Sputnik in October 1957. The United States followed suit in January 1958 after repeated failures. Nevertheless, Eisenhower and his administration were accused of allowing the Soviets to leapfrog the United States—to permit a missile gap. U.S. ICBM and **intermediate-range ballistic missile (IRBM)** programs had been delayed due to parallel development in rocket technology. Moreover, SAC had concentrated most of its bombers in a few bases, which rendered them vulnerable to Soviet attack. Finally, Soviet ICBMs might reach their targets faster than Washington could deploy SAC bombers. If this were true, then the Soviet's chances of executing a successful first strike had dangerously increased.

As European doubts concerning the credibility of the U.S. nuclear guarantee grew, Britain and France intensified their national nuclear programs. Neither London nor Paris was willing to forsake these new symbols of national power. In the race to produce nuclear arsenals, Britain outmatched France, as it was able to profit by its special relationship with the United States. What, however, was the significance for West Germany, whose importance as a U.S. ally was constantly rising? West Germany's point of departure was fundamentally different in this respect, as its representatives had agreed not to produce any nuclear weapons in the Paris Treaty of 1954. As a consequence, the Adenauer government had expedited the expansion of German conventional forces. The rising significance of the nuclearization of the European security political context, however, also combined with Europe's de facto dependency on the U.S. nuclear arsenal to deflate the position of conventional forces. Because of the emphasis placed by London and Paris on the development of national nuclear programs, Germany's rearmament program within NATO was apparently called into question. As a result, the German government set much store in gaining access to nuclear weapons, which had become important symbols of national sovereignty.

Eisenhower's answer: growing interest in arms control and nuclear sharing. How, then, did the United States avert Europe's loss of confidence and challenge to leadership? On the one hand, the Soviet threat throughout the 1950s forced the United States to moderate its bellicose demeanor. During his last years in office, Eisenhower's willingness to investigate a relaxation of superpower tensions increased—especially in relation to **arms control** and disarmament. Eisenhower left the White House disappointed that he had been unable to check the spiraling arms race. On the other hand, Eisenhower was prepared to consider schemes of nuclear sharing with European allies. The stationing of tactical nuclear weapons in Western Europe, especially in West Germany, after the Suez crisis was intended to counteract the European crisis of confidence. Control over the nuclear warheads, however, was retained by the United States and in accordance with legal provisions. In the wake of the Sputnik shock, the stationing of U.S. nuclear IRBMs became an ongoing theme among the Western allies. For the remainder of Eisenhower's second term in office in late 1960, the only tangible result of this debate was the deployment of land-based intermediate missiles (Thors and Jupiters) in Britain, Italy, and Turkey. The issue of control was bilaterally resolved between the United States and the state hosting the U.S. nuclear weapons, which led to the introduction of the so-called dual-key system.

President Eisenhower was too much of a pragmatist to fundamentally oppose the buildup of national nuclear forces among the European allies; this would change under his successor, John F. Kennedy. Eisenhower did not hamper the progressing British and French nuclear programs. Moreover, he did not categorically reject German demands to be accepted as a shareholder of the U.S. nuclear potential. In March 1958, the parliament of West Germany, following an unusually spirited debate, resolved to equip the German army with nuclear delivery systems. Before the year was out, the West German air force was conducting exercises involving the deployment of nuclear weapons, and construction projects for the building of depots that could house nuclear warheads were well under way. Even though control over the nuclear warheads in West Germany officially remained under U.S. jurisdiction, by the late 1950s West Germany had gained almost de facto access to the U.S. nuclear arsenal.

By sharing a small fraction of its potential for deterrence, the United States arrested the fragmentation within the Western bloc. Conversely, the United States was unable to undo any of the damage it had wrought in the eyes of the Soviets: West Germany had been reconstituted and was rearmed, and by the late 1950s West Germany had come close to accessing a nuclear weapons potential, albeit not its own. In the end, the Soviet nightmare had come true: through the process of containment, the United States had virtually equipped the principal enemy of the Soviet Union, the Germans, with the most destructive weapon ever built.

The Economic Integration of Europe

As opposed to the military integration of Western Europe, its economic counterpart developed along exclusively European lines, although the initial impulse came from across the Atlantic. After the conclusion of World War II, calls for a United States of Europe foundered on the hard realities of European history. For centuries, European nations had fought each other in one alliance or another. The upheavals caused by Nazi Germany's hegemonic aspirations caused another round of frenzied hostilities. Against the backdrop of innumerable divisions caused by ancient grudges and distrust, the political unification of Europe seemed improbable at best and unrealistic at worst.

Nevertheless, a group of idealists propagated the idea of a **supranational government** that would direct the future of Europe. The more moderate federalists represented one school of thought, whose principles would contribute to the gradual achievement of European union. The realists, who would never allow their respective national governments to delegate sovereign powers to a supranational body, ardently opposed them. From the confrontation between idealists and realists emerged a more pragmatic dialogue culminating in yet another school of thought. This last group—the **functionalists**—for the most part modeled its views on those of the realists. They did not pursue the vision of a united Europe. Notably, functionalists were prepared to work toward a more limited objective: incremental collaboration among European nations on mutual projects. The unfolding story of the European economic integration bore the imprint of all three intellectual traditions.

The financial infusion that the Marshall Plan provided as of May 1947 may be understood as the actual starting point of Europe's postwar economic integration. The benefits of the Marshall Plan were extended to various European countries. Stalin's refusal to allow his East European satellites to participate in the Marshall Plan marked the beginning of Western European recovery. As early as May 1948, delegations from Europe's states flocked to the Hague in order to found a supranational European representative body. The Council of Europe, as it was called, failed to appropriate the necessary powers to achieve its stated objective. Britain, in particular, opposed any move to endow the council with real power. The only power was vested in a council of foreign ministers. Without the right to pass legislation, the Council of Europe soon became a dead letter. Although the idea of European integration almost fell into desuetude, advances made were achieved along functionalist lines, that is, in the shape of tangible and limited projects. Not unlike the transition from the idea of the European Defense Community to a more pragmatic transatlantic alliance, the economic integration of Europe moved away from supranationalist tendencies toward **functionalism**.

The economic integration of Europe: from ECSC to EEC.   It was the French government that called on the nations of Europe to participate in a mutual undertaking beneficial to all. In early 1950, Robert Schuman, the French foreign minister, presented a scheme devised by the economist Jean Monnet suggesting the common use of European resources in the extraction of steel and coal. The economic integration process, though, was clearly motivated by security considerations: the Ruhr region, the mainstay of the German armaments industry during the two world wars, was to be rendered accessible for civilian use by its inclusion into a supranational decision-making process. By April 1951, West Germany, France, Italy, Belgium, Luxembourg, and the Netherlands signed a treaty establishing the European Coal and Steel Community; the ECSC soon took up operations. A transnational panel with the authority to regulate industrial output in the six member states governed the ECSC. By 1955, its successes had exceeded expectations.

Encouraged by the outcome of the joint venture, the signatories of the initial treaty decided to take a step ahead and renewed their bond as the European Economic Community. Between March 1957 and early 1958, the EEC was given the organizational structure to expand its activities; the Treaty of Rome formally transmuted the pragmatic and functional approach to European integration into a more ambitious undertaking. Economic growth in Europe soon outstripped that of the United States. The European Common Market established by the EEC allowed for lower tariffs within its boundaries. Improved conditions for importing and exporting goods accelerated the turnover rates and increased economic output, demand, and jobs. The overall effect was that Europe's recuperation from World War II came in a relatively short time. By the end of the 1950s, Germany, left with barely any infrastructure in 1945, had been transformed into one of the world's most prosperous nations by an economic miracle.

Even so, Europeans witnessed serious tensions in the long process toward integration. Whereas Britain engaged its resources in the politico-military integration of Europe without reserve, it remained aloof from economic development on the Continent. In the case of Britain, the bone of contention revolved around diverging interests in common markets. Following the decline of the British Empire after the war, Britain had embarked on the painful journey toward decolonization. Instead of holding on to its colonies, Britain had instituted the Commonwealth—an economic and political partnership with its former dependencies. The Commonwealth was a common market, and Britain had come to benefit by its low tariffs. Thus, the EEC constituted a rival project in which Britain would be among equals, whereas in the Commonwealth it held the position of primus inter pares. Moreover, the statutes of the EEC demanded a limited curtailment of national sovereignty and, likewise, the delegation of power to a supranational assembly. But Britain had vociferously opposed any abrogation of its sovereignty at an earlier stage and was not about to change its course.

The economic integration of Europe: EEC or EFTA?   France, ever distrustful of its old rival, was not keen on British participation. In any event, the Anglo-U.S. special relationship was irksome to French politicians in the postwar period. Humbled and relegated to the status of second-tier power by the twists and turns of World War II, France was not about to sanction the integration of the Western hegemon's surrogate in Europe. This was especially true because the EEC had evolved from a French proposal. When the EEC was founded in the late 1950s, Britain had refused to become involved, preferring to improve its transatlantic links rather than those with the Continent. In the early 1960s, with more and more colonies gaining independence, the British economy stagnated. The sole reliance on Commonwealth trade no longer represented a feasible solution for the future of the British economy.

Predictably, Britain sought to arrange a belated entry into the EEC, only to meet with internal as well as external opposition. Domestically, the Labor Party denounced the move. The avidly nationalist Charles de Gaulle, president of France, made use of an EEC proviso stipulating that new members could be admitted only if the EEC's governing body supported the applicant's entry unequivocally. According to EEC regulations, de Gaulle was able to single-handedly deny Britain its place in the Common Market. So it was not until after de Gaulle's tenure ended in 1969 that Britain joined the EEC (in 1973). In the meantime, Britain sought refuge in an alternate trade arrangement: the European Free Trade Association (EFTA), which was composed of Austria, Denmark, Norway, Portugal, Sweden, Switzerland, and the UK. In contrast to the EEC, which adopted common tariffs, EFTA members sought to mutually lower their tariffs. Thus, two economic international organizations coexisted in a state of friendly rivalry.

Finally, the EEC was split between two factions. The early successes of the ECSC, and later those of the EEC, encouraged the supranationalist movement to readvance the idea of a united Europe under a single government. The European Parliament in Strasbourg constituted the supranationalists' principal outlet. A convergence of power in the European Parliament would have threatened national sovereignty and was therefore thwarted by a significant number of **federalists**. Once again the realist movement in its federalist guise, which championed the retention of national sovereign rights, was at loggerheads with forces favoring undiluted integration. The balance of power obviously favored the federalists, as the European Parliament was not invested with legislative power. The protracted struggle between realists and idealists, fueled by divergent national interests and jealousies, derailed the process of European integration. Nevertheless, the successes of the ECSC, the EEC, and the EFTA constituted milestones on the road to a united Europe.

The Global Dimension of the Cold War: Taiwan, Suez, Guatemala, and Cuba

When the Cold War spilled into Asia, the world was divided into two antagonistic blocs. By 1955, the postwar system had been transformed into a bipolar international system. Facing the United States and its allies across an irreconcilable ideological, social, and political chasm were the Soviet Union, China, and their dependents. But the Cold War did not stop in Asia. Instead, it spread to envelope Latin America and the Middle East. Four examples will help to illustrate this phase in the expansion of the superpower conflict.

Crisis in the Strait: Taiwan

A potential flashpoint of the Cold War in Asia was the Republic of China situated on the island of Formosa, better known as Taiwan. The Republic of China was the immediate result of the civil war between Communists and Nationalists. When the Nationalist Kuomintang lost its struggle against the Communists on the mainland, General Chiang Kai-shek led his followers across the Taiwan Strait. The Japanese had recently ceded Taiwan to the Nationalists. In 1949, almost 2 million people followed Chiang Kai-shek into exile. Resistance by the indigenous population was ruthlessly crushed. Some 20,000 Formosans died as a result of the Nationalist takeover. With massive U.S. support, the Kuomintang was established as the undisputed ruling power on the island. Fearing attack by Communists from the mainland, the Taiwanese army grew to a half-million men. The Nationalists represented China at the United Nations until 1971. After the Chinese civil war, the West had not recognized Mao's communist government.

The first Taiwan Strait crisis.   In preparation of an impending invasion of the communist mainland, Chiang Kai-shek had the Quemoy Archipelago and the island of Matsu fortified and heavily manned. The latter lies only some eight miles off the Chinese coast. At the same time, Mao also laid claim to the offshore isles occupied by the Nationalists.

In January 1950, President Truman announced that the United States would not interfere should the Communists launch an invasion of Taiwan. The U.S. position changed after war broke out in Korea in June 1950, when the United States neutralized the potential conflict by deploying the Seventh Fleet to keep the belligerents apart. The United States would not brook communist Chinese military operations against Taiwan; neither would it permit Kuomintang forces to cross to the mainland. Despite the pressure exerted by an increasingly hawkish U.S. Congress, the Truman administration upheld its neutralization policy in the strait. With the inauguration of Eisenhower into office in January 1953, the U.S. stance on the Taiwan issue underwent drastic change. Eisenhower lifted the blockade of Taiwan and thereby permitted Chiang Kai-shek to move in excess of 70,000 troops to Quemoy and Matsu. In August 1954, Beijing declared that Taiwan had to be liberated. The United States immediately issued warnings that any action taken against Taiwan would prompt a determined response. Nevertheless, the People's Liberation Army commenced its shelling of Quemoy and the proximate Tachen Islands in September and continued its attacks until November.

The U.S. Joint Chiefs of Staff urged the deployment of nuclear weapons against communist China. Eisenhower refused to consider the use of atomic bombs in order to resolve the crisis. Meanwhile, a powerful pro-Taiwan lobby in the U.S. Congress had achieved a first success when Eisenhower concluded the Mutual Defense Treaty, which obliged the United States to take all necessary measures in the event of Chinese communist aggression against Taiwan. The treaty did not include the offshore islands. The fighting between Chinese Nationalist and communist forces in the Quemoy Archipelago, Matsu, and along the mainland coast escalated anew in January and February 1955. The U.S. Congress responded by passing and ratifying the Formosa Resolution, which pledged U.S. forces in defense of Formosa, the nearby Pescadores Islands, and any other territories that the president deemed necessary. At this stage, the United States emphasized a forceful nuclear rhetoric. In early March 1955, both Eisenhower and Secretary of State Dulles indicated that they were prepared to use nuclear weapons against communist China. As the United States was gearing up for war, opposition to escalation of the conflict in the strait, especially nuclear escalation, stiffened among NATO decisionmakers. Despite the Western alliance's almost unequivocal criticism, the United States expected to be at war with China by mid-April. Finally, on 23 April the Chinese signaled their willingness for negotiations with the United States and accommodation with the Nationalists. The first Taiwan Crisis was over.

The second Taiwan Strait crisis.   In the aftermath of the first crisis, Eisenhower sent a deputation to Taiwan to negotiate the withdrawal of Nationalist troops from Quemoy and Matsu. Chiang Kai-shek declined to listen despite the fact that the U.S. representatives pointed out to him in 1955 that his outposts on the offshore isles could not be properly defended. Subsequently, Eisenhower chose to equip the Nationalist army with air-to-air missiles and howitzers capable of firing nuclear shells. Moreover, the United States stationed surface-to-surface missiles on Taiwan. The virtual breakdown of bilateral U.S.-China talks taking place in Geneva at the same time corroborated the Chinese communist suspicion of a mounting threat in the strait. When Mao eventually turned his back on Khrushchev's principles of peaceful coexistence, he also signaled that the PRC would henceforward pursue a harder line toward Taiwan and the United States.

In addition, Mao challenged Khrushchev openly concerning the futility of fighting a nuclear war. Half of the world's population would, according to Mao, survive the devastation. In other words, Mao believed that the PRC would survive a U.S. nuclear strike (an eventuality for which provisions had been made). What had caused Mao to embrace such a cold-blooded logic? In the first place, the Chinese Communists reacted to the U.S.-sponsored qualitative upgrading of the Nationalist arsenal by readying their own offensive capabilities. Mao perceived a threat in the heavily fortified and reinforced offshore islands. In the larger context, Soviet advances in the development of long-range delivery systems for nuclear weapons (i.e., ICBMs) encouraged Mao to believe that the balance of power had changed in favor of the communist bloc. But apprehensions concerning the reliability of the Soviet nuclear deterrent within Chinese communist military circles subsequently exacerbated Mao's sense of insecurity vis-à-vis the United States.

It was not by chance that tensions escalated shortly after Khrushchev visited Beijing in late July and early August 1958. The subsequent communist attack against the Nationalist offshore positions was a sign that Mao directed at the Kremlin: the PRC would not depend upon the nuclear umbrella provided by the Soviets. Simultaneously, Beijing also signaled that in the event that China could not count on the unequivocal support of Khrushchev in a confrontation with the United States over Taiwan, Mao was prepared to keep the level of hostilities in the strait to a minimum. For various reasons, a Chinese deflation of its own aggressive posture toward the United States would damage Soviet foreign political objectives, for the Soviets had a vested interest in keeping up the pressure against the United States and its allies. Khrushchev conceded the issue and accordingly warned Eisenhower that any offensive action against the Chinese mainland would be viewed as a direct attack on the Soviet Union. It is important to understand that Khrushchev did not intend to threaten the United States with nuclear weapons; he meant to indicate his support for communist China.

Hostile relations between Mao Tse-tung and Chiang Kai-shek reached new heights when, as of 23 August 1958, communist Chinese troops again began shelling Quemoy and Matsu. In addition, Chinese patrol boats prevented Nationalist supply vessels from reaching Quemoy and Matsu and even went as far as openly threatening U.S. ships. Worse, an invasion from the mainland seemed imminent. Eisenhower saw in the communist attack a possible prelude in an attempted invasion and destruction of Taiwan. In accordance with the terms of the 1954 Mutual Defense Treaty, Eisenhower deployed the Seventh Fleet in the Taiwan Strait; U.S. troops stationed on Taiwan were reinforced; and Eisenhower's national security advisers again suggested using nuclear weapons against communist China. Dulles's rhetoric seemed to lend credence to such a position. Conversely, Eisenhower refused to act on recommendations of this stamp, but he would also not make any concession given potential hostilities. Eisenhower's determined stance took the Chinese Communists by complete surprise. The force of the U.S. response contributed to a deescalation of the crisis. At one stage, the Kremlin grew anxious enough to send Soviet foreign minister Andrei Gromyko on a diplomatic mission to Beijing.

Realizing that Eisenhower was in fact serious about containing communism on the mainland, Mao and his foreign minister, the redoubtable Zhou Enlai, called off the attack in October. The United States had seemed willing to face communist China in a direct confrontation. True enough, Eisenhower had decided that Taiwan was where the United States would draw the line. As a result of the abrupt cessation of hostilities, the battle for Quemoy and Matsu did not escalate into a Sino-U.S. war. It seems surprising that U.S. policymakers had even considered the possibility of using nuclear weapons because of a number of minor islands off the Chinese coast. But again, the Taiwan crisis of 1958 needs to be understood within the broader context of the Cold War and the comprehensive U.S. effort to hem in communism.

Despite the fact that Beijing continued to officially claim the disputed offshore islands, the Chinese Communists had learned two important lessons during the second Taiwan crisis. First, they realized that the Soviets could be trusted to deter an unwarranted attack against the Chinese mainland but could not be relied upon to support Chinese expansionism in the strait. Second, as long as the PRC continued to rely on the Soviet nuclear deterrent, the Kremlin would define the extent and intensity of Chinese communist military action against Taiwan and/or the United States in the strait. The latter lesson was coupled with a bitter admission for Mao and his adherents. It also fueled Mao's unmitigated and continuing criticism of Khrushchev's peaceful coexistence policy. The culmination of these tensions led to a Sino-Soviet estrangement: Soviet insecurity concerning the future Chinese communist policy toward Taiwan, then obviously under U.S. protection, led to the cessation of the transfer of Soviet nuclear technology to China. After June 1959, Beijing was compelled to begin its own nuclear program.

The Western Alliance at Odds in the Middle East: The Suez Crisis

The China-Taiwan example gives an impression of just how heavily contested a region Asia was during the Cold War. Initially, the European colonial powers sought to resuscitate their overseas holdings. In the second phase, conflicts between colonizers and nationalists, but also indigenous civil wars, became subject to the Cold War dynamic. This fateful concoction—the process of decolonization and the bipolar dynamic—extended into the Middle East, where two conflicting nationalist movements—Zionism and pan-Arabism—were fated to clash repeatedly. The superpowers' involvement in Middle East affairs during the opening phases of the Cold War was limited but tangible. The Suez crisis set the stage for one of the last European military adventures abroad.

In mid-1956, the refusal of the Western powers to support the construction of the Aswan Dam in Egypt gave the Soviets an opportunity to expand beyond the Iron Curtain. Soviet arms deliveries further served to destabilize the region. Finally, when Egyptian President Gamal Abdul Nasser nationalized the Anglo-French Suez Canal Company on July 26, 1956, Great Britain, France, and Israel, whose trade and security interests were suddenly jeopardized, decided to initiate a concerted military campaign against Egypt. This tripartite decision was eventually also taken under the pretext of Nasser having violated several UN resolutions. One such resolution, frequently breached by the Egyptians, forbade Egyptian customs and military to confiscate noncontraband cargos on either Israeli vessels or international freighters carrying goods for Israel; this further aggravated the tense relationships between the two states. But for Israel, the main reason to consider military action against the vociferous Nasser was the recent understanding between nationalist Egypt and the Soviet Union and, worse, the attendant influx of Soviet arms. The Israeli government believed that its Egyptian foe was poised to strike against the Jewish state; for their part, the Western powers saw a Soviet-Egyptian alliance.

The alliance against Egypt: Britain, France, and Israel.   For England and France, the Suez crisis constituted a pretext for a joint effort to overthrow Nasser's strongly Arab nationalist government, which had already caused the Western powers trouble in their respective overseas colonies. French interest in maintaining the colonial status quo ante in Algeria, as well as the brutal repression of the indigenous independence movement by the Pieds Noirs (the French settler movement in Algeria) led to Nasser's more or less open support for local Arab rebels. Aside from the outrage felt at Nasser's expropriation, Franco-British interference in the Suez crisis can be understood as a reaction to the dissolution of their colonial empires. The nationalist uprising headed by Nasser two years earlier had led to the deposition of the Egyptian monarch, King Farouk. The change in government implicitly spelled the end of British hegemony in Egypt and proved to be a hard blow for Britain's international image as a Great Power.

Without U.S. sanction or knowledge, the Israelis met the French during 22–24 October 1956 to coordinate the campaign against Egypt. The prime ministers of France and Israel—the British were conducting their negotiations through the French for fear of estranging their Arab allies—decided that the Israeli Defense Force should advance through Gaza and Sinai toward the Suez Canal while Anglo-French troops simultaneously concentrated on Cyprus and Malta. Before the Israelis could seize the canal, the Western powers would issue an ultimatum, calling on both belligerents to cease hostilities within twelve hours; the Anglo-French troops would subsequently occupy the Suez Canal in order to guarantee its safety. Naturally, the British and the French were interested in the reestablishment of the old Suez Canal Company.

The attack on Egypt and the Suez crisis.   Israeli troops advanced toward the Egyptian border in late October 1956. An Israeli maneuver led Nasser to believe that the Israeli forces were amassing in the vicinity of the Jordanian border. Border incidents involving Palestinian guerrilla and Israeli regulars had proceeded along these lines in the recent past. Consequently, Nasser positioned the bulk of his troops, some 60,000, in Egypt proper. Accordingly, the Israeli commander, General Moshe Dayan, did not anticipate too much serious resistance from the enemy. The Israelis struck fast and hard: Israeli paratroopers seized Mitla Pass after a short but bloody clash while motorized infantry occupied Gaza and the surrounding area. The campaign was developing well for Israel. Israeli troops crushed enemy resistance wherever they found it. The French had promised to provide air cover for the Israeli coastal strip while the bulk of the army marched on Egypt. For this reason, Israel was able to deploy its entire air force against Egyptian targets. During the Israeli raid on enemy airfields, most of the Egyptian aircraft were destroyed on the ground.

In accordance with the plan, the French issued their ultimatum only hours later, ordering Egyptian and Israeli forces to withdraw at least ten miles from the canal. Soon thereafter, Anglo-French troops moved between the Israeli Defense Force and whatever was left of the Egyptian army. By 30 October, Nasser finally understood the full scope of the Israeli attack: this was evidently no skirmishing party. He reinforced Egyptian troops in the field by adding another 10,000 infantry to the canal contingent. The French ultimatum expired soon after on the evening of 31 October; Nasser then decided to destroy all bridges over the canal. This occurred just hours before the Anglo-French air force had begun pounding Egyptian military airports. In order to save as many planes as possible, the Egyptians evacuated all intact aircraft to the surrounding Arab countries. Nasser ordered all nonengaged troops in the Sinai to retreat over the Suez Canal as quickly as possible. Despite the French ultimatum, Israeli units rapidly advanced on the canal; the Israelis met stiff resistance after contact with enemy forces, but by and large the Egyptians were immobilized due to lack of air support. On 1 November, fighting mainly rear-guard actions, some Egyptian contingents managed to escape over the Suez Canal before Nasser's orders to destroy the bridges were carried out.

The aftermath of the Suez crisis.   When news of Israel's preemptive strike against Egypt and Anglo-French collusion reached the outside world, U.S. President Dwight Eisenhower condemned the forward military action taken by the aggressors, some of whom were the closest U.S. partners in the Western alliance. Moreover, he immediately summoned a UN Security Council meeting. The Security Council became deadlocked thanks to Britain and France, but the UN General Assembly denounced Israeli action as overtly aggressive and furthermore accused the invaders of openly violating the UN Charter. Consequently, the United Nations issued a resolution that called on the Israelis to withdraw their armed forces behind the previously established armistice lines. Considering the fact that Anglo-British operations were designed to bring the Suez Canal Company back into the hands of its former owners, the irate U.S. reaction toward the coalition fighting against Nasser was in part a further manifestation of U.S. anticolonialism. Furthermore, the Suez crisis distracted world opinion from the brutal suppression of the Hungarian uprising and thus eased the pressure exerted by the United States on the Soviet Union.

Of course, Britain and France stoutly opposed the UN resolution but could not prevent its passage by overwhelming majority. Israel agreed to a cease-fire, which would effectively leave it possessing most of the military objectives, but its government was not yet willing to withdraw from conquered territory. It took severe pressure from diverse members of the United Nations to coerce Israel into conceding most of its gains. Equally, Anglo-French troops were to hand over control of the Suez Canal, which they had easily seized, to the United Nations. Soviet threats proved most effective, for the United States feared that if Egypt received more support from the Soviets that Nasser would be drawn deeper into a political alliance with the Eastern bloc. The fact that the United States had provoked Nasser earlier by denying support for the construction of the Aswan Dam project seemed to be of no importance at the moment. The United States reprimanded Israel and the Anglo-French coalition for their irresponsible actions, and Egypt was suddenly the object of a reconciliatory political course.

A few days later, UN peacekeeping forces occupied the demarcation lines along the Sinai and the Suez Canal. The flames of conflict had been smothered, but the Suez Canal, the powder keg of the Middle East, remained a potential source for further squabbling between the contending nations. Nasser immediately turned the Egyptian military debacle in the Sinai into a victory over Israel, the pawn of Western imperialism. The astonishing fact is that Nasser got away with his ludicrous propaganda; Arabs around the globe revered him as their protector. Conversely, the Israelis had successfully managed to destroy large amounts of Egyptian arms only recently sold to them by the Soviet Union. Furthermore, the

Israeli Defense Force had secured some of the prime military objectives in the war (e.g., the reopening of the Suez Canal to international trade and the occupation of the strategically vital Gaza Strip).

The darker side of the conflict did not reveal itself until weeks afterward. For Jews in Egypt, and for Arabs in Israel, there were tragic repercussions: an overzealous Israeli border patrol massacred fifty Arabs at Kafr Kassem, and Egyptian authorities persecuted and later expelled vast numbers of Jewish citizens. The war had not really shifted the balance of power in the Middle East, but it did reassert Israel's claim of national sovereignty. For Israel, the conflict would continue as long as Arab nations and their allies maintained their irreconcilable attitudes.

During the Suez crisis, Anglo-French colonial adventurism and Arab-Israeli nationalist tensions combined to plunge the Middle East into yet another war. On the level of superpower confrontation, the United States had lost the allegiance of Arab nationalists and frustrated the colonial pretensions of its principal European allies; the Soviets, for the first time, managed to extend their influence beyond the Iron Curtain despite Western efforts to the contrary. Essentially, the United States, not unlike the British, had to come to terms with the fact that it could not straddle two horses. Wooing Arab nationalism had not paid off.

The United States and the Western Hemisphere:
Guatemala and Cuba

Even stronger than in Asia, the paradox of U.S. foreign policy—that is, the conflict between historic U.S. idealism and the requirements set by the bipolar struggle—surfaced in Central America and South America, as well as in the Caribbean. In order to further illustrate this phenomenon in international relations, we will take a closer look at two examples: Guatemala and Cuba. The economic penetration of Central and South America by the United States since the nineteenth century had created a number of long-term structural problems. To begin with, U.S. financial interests had steadily cooperated with the local force of the day—usually one military dictatorship or another. In the first half of the twentieth century, the indigenous populations seemed to rise out of a torpor induced by repression, illiteracy, and poverty. Social justice increasingly came to be the rallying cry around which revolutionary movements formed to fight the land-owning aristocrats, the *caudillos*, and the military rulers, the *junta*.

The case of Guatemala. Ironically, in Guatemala, which had suffered the vicissitudes of numerous *juntas* since the previous century, it was the military that made possible an interlude in the seemingly endless string of military dictatorships. In 1944, a revolution supported by the middle class and segments of the military establishment paved the way to free elections. Under Juan Jose Arevalo from 1945 to 1951 and then Colonel Jacobo Arbenz Guzman, the country underwent sweeping reforms. The exploitation of the Maya, who had been pressed into forced labor, was ended, and the land was redistributed. Meanwhile, the *caudillos* and representatives of U.S. business and finance interests worriedly looked on as Arbenz implemented moderate socialist measures.

When the U.S.-based United Fruit Company was nationalized and only sparingly recompensed by the Guatemalan government, Washington cracked down hard. Arbenz's social reforms had caused the United States embarrassment and even provoked the apprehensions of policymakers fearing the loss of yet another state to communism. But the expropriation of a powerful U.S. corporation with connections in the corridors of power in Washington prompted the United States to let matters rest in the hands of the Central Intelligence Agency. CIA agents quietly made use of the discontented upper-class officers in the Guatemalan army to engineer Arbenz's ouster. In 1954, the legitimate government of Guatemala was yet again overthrown by the military. This time, however, the political situation was also dictated by U.S. fears of communist expansion and, less overtly, by longstanding U.S. economic interests. The reforms instituted by Arbenz were annulled, and the peasantry was again suppressed. In the wake of the 1954 coup, Arbenz went into exile and the new rulers began what, for lack of a better term, could only be referred to as a witch hunt against all socialist-inclined political groups in the country. Thousands fell prey to the ensuing purges.

The case of Cuba during the Eisenhower years.   One of the many Marxist-minded men who had believed in the reforms of Arbenz's government was a young Argentine medical doctor named Ernesto "Che" Guevara Serna. Guevara left for Mexico, where he met a group of like-minded Cuban revolutionaries led by the lawyer Fidel Castro Ruz. As in the case of Guatemala, a powerful U.S. interest group had established a significant presence on Cuba. Sugar exports to the United States constituted its greatest source of income. To ensure the safety of their investments, the U.S. investors lobbied Washington to support Cuban governments that would not interfere with their operations. After the Cuban elections of 1952, won by the liberal Partido Autentico, a military takeover headed by former Cuban General Chief of Staff Fulgencio Batista y Zaldivar had reestablished a dictatorship. Castro's attempts to seek redress by constitutional means were frustrated.

On 26 July 1953, Castro led a group of revolutionaries against the military barracks in Santiago de Cuba, the island's second largest population center. The attack was foiled, and Batista took his revenge by executing ten insurgents for every soldier killed. Castro and his brother were sentenced to lengthy terms in prison but were released early on condition that they leave Cuba. Castro and his followers elected to go to Mexico, where they founded the guerrilla organization named 26 July (the date of the attack on the Santiago barracks).

Meanwhile, conditions in Cuba deteriorated under a stagnant economy and the terror exerted by Batista's secret police. In November 1956, Guevara, Castro, and some eighty guerrillas left for Cuba aboard a yacht. The revolutionaries made landfall in early December and were intercepted by government troops. The majority of the tiny invasion force died in the encounter; twelve survivors, Guevara and Castro among them, fled into the mountains of the Sierra Maestra. From the safe haven of their mountain refuge, Castro's rebels conducted a series of stunningly successful military operations against Cuban regular troops. The region in which Castro's growing guerrilla forces held sway became a quasiautonomous unit, and by December 1958 Batista lost the strategically located city of Santa Clara to the revolutionaries. Despite the fact that Castro's own troops never numbered more than 300–800, they were able to occupy Havana in January 1959.

Batista had wisely fled Cuba for the United States on New Year's Eve. The one astonishing fact about events surrounding Castro's struggle for power is that U.S. troops stationed near Guantanamo never entered the fray. U.S. soldiers watched as the future course of Cuban history unfolded. Government troops, some 30,000 strong, simply disintegrated given the guerrillas' successes. In due course, Castro proceeded to expropriate large corporations, most of which were U.S.-based. If his redistribution of wealth did no more than earn him Washington's distrust, his increasingly socialist policy alienated U.S. policymakers. Initially, retaliation for the damage caused to U.S. investors was the reduction of sugar imports; economic sanctions were followed up by the unilateral severing of diplomatic relations on 3 January 1961 and the introduction of a comprehensive embargo. Castro defied the United States to do its worst. What the U.S. government failed to realize was that Castro would thus be forced to seek a new buyer for sugar exports and direly needed imports. Consequently, Cuba extended its feelers to Moscow, where Castro's revolution was greeted as a significant contribution to the socialist cause.

Cuba during the Kennedy years. After Eisenhower left office, the new U.S. president, John F. Kennedy, inherited the Cuban issue. Castro's rapprochement with Moscow was disturbing in and of itself, as the probability of Soviet influence in the Caribbean posed a direct challenge to U.S. hegemony in the Western Hemisphere. Worse was yet to come: Castro proclaimed the Cuban revolution to constitute a model for all the oppressed and downtrodden of Latin America. Conversely, thousands fled Cuba due to Castro's

Marxist reforms. With hopes for a better life, many Cuban refugees left for the state of Florida, where they founded the world's largest Cuban expatriate community. This migration from the Caribbean to the United States brought to the fore the domestic component of the Cuban problem: if the U.S. president wanted to canvas votes in Florida, he had to assume a tough stance toward Castro—at least rhetorically.

Assuming Eisenhower had toppled Arbenz in Guatemala a number of years earlier, he also authorized the CIA to plan for a comparable solution in Cuba. Accordingly, the CIA developed a scheme involving the recruiting, training, and equipping of anticommunist Cuban exiles. Basically, the idea was to launch an invasion for which the United States would provide aerial cover. As Kennedy moved into the White House, he was faced with a dilemma: if he did not want to appear as a soft Democrat, he would have to go through with the planned operations. At the same time, he feared that direct U.S. military involvement would strain relations with the Soviet Union, and creating potential complications shortly before Kennedy was due to meet with Nikita Khrushchev for the first time in Vienna was undesirable. Thus, Kennedy decided to furnish the Cuban exiles with planes, but no U.S. pilots would be involved in the invasion attempt. In the event, CIA pilots did fly the planes without the knowledge or consent of the president. Moreover, the architects of the plan repeatedly told Kennedy that Castro did not enjoy popular support and that his regime could thus be easily overthrown. The president would learn otherwise all too soon.

When some 1,500 Cuban exiles returned to the shores of their home island on 17 April 1961—at the Bay of Pigs—there was no popular uprising against Castro. Quite the opposite was the case, for the exiles had been expected by revolutionary troops at the site of their landing. The operation was a disaster. While Castro's propaganda capitalized on the botched invasion attempt, Kennedy had to admit that tiny Cuba had successfully defied the Western superpower. Nevertheless, Kennedy's address to the U.S. Society of Newspaper Editors a few days after the Bay of Pigs fiasco left little room for interpretation and was clearly addressed to the Soviets and their Cuban allies:

> Should it ever appear that the inter-American doctrine of non-interference merely conceals or excuses a policy on non-action—if the nations of this Hemisphere should fail to meet their commitments against outside Communist penetration—then I want it clearly understood that this Government will not hesitate in meeting its primary obligations which are to the security of our Nation![2]

U.S. interference in Cuba may have not brought the results it did achieve in Guatemala, but Kennedy's statement made it clear that he would never brook Soviet interference on America's doorstep. Yet it was the fateful convergence of U.S. business interests and the strategy of containment, rooted in the classical U.S. foreign policy dilemma, that set the Kennedy administration on a dangerous tack. The Cuba issue had not been resolved. Instead, it became an obsessive concern of U.S. domestic and foreign policy and would lead the world to the very brink of nuclear holocaust.

Competing Superpowers: Crisis and Stabilization, 1958–1963

Even though the Cold War expanded beyond Europe in the 1950s, Europe remained at its heart. This became fully evident when Berlin became the focal point of the conflict between late 1958 and early 1963. The crisis was caused by a reciprocal Soviet-U.S. distortion of perception: each saw the other as perpetrator of security infringements. It also caused a multiplicity of side issues that rendered the situation still more complex and compounded the mounting superpower tensions to boot. As a consequence, the Cold War pushed the world toward potential nuclear war in late 1962. The antagonists had, for all intents and purposes, reached the age of mutual vulnerability; that realization finally brought the leaders of the superpowers to deescalate the looming prospect of World War III. Paradoxically, the very threat of nuclear war made a return to a stabilization of the international system possible, for the subsequent relaxation of tensions was embedded in a stability predicated upon the superpowers' mutual recognition of a stalemate. The period between 1958 and 1963 laid the foundation for an astounding transformation of the European security system: from the Cold War to the long peace. Change, however, was tardy, and it did not come easily.

The Focal Point of Systems Competition: The Berlin Crisis

As Europe became the prize of superpower competition in the 1950s, Germany and its divided capital become the focus. By then Berlin was an object of superpower contention. As a response to Stalin's consolidation of the Soviet sphere of influence behind the Iron Curtain after the war, the Western military powers united the three zones of occupation under their command and, in due course, introduced their own currency. From 1948 to 1949, Stalin's forces unsuccessfully blockaded the city. The city of Berlin was then divided into a Soviet-occupied sector, and the three Western zones coalesced into West Berlin.

Almost a decade after those events, the situation had not changed. Berlin continued to exist as two separate cities, and the Eastern and Western positions on Germany had become even more firmly entrenched. Meanwhile, the internal bloc criticism leveled at Khrushchev's peaceful coexistence policy was gathering force—and not only from the Chinese hard-liners. Walter Ulbricht, head of state in East Germany, expediently used the situation to place his demand for a firmer policy toward the West and more substantial support for East Germany at Khrushchev's doorstep. The last point was especially pressing, as the continuing dissatisfaction with the government and living conditions in East Germany prompted many citizens to seek refuge in the West. This migration swelled to 2.6 million from 1950 to 1962. The loss of human capital proved to have a crippling effect on East Germany's economy: The draining of much-needed manpower had to stop; otherwise, Moscow would become exposed to continuous criticism from its own bloc partners.

There were other reasons for concern. Although prodétente groups within NATO increasingly questioned the tough U.S. stance toward the Soviet Union as the 1950s progressed, the Western powers were not willing to reconsider their position on Germany: reunification was considered a precondition to a pan-European peace settlement with the Soviets. Adenauer's influence in Washington had reached its apex, as the German chancellor proved successful in canvassing U.S. support—at least in principle—for the equipment of the West German army with U.S. nuclear weapons. Although overall control of U.S. nuclear devices in West Germany remained with the U.S. president, the deployment of nuclear weapons in Central Europe fundamentally threatened Soviet interests.

Not unlike Stalin in 1948, Khrushchev correctly identified Berlin as the weakest link in the Western bloc: the former German capital was the only outpost behind the Iron Curtain and, as such, was highly susceptible to Soviet machinations. Khrushchev used the vulnerability of West Berlin to create leverage in negotiations with the West. This time, however, the success of launching Sputnik and the advances made in nuclear delivery systems technology would not permit the West to brush off Soviet demands. Although it is hard to credit the superiority of Soviet strategic nuclear weapons at that time, Khrushchev proved a master at projecting a convincing image of Soviet nuclear strength.

Khrushchev's first ultimatum.   On 27 November 1958, Khrushchev demanded that the West agree to a peace treaty. No formalized treaty had hitherto conclusively defined the Western powers' relations with Germany after the war. Moreover, the Soviets based their demand on the articles of the Potsdam Accords for the constitution of a confederated German state within the boundaries agreed upon by the wartime Allies in 1945. A critical element in such an accord would be the exclusion of the two Germanies from the blocs. In the interim, Khrushchev wanted to institute a fundamental change in the status of occupied Berlin. The German capital was to be granted the privileges of a free city. In other words, Berlin was to be demilitarized. A retreat from Berlin would damage the United States's pivotal role of primus inter pares within NATO; going to war over Berlin was simply not an affordable option to the West, for the likelihood of nuclear escalation loomed large. Khrushchev therefore calculated that the West could be inveigled into accepting the position favored by the Soviet Union—that of maintaining the status quo. In the event that the Western powers chose to decline Khrushchev's offer within six months of its submission, the Soviet Union would turn over all access routes to and from Berlin to East German authorities. In that case, the West would be compelled to work with a state that it did not recognize. Unless the West complied with the Berlin ultimatum, Khrushchev would conclude a separate peace with East Germany.

Eisenhower and the Berlin crisis.   Under Eisenhower, the United States steered a course of stiff resistance to what was perceived as Soviet attempts at coercion. The Soviets, it was argued in Washington, were testing Western resolve and undermining NATO's cohesion by using their latest progress in the development of nuclear arms to exert pressure on Western Europe. Significantly, Eisenhower failed to see that Khrushchev's bluster was motivated by legitimate Soviet security concerns. The U.S. government interpreted Khrushchev's threat to Berlin as a consequence of recent Soviet advances in nuclear weapons technology. Ultimately, Eisenhower believed that Khrushchev was bluffing; the Soviets would not permit a direct superpower confrontation within Europe. The carefully laid Soviet plans thus did not come to fruition but instead had to be postponed. Khrushchev retracted the Berlin ultimatum, but only to await U.S. elections in the near future.

Kennedy and Khrushchev's second ultimatum.   In the aftermath of the Sputnik shock, criticism of Eisenhower for his apparent laxity in keeping up with Soviet arsenals allowed a young Democratic senator from Massachusetts to win the 1960 presidential election. John F. Kennedy's campaign was successful because he had promised, among other things, to close the so-called missile gap, which apparently placed the U.S. nuclear arsenal at a disadvantage compared to that of the Soviet Union. But the truth is that there never was a missile gap. Upon Kennedy's accession to office, the United States could field some 145 **submarine-launched ballistic missiles (SLBMs)** as opposed to only forty-five on the Soviet side and 550 strategic aircraft as opposed 175 for the Soviets. Only in the category of ICBMs did the Soviet Union (with thirty) outmatch the United States (with twenty). In short, the missile gap was not a U.S. problem; it was a Soviet reality. The crucial point, however, is that neither the U.S. public nor the U.S. allies in Western Europe were aware of this circumstance.

At a summit meeting in Vienna, Kennedy warned Khrushchev in early June 1961 not to underestimate the U.S. government's determination to oppose any Soviet attempt to jeopardize the Western presence in Berlin. Khrushchev then reiterated the threats initially made in 1958: all access to Berlin would be left under the aegis of East Germany unless the West agreed to conclude a peace treaty with the two Germanies within six months. The leaders of the superpowers even went so far as to explicitly confront one another with the possibility of war.

Kennedy and his staff approached Khrushchev's ultimatum entirely differently compared to the Eisenhower administration. First, Kennedy asked a simple question: Why was Khrushchev risking his prestige a second time after losing face over Berlin in 1958? Could he afford to expose himself to internal and external pressures again? Were the Soviets really trying to suborn the West by exerting pressure against a vulnerable outpost? Second, the problem of Soviet skepticism toward the U.S. nuclear guarantee in Western Europe, and toward Western determination to defend Berlin with nuclear weapons, remained. If the West continued its tough stance and Khrushchev acted on his threat, the conflict over Berlin would escalate into a nuclear confrontation.

Against this backdrop, the interpretation of Soviet motives for the Berlin ultimatum incrementally shifted under the new Democratic administration. Kennedy's advisers concluded that the Soviet Union's aggressive posture did indeed derive from legitimate security concerns. On the one hand, the mass immigration to West Berlin had assumed such dimensions that it undermined the stability of East Germany. On the other hand, Khrushchev genuinely feared the consequences of a rearmed West Germany that did not recognize the postwar boundary settlement in Central and Eastern Europe. What if the Soviet leader was *not* trying to willfully coerce the West and had instead embarked on a political course geared toward the stabilization of Cold War tensions in Europe?

If Soviet authenticity was thus accepted as a premise by the Kennedy administration, it followed that Khrushchev's demands for recognition of the Oder-Neisse Line and East Germany were part and parcel of his equilibrating policy in Europe. The Soviet position, however, was irreconcilable with that of the West Germans, for whom the recognition of East Germany was utterly unacceptable. Kennedy and his advisers were in a quandary. Given the new insight into Khrushchev's motives, the U.S. government reconsidered its own position toward the Soviet Union in relation to Berlin. Instead of forcing the issue in West Berlin, Kennedy's staff identified three essential Western interests: the right to self-determination of West Berlin; the retention of a full Western presence in West Berlin; and unrestricted right of passage to and from West Berlin. In the long term, the Kennedy administration moved toward a more cooperative position with the East. Basically, Kennedy was willing to consider acknowledging the Oder-Neisse Line and recognizing East Germany. Moreover, he was not averse to entering negotiations with the Soviet Union for two separate peace treaties for Germany while considering a German-German nonaggression pact (cemented by reciprocal security guarantees by NATO and the Warsaw Pact) as well as the creation of a nonnuclear zone in Germany.

The Berlin Wall as symbol of the status quo. The new U.S. policy regarding Europe amply illustrates that Washington and the Kremlin, in principle, had moved closer on their respective European policies. The Kennedy administration was prepared to accept the de facto partitioning of Europe as its willingness to engage resources beyond the status quo was rapidly decreasing. During this hiatus, Khrushchev felt confident enough to address a problem particular to Berlin. As Cold War tensions over Berlin received a significant impetus at the Vienna summit, the mass exodus of refugees from East Germany dramatically increased. With Soviet sanction, Ulbricht ordered all access to West Berlin closed. As of 13 August 1961, workers under armed guard commenced the construction of a wall that would effectively cordon off East from West.

With construction of the Berlin Wall, the Iron Curtain assumed a stony face. Although the U.S. government publicly protested the physical separation of West and East Berlin, Kennedy, behind closed doors, subscribed to the belief that the Berlin Wall would actually simplify matters in that it symbolized the superpowers' acknowledgement of the division of Europe. U.S. political reticence during the Berlin crisis, however, did not render justice to the contemporaneous and widespread European crisis of confidence, felt especially in Berlin, Bonn, and Paris. As part of an exercise in damage control, measures to prevent a serious rift in U.S.-German relations and to restore the confidence of the West Berlin citizenry became a top priority in Washington: Kennedy sent Vice President Lyndon B. Johnson to West Berlin and reinforced the U.S. garrison in West Berlin by a full battle group (1,500 men).

Despite growing interest in a peaceful settlement, superpower negotiations over Berlin came to a near standstill. There were two reasons for the impasse. First, West Germans and the French overtly opposed Kennedy's policy, for it compromised the future reunification of Germany while rendering probable the recognition of an East German communist puppet state. Second, Franco-German opposition viewed Kennedy's rapprochement with the Soviet Union as a sign of weakness, which in turn was indicative of growing U.S. nuclear vulnerability. The Europeans' point of view was compounded by Kennedy's expedient use of the missile-gap thesis during the U.S. elections of 1960; by Soviet advances in nuclear weapons technology; by the new U.S. administration's shift from a strategy of massive retaliation to a policy of flexible response; and the parallel U.S. support for a conventional, as opposed to a nuclear, option for NATO.

Franco-German opposition limited Kennedy's ability to realize a bilateral rapprochement with the Soviet Union, for he could not risk jeopardizing his country's relations with two of the three principal European allies. In the crisis of confidence, which lasted throughout the fall of 1961 into early 1962, the United States reacted by launching an information campaign concerning the missile gap. Anything less than a full disclosure of the U.S. nuclear potential would likely end in European recriminations. Fundamentally, the message of Kennedy's administration to European skeptics was that its own second-strike potential was higher than the Soviet Union's entire nuclear arsenal and that the United States therefore did not act out of weakness.

This signal was appreciated by the West Germans as well as the Soviets, whose interpretation was markedly different. To Khrushchev and his associates in the Politburo, the divulgence of U.S. nuclear superiority at a crucial juncture in bilateral superpower negotiations translated into a fundamental questioning of the nuclear balance. Khrushchev concluded that in the long term the Soviet Union had to close the qualitative missile gap by achieving quantitative parity. In the short term, Khrushchev had to respond to the blatant U.S. challenge: stationing medium-range ballistic missiles (MRBMs) and IRBMs on Cuba, the Soviet leader carried the nuclear threat to America's doorstep.

The Significance of the Cuban Missile Crisis
in the Context of Systems Competition

In a televised speech on 22 October 1962, President Kennedy announced the CIA's discovery of Soviet missiles on Cuba, and thus came the most frightening fortnight of the Cold War: the two superpowers faced off over nuclear missiles. In the wake of Kennedy's TV address, the United States and Western Europe were astounded and perplexed by the Soviet move. Essentially, the Soviets had stationed nuclear missiles in the Caribbean just off Florida's coast. And although 1962 saw the superpowers nearing mutual nuclear destruction, the events led to a calmer phase of the Cold War.

The settling of the crisis.   In August 1962, there were indications that the Soviet Union was expanding its arms shipments to Cuba. What concerned Washington was the realization that the Soviets were constructing surface-to-air missile (SAM) launch sites on Cuba. The discovery of SAM installations prompted an intense domestic debate in the United States over the meaning of the Soviet shipments to Cuba. The director of the CIA, John A. McCone, argued that the stationing of defensive surface-to-air missiles would make sense only if the Soviets could defend the deployment of offensive MRBMs. But others countered that the Soviets were unlikely to install an offensive nuclear capability in Cuba, for that would be too blatant a provocation. In light of mounting domestic pressures and growing criticism from hard-liners, Kennedy decided to reassure U.S. citizens. On 13 September, he addressed the nation and committed to act should Cuba acquire the capacity to carry out offensive actions against the U.S. homeland. In a joint resolution a few days later, Congress reinforced this message, stating that the nation was determined "to prevent in Cuba the creation or use of an externally supported military capability endangering the security of the United States."[3]

The analysis of aerial photography made by two U.S. reconnaissance planes over Cuba on 14 October corroborated John McCone's thesis. The U-2 spy planes provided the first hard evidence of Soviet MRBM sites on Cuba and confirmed twenty-four SAM sites. The Soviets were indeed constructing launching pads for nuclear weapons. On Tuesday morning, 16 October 1962, Kennedy was told that the Soviet weapons on Cuba were offensive, not defensive. At the White House, the principal advisory panel on security—the **National Security Council Executive Committee (ExComm)**—met to review all possible options. Full-scale invasion by sea and air, surgical air strikes, and a naval blockade were among the possible solutions outlined by the advisers. After five days of analysis and debate, Kennedy decided to cordon off Cuba by sea. The president went public on 22 October, demanding that the Soviets immediately withdraw their missiles from Cuba. The U.S. public's reaction to the stationing of Soviet tactical and intermediate-range nuclear weapons just off southern Florida was frantic.

A naval blockade was to be the first step in U.S. plans to lend their ultimatum weight. On 24 October, the U.S. Navy, within the 500-mile perimeter established around Cuba, intercepted two Soviet transport vessels suspected of carrying more nuclear weapons. The blockade fleet was under orders to attack escorting Soviet submarines unless they surfaced. The Soviets stopped their vessels. When intelligence reports started to trickle into Washington indicating that the Soviet ships were turning around, Secretary of State Dean Rusk uttered his famous comment: "We are eyeball to eyeball, and the other fellow just blinked."[4] Civilian shipping was permitted to pass the U.S. blockade in the following five days.

The U.S. blockade was accompanied by a series of military and diplomatic moves and countermoves. On 26 October, the first cause for hope emerged: the senior intelligence official at the Soviet embassy in Washington suggested outlines for a possible accommodation in a talk with a respected ABC News correspondent. Later in the day, the State Department received a letter from Khrushchev to Kennedy proposing a deal along the following lines: the Soviets would remove their nuclear weapons from Cuba if the United States agreed to guarantee Cuba immunity from attack. Significantly, Khrushchev warned Kennedy "should war indeed break out, it would not be in our power to contain or stop it."[5] The cautious optimism of Friday night, however, soon gave way to the blackest hour of the crisis on Saturday. While the ExComm was meeting to consider a positive reply to Khrushchev's letter, Radio Moscow broadcast a second message from the Soviet chairman in which he demanded a quid pro quo: Soviet withdrawal of nuclear weapons in Cuba for U.S. withdrawal of nuclear weapons in Turkey.

Obviously, Khrushchev's move was politically motivated. A U.S. retreat from Turkey would allow Khrushchev to magnanimously reciprocate U.S. cooperation to end the nuclear deadlock. The U.S. missiles stationed in Turkey had become obsolete, and the Americans had considered removing them as early as 1961. But Khrushchev's demand was intended to legitimize the presence of Soviet missiles on Cuba. If Kennedy accepted the deal, his government would effectively justify Soviet operations in Cuba. To make things still more difficult for the United States, its NATO allies would almost certainly condemn such an agreement with the Soviets over Cuba as a sellout of European security interests for the sake of U.S. interests in the Caribbean. Under such circumstances, a public deal would not be possible.

In the interim, a U.S. reconnaissance aircraft was downed over Cuba. Almost insignificant of and by itself, this event took on exaggerated proportions in the charged atmosphere of crisis. Another U-2 plane had been shot at by antiaircraft batteries in Soviet airspace, which compounded the situation. The crisis had brought the superpowers to the edge of war. Khrushchev and Kennedy were aware of the probable risks of continuing the confrontation. Khrushchev was prepared to withdraw the Soviet missiles deployed on Cuba in return for Kennedy's guarantee not to attack Cuba. In his letter of 26 October 1962, Khrushchev indicated that he agreed to resolve the crisis by peaceful means. Kennedy, too, was inclined not to allow the obsolete U.S. missiles stationed in Turkey to stand in the way of a mutually acceptable, peaceful solution. President Kennedy's brother, Robert Kennedy, clandestinely informed the Soviet ambassador in Washington, Anatoly Dobrynin, that the U.S. government was willing to withdraw its missiles from Turkey in exchange for the removal of all Soviet missiles on Cuba—but only if the Soviet leadership agreed not to make the agreement public. Furthermore, Kennedy took care to respond only to Khrushchev's initial proposal, which had not been made conditional on simultaneous withdrawal of U.S. installations in Turkey. The U.S. military was then put on alert and commenced preparations for an invasion of Cuba on 27 October.

As the world held its collective breath, one question came to obsess presidential advisers in Washington: Would the Soviets yield? On the morning of Sunday, 28 October, an address transmitted via radio apprised the ExComm of Khrushchev's decision to end the crisis. Kennedy accordingly called off the naval blockade as the Soviets proceeded to remove all weapons from Cuba. Castro was bitterly disappointed by his communist allies. He accused Khrushchev of having used Cuba in order to further the political ends of the Soviet Union. Not a word of the deal concerning the U.S. withdrawal of missiles in Turkey was announced to the public. Quietly, the last Jupiter missiles left Turkey in April 1963. Effectively, the public perception of events during the Cuban missile crisis was that the Soviets had lost a high-risk gamble. Eventually, the man who would be held responsible for the Soviet Union's loss of prestige would be Nikita Khrushchev himself.

The central lesson: from crisis bargaining to not losing control. For the first twenty-five years following the Cuban missile crisis, the central lesson had been that the resolution of this historic incident represented a successful model of crisis management. For the duration of that period, the idea that the Cuban missile crisis had been handled with great aplomb on the U.S. side was largely perpetuated by Robert Kennedy's *Thirteen Days: A Memoir of the Cuban Missile Crisis*, Graham Allison's *The Essence of Decision*, and statements by close witnesses of the crisis such as Arthur Schlesinger Jr., who boldly stated that John F. Kennedy's actions throughout October 1962 had been a "combination of toughness and restraint, of will, nerve, and wisdom, so brilliantly controlled, so matchlessly calibrated, that it dazzled the world."[6] The myth of competent crisis management, however, was debunked toward the end of the 1980s with new archival and other evidence as well as conferences on the event. Only then did historians and other experts realize just how close the crisis had come to spinning out of control. It was also discovered that the political leaders of the two superpowers had come dangerously close to losing control of the situation themselves. The new revelations about the Cuban missile crisis emphasize the extent to which decisionmaking in Washington, Moscow, and Havana was characterized by flawed communication and miscalculation. A brief discussion shows the extent to which misperceptions colored the leaders' actions.

Kennedy's sense of urgency. Why were U.S. policymakers shocked by the installation of Soviet nuclear weapons in the first place? And why did Kennedy and his advisers reach an immediate consensus on the necessity of the United States to react with more than diplomatic means to what they perceived as a reckless initiative? After all, the Soviet Union had existed under a comparable threat of nuclear attack by the United States and its allies for a considerable period. Whenever Khrushchev took leave of his duties in Moscow to spend a vacation at the Black Sea, he was faced with U.S. nuclear weapons installations across the border in Turkey. The principal reason for Kennedy's, and his advisers', irate response was aptly encapsulated in Kennedy's first reaction upon receiving the information, for he believed that "there had been a concerted Soviet effort to mislead the United States government and its president with a *fait accompli* at some moment of Khrushchev's choice."[7] Kennedy felt particularly deceived because of the secrecy of the Soviet move. Moreover, when Kennedy met with Soviet Foreign Minister Andrei Gromyko on 18 October, the latter denied that Soviet military aid to Cuba was in any way of an offensive character. Kennedy had decided not to discuss U.S. awareness of the missiles with Gromyko. However, he interpreted the Soviet foreign minister's statement as a lie and felt betrayed by the Soviet government.

Initially, Kennedy thought that Khrushchev had made his decision to station missiles in Cuba despite U.S. warnings to the contrary. The problem with such a position was that the warning issued by the Kennedy administration came too late for the Soviets to beat a graceful retreat. Why did Kennedy fail to issue a warning earlier? This can only be explained by a strong belief, particularly in the White House, that Khrushchev would never dare to deploy nuclear missiles to Cuba. From a U.S. perspective the unacceptability of Soviet missiles in the Western Hemisphere was so self-evident that no one saw a need to communicate that fact.

Khrushchev's motives.   What motivated the Soviet leader to implement his personal idea to deploy nuclear missiles in Cuba? The Soviet engagement on Cuba was primarily a matter of superpower prestige: Moscow had thereby established a presence in the Western Hemisphere. But the United States had already attempted to overthrow Fidel Castro's government. U.S. attempts to isolate Cuba diplomatically, militarily, and economically did not, however, stop with the abortive Bay of Pigs invasion of April 1961. In late 1961, Kennedy authorized the covert Operation Mongoose, which was geared toward the overthrow of Castro in October 1962, the very time that the lately discovered Soviet deployment of nuclear missiles erupted into an international crisis. It was clear that the final success of the operation would rest on decisive military intervention. Parallel to the program, U.S. forces carried out a series of highly visible military exercises, clearly simulating an invasion of Cuba. Moreover, the Cubans and Soviets were well aware of these developments, for Cuban intelligence had managed to penetrate the CIA. Clearly, Khrushchev expected the worst, that is, he apprehended a U.S. invasion of Cuba.

In addition, Khrushchev perceived the missile deployment as a means to redress a highly unfavorable strategic balance. By early 1962, it was clear that the United States possessed a substantial nuclear superiority.

"The Americans," Khrushchev wrote in his memoirs, "had surrounded our country with military bases and threatened us with nuclear weapons, and now they would learn just what it feels like to have enemy missiles pointing at you; we'd be doing nothing more than giving them a little of their own medicine."[8] Ostensibly, the Soviets had increased their strategic arsenal when they dispatched some forty missiles of inferior quality to Cuba. The explanation for this was that the Soviet ICBM program had made only very slow progress—a fact that was hidden to the West for all of Khrushchev's forceful nuclear rhetoric.

Conversely, the Kennedy administration failed to understand the Soviets' perspective on their engagement in Cuba. President Kennedy did not think that Khrushchev would perceive U.S. action against Cuba as an indication of an impending invasion. U.S. policymakers underrated the significance that Khrushchev attached to his plans for nuclear deployment in the Caribbean aiming to redress the strategic imbalance between the superpowers. They failed to anticipate how desperate the Soviet position seemed in Moscow. Instead, Kennedy believed that the missiles in Cuba had only a marginal impact on the overall strategic nuclear balance. There would be little difference between missiles launched from the territory within the Soviet Union or from Cuba: the threat would remain practically the same. What would change, however, was the perception of the balance of power in the context of the Cold War and its impact on the political balance between the superpowers.

The nature of the Cuban missile crisis was political and not strategic. Indeed, in the first place it was domestic pressure over the meaning of the Soviet arms shipments to Cuba that had forced Kennedy to challenge the Soviet Union openly. For if Kennedy appeared any less committed to a hard line against the Soviet menace than Eisenhower had been before him, he stood to loose his bona fides with his constituents. Following the fiasco at the Bay of Pigs, another setback connected with Cuba would have spelled the end of Kennedy's domestic political credibility.

Neither side could afford a loss of face. This was as true for Kennedy as for Khrushchev. The Soviet leader was committed to an all-out defense of Cuba. He would make sure that there would not be a second Bay of Pigs, if only because his détente policies had earned him the enmity of hard-line communist forces in the Eastern bloc. Essentially, his political career was at stake over the Cuban missile crisis. In summary, Khrushchev's volatile policies at home had not endeared him to his colleagues in the Politburo, whereas Kennedy was new in power and had to prove to his domestic opposition (i.e., the Republican Party) that he could be as tough on communism as Eisenhower had been. In this sense, the Soviet-U.S. confrontation over Cuba was also a political issue intimately linked to the political careers of the Eastern and Western leaders.

On the Road to Stabilization: Bipolarity and the Reciprocal
Acceptance of the Territorial and Nuclear Status Quo in Europe
The Cuban missile crisis had its roots in a Cold War environment shaped by tensions over the Berlin issue. If the Cuban missile crisis is juxtaposed with the Berlin crisis, a question arises as to the significance of the Cuban missile crisis vis-à-vis the tug-of-war over Berlin. To begin with, the psychological effects of the Cuban missile crisis on the U.S. government loomed large in the sense that the Soviet action corroborated the superpower acceptance of the territorial status quo in Europe. In the early stages of the crisis, Kennedy and his advisers were convinced that the stationing of missiles on Cuba was part and parcel of a comprehensive Soviet plan to increase pressure on the Berlin issue. If truth be told, Khrushchev had said as much in his second Berlin ultimatum. If the United States undertook steps to invade Cuba, then the Soviets would move on Berlin in force. This allowed for the superpowers to find consensus over Cuba but would leave the United States at a disadvantage concerning Berlin. When Kennedy ordered the U.S. Navy to blockade Cuba in late October 1962, the Soviet reaction, as expected by the White House, failed to materialize. Surprisingly, the Soviets did not escalate the conflict in Europe. The failure of a Soviet response implied that Khrushchev was not too concerned with Berlin but instead was interested in the defense of Cuba.

Lastly, the Cuban missile crisis improved the superpowers' faith in the nuclear status quo in Europe. The drama that surrounded the crisis sensitized the leaders of East and West to the authentic and inescapable dangers of nuclear war. The deadlock forced both sides to reconsider the consequences of their respective actions and to prevent—at all costs and by all means necessary—the escalation of a nuclear war. Kennedy had already spelled out before the UN General Assembly in late 1961:

> War appeals no longer as a rational alternative. Unconditional war can no longer lead to unconditional victory. It can no longer serve to settle disputes. It can no longer be of concern to great powers alone. For a nuclear disaster, spread by winds and waters and fear, could well engulf the great and the small, the rich and the poor, the committed and the uncommitted alike. Mankind must put an end to war—or war will put an end to mankind.[9]

It was in this context that Kennedy—whose domestic political success had strengthened his position in relation to his opponents at home—and Khrushchev—inclined to introduce a friendlier foreign policy toward the United States—were able to recommence superpower relations on an improved basis.

In the aftermath of these two crises, the tensions dominating superpower relations since the conclusion of World War II eased. Kennedy and

Khrushchev both accepted the territorial and nuclear status quo in Europe. Khrushchev indicated that he was willing not to use the Soviet stranglehold on Berlin to pressure the Western bloc in the future and that he would accept the fact of a divided Berlin. By signing the Limited Test Ban Treaty in 1963, Kennedy made it understood that his government would continue to support the principle of two nonnuclear German states. In order to satisfy the security interests of West Germany, U.S. troops were stationed there on a permanent basis. The very drama of the critical events that occurred in 1962 opened the way to the establishment of informal channels between East and West: a direct telephone line (the so-called Hot Line) between the White House and the Kremlin was installed. Improved communication and concurrence on central issues of the Cold War resulted in a short period of relaxation in 1963. This phenomenon is referred to by historians of this period as the "little détente."

During the 1960s, however, superpower competition escalated into renewed hostilities and a resuscitation of the Cold War. The arms race received new impetus when the Soviets decided to achieve quantitative nuclear parity with the United States. In the U.S. government, powerful factions strove for the maintenance of nuclear superiority. Finally, the Soviet Union's gradual expansion of influence in the third world caused significant friction and was duly reciprocated by the United States (e.g., in Vietnam). The bipolar structure, it seemed at the time, had again assumed the role of a defining characteristic in international relations. The Soviet Union imposed the Pax Sovietica on its sphere of influence, and the United States enforced the Pax Americana in the Western Hemisphere: the international system was thus subjected to a balance of terror. In truth, however, the international system had undergone a fundamental change since 1945. Although not readily apparent, the bipolar structure had disciplined and controlled the emerging new forces.

IR Theory and Key Concepts

Federalism
Federalism is a vision of regional and or international relations favoring a supranational government with authority in certain areas over constituent states. At its most extreme, federalism pursues world government as the penultimate objective of idealist forces. As stated previously, federalism can also be applied on a state or regional level, as is evidenced by the European federalists in the development of the European Community (EC) and the European Union.

Functionalism

Functionalism emphasizes purposes and tasks in the context of international relations, especially as practiced by organizations. Arguments have been raised to the effect that the growth of organizations, specifically international organizations, occurred in response to the rising number of purposes and tasks demanding attention. In its capacity as a theory of **regional integration**, neo-functionalism focuses on premeditated political action and profitable reaction by elites who act cooperatively in the implementation of specific tasks as opposed to broadly defined policies. According to the mainstream in the regional integration literature, especially the literature relating to Europe, the concept of spillover refers to a process during which the satisfactory cooperation by states in a specific, and frequently technical, dimension prompts the involved parties to extend their mutually beneficial ties into proximate areas of cooperation and/or broader collaboration. The motivation and rationale behind functionalist approaches is the successful culmination of the spillover effect and not a highly regulated program of international cooperation sponsored by states. Essentially, functionalism is based on voluntarism and is therefore self-regulatory.

Liberalism and Capitalism

Liberalism refers to a political philosophy with origins in the seventeenth and eighteenth centuries (especially John Locke, 1632–1704) that emphasizes individual liberty to be achieved through minimal state interference. Laissez-faire government—one that upholds law and order but is otherwise legally constrained or not granted authority to infringe on the rights of citizens and subjects—is thereby considered to be a liberal government. Classic liberalism subscribes to the tenet of free-market principles with little or no interference on the part of the government both at home and abroad. It also implies government support for free-trade policies and the nearly unfettered conduct of commercial activity in domestic and international markets. As opposed to classic liberalism, the contemporary usage of the term *liberalism* in the United States usually refers to the augmentation of individual rights through government action.

Capitalism is an economic system or mode of production that postulates the private ownership of the means of production and a free market. One who owns the means of production is a capitalist or, alternatively, a bourgeois.

Key Terms

- the postwar alliance systems: NATO, SEATO, and the Warsaw Pact: The North Atlantic Treaty Organization is the result of the unsuccessful attempt by the former Great Powers of Europe to establish a common security policy for Europe. Instead, the focus shifted west, across the Atlantic. NATO became the Western postwar defensive alliance. The Warsaw Pact was the Soviet response to NATO and West Germany's conventional rearmament and constitutes the eastern antipode to NATO. The South East Asian Treaty Organization exemplifies the postwar Western security policy trend in establishing regional security systems and alliances. SEATO is the Asian version of NATO, though the member states' commitment to mutual defense is not as stringent as that of NATO member states.
- collective security: Collective security is agreement by all countries to automatically punish aggressors. As opposed to an exclusive defensive or offensive alliance, collective security is inherently inclusive.
- colonialism and imperialism: Historically, colonialism is defined as the efforts of the Great Powers of Europe to establish territorial dependencies overseas. In antiquity, the concept of imperialism denoted the territorial expansion of a power and its ability to create dependencies, which were subject to a power's center. John Hobson's and V. I. Lenin's models are predicated on economic and historic-dialectic determinants.
- rollback: John F. Dulles's rhetoric of rollback in the post-Stalin era was intended to weaken Soviet predominance and influence in Eastern Europe. Effectively, the rhetoric of rollback instilled Eastern Europe with hopes of U.S. military support for anti-Soviet revolutionary movements, which were—as in the case of Hungary in 1956—not fulfilled.

New Problems, (C)old War:
Three Perspectives, 1963–1968

THE THAW IN THE COLD WAR THAT FOLLOWED THE RESOLUTION OF THE BERLIN crisis and the Cuban missile crisis did not last long enough to fully materialize as a genuine relaxation between the superpowers. At that time, the international bipolar system had indeed achieved a measure of stability. By the mid-1960s, however, superpower competition had reached a new stage, the most extreme implications of which were encapsulated in the notion of mutually assured destruction, coined by U.S. Secretary of Defense Robert McNamara. Ironically, MAD would provide the world with the most efficacious deterrent against nuclear war. This grotesque equilibrium was predicated on a choiceless choice: static balance, or annihilation. But in order to maintain this balance of terror, the superpowers were forced to keep their nuclear arsenals on par and up to date. This compulsive Cold War dynamic resulted in a self-perpetuating arms race that extended far beyond Berlin and Cuba.

Conversely, the stasis caused by the bipolar nuclear balance of peril created unpredictable imbalances within the Western and Eastern blocs. The relative loss of internal stability within the blocs surfaced as new uncertainties were expressed in Europe and Asia—especially by parties that stood to lose the most in military conflicts below the threshold of nuclear war. This novel skepticism in the Eastern and Western blocs increasingly challenged the credibility of superpower commitments to nuclear defense. For their part, the superpowers were suddenly faced with the fait accompli of having to manage contumacious allies, which in turn led to a gradual diminution of their respective hegemonic status'.

In the West, the U.S. demonstration of anticolonialism directed against Britain and France in the 1950s combined with the European crisis of confidence in the U.S. nuclear guarantee to create a resounding challenge to U.S. leadership while also creating an impetus for national nuclear weapons development programs among the European allies. Moreover, the

United States became mired in a long and costly conflict in Vietnam, which left its European allies more room for initiative and also served to consolidate their skepticism toward the U.S. commitment to the defense of Europe.

In the East, the progressing Sino-Soviet disassociation culminated in the creation of two communist poles. At that stage, Maoist China became a contender for the role of principal communist state in the Eastern bloc, as national liberation movements in the third world and disgruntled Soviet clients (e.g., East Germany and Albania) turned to China for aid. In the case of Czechoslovakia, Soviet preponderance in the East was overtly challenged, and North Vietnam sagaciously permitted the contending communist powers to woo it with promises of support. And where the West emerged from this latest threat to its internal cohesion stronger than before, the East turned rigid in an attempt to establish control over its allies. The principal difference between the Eastern and Western developments was this: whereas the West responded to its internal crisis by addressing its difficulties and, in the process, underwent a genuine, if difficult, transformation toward integration, the Soviet Union turned to heavy-handed centralization that arrested any chances for development.

The evolving nuclear stalemate enhanced the willingness of policymakers in Washington and Moscow to accept the status quo as the basis for their bilateral relations. The times had passed by the principle of victory through force. The faith that the West had placed in liberation, rollback, and driving wedges could no longer be upheld. The danger of nuclear war could only be kept in check if the superpowers created a compromise in the context of which *both* were able to forgo the nuclear option. The superpower consensus after Berlin and Cuba was exclusively that: a Soviet-U.S. common denominator in bilateral policy leaving enough room for alternatives to direct confrontation.

The limits of bilateral relaxation in 1963 were indeed restrictive. Progress in arms control and disarmament were confined to the Limited Test Ban Treaty, and a major breakthrough in the context of bilateral negotiations was scarcely to be expected. In due course, the Cold War became palpable again in the superpower capitals. In Moscow, communist hard-liners—supported by Khrushchev's Chinese critics—were actively undermining the Soviet chairman by accusing him of having compromised Soviet interests during the Cuban missile crisis and having shamefully betrayed Castro, the Soviet Union's most valuable ally in the Western Hemisphere. To many among the Soviet leadership, the Cuban missile crisis and the Berlin crisis demonstrated the critical importance of achieving a quantitative nuclear parity with the United States. Conversely, in Washington the contradiction between rapprochement with Moscow and fighting communism in Asia became ever more glaring, as U.S. GIs were drawn deeper into a guerrilla war fought in the jungles of Vietnam.

Simultaneously, relations within the blocs were characterized by a diffusion of power or, rather, a devolvement of power from Washington and Moscow to the most influential allies—the NATO member states on the one side, and China on the other. Not all of the relevant players did take the nuclear stalemate for granted in the 1960s. As a consequence, allies' insecurities regarding the credibility of the nuclear guarantees of the two hegemons had repercussions for the superpowers. Time and again, the United States and the Soviet Union attempted to regain the confidence of their allies by bolstering and substantiating their capacity for nuclear deterrence and, implicitly, for the protection of U.S. and Soviet confederates. Ultimately, this vicious circle, rooted in the internal instability of the blocs, reinforced the superpowers' compulsion to maintain bilateral nuclear parity. The arms race had become an inescapable, self-sustaining fact in the logic of the bipolar international system shaped by the Cold War.

At the same time, the proliferation of nuclear capabilities within Britain, France, and China illustrated that the international system had lost one of its key bipolar elements. Despite the fact that none of the secondary powers proved capable of building a military force rivaling those of the superpowers, Moscow and Washington no longer had at their disposal exclusive nuclear deterrents. Moreover, the effects of **nuclear proliferation** on the international system remained unclear, and the adoption of a skeptical view of future trends seemed appropriate. Even though technical and financial obstacles to developing nuclear weapons had become greater with the signing of the Limited Test Ban Treaty—according to which no nuclear testing was to be conducted in the open seas, the atmosphere, and in space—the very fact that France and China were not among the signatories demonstrated that the problem caused by nuclear proliferation was far from being solved. Only toward the close of the decade was significant progress in this matter achieved.

In addition to new uncertainties related to power diffusion and credibility, the emergence of nationalism in the third world accentuated differences in interests, economic models, and social structures between, but also within, the two blocs. The period between 1945 and the highest tide of the Cold War, in the early 1960s, was marked by the superpower struggle over the control of Europe. Before, little notice had been taken of other regions, with the exception of Asia and the Middle East, where the process of decolonization constituted more of a legacy problem than a novel phenomenon. It was in Asia that the curious admixture of decolonization and the Cold War occurred—notably in Korea in the 1950s, and increasingly in Indochina during the early 1960s. As far as decisionmakers in Washington and Moscow were concerned, the battlefields of Asia represented mere sideshows. Each superpower sought to impose its control on those regions within its respective sphere of influence. Outside these spheres the superpowers sought only to recruit other states into their alliance systems. This perspective underwent a remarkable change in the early 1960s.

Significantly, as the Cold War in Europe stabilized in the shape of the mutual superpower acceptance of the territorial and nuclear status quo, its focus shifted elsewhere. Although the achievement of stability in Europe had averted a direct nuclear superpower confrontation, it is important to remember that the antagonists had really faced not much of a choice: the stakes for Europe were too high. Yet the dynamic of the Cold War—competition between two diverging value and social systems—was still very much alive. One of its manifestations was the arms race following the Berlin and Cuban missile crises. Its equivalent in the realm of conventional conflict materialized outside Europe. Because nuclear war with its focal point in Europe was not a viable option (after all, there would be no victors in such a war), and while systems competition continued unabated, the Cold War required an outlet, and it found one beyond the bounds of Europe. Thus, the third world (a geographic compound consisting of Africa, Asia, Latin America, and the Middle East) became the battlefield of the Cold War antagonists in the early 1960s.

The nascent states of the third world that had only recently become independent, or were still in the process of fighting a war of liberation, had their own problems and agendas. Nevertheless, they almost invariably became pawns of the superpowers and were used as proxy warriors of the superpowers on a substitute battlefield. In reaction to this trend, the third world states attempted to create a third pole in the international system by opting out of or opposing the Cold War; or by instrumentalizing the Cold War for their own purposes. In any event, the heightened significance of the third world in the wider context of the Cold War increased the number of actors involved and, as a corollary, contributed to the involution of the international system.

Toward Integration: The First World in the West

The growing integration in the West was the result of a dolorous process on both sides of the Atlantic leading toward an uneasy and unpalatable consensus in matters of internal and foreign policy. The Western progression toward integration was not achieved without a price: having to cut one's losses, so to speak, notably in Europe. The nuclear impasse between Washington and Moscow did not allow for the progressive settlement of those disputed issues—German reunification and French (and, to a lesser degree, British) independence—which were top priorities on the political agendas in Bonn, Paris, and London. The problem with the flexible bilateralism of 1963 was clear enough: although it constituted a logical and sensible reply to the nuclear abyss, it did not do justice to Eastern or Western allied concerns, which were historically, and not rationally, motivated. The erosion of cohesion that followed in the wake of the internal crises of confidence in the Eastern and Western blocs badly damaged the hegemonic position of the superpowers within those blocs.

The United States and the Vietnam War

To U.S. policy planners in the State Department it became apparent that U.S. Central European policy, in light of the yearning for reunification within the divided German nation, could not confine itself to a freezing of the status quo without significant reform in the long term. In an increasingly multipolar world of diffused power and with détente well under way, the growing desire for a solution to the German question had to be met by the implementation of proactive policy. An extended détente could be expected only as the result of a long-term, fluid historical process, not of a static deadlock in the form of a final, imposed settlement. Against this backdrop, Washington began to adjust its Central European policy. On the one hand, Lyndon Johnson's administration gave unstinting support to political forces in West Germany who understood that reunification hinged upon a flexible process of cooperation, but this was wholly inconsistent with the unyielding stance as exemplified in the Hallstein Doctrine. On the other, the U.S. Central European policy underwent a transition from driving wedges to building bridges, the objective being to render the boundaries between Eastern Europe and Western Europe more pervious.

A stronger participatory integration of allied interests in the U.S. policy on Europe, however, could not be achieved without a diminution of hegemonic influence exerted by the United States within the Western bloc. Thus, leadership in the West had to be based on persuasion rather than control. The realization by the United States that it had overcommitted its forces not only in Europe but also worldwide was lastly brought about by a conflict the cost and longevity of which swallowed much of its resources: the Vietnam War. The gradual escalation of the conflict in Indochina beyond the threshold of war occurred in the mid-1960s, but the U.S. withdrawal had to wait until the early 1970s and was not complete until 1975. The setbacks suffered during the latter phases of the Vietnam War had an adverse, twofold effect on the United States, one of which affected U.S. society, the other its foreign political objectives. When the two interacted and reinforced the other, the U.S. position relative to the pursuit of military intervention in Vietnam became untenable.

The impact of the Vietnam War on U.S. society was significant, and its reverberations can be felt to the present day. As the war in faraway Vietnam turned into a protracted nightmare, voices of protest against the bloodshed and senseless expenditures were raised at home. The issue profoundly divided and disillusioned U.S. society. What were young Americans dying for in a remote corner of the world? Why were direly needed U.S. finances being gobbled up by a seemingly nonsensical military campaign in a foreign country? Answers to these questions were hard to come by; the objectives of containment were barely understood or rejected as anachronisms; and, accordingly, successive U.S. governments under Lyndon B. Johnson and Richard Nixon began to lose the confidence of the people.

Domestically, two successive U.S. administrations witnessed the division of U.S. society and the alienation of an entire generation. In Europe, Johnson and, to a lesser degree, Nixon faced a strategic dilemma: Could the United States uphold its financial and military commitments to defend Europe from Soviet aggression while the Vietnam War was depleting the treasury and tying up the greater part of U.S. conventional military resources? After the mid-1960s, U.S. domestic pressure was translated into an organized popular resistance to the further conduct of the war, as well as congressional opposition to government overspending in both Asia and Europe. President Johnson was compelled to curb expenditures one way or another. His was the thankless task to decide where the cuts were to be made. If he withheld funds from the war effort in Vietnam, Johnson would jeopardize a U.S. victory. Yet if the U.S. government ordered a reduction of its military presence in Europe, the European allies—who had begun questioning the U.S. ability to protect Europe from Soviet aggression and the legitimacy of U.S. military intervention in Vietnam—would interpret such a step as being the first in a gradual withdrawal of all U.S. forces from the Continent. Only the U.S. ability to honor its pledges for the defense of Western Europe would suffice to prevent the dissolution of NATO. The resolution of such a complex set of problems would, as we will see below, demand determination on the part of all members of the Western alliance. At this stage, it is important to understand that the Vietnam War, costly in terms of human lives and finances, was politically damaging at home and abroad.

The United Kingdom: A Realm Apart?

Although Britain vied with France for influence in the Western alliance, its principal concern was a financial recovery, which it hoped to achieve by ridding itself of costly colonial liabilities. While its rivalry with France over influence in Western Europe in the 1950s and 1960s was real enough, Britain thus continued the painful process of decolonization, quitting its Mediterranean stronghold of Cyprus in 1959 and releasing West Africa into independence at about the same time. For its part, France was in the midst of waging war against the Front de Libération Nationale (FLN) in Algeria. In the early 1960s, Britain quickened the pace of colonial disengagement by repeating the West Africa experience in eastern and central Africa. There, however, British efforts at withdrawal were resisted by the various white minorities that had come to dominate most of the natural resources and that had, throughout the years of white rule, monopolized political power. Displacing white elites proved far more difficult than withdrawing a standard British colonial administration, as the white settlers retained a vested interest in the continued presence of the motherland and, if necessary, would hold on to power without British support.

Although settlements were reached in Tanzania and Kenya, the situation in Rhodesia went from bad to worse, ending with the white minority's peremptory declaration of independence in 1965. The Rhodesian regime took all necessary measures to suppress the blacks' aspirations toward majority rule. Britain responded with an economic embargo. But the white Rhodesian leader, Ian Smith, managed to evade the strictures of British economic sanctions by slipping contraband into the country through Portuguese Mozambique. In the case of Rhodesia, British plans to incrementally devolve government on the indigenous populations of its former African colonies backfired, as Smith and the white Rhodesian elite remained in power until 1979, when they were forced to relinquish control. Britain had little to do with the change of regime, which underscored the decline of its influence in the former colonies.

Despite the diverging national interests of the former Great Powers, the process of European economic and military integration moved apace. Significantly, Britain's contribution to the maintenance of the Western alliance was its commitment to the transatlantic alliance. As the resurgence of postwar nationalism and the colonial legacy withered in light of the overwhelming need to cooperate in the defense and reconstruction of Europe during the 1950s and 1960s, the countries of the old Continent for the first time also shared and saw the benefits of mutual assistance. Again, it was British policy within, and its conception of, NATO—"to keep the Russians out, the Germans down, and the Americans in"—that constituted the backbone of the Western alliance in Europe.[1] Indeed, Britain was in the vanguard of the Atlanticist faction in Europe. Representative of this evolving sense of unity was the solution that the Europeans—minus France—and the Americans found in 1966 to cement their relationship and to secure the safety of Western Europe—a process that will be discussed in more detail below.

France and the End of the Fourth Republic

As West Germany successfully reintegrated into the community of European states, and Britain struggled to bring its colonial engagements to a close, France was wracked by internal turmoil after the war. With its economy in tatters and no decisive leader at the political helm, France suffered from inflation, frequent strikes, and backward-looking industries. On one issue, however, French political elites agreed wholeheartedly: the loss of prestige suffered in the course of World War II irked parties on the left and the right. Having been overshadowed by a superpower was a reality that the French struggled to face. In fact, as time moved on the French were hoping to provide the world with a third superpower between the chief antagonists of the Cold War. The special relationship between the Anglo-Saxon powers—Britain and the United States—undermined French aspirations to become the principal Great Power in Europe. Worse still, the French perceived British coziness with the United States as a further indication of waning French influence in international politics. This perceived decline was abruptly halted with a crisis in government brought about by French rebels in Algeria and that threatened to culminate in civil war. The crisis marked the end of the Fourth Republic and brought about the return of General Charles de Gaulle to power in 1958 and the foundation of the Fifth Republic.

But the resuscitation of French self-esteem also led to friction with its Western allies, as its claim to leadership in Europe could no longer be easily sidelined. De Gaulle demanded that justice be done to France's renewed rise to power in the counsels of NATO. He consistently challenged the U.S. leadership role, refused permission for the deployment of U.S. nuclear weapons on French soil, and accelerated the development of the Force de Frappe (an independent, sovereign, and powerful French nuclear deterrent) at the same time. Concurrently, he also portrayed himself as the principal advocate of a Franco-German rapprochement in order to extend French preponderance on the Continent. The Franco-German Treaty of Friendship of January 1963, signed by de Gaulle and Adenauer, demonstrated to the latter the ill effects of moving closer to Paris at the expense of the transatlantic relation. Germany remained highly dependent on the United States for protection of German territory against Soviet aggression and would not jeopardize such vital interests for the sake of improved relations with France. Finally, de Gaulle responded to the Anglo-U.S. rejection of his demands by withdrawing all representation from the integrated command of NATO in 1966.

France did maintain its association with the Western bloc and supported the United States throughout its confrontation with the Soviet Union. In all other spheres of interaction with the United States, however, de Gaulle steered an increasingly anti-U.S. course. Openness toward China in 1964, economic overtures to the East, and de Gaulle's visit to Moscow symbolized the general's vision of an independent and powerful French state within the Western bloc. The French drive for independence and leadership on the Continent was exemplified by France's stubborn veto of British membership in the Common Market. By the time students took to the streets in Paris in May 1968 to protest Gaullist paternalism and authoritarian rule, France had become fully disillusioned with his leadership. De Gaulle's prestige—if not that of France—never recovered from the political divisions of 1968. Despite the widespread and deep-rooted conservatism of the French, de Gaulle was forced to step down in 1969 following the unsuccessful outcome of a referendum. Gaullism as a political movement remained a powerful nationalist force in the country for decades to come. In a sense, the resilience of Gaullist tendencies in the French electorate remains a tribute to the achievements of the man who made France great again.

Germany: An Opening to the East

When the long tenure of Konrad Adenauer ended in 1963, another conservative, Ludwig Erhard, succeeded him. When Erhard fell from power following his fruitless attempt to postpone the balance-of-payments owed to the Western allies for the defense of West Germany, Kurt Georg Kiesinger was elected the next chancellor of West Germany in 1966. In the same year, the election of Willy Brandt, the former mayor of Berlin, as foreign minister under Chancellor Kiesinger ushered in a new period of foreign policy. Brandt was committed to a full reversal of Adenauer's political practice vis-à-vis the Soviet satellites in Eastern Europe. In contrast to Adenauer, Brandt realized that twenty years of Soviet suzerainty in Eastern Europe indicated that little would change in the near future pertaining to German unification if West Germany remained incommunicado. The turnabout in German foreign policy had a precedent in Johnson's belief in the necessity of détente. Johnson saw the impasse between the two Germanies as the greatest obstacle to unification. In this atmosphere, Brandt took his first, tentative steps toward what would later be known as **Ostpolitik** (eastern politics), that is, a policy to achieve improved relations with the Eastern bloc.

What would have been inconceivable under Adenauer served Brandt as a preliminary when he launched his foreign political offensive. Brandt was willing to explore any means necessary to bring about a rapprochement with East Germany—even if this meant extending factual rather than legal recognition to East Germany and the European frontiers that emerged as a consequence of the Allies' victory. In this context, the new West German government was even willing to go so far as to break a postwar taboo: recognizing the Oder-Neisse Line. Effectively, Brandt was a pragmatist and would not condone any German attempts to regain the territorial losses of World War II. His government repudiated Adenauer's claims for the restitution of the East Prussian, Polish, and Sudeten territories lost to Germany after 1945.

The East Germans and their Soviet masters did, however, not grasp the olive branch extended by Brandt, as they were primarily interested in a de jure recognition of East Germany's socialist government. By implication, the legal and diplomatic recognition of East Germany by Brandt's government would serve the Soviets as an act of affirmation in their endeavor to bring about a German state in their image. Worse, it would render permanent the perfunctory division of Germany and undermine Adenauer's claim to West Germany's sole right to represent all Germans. Consequently, any West German government could not accede to East German and Soviet demands; such an act would undermine the very tenets of West Germany. The more practical side of Brandt's opening to the East was made manifest in a meeting with Willy Stoph, the representative of Walter Ulbricht, at Erfurt on 19 March 1970. The result of improved relations between the two Germanies led to the Basic Treaty of 1972. Although East Germany was not accorded diplomatic recognition, measures designed to bring the two states to take up cooperative relations in cultural and economic matters proved successful and encouraging.

Brandt's Ostpolitik was responsible for a gradual easing of tensions not only between the two Germanies but also in time between the superpowers. Brandt's initiative lifted the question of post–World War II borders on the Continent out of the bilateral Soviet-U.S. little détente of 1963 and refocused the issue within the broader multilateral context of a pan-European security system. In 1968, West Germany established diplomatic relations with the most Western-minded of the East European states: Marshal Tito's Yugoslavia. By 1970, the Soviet Union had concluded a nonaggression treaty with West Germany, and in that year Brandt recognized the Polish frontier of 1945. Brandt's accession to the Oder-Neisse Line, however, was designed to propagate Ostpolitik. Unless the governments of the countries that had been at war with Germany did not conclude a peace treaty with West Germany, no agreement made on the part of Brandt's government would possess the force of legality. Oddly enough, Germany had made no formalized peace or war relations with the victors of World War II or any of its cobelligerents. Brandt's successors would make use of early German republican legalism when East-West relations reached a second nadir in the 1980s.

NATO: From Crisis to Reform, 1966–1969

The interests of the most significant NATO member states were diverging by the mid-1960s. Even as NATO moved toward a crisis, the harbingers of reforms made themselves felt, for the prerequisites for defining a new vision of the alliance had markedly improved. In Washington, the idea that NATO should preserve its military functions while expanding to encompass

Henry Kissinger's proposed "Atlantic Commonwealth" was gaining ground. In the wider context of détente, the Western alliance required a new mechanism in order to more effectively share political decisionmaking. The realization struck West German leaders in Bonn that their objectives could be substantiated only if they were willing to pursue a diplomatic course of action that prioritized the incremental economic and cultural rapprochement between East and West. And the more France distanced itself from NATO, the more Britain emphasized the transatlantic, rather than the European, integration process.

The change NATO underwent in the course of these developments caused friction within the alliance. In the final analysis, it was the very institutional structures of NATO that proved instrumental in forging a convergence of European security perspectives among the United States and its allies. The debate revolved around a number of issues that, albeit not concurrently at the center stage, were nevertheless intricately connected: the strategy and the role of tactical nuclear weapons in Europe; burden-sharing and decisionmaking; and the military and political roles of NATO.

The debate on strategy: from massive retaliation to flexible response.   In the wake of the Berlin crisis and the Cuban missile crisis, the superpowers drew lessons from past events. In the West, especially in the United States, policymakers came to understand that a nuclear confrontation was unthinkable. Under the auspices of President John F. Kennedy and Secretary of Defense Robert McNamara, a decisive revolution of strategic thought took place. In this case, the conceptual terminus a quo was vested in Dwight Eisenhower's strategy of massive retaliation: every aggression perpetrated by the Soviet Union would prompt an immediate nuclear U.S. response—independent of the Soviets' choice of offensive means. The Sputnik shock of 1957 and the Soviet capability to threaten U.S. territory, which had come in range of Soviet strategic nuclear weapons, rendered massive retaliation obsolete.

At the beginning of the 1960s, the incoming Kennedy administration criticized massive retaliation for its lack of flexibility and infeasibility. It proposed a new concept: flexible response. This novel strategy came to the fore during the Cuban missile crisis in October 1962, when Kennedy ordered a blockade of Cuba instead of a full-scale invasion: this was a graduated U.S. response to a Soviet action, which prevented an escalation of the crisis. The lesson learned was that the United States and, by extension, NATO ought never again become the object of circumstantial, military, and political forces but should develop the capability to shape situations. The rigidity of massive retaliation and the single course of action it left open to decisionmakers was, therefore, sidelined in favor of a strategy that would allow the U.S. president and European allies as many options as feasible according to circumstances. Operationally, the significance of the new strategy was that it would permit the West to plan and control a graduated escalation—initially with conventional means and, failing that, with a selective nuclear response that could be expanded into a full nuclear confrontation. The new paradigm became known as the *strategy of flexible response*.

On the bilateral level, flexible response was a logical answer to the flaws of pre-Cuban U.S. military doctrine. The trouble in Europe began as flexible response percolated through NATO ranks. Kennedy's faith in flexible response was unveiled to the European allies at a NATO meeting in Athens in May 1962, where McNamara introduced the new strategy. Significantly, the implementation of flexible response in the United States had proved difficult and had encountered hostility from the military; by contrast, it took the Europeans years to come to terms with McNamara's idea. The reasons for European resistance to flexible response were manifold. To begin with, Western European parties faced different domestic pressures and divergent foreign political interests, also determining their political agendas according to specific national circumstances, such as geography.

West Germany feared that flexible response would erode the credibility of the Western nuclear deterrent by introducing a scalable, conventional element into Germany's defense. West Germany's geographical position rendered it highly vulnerable to potential Soviet aggression. For this reason alone, West Germans did not take kindly to the notion that the Western nuclear deterrent was to be diluted in the name of strategic flexibility: raising the nuclear threshold could well culminate in decoupling. Germany would, after all, be the first to feel the consequences of failure.

Despite cordial relations with the United States, Britain was stung by McNamara's criticism of national nuclear weapons programs. The British nuclear potential had a strategic as well as a purely political significance by bolstering British prestige. McNamara argued that "weak nuclear capabilities, operating independently, are expensive, prone to obsolescence and lacking in credibility as a deterrent."[2] But his pragmatism did not allow for Britain's self-perceived role as a Great Power. It might be added that Eisenhower's snub of the British during the Suez crisis six years earlier was not easily forgotten. Britain was also torn between its allegiance to the special relationship with the United States and its stakes in continental relations and European integration.

French opposition was the most vocal and determined. General de Gaulle pursued a policy geared toward the establishment of an independent, sovereign, and powerful French nuclear deterrent—the Force de Frappe. French nuclear capabilities, however, were not designed to meet the demands of flexible response in the first place. De Gaulle's nationalist policy was responsible for obstructing all efforts deviating from a nuclear trip-wire strategy in Europe and thus became the catalyst for a serious crisis within NATO. The motivation behind de Gaulle's policy of disassociation was that he wanted to emerge as the leader of a loosely integrated Europe (with West Germany playing the part of junior partner), which might be turned into a third force beyond the two antagonists of the Cold War. The deadlock created by French opposition to the United States in the Western alliance was resolved only after two significant developments. First, the Adenauer era ended in 1963 and the political opposition gained power in Britain in 1964, which smoothed the way toward a U.S.-European under-standing by reducing fundamental objects of contention to interpretative nonissues; second, in opposition to U.S. preponderance in the Western alliance, France quit the NATO integrated command in early 1966. The way toward a resolution of NATO's crisis of confidence was at last open.

The burden-sharing debate: the Offset negotiations.   At that time, the three remaining principal members of the Western alliance—the United States, West Germany, and Britain—faced serious financial problems. The United States was fighting an expensive war in Vietnam. Congressional pressure under the leadership of Senator Mike Mansfield sought to limit fiscal drainage by moving Kennedy's successor, Lyndon B. Johnson, to accept a political quid pro quo: qualified congressional support of his policies at home and the pursuit of war in Vietnam for a reduction of forces in Europe. Thus if Johnson elected to reduce the U.S. military presence in Europe while the Western alliance underwent a crisis of confidence centered on the potency of the U.S. deterrent—further compounded by a tendency toward fragmentation—then NATO would likely disintegrate. Yet the United States could not uphold its engagement in Asia while bearing the same heavy bur-den in Europe. A compromise would be the only viable option. In accor-dance with the so-called Offset Treaties, West Germany was bound to absorb a significant part of the financial burden incurred by the Western allies in its defense. The Offset deal stipulated that West Germany was to compensate its allies for their expenditures by a balance-of-payments in the shape of military hardware purchases in the United Kingdom and the United States.

   In the summer of 1966, West Germany made clear its inability to honor the Offset payments for Great Britain's British Army on Rhine (BAOR). Meanwhile, the British economy weathered a severe crisis, which ham-pered its ability to maintain BAOR at full strength. And Johnson apparently considered the withdrawal of 15,000 troops from Europe for redeployment in Vietnam. In this situation, NATO faced a twofold problem. On the one hand, a British withdrawal would certainly set the trend for a general allied troop reduction in Europe, which in turn would fuel West German fears of abandonment; on the other hand, the redeployment of Western alliance troops would call into question the fundamental precept of flexible response within NATO—that of increasing conventional forces for the sake of expanding Western options in the event of a confrontation with the Soviet Union and the Warsaw Pact. By extension, such a development would cast doubt on the future viability of the Western alliance.

On the initiative of Johnson, the three leading NATO members engaged in trilateral negotiations toward a resolution of the Offset and troop reduction issues in October 1966. In the course of the Offset negotiations, the parties came to understand that no new strategy for NATO could be ratified unless they first concluded the trilateral talks satisfactorily. In February 1967, Johnson could no longer postpone a decision on the reduction of U.S. troops stationed in Europe: congressional pressure was mounting, and the European quandary remained painfully obvious. Senator Mansfield clamored for the recall of U.S. troops from Europe, arguing that the United States could not be expected to simultaneously pay the lion's share of Europe's defense, pursue the war in Vietnam, and not redeploy sorely needed U.S. regiments from Europe.

At this stage, Johnson's advisers proposed three schemes relying on the idea of dual basing, or rotating, U.S. conventional forces in Europe. In other words, a U.S. troop reduction would not be irrevocable. Instead, U.S. divisions would merely be redeployed elsewhere while continuously assigned to NATO. In the event of crisis, the dual-based divisions would be recalled and airlifted to their European postings. During their absence, the dual-based contingents' equipment would remain in Europe. Moreover, dual-based troops would be subject to a carefully planned rotation schedule allowing for their periodic redeployment and training in Europe. Such a course of action had a better chance to render the likely troop reduction politically palatable to West Germany. The first advisory proposal was that of rotating two U.S. divisions and six air wings; the second suggested redeploying half that amount; and the third recommended that Johnson desist from moving any troops whatsoever.

In April 1967, the three parties to the Offset negotiations were finally able to arrive at a compromise despite a definitive removal of U.S. troops from Europe. The United States designated three brigades of a division, as well as ninety-six aircraft of three wings, for rotational transatlantic duty. The British, who had warned West Germany that they would disestablish BAOR in the event that no satisfactory balance-of-payment could be arrived at, ended up withdrawing a single brigade from the Rhine. The financial divergence between the West German and British positions in the negotiations had amounted to some U.S.$40 million. Johnson then suggested that it made little sense to abandon NATO for a pittance and shamed the contending allies into contributing money themselves. On the whole, how-

ever, these qualified successes were made possible only by major concessions granted by the West Germans, which allowed for an improved balance of the allies' burden-sharing. In order to forestall a general recall of
allied troops from West Germany, Johnson opted for the rotation/dual-bas-
ing scheme, which would least compromise U.S. credibility in the defense
of Europe. Rotation/dual-basing also permitted Johnson and his advisers to
stave off further demands by Congress for the recall of U.S. troops from
Europe—at least temporarily.

The role of tactical nuclear weapons in Europe: MC 14/3. The circumscribed withdrawal of conventional forces from Europe was the diametric
opposite of McNamara's stated policy objectives of flexible response. Yet it
is important to understand that the minimal allied troop reduction on the
Continent was also the best possible political solution causing the least possible damage to allied conventional military capabilities in Europe.
Moreover, the resolution of the Offset negotiations established the basis for
NATO's strategic transition from the almost exclusive reliance upon
nuclear weapons as a deterrent to the scalable and controlled deployment of
conventional and nuclear forces as set forth in flexible response.

In December 1967, NATO's supreme political body, the North Atlantic
Council, formally ratified the new strategy of flexible response in the shape
of a document entitled MC 14/3. According to MC 14/3, any provocation or
aggression committed by the Soviet Union or the Warsaw Pact would no
longer prompt a massive nuclear retaliation but instead would be confronted with a credible and adequate conventional or nuclear deterrent.
Effectively, MC 14/3 amounted to a compromise between the political
necessities of the U.S. and European security requirements. The United
States achieved almost all of its objectives for NATO but had to accept cur-
tailments of its initial demand for an augmented conventional defense for
Europe. In turn, the Europeans, specifically the West Germans, had to agree
to a longer conventional defense phase in the event of attack from the East
and, as a corollary, were compelled to embody the requisite regiments and
accept a higher nuclear threshold. Still, the Europeans had managed to convince the United States of the necessity for an enduring and credible
nuclear deterrent in Europe. The United States was to support the principle
of forward defense, that is, a commitment to defend Europe along the West
German–East German frontier with theater nuclear weapons (i.e., tactical
nuclear weapons).

*A new balance between the political and the military functions of the
Western alliance: the Harmel Report.* In 1967, NATO also reviewed its
political role vis-à-vis the rise of détente while considering the effects of its
own recent crisis. The Harmel Report, named after the foreign minister of

Belgium who had suggested the venture in 1966, was to investigate the possible necessity for NATO to reappraise and adjust its policy and future tasks in a changing security system. Moreover, the Harmel Report scrutinized the tendentiously diverging positions of the Western alliance members. In terms of foreign policy, the members almost invariably disagreed. According to the final analysis of the report, several issues were responsible for fragmentation in the Western bloc in 1966 and 1967: the U.S. pledge to wage a victorious war in Vietnam; the German question; the pains of European integration; the turbulent French break with NATO; NATO's multilateral relations with the Warsaw Pact; and the wearying discussions on strategic reform.

Against the background of these developments, the Harmel Report established a new balance between the military and political functions of the alliance. While NATO would "maintain adequate military strength and political solidarity to deter aggression and other forms of pressure, [as well as] to defend the territory of member countries if aggression should occur," the way to peace and stability rested "in particular on the use of the alliance constructively in the interest of détente."[3] The conclusion of the Harmel Report was, understandably, well received in Washington, as it reflected the U.S. conception of NATO. The U.S. government believed that the report "is a sustained attack upon 'outmoded nationalism' and 'illusory neutrality,' and therefore upon much of the substance of Gaullist policy."[4]

Nuclear control versus nuclear proliferation: the Nuclear Planning Group. Tensions among the Western allies culminated in French withdrawal from NATO's integrated command structure and introduced an innovative strategic paradigm with flexible response; they also engendered a climate in which the necessity for integrating nonnuclear member states in nuclear planning became apparent. In terms of Western alliance cohesion, this issue was especially important to the West Germans. As early as 1962, McNamara introduced the notion of increased co-option of Western alliance members in the planning processes of nuclear strategy within NATO. During the ministerial summit at Athens in 1962, Western alliance members agreed to abide by the so-called Nuclear Guidelines, which called for consultation prior to deployment—with the sole caveat that they would not apply in the event of a Soviet preemptive strike. In any event, the phrase *nuclear sharing* could not justifiably be applied to NATO until the mid-1960s, as the U.S. Joint Chiefs of Staff and the U.S. intelligence community vetoed the exchange of requisite but classified information for security reasons.

Under various guises, the projected Multilateral Nuclear Force (MLF) was tabled time and again and proved infeasible for a number of political and military reasons. Conversely, U.S. government institutions, especially the State Department, saw in the realization of MLF a powerful tool to quiet West German fears about an insufficient nuclear deterrent for Europe while also requiting German desire for participation in the nuclear weapons decisionmaking process. One of the principal problems with the MLF was that it constituted a competing and contradictory option to flexible response; the Western allies could afford to implement either MLF or an augmentation of conventional forces—but not both.

Thus, nuclear sharing remained a paper tiger until McNamara instituted the Nuclear Planning Group (NPG) in 1967, which emerged in a more consolidated shape from its predecessor, the ad-hoc Nuclear Planning Working Group. In conjunction with NATO's Nuclear Defense Affairs Committee, the Nuclear Planning Group developed into the principal forum for the exchange of information concerning nuclear questions in general, as well as for the participation and definition for nuclear weapons systems within NATO. Certainly the most important early question that the NPG addressed was the clarification of the role that theater nuclear weapons were to play in the larger strategic scheme of the Western alliance. Moreover, the NPG was responsible for increasing transparency in the U.S. nuclear planning process while simultaneously supporting a number of relevant NATO programs. The NPG helped to reduce European fears of disengagement from the Continent's defense. Increased alliance consultation helped provide a collective solution to the touchy question of independent German nuclear access. This alliance breakthrough paved the way for successful negotiation of the **Nuclear Non-Proliferation Treaty** in 1968.

By 1969, the Western alliance had weathered a stormy decade. Compromise had been achieved at considerable cost. For the cohesion of NATO, however, the resolution of the European crisis of confidence culminated in a new sense of purpose; reform was the answer. However, the same cannot be said for developments in the East, where a number of forces undermined the authority of the Soviet Union, which responded to this challenge with heavy-handed authoritarianism.

The Danger of Disintegration:
The Second World in the East

While the Western bloc's integration proceeded apace, not all was well in the East. Centralization became a necessity dictated by a new set of political circumstances, as Moscow's absolute claim to leadership was exposed to internal bloc, as well as domestic, challenges. Fundamentally, the problem was caused by fearful stagnation of the Soviet leadership in light of a potential nuclear confrontation. The balance of terror with the United States created new strains in Moscow's relations with the governments in East Germany and China. Communist leaders like Walter Ulbricht and Mao Tse-tung grew apprehensive about Soviet incentives to maintain the status quo instead of supporting revolutionary aims and interests of allies. Perceived Soviet timidity drove Mao toward independent nuclear development and a separate road to socialism.

The rise of communist China created a direct challenge not only to Moscow's influence but also to its basic revolutionary claims. China became an alternative source of aid and encouragement for national liberation movements in Southeast Asia, and even communist states in Eastern Europe, including Albania and Romania, began to look to Beijing for support. The bipolar world of the Cold War was in the process of assuming a new shape: it was turning triangular. A direct consequence of the fragmentation of the Eastern bloc was the rapprochement between the Soviet Union and the United States in the early 1960s, as well as China's opening to the United States ten years later.

Khrushchev's Downfall and the Demise of Peaceful Coexistence

The Sino-Soviet conflict undermined the Western myth of international socialist solidarity pitting the vast forces of global communism against a fragmented and idiosyncratic free world. In the Soviet Union, Nikita Khrushchev's ascendancy had been initiated with a repudiation of Stalinism, as well as a fundamental change in foreign policy in favor of peaceful coexistence. Khrushchev's volatile and impulsive foreign policy failed to earn him the prestige he had sought. Although the Soviets' conciliatory demeanor allowed détente to germinate, Khrushchev's standing in the Politburo and among his allies was badly damaged by repeated Soviet debacles in the superpower struggle for global preeminence. In the end, Khrushchev became the casualty of his own inflated rhetoric, nuclear boasts, and gusto for brinkmanship. His policy, however, was better than its reputation. Because of the Berlin crisis, the United States was prepared to accept the status quo in Europe, and due to the Cuban missile crisis, the pressure on Cuba exerted by the United States decreased. Nevertheless, Khrushchev's image was tainted by the perception that he and his rhetoric had involved the Soviet Union in Berlin and Cuba, whereby the Soviets eventually had to bow to Western strength.

Khrushchev's fruitless challenges to the West compelled the Soviet Union to moderate its foreign political tone. Moreover, Khrushchev's erratic domestic policy led to food shortages. Finally, in 1964 Khrushchev was forced to resign. His opponents at once secured power in the Communist Party. As in the days following Stalin's death, the Politburo was loath to install a single successor. Accordingly, three prominent party members were installed in leading positions, though only one of them would emerge as the undisputed head of state. Leonid Brezhnev was not nearly as forward as Khrushchev had been. In his rhetoric of nuclear superiority, Khrushchev bolstered the so-called nonmilitary superiority of the Soviet system at the expense of conventional forces. At Brezhnev's accession to power, the indicators for the priorities of the new regimes suggested another course: the new man in the Kremlin emphasized the importance of augmenting the military's capabilities in order to compensate for other shortcomings in the Soviet system.

Between 1964 and 1974, the Soviet armed forces secured for themselves the lion's share of the annual fiscal income. The Soviet rearmament and stockpiling was again dictated by the harsh logic of the Cold War. Recent Soviet troop cuts under Khrushchev, as well as Western nuclear superiority, threatened to unhinge the paradoxical safeguard of mutually assured destruction. Therefore, the lagging Soviet armament programs had to keep pace with the latest Western developments. Chronic underproduction resulting from the disadvantages of a command economy, however, bedeviled Soviet efforts at closing the military gap. Only at the expense of improved quantity and quality of consumer goods could the Soviet Union continue to allocate disproportionate amounts of money to rearmament. Consequently, the continuous lack of staple goods caused dissent within the Soviet Union. Economic weakness thus came to pose the greatest threat to the empire.

Divergence and Discord in the Warsaw Pact:
Albania, Romania, and Poland

Khrushchev's gambles over Berlin and Cuba had doomed his attempt at demilitarization. At the same time, the Warsaw Pact began its transformation from a diplomatic alliance to a military tool; this process came to a conclusion under Brezhnev. The Warsaw Pact commenced initial maneuvers in which the participating troops would exercise a deep thrust into Western Europe. Such a scenario, however, was predicated upon the assumption that the Eastern European allies would be exposed to large-scale destruction. Against this backdrop, the pressure increased on the part of Warsaw Pact members for more say in affairs. The spectrum of positions within the Warsaw Pact ranged from demands for soft reform, to something closer to an alliance of equals, to a marginalized role for the Soviet Union in a weakened alliance, to leaving the Warsaw Pact altogether.

Soviet-Albanian relations had suffered a dramatic downturn even before the commencement of the Cuban missile crisis. Albania's support for China in the wider context of the Sino-Soviet ideological dispute had driven a wedge between the two socialist states. Toward the end of 1961, Moscow decided to end diplomatic relations with Albania, forced the closure of the Albanian embassy in Moscow, and withdrew the Soviet diplomatic staff from Tirana. In the course of the 1960s, ties between the two states deteriorated further. As a response to the Soviet-led invasion of Czechoslovakia, Albania withdrew from the Warsaw Pact in 1968.

With Albania's exit from the Warsaw Pact, the role of maverick went to Romania. In Bucharest, the leadership decided that it would seek to disengage Romania from the Warsaw Pact. In the course of a secret conversation in October 1963, the Romanian foreign minister indicated to his U.S. colleague that his country had not been consulted over the Soviet decision to place nuclear missiles in Cuba. At the same time, he emphasized that Romania would act neutrally in the event of a superpower confrontation in order to prevent a military strike by the United States. When asked by Dean Rusk whether there were any Soviet nuclear weapons stationed on Romanian soil, Corneliu Manescu replied that such was not the case and offered the United States an opportunity to verify.

Despite the fact that the subject and contents of this parley remained unknown to the public until the 1990s, the dissatisfaction of the Romanian leadership with the Warsaw Pact in the mid-1960s was no secret. Romania was bent on curtailing Soviet power within the Warsaw Pact; its representatives emphasized the principles of national independence and sovereignty, equal rights, and noninterference as the basis for cooperation among member states. Although the Romanian leadership did not directly challenge the Soviet Union and never cut its ties with the Eastern bloc, the view that the Warsaw Pact constituted nothing but a noncommittal club for discussion and debate was not well received in Moscow. The more the Soviet Union worked for the military integration of the Eastern bloc, the less Romania actively participated in the military command of the Warsaw Pact.

The Polish government sought to work not against but in close cooperation with Moscow to advance reform in the Warsaw Pact. The Polish vision was clearly influenced by the institutional structures of NATO. The Political Consultative Committee was to be consolidated and expanded into a forum for systematic consultation on specific policy issues, in which member states were to participate in a dialogue among equals. Concerning military issues, the consultative position of the member states was to be augmented—especially in relation to the authority of the Soviet supreme commander. The demand for reform and a consultative capacity within the Warsaw Pact appeared still more important when set against the backdrop of Brezhnev's policy of modernizing and expanding the nuclear and conventional forces of the Soviet Union. Not only in Warsaw but also in Prague a growing number of top military personnel realized the looming threat of total destruction in the event of a general war between the two alliance systems. Although minor reforms were tolerated and remained in keeping with Brezhnev's gradualist approach, any attempt at reconfiguring the social system, for example, by rendering it more pluralistic, would be nipped in the bud.

The Prague Spring

The dreaded moment of radical change occurred in the least likely place in the Soviet sphere of influence. Since the early 1950s, Czechoslovakia had been under the firm and paternalistic governance of an old-school Stalinist by the name of Antonin Novotny. More than a decade after he had acceded to power, Novotny still directed the fate of his country. In the interim, he had become intensely distasteful to a growing number of the Czech intelligentsia and had made himself singularly unpopular within the Communist Party. With the approval of Brezhnev, Novotny was removed by his own colleagues and replaced by the reformist Alexander Dubcek in 1967.

Dubcek was a Communist, but his view of communism did not conform to Moscow's orthodoxy. The excesses of law enforcement were drastically curbed, restrictions on travel were quickly eliminated, and freedom of the press became a common good. Czechoslovakia turned into a hotbed of debate and criticism freely directed at the party. The improvements enjoyed immense popularity but also startled the Soviets, who had not expected such developments from a dependency they held to be securely within their grasp. With the suppression of the Hungarian uprising still fresh in mind, member states of the Warsaw Pact sent their representatives to Prague in a frantic effort to persuade Dubcek that his reforms were endangering the fruits of the changes he had hitherto wrought. In any event, there was little enough Dubcek could have effected—even had he wanted to.

When the vanguard of revolutionary change in Czechoslovakia submitted arguments for a withdrawal from the Warsaw Pact for benign neutrality, Brezhnev realized that Dubcek's chance to remedy the situation had already passed. In fact, the Czechoslovak reforms—also known as the **Prague Spring**—had thrown the Soviets into disarray; Brezhnev and his advisers disagreed what response would be appropriate. The speed with which Dubcek was hoping to accomplish his "socialism with a human face" was the diametric opposite of Brezhnev's incremental reform policy. It may also be remarked that whereas the Soviet Union achieved no real solution to the domestic problems of economic stagnation, the Prague Spring actually yielded results. But Soviet fears of Dubcek having lost control over the reform movement won out in the end.

The reasons for Soviet apprehensions were by no means negligible, for the Prague Spring began to inspire mostly non-Russian member states of the Soviet Union. If the reformist euphoria spilled into the Soviet Union, the inner cohesion of the East would be severely threatened. By August 1968, the Hungarian precedent loomed large. On 20 August 1968,

Brezhnev set into motion plans to eliminate the achievements of the Prague Spring. With the notable exception of Romania, members of the Warsaw Pact complied. For the first time since Adolf Hitler's motorized divisions crossed into Czechoslovakia in 1938, Warsaw Pact troops—conspicuous among them an East German contingent—invaded the country and occupied Prague. In the vein of previous Soviet armed interventions in Eastern Europe, the more pliant Gustav Husak quickly replaced Dubcek.

The Brezhnev Doctrine and the Militarization of the Warsaw Pact

The Czechoslovak example demonstrated the weakness of an empire unable to accommodate substantive and needed reform. The very fact that the Soviet Union used the combined might of the Warsaw Pact to quell progressive reforms in Czechoslovakia revealed how brittle Soviet communism had become. Soviet use of force to prevent political liberalization in Czechoslovakia was no longer a last resort to an insoluble situation. Instead, it had become a substitute for lacking ideological attachment and popular support. In summary, a quarter-century after its inception in Eastern Europe, communism had repeatedly failed to convince and convert the people. Instead, the Soviet Union was demonized as an oppressive power, and its actions betrayed the shallowness of its tenets. To many Eastern European progressives, the age of communist ideals and ideology had passed—abetted by the cynicism of Soviet power politics.

In the long run, the peoples of Eastern Europe would again look to nationalism. Nationalist tendencies were extant in Tito's Yugoslavia, Gomulka's Poland, and, for a short while, in Nagy's Hungary. Conversely, the Soviets argued that their course of action had been legitimate, as Dubcek's reforms had been intended to foment a nationalist counterrevolution within the Soviet sphere of influence. Worse, Czechoslovakia had been on the verge of defecting to the West. The Soviet position and its concomitant rhetoric, originally published as an article in the Soviet newspaper *Pravda*, soon became known as the **Brezhnev Doctrine**, which stipulated in no uncertain terms that a communist state was within its rights to intervene in the internal affairs of an Eastern European state if such action would prevent the reintroduction of a capitalist social system. Notably, the Soviet intervention, with troops furnished by fellow socialist East European states, stood in direct contravention to the terms of the Warsaw Pact of 1955. The Brezhnev Doctrine was a stopgap measure, for in the long run it only helped to hasten the dissolution of the Soviet Union. In the event, it would prompt the Soviet Union to invade Afghanistan, where indigenous irregulars would finally bring to light the feebleness of Soviet might and extract a heavy price for imperial overextension.

One consequence of the Prague Spring was the rapid militarization of the Warsaw Pact. Initially, the Warsaw Pact had served to establish an official equivalent to NATO. At the time, the Soviets had claimed that the military alliance to which most East European socialists acceded in 1955 was established as a response to West Germany's entry into NATO. But when de-Stalinization had threatened Soviet supremacy in Poland and Hungary during the 1950s, the Warsaw Pact's purely political and diplomatic function was augmented by a military dimension. During the 1960s, the Warsaw Pact served the Kremlin as a convenient bargaining tool within the context of East-West diplomacy. Equally, its military aspect gradually came to serve as the Soviets' police force in independent-minded East European states.

With the unexpected turn in Czechoslovakia, the Warsaw Pact was reconstituted as a multinational intervention force. Led by the Soviet Union, member states would put their troops at the disposal of Soviet security interests throughout Eastern Europe and legitimize future intervention against rebellious satellite states by painting a gloss of multilateral action over Soviet repression. In the wake of the Prague Spring, the Soviet Union convoked members of the Warsaw Pact in order to restructure its military organization. Moreover, the Soviet Union proceeded to tighten cohesion and augmented the command structure with a military, scientific, and technical committee. The winds of change, however, also affected Soviet predominance. In the early 1970s, a growing number of crossnational treaties allowed non-Soviet pact members to oppose Soviet hegemony. Although not endowed with equal power, East European countries had seriously undermined Soviet power within the communist bloc. The Soviet Union was left with one sensible alternative: use the plenary meetings of the Warsaw Pact to coordinate defense and control in Eastern Europe.

The Sino-Soviet Rift in the 1960s: The Ussuri Crisis

The Soviet Union's growing interest in the full integration of East European states into the Warsaw Pact's military structures could be ascribed to worsening Soviet relations with China. Ideological criticisms reinforced by Mao's repeated challenges to Soviet supremacy within the international communist bloc had rendered transparent a Sino-Soviet divergence toward the end of the 1950s. Mao had singled out Khrushchev's policy of anti-Stalinism and his new policy of peaceful coexistence with the West for frequent, vituperative attacks in his own speeches. Due to Khrushchev's apprehensions concerning Mao's cold-bloodedness over the second Taiwan Strait crisis in 1958, China had been abandoned to pursue its own nuclear weapons program. In reaction to these adverse developments, Maoist China began to cultivate its own clients in the Eastern bloc and the third world, thereby offering itself as an alternative communist power to the Soviet Union.

In October 1964, China detonated its first atomic bomb. Emboldened by recent successes, China's competitive behavior toward the Soviet Union and its persistent reaches for influence within the Eastern bloc increased tensions. As the 1960s progressed, the Sino-Soviet ideological contest erupted into open violence in a border dispute over a number of islands located in the Ussuri River. In March 1969, Soviet and Chinese troops clashed on one of the islands. The Soviets beat back a Chinese attempt to overrun their positions and promptly retaliated. Troops on the Sino-Soviet border were massing. The fighting left some 800 Chinese and sixty Soviet soldiers dead. Despite a cease-fire, a Sino-Soviet confrontation remained a probability for another decade.

The Problem of Managing Alliances

In the period between 1963 (the conclusion of the confrontational phase of the Cold War) and the late 1960s and early 1970s (the beginning of a relaxation of superpower relations), the Western and Eastern blocs came under considerable internal pressures. The two hegemons faced new challenges in their respective blocs deriving from a general sense of insecurity and unease relative to the nuclear and territorial status quo. In the West, European U.S. allies challenged the U.S. ability to guarantee European safety with a nuclear deterrent that was increasingly called into doubt and also questioned the U.S. claim to lead the free world in the struggle against global communism. In the East, the Soviet Union's position as paramount power in the communist bloc was rivaled by Maoist China, and the rigid social and political stasis settling in after Khrushchev's fall from power in 1964 kindled opposition in the Soviet Union and throughout the Warsaw Pact territories.

The hegemonic response to this new set of problems diverged fundamentally. On the one hand, the United States compromised on its own political and strategic objectives while confronting allies with sometimes unpalatable options. Nevertheless, U.S. alliance management was based on a measure of choice over rigid dogmatism. President Johnson and Secretary of Defense McNamara were willing to expose the Western alliance to the arduous task of achieving a viable working consensus and accepted the risk of fragmentation within NATO and of having to cut their losses. As a consequence, France withdrew from NATO's integrated command structure and U.S. influence. Ultimately, it was the Western resolve to face the causes behind the disintegrative tendencies that threatened the cohesion of NATO, as well as the process of weathering the crisis, which resulted in a genuine integration of the Western alliance.

Seen on a security-political level, decentralized and disconnected structures of Western interaction were the principal source of long-term strength. This became evident as the political structures of the Western bloc absorbed disputes, tensions, and disagreements far better than did the authoritarian instruments of the East. In particular, Western institutions, based on a common set of values, provided a working environment in which diffused responsibility had left its mark. For these reasons, the United States was able to credibly portray itself, and be considered by its allies, as a benevolent hegemon.

In addition to the changes in traditional security policy, the expansion of national economies in East and West since the 1950s added a new dimension to the relations between the major powers in international politics. In the West, the United States was faced with a situation in which it was compelled to shift the increasing financial burden of defense to its allies—but without relinquishing control over military forces. For the East, the problem caused by capitalist-economic development was vested in the pressures created by diametrically opposed objectives: On the one hand, the Eastern bloc sought to close the gap vis-à-vis the rapidly expanding Western economies; on the other, it attempted to acquire Western technology and capital to achieve its first goal without creating any dependencies on the West that could threaten socialist society.

Indeed, the Soviet Union's approach to the management of the Eastern bloc was to view any call for internal bloc reform as a challenge to supremacy. As the Western alliance became more porous and multilateral, the communist states grew more politically rigid and hegemonically constrained. In the case of Maoist China, whose criticism and mounting hostility led to tensions within the Eastern bloc and a weakening of Soviet preponderance, forceful confrontation constituted a plausible course of action for a superpower. Conversely, the heavy-handed Soviet policy toward Eastern European allies, particularly Czechoslovakia, drove it to reinforce the immobility of communist politics and society, which had initially given rise to the call for reforms. The Soviet refusal to countenance any measure of independence and self-determination for its allies also manifested in increased centralization of power in the East, which could be upheld only by stifling dynamism in its own ranks. Indubitably, Soviet centralization achieved a high degree of integration, albeit only in a timesaving fashion. Deprived of any measure of choice, the rigid cohesion of the Eastern bloc was not built on a durable foundation.

The Maoist challenge, unrest in Eastern Europe, a tottering domestic command economy, and a nuclear disadvantage in the arms race did not keep the Soviet Union from struggling against the United States by conventional means. Following the Berlin and Cuban missile crises, Europe—the center of the Cold War for two decades and where the balance of terror was firmly established by the deployment of tactical nuclear weapons—no longer provided either side a tenable battleground. The risk of nuclear war being sparked off by hostilities in Europe was simply too great for East or West. Superpower competition in a more or less conventional fashion therefore took place far away from Europe. We have already focused on the Cold War spillover into Asia during the late 1940s and 1950s. The only difference to the previous phase of the Cold War was that in the 1960s and 1970s the superpowers shifted some attention from Europe and Asia to Africa, the Middle East, and Latin America. As early as Khrushchev, the Soviet Union had earmarked developing countries as an ideal theater of war.

The Global South (the Third World)

The focal point of the Cold War was in Europe. Despite being superseded by the superpowers after World War II, Europe's military and economic potential remained a crucial factor in deliberations between East and West. The pivotal European role was seen in repeated crises over the divided city of Berlin. In the fall of 1961, the superpowers actually faced off at Checkpoint Charley as U.S. and Soviet tanks moved to within a short distance. The image of the clash at Checkpoint Charley called to mind the risk of military escalation in Europe. The memory of world war was too recent. In retrospect, however, the Cold War was also responsible for the maintenance of the long peace in Europe. Notably, Europe experienced an almost unprecedented half-century of peace.

This did not hold true for regions outside the immediate spheres of influence. In fact, quite the contrary seemed to apply, especially as events in Asia, Africa, Latin America, and the Middle East unfolded. Systems competition did affect all these regions, and the Cold War had a global impact. But the interaction between the bipolar international system, and the political, economic, cultural, and historical idiosyncrasies of these regions culminated in different outcomes. Thus, when the Cold War met the third world, the superpowers more often than not failed to perceive the variegated strata of conflicts in which they had become involved. Washington and Moscow attached little importance to the internal structures, economic problems, and regional security requirements of states belonging to the third world. The United States and the Soviet Union were more interested in acquiring new allies. With the elimination of Europe for a viable battleground of the Cold War, the outcome of the superpower conflict would be decided in the third world.

A comparable absence of violence in the third world was lacking, as were the deterrents keeping the superpowers from making liberal use of indigenous unrest. With the notable exception of Cuba, no nuclear weapons were stationed in the third world for very long. But the Cold War did spill over (the wars in Korea and Indochina being prime examples). Aside from Vietnam, however, superpower confrontation shifted from Asia to Africa in the mid-1960s and 1970s. There, the superpowers competed for the allegiance of new African nations in an attempt to cement and expand their respective spheres of influence. The economic and political needs of the new African nations, however, did not overly concern the Cold War antagonists.

Any addition to the camp of one superpower constituted a loss for the other. As part of the Western Hemisphere, Latin America was the immediate object of U.S. national security concerns. Its nations were exposed to severe pressures as pervasive social injustice opened the gates to social revolution based on communist ideals, which in turn was interpreted by the United States as constituting a Soviet-sponsored incursion into its sphere of influence.

In the Middle East, the superpowers were represented by proxies who faced off in a series of nationalistic wars. But here the logic of regional dynamics and national interests circumscribed the influence of the superpowers. The third world thus provided new ground for systems competition between East and West; it was where the superpowers could fight **limited wars** without fear of initiating a nuclear holocaust.

Paradoxically, the emergence of proxy warfare in the third world appeared at the moment the struggle in Europe began to ease. Following 1963, Khrushchev and Kennedy concluded that global peace could be maintained only by maintaining the nuclear and territorial status quo in Europe. Obviously, in the minds of the leaders of East and West, the same analysis of national security policies did not apply to the third world; quite the opposite in fact. Washington and Moscow increasingly pursued a course of action geared toward systems competition in the third world, as the limits of power and conflict in the first world and **second world** had been explored and tested; strategic preeminence in the third world had yet to be defined.

The starting point of this new development was a Khrushchev speech in January 1961, in which he called upon comrades to support wars of liberation in the colonies still dominated by the **imperialist** West. In his speech ("For New Victories of the World Communist Movement"), the Soviet leader distinguished three types of war: world war; local war; and the national war of liberation. World wars, Khrushchev maintained, would not occur, as the balance of terror guaranteed mutually assured destruction. The probability for local war was admittedly higher, but Khrushchev rejected this as too prone to escalate into nuclear war. Wars of national liberation, however, were likely to occur, indeed, unavoidable as long as capitalist imperialism continued to hold sway. Thus, Khrushchev concluded, world communism would decide the great test in its favor. Wars between nations were not a prerequisite for the ultimate success of communism.

Kennedy attached great weight to Khrushchev's pronouncement and interpreted it as a challenge to U.S. supremacy in the third world. Against the backdrop of Khrushchev's new policy, Kennedy's growing interest in the maintenance of improved relations with the nations of Asia, Africa, and Latin America thus became clear. The fear of national wars of liberation also had a significant impact on the shift from the strategy of massive retaliation to flexible response. Aside from an intense buildup of conventional forces, Kennedy called to life multiple counterinsurgency units specifically trained to fight in guerrilla wars.

The Cold War in the Third World

Thus, the stage was set for conflict in the third world. What, however, constituted the third world? In the three decades after the conclusion of World War II the nations of the world gradually emerged into three distinct groups. The prosperous **first world** included the highly industrialized nations of the West, that is, North American countries as well as Western and, partially, Central European nations. Together they formed the Western bloc. The second world comprised the Soviet Union, its Eastern European dependencies, and the People's Republic of China. By and large, the countries of the second world were congruent with those of the communist (Eastern) bloc. The first world and the second world have also been defined as **the North**. By contrast, the third world—defined as **the South**—was the global poorhouse. It was made up of all the developing countries in Asia, Africa, the Middle East, Central America, and South America.

This nomenclature, however, should not be understood as a comprehensive definition (Australia and New Zealand, for example, were commonly counted among the countries of the North, whereas Japan was held to be a Western country). In the case of China, the frailty of this set of definitions becomes glaringly obvious, as it is an Eastern country by virtue of its social system, but Chinese military capabilities and its economic potency ranked it among the developing states of the third world. It follows that any definition of the third world was at best an ancillary tool, its merits of limited value.

Two important criteria for defining the third world played an important role. First, "third world" acted as a generic term for states that pursued a policy of nonalignment during the Cold War. In this sense, the term was first used at the **Bandung Conference** of 1955, which gave birth to an incipient Non-Aligned Movement. Second, the term was further applied to describe states in a condition of significant economic and social underdevelopment. Conversely, both criteria (nonalignment, and social and economic underdevelopment) did not apply equally to all third world states at all times. In the harsh reality of the Cold War, the countries of Asia, Africa, Latin America, and, to a lesser degree, the Middle East were more or less committed to either the East or the West. A few actively sought to capitalize on the bipolar divide by playing off one superpower against the other.

The third world comprised highly disparate elements in regard to economic potential. Around 1960, however, countries in the third world made up 65 percent of the global population but produced only 25 percent of the world's foodstuffs and about 18 percent of all industrial products. Their share of the global income did not exceed about 20 percent; implicitly, then, global wealth was concentrated in the West and the East. In this set of circumstances, the wealthy North contributed development aid to the states of the poor South. Between 1960 and 1962, the United States spent U.S.$3.8 billion on development aid, and the Soviet Union invested some U.S.$1.1 billion during the same period. The proportion of the distributed development aid is indicative of the East-West divide. With these investments, the countries of the North were hoping to create favorable political and economic circumstances for themselves. Frequently, third world countries were able to manipulate the hopes and aspirations of the Cold War antagonists to their own benefit.

In the late 1960s, the third world paradigm shifted as circumstances underwent significant change. Economically and socially, the third world constituted a heterogeneous group of states. Due to the exploitation of natural resources (e.g., crude oil) or the development of advanced technology, some states in the third world in the 1960s achieved incomes comparable to those of the West in the 1970s. More recent success stories in Taiwan, South Korea, and Singapore called into question the validity of any typological definition. This uneven economic development in the global South during the 1970s and 1980s rendered the third world terminology of the 1960s, with its attendant homogenous implications, obsolete. Instead, as of the early 1970s the focus shifted to developmental issues in the context of the North-South divide and thus gave rise to the conception of asymmetrically developing states.

The founding of the Non-Aligned Movement. The Cold War left its marks upon most parts of the third world. The antagonism between East and West surfaced in areas where communist groups had gained significant influence. On the one hand, such a process was evident in Asia, where the defeat of Japan led to a power vacuum and concomitant destabilization in adjoining countries, such as Korea and China. On the other hand, national liberation movements sought proximity to Moscow in the wider context of decolonization and their struggles against the European colonial powers embedded in the Western bloc. Such a trend opened doors to Soviet communist influence in the third world that prompted decisive action on the part of the United States. Consequently, the relatively young states of the third world found it difficult to tread an alternative third path between East and West. But this was the final objective of 340 delegates from twenty-three Asian and six African states convening at Bandung, Indonesia, in 1955. The Non-Aligned Movement, as it was known after 1961, sought to establish itself as a third force between the two blocs. The first task on the Non-Aligned Movement's agenda was the definition of mutual interests for themselves and those states remaining under colonial tutelage. The issue was primarily influenced by a nonaligned movement effort away from the West, whence the colonial powers originated.

During the 1950s, the Soviet Union repeatedly endeavored to instrumentalize the Non-Aligned Movement for its own purposes. Khrushchev's initial attempts, however, met with a lukewarm reception. Non-Aligned Movement fears of being drawn into the bipolar struggle at that time exceeded anything the Soviets could offer. The will of the Non-Aligned Movement not to become the pawn of either superpower was made manifest in the criteria governing admission to the movement, which was formulated at the first official meeting in 1961. Significantly, the criteria for admission to the Non-Aligned Movement were adumbrated rather than formulated, a circumstance that left these stipulations open to lax interpretation. Thus, the Non-Aligned Movement states defined the following guidelines:

- A policy governed by the principles of peaceful coexistence;
- Support for national liberation movements;
- Strict nonalignment and nonparticipation in Cold War military alliances;
- Refusal to host military bases of the Great Powers or the superpowers; and
- Nonparticipation in any defensive treaty connected to conflicts including any of the Great Powers or either one of the superpowers.

In the 1960s, the Non-Aligned Movement states abandoned their passive position toward the superpowers for an active policy geared toward the launching of peace initiatives directed at East and West. This novel awareness reflected the rapid growth of the Non-Aligned Movement. At a second conference in Cairo on 5–10 October 1964, the twenty-five founding members had brought their number up to forty-seven participating states. By 1973, the movement counted seventy-six member states and three years later had grown by another three delegations.

During the 1970s, the main theme of the Non-Aligned Movement shifted away from security policy toward issues of an economic and developmental character. On the one hand, it was the onset of détente that permitted the new departure of the Non-Aligned Movement. On the other hand, the Western model for aid in developing countries sorely disappointed third world developing states. Increasingly, the Non-Aligned Movement states of the third world came to blame the capitalist system for the miseries experienced in developing countries. The policy of the West was perceived as a new kind of imperialism, reinforcing the dependency of the third world on the first world. Put in another way, the poverty-ridden South accused the wealthy North of fostering the **development of underdevelopment (dependency theory)**, that is, supporting economies in the South so they could function yet not achieve self-sufficiency due to crippling balance-of-payments to creditors in the North.

The communist bloc, with Cuba, China, and the Soviet Union in the vanguard, expediently used this new situation in North-South relations. The communist countries spread the thesis that Western imperialism under the leadership of the United States bore sole responsibility for ongoing humanitarian disasters, economic hardship, and indebtedness in the third world. Conversely, they maintained that they were natural allies in the struggle against Western imperialism. Subsequently, more and more members of the Non-Aligned Movement were drawn into the bipolar dichotomy. During the late 1970s, the well-established and repeatedly postulated neutrality of an entire group of nonaligned states was portrayed as a supine and expedient lack of a clear position in international relations. Ultimately, the task set by the Non-Aligned Movement was a formidable one: the avoidance of being drawn into superpower competition. At the same time, between the 1950s and 1970s the third world gained significance in global politics. Although the Non-Aligned Movement never achieved superpower status, member states wielded respectable power in the United Nations, where they controlled a majority in the General Assembly. This allowed the nonaligned states to shape the UN agenda. As time moved on, the two superpowers were compelled to acknowledge the significance of the third world in global politics. As early as the 1970s, it became apparent that the developing states would in the long term work toward a change in the international system.

Asia: After French Tutelage, U.S. Intervention in Indochina

In accordance with the articles of the 1954 Geneva Conference, France withdrew its troops from Indochina. Moreover, the terms of the conference called for internationally supervised elections to be held in July 1956. The United States, which held the status of observer, was not among the signatories of the Geneva Conference but promised to abide by its stipulations. From the outset, the United States sought to back Bao Dai (1913–1997; the last ruler of the Nguyen Dynasty) and inconvenience Ho Chi Minh's government in the north. U.S. military, political, and economic aid for the south was in keeping with the support they had given the French in Indochina after World War II.

The elections never took place. Bao Dai's position was severely undermined in the autumn of 1955 by his own prime minister, Ngo Dinh Diem.
Following a referendum, the monarchy was abolished, and Diem became
the first president of the Republic of Vietnam (South Vietnam). What
endeared Diem to the United States was his long-standing record as an anticommunist. With the connivance of Washington, Diem boycotted the terms
of the 1954 Geneva Conference. Ever-increasing financial and military aid
from U.S. patrons allowed Diem to set himself up as an autocratic, paternalistic ruler. But his refusal to allow elections to proceed in 1956 caused
widespread dissent, especially among former members of the Vietminh
resistance. Diem's heavy-handed suppression of political dissent in the
south inflamed the opposition still more. Militating against the South
Vietnamese regime was the lack of genuine land reforms. Meanwhile,
Communists implemented thorough property redistribution in the north. As
four-fifths of the southern population consisted of peasants in rural areas,
Diem's conservatism served to raise the countryside against his government.

Tensions in South Vietnam escalated between the mid-1950s and early
1960s. Diem responded by interning the political opposition; paralleling his
political suppression was the wholesale persecution of Buddhists. Driven
underground, various factions terrorized by Diem combined to establish the
National Liberation Front (NLF) and commenced guerrilla operations
against government troops. The NLF guerrilla forces were colloquially
known by the derogatory term "**Vietcong**" (Vietnamese Communists). In an
effort to take charge of the deteriorating government position in the countryside, Diem advanced a scheme whereby entire villages were forcibly
resettled to so-called strategic hamlets. Furthermore, Diem installed clients
as village heads. From the outset, the Vietcong marked Diem's choices for
death, and many were murdered. In urban areas, Diem's nepotism
estranged all segments of society; a coup sponsored by his own army
failed. To make things worse, his U.S. backers, after concluding that Diem
was the wrong man to spearhead the struggle against communism, left him
to his own devices.

Again, the United States connived at a plot originating in the South
Vietnamese armed forces, when, in November 1963, the Diem regime was
violently overthrown by a group of army officers. Diem, his brother, and
members of his coterie were hunted down and killed. The new regime
stepped up the campaign against the rural insurgents, only to discover in
1964 that the Vietcong was gaining ground and support. For a while, U.S.
government observers grew so perturbed at the situation that the U.S. military advisers in Vietnam were soon complemented by counterinsurgency
units. Under Kennedy's presidency, the U.S. contingent in South Vietnam
had grown to 15,000 men. By late 1963, when Lyndon Johnson succeeded

Kennedy, the threat of an NLF victory had become tangible. The rationale behind the ensuing U.S. intervention in Vietnam—that is, the so-called Americanization of the war—must be sought in the rhetoric of the Domino Theory. If the NLF won the battle for the south, then Vietnam would be lost to the West. In the wake of Vietnam, other Southeast Asian states would follow. Put simply, the U.S. government viewed the NLF as being guided in all things by Hanoi, which in turn was nothing but an extension of Beijing and Moscow: efforts to bring about the fall of Vietnam were conceived of and masterminded by the communist enemy of the free world. To Lyndon Johnson, the conflict in Vietnam was not a civil war but a battle to contain aggressive communist expansion.

Conversely, the NLF charged the United States with duplicity for not having followed the articles of the 1954 Geneva Conference. More specifically, it criticized the presence of U.S. troops on Vietnamese soil while claiming that it was combating an illegitimate government without a popular mandate. Evidently, the NLF largely conducted its own struggle against the South Vietnamese government. Indeed, this situation lasted until the war between North Vietnam and South Vietnam experienced a new twist—unmitigated U.S. intervention.

The Americanization of the Vietnam War.   The pretext for a U.S. entry into the war occurred in August 1964. Allegedly, the U.S. destroyer *Maddox* had been the target of North Vietnamese aggression in international waters. A second attack a couple of days after the first incident near the Gulf of Tonkin, on the Vietnamese seaboard, prompted Johnson to seek congressional support for counterstrikes. The **Gulf of Tonkin Resolution** left the president with virtually free reign to conduct military operations against the North Vietnamese. The resolution rendered an official declaration of war, necessitating majority congressional support, obsolete: it constituted a carte blanche. Following limited air strikes against the north in February 1965, U.S. troops were deployed in earnest. A new *junta* had toppled the old. General Nguyen Van Thieu emerged as the undisputed victor of the recent power struggle in Saigon. Under his leadership, the **South Vietnamese Army (ARVN)** descended upon the Buddhists of Hue and refused any kind of accommodation with the NLF.

The novelty of the Vietnam War was use of massive firepower on the part of U.S. troops. Ever-increasing fatalities on the communist side seemed to suggest that Nguyen and his U.S. allies were deciding the war in their favor. But surprisingly, the more Vietcong were killed in action, the more flocked to their banners. Moreover, Hanoi actively supported the guerrillas militarily. Decisionmakers in Washington duly arrived at the conclusion that they were not going to win this war in a hurry. The longevity of the war catalyzed a growing domestic opposition in the United States, as well as, among U.S. allies in Europe, widespread skepticism toward the legitimacy of military intervention in Vietnam.

The Vietnamization of the Vietnam War and the beginning of U.S. withdrawal.
In Vietnam the war had dragged on in a desultory fashion, going from bad to worse. Between 1965 and late 1967, U.S. commander General William Westmoreland believed that regular combat troops and superpower military hardware could crush the Vietcong and its North Vietnamese allies. By the end of this period, he was no longer certain. What President Johnson knew for sure was that the U.S. commitment of 500,000 soldiers was hurting the domestic economy. It was time to pull out before U.S. public opinion turned against Johnson himself. But extracting the troops proved more wearisome than intervention had.

In early 1968, the Vietcong and the massed North Vietnamese Army launched a counterstrike during the Tet holiday. Known as the **Tet Offensive**, the communist attack gathered momentum and penetrated far into the south. Vietcong commandos even breached the perimeter of the U.S. embassy compound in Saigon. Any illusions the United States might have held of winning the war were shattered in the wake of the Tet Offensive. On the home front, unfolding events eroded Johnson's chances to be reelected to a second full term; in fact, the Tet Offensive hastened Johnson's decision not to run in 1968. Stung by the audacity of Tet, U.S. retaliation was massive. The U.S. counteroffensive destroyed the Vietcong as a fighting force. Tragically, U.S. troops were forced to destroy cities and villages in order to save them from communism. By 1969, the U.S. endeavor to stem the communist tide in Vietnam had degenerated into an absurdity.

The new U.S. president, Richard Nixon, was committed to the extraction of U.S. troops in Vietnam. Nixon attempted to de-Americanize (or Vietnamize) the war by incrementally reducing U.S. troops and increasing military and financial support for the ARVN. But no matter how well equipped the ARVN troopers were, the superior morale and combat experience of the North Vietnamese began to pay off. In January 1969, the U.S. diplomatic offensive led by Nixon's National Security Advisor, Henry Kissinger, brought together all parties to the conflict: the United States, North and South Vietnam, and the NLF. Talks deadlocked over a timetable for the complete withdrawal of U.S. troops in Vietnam and the election of a new government in the south.

Nevertheless, by February 1969 some 400,000 U.S. soldiers had left Vietnam. Instead of exerting a stabilizing influence, the talks seem to have exacerbated the situation; in 1971 ARVN contingents crossed into Cambodia and Laos to destroy the Ho Chi Minh Trail, North Vietnam's main supply route. The expansion of the war provoked severe censure for

Nixon. Even worse, the northern enemy routed the South Vietnamese invaders. Thus did Nixon's campaign for an honorable peace gain a new impetus. In 1972, secret talks in Paris between Kissinger and the North Vietnamese plenipotentiary, Le Duc Tho, achieved a breakthrough. Despite assurances of continued U.S. support, the terms agreed upon in the peace preliminaries were rejected by South Vietnamese President Nguyen Van Thieu. Over Thieu's protests, Nixon signed the peace treaty with North Vietnam in January 1973 to end direct U.S. involvement in Vietnam; all troops were withdrawn by 1975 with the fall of Saigon.

The ARVN's struggle against the Communists dragged on until April 1975, when the North Vietnamese Army marched into Saigon unopposed. A few months prior to the North Vietnamese victory, southern troops had panicked and disintegrated given an imminent enemy offensive. Over the course of years, the cost of war to the Vietnamese was enormous: the south lost 200,000 troops killed in action; the north had lost about 1.1 million killed and more than 500,000 wounded. Civilian deaths has been estimated to be in the millions. Conversely, the United States mourned 58,000 killed and more than 300,000 wounded. Financially, the damage to the United States was severe. The entire campaign cost U.S.$165 billion. To this day, the specter of Vietnam reminds Americans of failed foreign intervention.

Africa: British and French Colonialism

Following the footsteps of Asian national liberation movements, Africa's progress toward independence shared with its predecessor the twin evils of colonialism and, later, the Cold War dynamic. The European colonization of Africa was motivated by economic profit. As opposed to the colonization in Asia, European activities in Africa were fairly recent and more short-lived. The principal European colonizing powers in Africa were the British and the French.

The European presence for a long time stifled African political awareness. To begin with, the boundaries established by the European colonizers took scant heed of ethnic and demographic realities: they were artificially imposed. Tribes were separated and often forced to mingle with traditional enemies. During the age of nascent African nationalism, the arbitrary frontiers would account for many of the intra- and interstate conflicts, which followed in the wake of decolonization. The natural collective self-defining unit in Africa was tribal, not national. Effectively, tribalism retarded nationalism. For this reason, and because of European military superiority, the indigenous populations in the African colonies did not rise against their masters.

British disengagement and the beginning of African decolonization. The British undermined their subjects' aspirations for full independence by applying the maxim of divide and conquer. As in India, they granted local rulers partial autonomy and the protection of their arms in exchange for loyalty. These quasifeudal arrangements worked until World War II. During that war, colonial troops in Africa witnessed the Allied struggle for the defense of democratic principles firsthand. Another parallel that can be drawn in relation to the decolonization of Asia is the emergence of a European-educated African elite. Elites brought with them a Western consciousness regarding the right to self-determination.

Earlier Asian examples and the emergence of the United Nations inspired new nationalist leaders. Vocal and articulate demands for independence were the result of the past war—and of a vision of a bright future. Concurrent to this development were the superpowers' firm anticolonial stances and the colonial powers' realization that their poverty-stricken dependencies would increase domestic financial burdens. In the late 1950s, Britain, receptive to its need to disengage from its former empire, initiated the process of African decolonization. The Gold Coast in British West Africa became independent as the state of Ghana in 1957. Once this process was under way, the rise of nationalism and the call for independence spread. In 1961, Malawi followed Ghana into independence, shortly succeeded by Kenya and Zambia in 1963.

French colonialism in Algeria.   In contrast, the French did not so much attempt to govern their colonies as to assimilate the peoples in them. French colonialism was possessed of a paternalistic cultural imperialism. The loss of Indochina in 1954 strengthened French resolve to hold on to Algeria at all costs. Events in Algeria were inextricably linked with the fate of the Fourth Republic. In an atmosphere of domestic unrest under the Fourth Republic, France set out to hold on to the vestigial trappings of its might. During the devastating First Indochina War, French expenditures for the maintenance of colonial possession in Southeast Asia rose to consume 10 percent of the national budget. In excess of 70,000 French servicemen did not return home.

In the 1950s, seeds of unrest were germinating in French North Africa. By the time France had concluded a humiliating armistice at Geneva in 1954, Algeria rose in revolt. In the turmoil that followed, a financially and militarily exhausted France was compelled to release Morocco and Tunisia from French colonial rule in 1956. Disengagement from the Algerian conflict proved more difficult. The Algerian question split France into two camps: those who vociferously demanded that the Algerian revolt be crushed and gave their unconditional support to the French settlers in Algeria (the Pieds Noirs) and those too weary to see any purpose in a continued French military presence or the concomitant bloodletting overseas. Unlike the British, who had the good sense to view overseas possessions more pragmatically, the French strongly felt that the maintenance of empire was a symbol of national grandeur. French obstinacy was reinforced by the decisive victory of the Vietnamese over French armed forces at Dien Bien Phu during the First Indochina War.

Thus, the war in Algeria dragged on while the political situation in Paris gradually turned untenable. Meanwhile, the Algerian resistance fighters of the National Liberation Front (FLN) doggedly fought on and achieved partial success in operations against collaborators, the French colonial administration's police, military forces, and the Pieds Noirs. Repeated French victories proved useless in light of the FLN's tenacity; successive governments of the Fourth Republic despaired over the Algerian question. By 1958, even the Pieds Noirs feared that Paris would seek a settlement with the insurgents behind their backs. The crisis broke out in April 1958, when the leading French generals in Algeria openly defied their government. Meanwhile, in Paris all attempts at forming a coalition government failed. With the French armed forces split between supporters of the French Algerian rebels and advocates of the Fourth Republic, the threat of civil war loomed large.

General Charles de Gaulle seized the moment to return to French politics. In Paris, the president of the National Assembly seemed to foist a politician on the army who at best was considered an unpalatable designate. The politicians' failure to form a government in the crisis-ridden month of May allowed de Gaulle to publicly place himself at the disposal of the republic. De Gaulle thereby set himself beyond direct parliamentary control. When the French rebels planned a coup to displace the last government of the Fourth Republic by the end of the month, the president of the National Assembly, in a last, desperate attempt to save the country from civil war, invited de Gaulle to take the reins of power. The aging general, however, would consent only if the National Assembly backed his plans to introduce a new constitution. The transfer of constitutional power, despite some smatterings of legality, occurred under duress: otherwise, it would hardly have been possible for de Gaulle to set his own conditions for accepting the position of head of state.

The final years of the war in Algeria were marked by de Gaulle's equivocal policy. He placated the Pieds Noirs by promising to use a firm hand in dealing with the FLN while he was taking his cues from public French opinion, which increasingly tended toward peace and disengagement in Algeria. By 1961, de Gaulle went public with his intention to sue for peace, whereupon extremists among the French settlers in Algeria known as the Secret Army Organization (OAS) and a sizeable portion of the French army sought to undermine the peace process. The general used his stature and renown to keep the army in check and avert the renewed possibility of civil war. Despite OAS terror and several attempts to assassinate de Gaulle, France concluded a peace with the Algerian resistance in 1962. Meanwhile, on the domestic front, de Gaulle had made good use of the special powers conferred upon him by the National Assembly for the duration of six months. With a consultative committee, de Gaulle drafted a new constitution, which easily passed a referendum in September 1958 and came into force in January 1959. The constitution of the Fifth Republic gave the president extended powers. De Gaulle was not loath to make use of those powers if he could thereby lead France to renewed greatness. Gaullist France aspired to become no less than the preeminent continental power of the postwar period.

Significantly, events in Indochina and Algeria did not affect the remainder of France's dependencies in Africa; when de Gaulle rose to power, the French were quick to opt for indirect control of their African possessions. De Gaulle offered twelve colonies in sub-Saharan Africa the option to remain within a French-dominated assemblage of states sharing French cultural values or, alternatively, full independence. With the sole exception of Guinea, the colonies elected to maintain ties to France with only limited autonomy. The gist of de Gaulle's offer was that France would be able to cut off all economic and military aid for the more independent-minded colonies should they choose to disassociate from France. This is exactly what he threatened to do in the case of Guinea. Guinea held out and came to define courage in the face of insurmountable odds along the path to independence.

By 1960, however, France suddenly released all its sub-Saharan colonies. This unexpected turn left the former French colonies little time to prepare for self-governance. Accordingly, sub-Saharan Africa descended into turmoil and conflict. France had not so much granted outright freedom as abandoned its colonies to unexpected freedom, which brought a host of problems. More generally, the European colonial powers' timetable for decolonization did not consider the political, economic, or social readiness of their colonies for independence. If anything, European affairs dictated the time when it was convenient for the colonial powers to end their presence in Africa.

The Horn of Africa and Angola.   The end of decolonization left struggling African states to tackle the fundamental problems of colonial legacy. The most fundamental problem remained the artificial boundaries the Europeans had drawn and that themselves were artifacts of European power politics. These borders were defined by European spheres of influence, which in turn had been shaped by the national interests of the colonizing powers. The abrupt departure of the colonizers left the new African states open to influence by the superpowers. The crushing financial burdens resulting from border and civil wars rendered many susceptible to the lure of superpower friendship. Two case studies illuminate the nature of the superpowers' intervention in Africa: the Horn of Africa and Angola.

In the case of the Horn of Africa, hostilities had the character of inter-state conflict. Ethiopia had been invaded by Italian troops in 1936; its emperor, Haile Selassie, was ousted while the country fell under foreign occupation until liberated by Allied troops in 1941. With the return of the old emperor, Ethiopian authorities launched a successful campaign to modernize the backward country. Selassie's enlightened rule ushered in an age of constitutional monarchism, industrialization, and significant advances in education. This all came to an end when the aged Selassie was overthrown during a coup led by army officers in 1973. The emperor and his family were murdered. Only in 1977 was the new ruler of Ethiopia, Colonel Haile Mengistu, able to firmly establish his rule. In contrast to Selassie's government, which had received much support and encouragement from the United States, Mengistu turned violently Marxist. Realizing the strategic import of the African Horn and its proximity to the Red Sea, the Soviet Union used Mengistu's leanings to further its influence in the region.

The story of adjacent, independent Somalia began in 1960, when British Somaliland was reunited with its other half under Italian colonial rule. Although the Somalis constituted one of the homogenous nations of Africa—they were united by a common ethnic heritage and shared a common language and Islamic faith—they were divided by a multiplicity of warring clans. The Republic of Somalia, founded in 1960, witnessed a military coup headed by Major General Muhammad Siad Barre nine years later. The Somali revolution was subsidized by the Soviet Union. Since the inception of the independent Somali state, the Ogaden area on the Somali-Ethiopian frontier had become a focus for conflict. The Ogaden had been apportioned to Ethiopia in the wake of British withdrawal after World War II; the Somalis had consistently claimed the Ogaden, as many of their nomadic countrymen dwelled in that area. Skirmishes along the frontier became commonplace until erupting into full-scale war (1977–1978). Mengistu seized power in Ethiopia when the war with Somalia broke out. Moreover, he was also trying to return the renegade province of Eritrea to the Ethiopian fold.

Beset by two enemies, Eritrea in the north and Somalia in the southwest, Mengistu became dependent on aid from Moscow. Due to the Ethiopian-Somali conflict over the Ogaden area, the Soviet Union was compelled to make a choice. Hitherto the Soviets had remained content to cynically supply both sides; such a position had, however, become untenable. Brezhnev sided with Mengistu's more powerful dictatorship; as a consequence, Somalia turned to the United States. The tragedy of the Ogaden conflict lies not only in the superpowers' exploitation of the Ethiopian-Somali conflict alone but also in the dreadful price these countries' populations paid to purchase weaponry. Several droughts and the lack of financial means to contain humanitarian calamities brought about widespread famines in Ethiopia and Somalia. While the people starved, the warring governments had emptied their respective treasuries to purchase advanced Eastern and Western weaponry. To the superpowers, support for the African belligerents was dictated by the logic of the bipolar world. Whichever superpower gained the predominant position through its proxy warrior would be enabled to indirectly control the strategic Horn of Africa.

The Cold War in Angola. The situation in Angola differed from that in the Horn of Africa in that it produced one of the longest civil wars. Although several foreign powers intervened on behalf of the conflicting Angolan parties and despite superpower involvement in the later stages of the war, fighting in Angola was underpinned by ethnic tensions. Before Angola achieved independence from Portugal in 1975, numerous guerrilla groups had been fighting against colonial rule in a protracted war of independence. After 1975, three militant groups representing different tribes vied for power. The right-wing National Liberation Front (FNLA), which during the war of independence against Portugal had received support from China and North Korea, represented the Bakongo from Angola's northwest; the equally anticommunist National Union for Independence seceded from the FNLA under the leadership of Jonas Savimbi and drew most of its support from the Ovimbundu, the largest tribe native to Angola; finally, the communist Popular Movement for Liberation (MPLA) endeavored to project its appeal to all tribes.

The right-wing factions sought support from the West and its African exponent, the Republic of South Africa. By contrast, the MPLA appealed to the communist bloc and, after 1975, received substantial military aid. Moscow called on Fidel Castro to furnish 15,000 Cuban troops to aid the MPLA. Backed by 5,000 South African regular troops, the FNLA fought the MPLA but proved unable to dislodge the leftist movement as the most powerful of parties to the conflict. The MPLA controlled twelve out of sixteen Angolan provinces. In 1976, the MPLA and its Cuban allies inflicted multiple defeats on enemy troops. As a consequence, South African troops withdrew from the conflict; their only interest had been to cut off rebels in neighboring Namibia, who had been operating out of Angola. The National Union for the Total Independence of Angola (UNITA) and the FNLA continued guerrilla operations against MPLA-controlled areas and often continued to cooperate with the South African armed forces and the CIA.

In the meantime, the Marxist MPLA had been able to establish a semblance of government in the greater part of Angola. But Savimbi's UNITA continued to cause Marxist Angola severe economic damage. Its campaign lasted until 1989, when South Africa's forces were tied down in Namibia. Even though UNITA was weakened by the dwindling support of Western and conservative African countries, Savimbi doggedly continued to fight the Marxists. Only in June 1991 did the parties to the civil war agree to an armistice. All foreign troops were withdrawn, and new elections were to be held. But the peace did not hold for very long. Elections monitored by the United Nations returned an MPLA majority to parliament in September 1992. UNITA refused to recognize election results and resumed hostilities until another armistice was concluded in 1994. Fighting in Angola continues to the present day.

The main lesson to be drawn from the protracted Angolan civil war is that it would have occurred with or without superpower interference. The ideological component did, however, partially account for the escalation of hostilities in Angola; some blame must also be accorded to the tribal divisions. The superpowers and their allies, such as South Africa and Cuba, are to blame for the intensification and expansion of the civil war. By supplying weapons, intelligence, regular troops, and irregular troops, the superpowers sought to secure their own national interests in that area. Moreover, the concept of the zero-sum game, which had a defining influence on the outlook of so many hawks in Washington and Moscow, disallowed retreat from the scene of battle in Angola; the defeat of either one among the Angolan factions would have carried with it a loss of face not easily suffered by the "losing" superpower. The Cold War had thus resurfaced in an existing conflict and found in Angola an alternate theater of war for continuing superpower competition.

Latin America: The Backyard of the United States

Latin America, comprising the states of Central and South America, shared many of the typical problems of the third world. But on top of endemic social and political crises and humanitarian catastrophes, the states of Latin America were beset by intermittent military dictatorships. The national elites were steeped in the sociocultural mores of their Spanish and Portuguese ancestors. A landowning aristocracy more often than not combined to form wealthy oligarchies. Frequently, the landowning minority owned sprawling estates—the so called *latifundia*—while the workers either did not possess sufficient arable land to feed their own families or were forced to turn into laborers (*campesinos*) existing at subsistence levels.

Blatant social injustice was a pervasive feature of Latin American life. It accounted for many of the social upheavals in the twentieth century. Because the nature of Latin American popular grievance was usually of a social nature, the often highly polarized conflicts between the haves and have-nots of the postwar period became susceptible to external influences such as Marxist-socialist ideologies. And as we have seen with the example of Africa between 1950 and 1970, wherever popular unrest was harnessed under the banner of socialist ideologies, communism was quick to follow.

The major difference between Africa and Latin America was geographic; whereas the former seemed remote from both superpowers, the latter was in the backyard of the United States. Therefore, it was the proximity of Latin American states that prompted the United States to exercise tight control over political developments of that region. Following Spain's departure from the North American continent in the early nineteenth century, the United States rose to become the principal power in the hemisphere. U.S. predominance was institutionalized with the Monroe Doctrine, promulgated in 1823, which set forth the U.S. mission as the guarantor of liberty in the Western Hemisphere. In the early twentieth century, the Monroe Doctrine was amended and expanded to include the right of armed intervention in the internal affairs of Latin American countries by the **Roosevelt Corollary**. Following World War I, the United States had established a practice of overthrowing and instituting Latin American governments according to the requirements set by U.S. economic interest groups. During World War II, relations between North and South America relaxed somewhat. But the prewar trend of asserting U.S. hegemony in Latin America returned with a vengeance after 1945. The reason for the U.S. return to a policy of direct interference in Latin American politics was the formation of the ideological blocs and the onset of the Cold War in Europe and in Asia.

Social injustice and unequal distribution of land in Latin America authenticated the image of insurgency and political unrest perceived in Washington. During the Cold War, attempts to introduce even moderate land reform in Latin American states raised the specter of communism in the minds of U.S. policymakers. The principal tool employed by successive U.S. governments to render Latin American governments tractable was the development of underdevelopment, the concept of which is fairly banal: in order to reduce their countries' dependency on the United States, Latin American leaders required U.S. economic aid. The United States was able to take advantage of this situation by threatening to terminate financial aid for any state likely to defect. This is exactly what happened to Cuba after Castro's victory in 1959. Unlike Europe, Latin America was not to benefit from the fruits of the Marshall Plan. A similar financial aid package for Latin America did not become apparent before 1961, when President Kennedy announced that the United States would spend some U.S.\$20 billion to promote democratic values and political reforms in a gargantuan effort designated as the Alliance for Progress. Kennedy did, however, attach some less altruistic strings, for example, the demand that troops in the employment of Latin American states be trained in counterinsurgency programs designed to combat socialist guerrillas in Latin America.

The explosive mixture of U.S. **interventionism**, U.S. business interests that relied on their government to secure their investments, if necessary, by force, and the compulsive paranoia of the bipolar system combined to turn Latin America into another battlefield of the Cold War. In order to protect economic and political interests in their backyard, successive U.S. postwar governments were willing to abet military dictatorships—so-called *juntas*—and, if convenient, lend a hand to suppress social justice movements turning to Marxist ideology and erupting into political violence. As Kennedy put it:

> There are three possibilities in descending order of preference: a decent democratic regime, a continuation of [a right-wing dictatorship] or [a left-wing dictatorship]. We ought to aim at the first, but we really can't renounce the second until we are sure that we can avoid the third.[5]

In other words, whatever party proved willing to safeguard U.S. interests in Latin America could count on U.S. financial and military support.

But the vicious circle of Latin American politics was not the exclusive preserve of exogenous factors. In addition to the chronic U.S. interventionism perpetuating Latin American dependency, the widening gap between the wealthy and the poor entrenched in Latin American society by the Spanish colonial legacy was mainly responsible for widespread popular grievances; it also served to increase the attractiveness of Marxism for the poor masses. The *latifundistas* saw any attempt to redistribute land as a challenge to their power, privileges, and conservative values. In such an event, landowning elites could call on the other major conservative power in the country to protect their interests: the army. Armed forces in Latin America had no long-standing tradition of civil-military relations; neither was the concept of democratic control over the armed forces ensconced in their respective national political cultures. Therefore, the militaries were rarely subject to a higher authority exerted by the democratic state. The constitutions of Latin American countries safeguarding the due process of law, parliamentary prerogative, and, more generally, democratic values were rarely respected. But as long as Latin American armies kept leftist governments out of power, they could rely on the support of the United States. U.S. apprehensions of communist expansion in Latin America kept dictatorial regimes in power, and the *juntas'* repeated failures to achieve social justice provoked socialist revolutions and revolutionary movements.

Central America: Nicaragua.   One specific example from Central America and a second from South America will serve to illustrate the impact of the

Cold War on Latin America. During the early twentieth century, the United States indirectly controlled the fate of Nicaragua in Central America. In order to protect strategic bases, U.S. Marines intermittently occupied the country. The longest periods of occupation were from 1912 to 1925 and from 1927 to 1932. During the latter phase of occupation, a national liberation movement under the leadership of Augusto Cesar Sandino fought against U.S. troops. Following the withdrawal of the Marines, U.S.-Nicaraguan relations relaxed. In their wake, the United States left behind a national guard that it had trained and equipped. The commander of the national guard, Anastasio Somoza Garcia, engineered Sandino's assassination and persecuted his followers in 1934. The Somoza clan proceeded to seize the reigns of power and manipulated rivalries within the Nicaraguan middle classes to suit its own ends. Three generations of Somozas stripped the country economically while enlarging their own fortunes in the process. Nicaragua had effectively become a single *latifundia* owned by the Somoza family.

In 1972, a cataclysmic earthquake destroyed Managua, the capital of Nicaragua. Somoza and some highly placed officers in the national guard, which had been turned into the dictator's private army, systematically looted the city while selling relief supplies received from various international organizations to the stricken denizens of Managua. The blatant nature of Somozista abuse provoked widespread dissent and opposition among cross-sections of Nicaraguan society. By the 1970s, even the middle class was determined to oust Somoza. In 1975, a Marxist guerrilla force (the Sandinistas, named after the resistance fighter Sandino) launched an effective offensive against barracks of the national guard. The brutality of Somozista reprisals won the Sandinistas widespread support. On 10 January 1978, the national guard murdered Pedro Joaquin Chamorro, the editor in chief of a liberal newspaper, whereupon national unions called for a general strike. While the country was paralyzed by the general strike, the Sandinistas successfully occupied the presidential palace and blackmailed Somoza, who was forced to release a number of opposition detainees and part with funds. Somoza's handling of the hostage situation cost him the loyalty of many in the national guard.

The Sandinista successes, the enemies Somoza had made in the bourgeois camp following the 1972 natural disaster, and the election of U.S. President Jimmy Carter all contributed to the downfall of Nicaragua's dictatorship. The Sandinistas and their liberal allies had set in motion the inexorable process of revolution. Carter was not willing to give Somoza unlimited support; a champion of human rights, the U.S. president was not inclined to overlook the blatant transgressions in Nicaragua. Following the execution of a U.S. journalist by the national guard while film cameras were recording the scene, Carter was in a position to force an end to the

U.S. government's sale of arms to the Somozistas. In July 1979, Somoza's hold on power slipped. He fled to Florida, where he asked for political asylum after he had plundered the country's treasury. The Sandinistas seized power after dispersing residual forces of the national guard. With Vietnam still fresh in the collective U.S. mind, Carter was loath to intervene in Nicaragua. Instead, he gave the Sandinista government some financial support for the reconstruction of the blighted economy, whereby he hoped to retain a last hold on Nicaraguan affairs. When the Sandinistas in power shifted still farther to the left, Carter, in a final act before he left office, cut off all economic aid in 1981.

The next president, Ronald Reagan, saw in the predominantly Marxist Sandinistas another Soviet threat to U.S. security. Accordingly, Reagan lavished some U.S.$30 million on a covert war against Daniel Ortega's Marxist government in Managua. Washington was aware that the Sandinistas had been enjoying limited Soviet support since their accession to power. The severance of the ties of dependency that had kept Nicaragua in the U.S. orbit, and its substitution with Soviet aid, incensed members of Reagan's administration. Reagan reacted by directing the CIA to assemble, equip, and train the vestiges of the Somozistas to be a viable counterrevolutionary force. The contras, as the counterrevolutionaries were called, enjoyed little popular support in Nicaragua by virtue of their controversial past under the Somoza regime. At home, Reagan ran into increasing difficulties in his dealings with Congress. U.S. apprehension of a second Vietnam accounted for the tepid congressional reception to Reagan's scheme to topple Ortega and the Sandinista government. In response to the mounting U.S.-contra pressure, Ortega sought closer relations with the Soviet Union. Ever since the Sandinistas had seized power after the civil war, they had received military aid from the Soviets. Ortega's visit to Moscow changed the nature of Nicaraguan-Soviet relations in favor of the Sandinistas. As a result, Soviet economic aid poured into the country.

The U.S. Congress took a dim view of the Sandinistas' diplomatic dalliance with the Soviet Union and, consequently, released direly needed funds for the contras. Meanwhile, the communist bloc had fortified the Sandinista forces with arms deliveries and many military advisers. Between 1983 and 1986, the extant foreign advisory corps, numbering approximately 3,000, was augmented to almost 7,000. The United States responded in kind by increasing the Honduran military establishment, by dispatching military advisers to adjacent El Salvador, and by furnishing the contras with still more arms and operations bases along the Honduras-Nicaragua border. Even before this buildup on both sides, a number of Latin American states known as the Contadora Group had launched a peace initiative, according to which all parties to the conflict were to withdraw all foreign military personnel. The Sandinistas readily agreed, but the Reagan administration demurred. To Reagan, the overthrow of the Marxist regime in Managua was a matter of maintaining U.S. credibility among its allies elsewhere in the world. The Reagan argument pointed to the fact that if the United States proved unable to defend its own interests on its doorstep, then it could not expect its allies to have faith in its ability to protect them and their interests.

But in the mid-1980s, Congress had again grown weary of protracted fighting in a foreign country. The contra offensive was stymied by dwindling funds and successful Sandinista countermeasures. Reagan, however, was determined to crush the Sandinistas by whatever means necessary. The Iran-contra affair involved the illicit transfer of profits made in clandestine arms deals between a U.S. government agency under the direction of Colonel Oliver North and Iran, a state hostile to the United States, to the contras. Reagan's financial contributions to the contras were made in direct contravention of U.S. law. The operation was discovered in late 1986. Congress, upon discovering Reagan's backdoor maneuver, immediately canceled all support for the contras. Meanwhile, the Contadora plan to end hostilities in Nicaragua foundered and came to an end in 1987. A new approach was then formulated by the Costa Rican President Oscar Arias, who intended to defuse the conflict by fostering the political dialogue and by curbing the military buildup in the area. The Sandinistas again were prepared to cooperate; Reagan's position on Nicaragua had become untenable, which compelled him to abandon the contra strategy. Ortega agreed to free elections in 1990 and promptly lost to Chamorro's widow, Violetta, who headed a coalition government and did much to heal the rift in Nicaraguan politics. Nicaragua's greatest problem to date remains foreign debt and reduced economic production.

South America: Chile.   Even by the harsh standards of South American political history, Chile stands out as an example of U.S. intervention. The only common denominator that Chile shared with Nicaragua was the relatively late advent of military rule. The armed forces of Chile behaved in an uncommonly impartial manner, allowing Chilean democracy to prosper in the postwar period. Significant U.S. investments in Chile ensured that local politics fell under U.S. scrutiny. Most of the copper used by U.S. industry was imported from Chile; U.S. corporations, in fact, owned most of the mines. Therefore, the United States was prepared to take all measures necessary to protect commercial interests in Chile. During the 1964 elections, the CIA bolstered the campaign of the Chilean Christian Democrats with U.S. funds. The Christian Democratic candidate, Eduardo Frei, endeavored to thwart his contender, the Marxist Salvador Allende. With the covert support of the United States, the election was won by Frei. He proceeded to implement moderate reforms, which were too egalitarian for the landowning elites and discounted as mere superficial treatments by the political left. All the while, Frei's government benefited from Kennedy's Alliance for Progress program, which poured vast amounts of money into Chile. When the elections of 1970 led to a narrow Marxist victory, the United States grew uneasy.

Allende embarked on a number of socialist reform programs, increasing wages, nationalizing foreign-owned companies, and redistributing the *latifundias*. A fall in the price of copper early during Allende's tenure as president threw the economy into disarray. Economic setbacks weakened Allende's influence, and by 1972 the conservative opposition was attempting to oust the socialists from power. The United States supported conservative schemes to bring the country to a standstill: The CIA was instrumental in organizing strikes; President Nixon also cancelled all trade with, and financial aid for, Chile. The eruption of open conflict was a matter of time. Allende's supporters were armed in response to potential army interference. The Chilean army struck in September 1973 by bombing the buildings of parliament. During the ensuing gunfight, Allende himself was shot to death.

The leader of the coup was one of Allende's confidantes in the army: General Augusto Pinochet. Pinochet had used Allende's trust to plot against the leftist government with the support of the CIA. A U.S. hearing in 1974 revealed the full involvement of the CIA in Allende's overthrow. In fact, the CIA had spent U.S.$3 million in order to keep Allende from gaining power in 1970 and had invested another U.S.$8 million to undermine his government. In any event, Pinochet reversed all socialist achievements and began a reign of terror by launching a wholesale persecution of the Chilean political left. Labor unions were outlawed, and civil liberties as well as parliamentary rule were abolished. U.S. companies again took over the property nationalized under Allende, and successive U.S. governments gave Pinochet's *junta* unstinting support throughout the 1970s and 1980s. Pinochet consistently fulfilled his part of the bargain with U.S. business interests by opening the country to foreign investments and by keeping the political climate stable with the support of the military.

Repression in Chile grew worse in the 1980s, and in 1990 mass demonstrations forced Pinochet to permit a national referendum. The outcome of the vote was a foregone conclusion. Civilian rule was to be reestablished. The new government proved successful in boosting the national economy, and the international trade volume soared throughout the 1990s. Pinochet, however, could not be dislodged constitutionally until 1997; the new constitution composed by Pinochet was the *junta*'s condition for a temporary abrogation of power. Pinochet still controlled the army and was even granted the implicit right to intervene in civilian affairs again by the new constitution; it took another three years for the Chilean courts to withdraw Pinochet's immunity. In 1998, the former dictator's tribulations began with a Spanish demand for extradition on charges of torture. Pinochet, who was in Britain, was put under house arrest for sixteen months. The British authorities declared Pinochet, who was suffering from diabetes and mild dementia, unfit for trial and permitted his return to Chile. By mid-July 2001, the sitting Chilean president moved to indefinitely postpone the trial of Pinochet; the judges of the high court decided to stay all judicial proceedings on the grounds of the defendant's ill health.

The end of the Cold War combined with mounting popular unrest thus made possible the transition from military to civilian government in Chile. More generally, it can be said that with the disappearance of the Soviet Union U.S. fears about communist infiltration on the U.S. doorstep abated. The gradual drift away from the *juntas* in the late 1980s and early 1990s toward democratically elected governments emphasizes the enormous impact that the Cold War had on shaping the postwar history of Latin America.

The Middle East: Zionism and Pan-Arabism

Following a long spell under the rule of the Ottoman Empire, Palestine passed into British hands after 1918 along with the lion's share of the Middle East. Palestine was entrusted to Britain by the League of Nations as a mandate. The indigenous peoples were Palestinian Arabs, but since the late nineteenth century immigration had been swelling Jewish ranks. The rise of nationalism in nineteenth-century Europe had also given birth to Zionism, a Jewish nationalist movement that had as its declared objective the foundation of a home for the dispersed Jews in the Diaspora. By the time the British Empire encompassed much of the Middle East, some 650,000 Palestinians lived alongside 68,000 Jews. The Balfour Declaration of 1917 promised the Zionists British support for the establishment of a Jewish state. The concurrent rise of Arab nationalism as a consequence of the recent foundation of an Arab kingdom in modern Syria, and what was perceived to be a Jewish encroachment upon Arab land in Palestine, increased tensions throughout the Middle East. Since the inception of their movement, Zionists had busied themselves with purchasing land required for the establishment of Jewish settlements in Palestine. Although Arab landlords gladly sold the drought-ridden plots, the expanding presence of Jewish settlers fanned Arab fears. Open hostilities between Jews and Arabs erupted in 1920. In the following decade, Arab demands for the restriction of Jewish immigration, and Jewish demands for a greater influx of their coreligionists, bedeviled successive British administrations.

The rise of the Third Reich in the 1930s ushered in a period of Jewish mass migration to Palestine. Despite British controls, Jewish immigration peaked at 62,000 in 1935. Discontent among the Palestinian farmers dispossessed by Jewish land purchases was used and polarized around the Palestinians' Muslim leader, Haj Amin. By 1936, he had roused the Palestinian masses to fight against continued Jewish immigration as well as the British presence. The possibility of open conflict became tangible. The British moved in reinforcements and defused tensions.

Based on the results of an investigation conducted subsequent to the then-recent upheaval, British policymakers concluded that Palestine would eventually have to be partitioned. The Arabs rejected the plan. Conversely, the Jews were willing to at least consider it. In 1939, the Arabs rose in arms. The British proceeded to crush the insurrection but simultaneously sought to retain overall Arab allegiance. British strategy was informed by considerations of the impending war in Europe. Securing the usually fickle Arab loyalty in light of a confrontation with Nazi Germany was accorded priority over maintaining cordial relations with the Jewish minority in Palestine. Accordingly, Britain was willing to partially meet Arab demands by further restricting Jewish immigration. But the Holocaust in Europe had a deep impact on the British difficulties in Palestine. The Nazi butchery of European Jewry after 1939 meant a renewed increase of clandestine Jewish immigration. Abetted by Jewish immigration organizations such as Mossad Aliah Beth, the flow of refugees into Palestine continued unabated. British and world indifference to the fate of Nazi victims also contributed to the radicalization of Zionist-Jewish resistance to British rule in Palestine.

The Israeli war of independence.   The continued rise of Arab nationalism, Arab solidarity in the Middle East, and the desperate Jewish struggle for the foundation of a state in Palestine put Britain under increasing pressure to abandon its mandate. As the confrontation between the diametrically opposed Arab-Jewish interests was almost certainly leading to war, Britain expediently turned over the Palestinian problem to the United Nations. Britain was keen on maintaining good relations with the Arabs, if only to serve its own economic interests. Moreover, the Palestinian mandate compelled Britain to commit 100,000 troops to keep the peace between Arabs and Jews. The withdrawal of British troops was scheduled for May 1948, but hostilities broke out as early as December 1947. Although the United Nations had voted in favor of partition, the Arabs proved unresponsive to repeated UN initiatives. Consequently, the Jews began arming their underground army, the Hagganah. The mufti of Jerusalem, acting in his capacity as the principal Arab religious leader in the area, served as a focal point for Arab resistance and preparation for the first round in the battle of supremacy in Palestine. He also tapped into the reservoir of Arab nationalist goodwill, which transcended national boundaries, in order to raise troops from adjacent Arab countries.

At this stage, the Soviet Union, fostering hopes of shaping a socialist-dominated Jewish state, instructed the Czech government to supply the Jews with arms. The fiercest fighting erupted around Jerusalem, a city venerated by Jews as well as Arabs. In other parts of Palestine, Arabs and Jews clashed. Palestinian Arabs and troops of the Arab Legion—a volunteer force composed of troops drawn from the armies of the outlying Arab countries—beset the Hagganah from within and without. Unperturbed by the Arabs' numerical superiority, David Ben Gurion, a leading figure of the Jews in Palestine, proclaimed the state of Israel on 14 May 1948. The fighting continued until the United Nations imposed a cease-fire on both sides by mid-June. The ensuing calm only served as a pause before hostilities resumed. With the material support of Czechoslovakia and France, Israel fought the advancing Arab armies to a standstill. By early 1949, the Egyptians, the last of the Israeli opponents, were defeated. David had prevailed over Goliath—at least for a short while. One of the immediate consequences of the Israeli war of independence was the displacement of hundreds of thousands of Palestinian Arabs. They were forced to eke out an existence in neighboring Arab states or, more frequently, languished in abject poverty in one of the many refugee camps in Lebanon and Jordan. Conversely, many Jews who had settled in Arab countries were driven out of their homes and forced to seek refuge in Israel.

The Desert Wars: Suez, the Six Day War, and the Yom Kippur War.   Of the repeated Arab-Israeli wars fought over the next quarter-century, all were motivated by the enmity of the Arabs for the Jews. The Arabs came to see in the state of Israel a slur on their pride spawned by Western imperialism. The Arab point of view was reinforced by the Eastern and Central European origins of many Jewish immigrants. When the Cold War intruded on the Middle East, however, the conflicts grew fiercer and were fought with ever-improving weaponry supplied by the superpowers or their clients. But to the last, the Arab-Israeli wars were all fought for reasons indigenous to the area, not because of the Cold War; superpower interference intensified the conflicts but, as it turned out, never molded them.

Following the Suez crisis, in which Britain and France allied with Israel against Colonel Gamal Abdul Nasser, the United States included the Middle East in its strategy of containment (the so-called **Eisenhower Doctrine** of 1957). In response to expanding Soviet influence in Syria, Egypt, Yemen, and Libya, the United States began taking a special interest in Israel. Conversely, the beginning of a long-standing alliance with Israel made it impossible for the United States to recruit Arab states for the purposes of containment, as the one thing that all Arab nations shared was a mutual hatred for Israel. As Nasser's pan-Arab rhetoric grew more aggressive in repeated calls to crush Israel, the uneasy cessation of hostilities became subject to rising tensions. The bellicose Syrians provoked Israeli retaliation on its northern border, as well.

In 1964, Arab leaders convened in Cairo. Nasser gave his wholehearted support to the establishment of the Palestine Liberation Organization (PLO) under Yassir Arafat. The Arab nations also resolved to maintain their refusal to recognize Israel. Guerrilla attacks carried out by the Syrian-sponsored PLO on Israeli territory provoked harsh retaliatory measures. The Soviets intentionally misconstrued Israeli military countermeasures to make the Egyptians believe that Israel was about to strike Syria. Egypt mobilized its army and reoccupied the Sinai, hitherto held as a buffer zone by UN troops, and stopped Israeli commerce in the Gulf of `Aqaba. Jordan and Egypt concluded an alliance, subsequently joined by Iraq. Iraq's accession to the treaty occurred on 4 June 1967.

On 5 June, Israel's new minister of defense, Moshe Dayan, ordered an all-out preemptive attack on hostile positions. The ensuing war lasted for six days (hence it became known as the Six Day War) and left the Arab would-be attackers reeling. After barely one week, the Israeli army occupied Sharm El-Sheikh, controlled the Sinai Desert, drove Jordanian troops out of Jerusalem, and savaged the Syrian army in the Golan Heights; the Israeli air force completely destroyed the combined aerial arsenal of Egypt, Syria, and Jordan on the ground in the first twenty-four hours. The Six Day War impressively demonstrated Israel's military capability. It was one of the most conclusive military victories of the recent past, a crushing humiliation of pan-Arab nationalist pride. Syria lost the Golan Heights, Egypt lost vast tracts of the Sinai, and Jordan lost the greatest of all prizes: the old town of Jerusalem. Jordan also lost the West Bank on its frontier with Israel.

On 22 November 1967, the UN Security Council passed Resolution 242, which outlined a Middle East settlement. It obliged Israel to return its recent conquests while guaranteeing the safety of its prewar borders and expressed the necessity of providing a satisfactory solution to the problem of Palestinian refugees. But the Arab nations in 1967 reaffirmed their refusal to recognize Israel and rejected peace negotiations with Israel as long as Palestinians' rights in Israeli territory were not given due consideration. Palestinian guerrillas intermittently raided Israeli territory and employed terrorist tactics abroad to strike at Israel wherever possible. Skirmishes with Egyptian forces in the Sinai continued into 1970, when a cease-fire was agreed upon. Nasser died that same year and was succeeded by Anwar Sadat. Sadat was faced with two choices: accept Israeli terms for peace, or launch another attack. In the event, Sadat chose to go on the offensive. A combined Egyptian-Syrian surprise attack on 6 October 1973—the Jewish Day of Atonement (Yom Kippur)—caught the Israelis unprepared. The Israelis, however, adjusted their defensive strategy to most effectively counter the two-pronged attack. The Syrian advance was eventually stopped in the north. In the Sinai, Israeli General Ariel Sharon's tanks outflanked an entire Egyptian army and cut off any retreat.

At this stage of the war, the superpowers intervened after the Arab nations imposed an oil embargo on any country aiding Israel. The United States had supplied vast amounts of arms to the Israelis, which had helped turn the tide of the war. But it also meant that the United States would be subject to the oil embargo. Western Europe was also penalized. President Nixon and Secretary of State Henry Kissinger realized that the time for negotiations had arrived. When Brezhnev invited the Americans to cooperate in Middle East affairs, Kissinger agreed to bring about a cessation of Israeli-Egyptian hostilities. The U.S.-Soviet plan was presented to the United Nations and went into effect on 22 October. But when the Israelis shifted their contingents around the trapped Egyptian army, Brezhnev threatened to take all necessary steps to force Israeli compliance with the terms of the truce. In the United States, Soviet saber-rattling was taken seriously enough for U.S. forces around the globe to be put on a state of high alert. Not since the Cuban missile crisis had the world been closer to the possibility of a nuclear war. At the first opportunity, Kissinger capitalized on the decisive U.S. response while telling Brezhnev that direct Soviet intervention in the Middle East was not acceptable. If the Soviets abandoned their idea of interfering in the Middle East, there would be no need to let the crisis continue. Brezhnev shared Kissinger's fears of an escalation of a local war into a potential global conflagration. The superpowers subsequently hammered out a plan to position UN peacekeeping troops between the belligerents. No Soviet or U.S. soldiers would join the UN forces.

The Yom Kippur War cost all parties dearly. Nevertheless, the early fortunes of the Arabs served to restore some of their self-esteem, whereas Syria and Egypt had finally come to terms with the improbability of completely dislodging the Israelis. On the other side, the Israelis had again proven their determination to fight against overwhelming odds and claim victory. Peace, however, would prove cheaper to the Israelis, too. Accordingly, they were willing to trade land for peace. Their U.S. patrons encouraged an Israeli-Arab rapprochement for the simple reason that a durable peace in the Middle East would limit Soviet possibilities for interference. In that sense, the Egyptian-Israeli treaty validated at Camp David in 1978 did lay the foundation for peace in the Middle East, but it also served to protect U.S. regional interests in the context of the Cold War. Therefore, it can be said that superpower competition in that particular region raised the intensity of the Israeli-Arab wars; but neither the United States nor the Soviet Union was able to reduce the belligerents to the level of obedient proxy warriors. Arabs and Israelis would continue to accept the bounty of superpower support but were loath to take even indirect orders from Washington or Moscow.

IR Theory and Key Concepts

Claims by realists concerning their seemingly scientific approach and methods (as, for example, maintained by Hans J. Morgenthau et al.) came under scrutiny and were challenged by former natural scientists working in the field of international relations in the United States. These pundits, and a group of researchers trained in the behavioral sciences, undertook to study the effective behavior of actors in international relations, as opposed to the significance and meaning attributed to actor behavior. In due course, their efforts and concomitant criticism of traditional international relations culminated in the second great debate: traditionalism versus behavioralism.

The Second International Relations Debate:
Traditionalism Versus Behavioralism

Traditionalism is a school of thought in international relations that focuses on the study of political philosophy, diplomatic history, and international law to advance understanding in their field of study. Approaches that employ scientific methods, such as statistics and formal hypothesis testing in an attempt to base findings on (semi-) empirical data, have incurred the lasting distrust of traditionalists. Conversely, behavioralism describes an approach to the study of politics that emphasizes the actions and interactions among units. This task is conducted by employing scientific methods of observation and is, if feasible, geared toward the inclusion of quantifiable variables.

The Rhetoric of National Liberation and
Revolution in Radical Europe and the Third World

Although Marxist theory gave rise to notions and even conceptions of structural inequality, they came to the fore in Lenin's work, closely followed by E. H. Carr's early ideas on the unequal distribution of wealth. More recently, Johan Galtung's structuralist theory of inequality provided a more comprehensive paradigm of structural inequality. As opposed to Marx and Lenin, Galtung, who scrutinized the mechanisms of imperialism, no longer subscribed to the belief that imperialism essentially constitutes an economic relation based on capitalism. Galtung held that imperialism caused the perpetuation of inequality within and among nations. According to his definition, imperialism is a structural relation of political, economic, military, cultural, and communications dominance. Galtung's definition is predicated upon a comprehensive understanding of structural dominance. Structuralist and neo-Marxist theories of inequality, built upon the concept of exploitation and neocolonialism, provided the basis for the radical fringe in Europe, which generally advocated wars of liberation in the third world. The intellectual basis for the revolutionaries struggling against repressive regimes in the third world was therefore essentially Marxist. For example, the Dependencia (dependency) school of thought prominent throughout Latin America, and the attendant paradigm of the development of underdevelopment, are both derived from theories related to the unequal distribution of wealth.

Key Terms
- nuclear proliferation and arms control: The major source of instability in the Cold War international system was the arms race and the parallel spread of weapons of mass destruction, particularly nuclear weapons. This phenomenon was proliferation and nuclear proliferation, respectively. The problem was understood, and, accordingly, bilateral efforts were under way to constrain and limit the expansion of such weapons. This endeavor was referred to as arms control, an objective that is to be carefully distinguished from disarmament, which postulates the total reduction of the deadly arsenals.
- deterrence and mutually assured destruction: The process of deterrence is based on the assumption of rational interaction between actors (e.g., one actor threatens some sort of action to prevent some other action by a second actor). This constitutes an attempt at deterrence. In order for deterrence to function, the second must convincingly perceive that the cost is higher than the gain. In accordance with the precepts of rational interaction, the second will forsake its plan because it brings more costs than gains. Moreover, deterrence is predicated on the first actor's ability to properly assess the second actor's weighing of the cost and benefits. U.S. Secretary of Defense Robert McNamara of the Kennedy and Johnson administrations frequently employed the idea of mutually assured destruction. MAD was a defining feature of the bipolar Cold War international system in which a relative equilibrium of mass destruction by nuclear arms underpinned a precarious balance of power. The stability of the Cold War balance of power was

dependent upon functional deterrence, for if two actors comprehend and agree that the deployment of nuclear weapons will lead to escalation and substantial losses for each side, then, as rational actors, both have no motive to deploy nuclear strike capabilities against the other. This perspective is only valid as long as both actors are deterred from using nuclear weapons by a relatively equilibrated and static balance of terror. MAD constituted a tenuous balance of power and was easily upset by innovation and progress, for example, the Soviets' development of **antiballistic missiles (ABMs)** and the U.S. move toward multiple independently targetable reentry vehicles (MIRVs)—a qualitative innovation in nuclear weapons technology of the early 1970s.

- massive retaliation versus flexible response: Massive retaliation constituted the official security policy of the Dwight Eisenhower administration during the 1950s. The strategy of massive retaliation advocated a disproportionate U.S. nuclear retaliation against the Soviet Union and the Eastern bloc in the event of any kind of military aggression, limited or more comprehensive, from a communist power. In the face of increasing U.S. exposure to Soviet nuclear weapons, the John F. Kennedy administration sought a new approach to counter the threat of nuclear war. Kennedy focused on the development of U.S. conventional forces that were to be used as a first option in the event of armed confrontation and encouraged differentiated thinking on the deployment of nuclear weapons and its consequences. Under Kennedy, the U.S. government turned from massive retaliation to a strategy of flexible response. Flexible response incorporated a sophisticated command-and-control structure and was intended as a strategy that left open multiple options for crisis response. The strategy of flexible response was conceived within the overriding concern to permit the U.S. government to investigate the extent and limit of adversarial cooperation; the terms of a confrontation; the choice of weapons employed by the enemy; and how armed hostilities could be brought to a close. In other words, the strategy of flexible response prioritized the prevention of rash or ill-judged reactions by seeking to keep as many options open for the—not necessarily peaceful—resolution of a crisis.

- game theory: Game theory is a decisionmaking and analysis

method predicated upon presumed actor rationality in competitive environments. Game theory operates within a set of general assumptions. To begin, actors attempt to avoid loss and increase gain. Frequently, actors are compelled to work with incomplete data and remain uncertain as to the quality of their decisions. Thus, general conditions force actors to prioritize, appraise, and assess options while forecasting the next steps of other actors. A zero-sum game involving two players leaves little room for alternatives, for what one player gains, the other loses. Conversely, in a two-person game that is not constrained by the zero-sum axiom—a so-called non-zero-sum or variable-sum game, winning and losing is not strictly equal. Thus, it is conceivable that either side may gain or lose. This type of situation is a positive-sum game. In certain situations, both participants can win or lose different amounts. If a situation includes more than two players, then it is an *n*-person game. Game theory proved instrumental in the development of deterrence strategies by describing models of deterrence and by projecting arms race spirals. Moreover, game theory has also provided a basis for inquiring into the behavior of competing states in an anarchic international system and their inclinations toward cooperation. A problem presented to users of game theory is that certain situations may offer single actors, such as a state, a better option by deciding on remaining aloof instead of entering cooperative relations with other state actors.

The Rise and Fall
of Détente, 1968–1979

THE CONFRONTATIONAL PHASE OF THE COLD WAR CULMINATED IN A BRIEF PERIOD of diminished superpower tensions in the wake of the Berlin and Cuban missile crises. This was largely due to the relative stabilization of the European security system in the early 1960s and resulted in what has become known as the little détente of 1963. Relations between the Soviet Union and the United States, however, became strained again shortly after 1963. In the aftermath of the Cuban missile crisis, the Soviet leadership embarked upon the ambitious project of achieving a quantitative nuclear parity with the United States in the shortest possible time. In the West, the Soviet plan to expand their nuclear arsenal caused consternation, and it certainly alarmed the United States. The resulting production of ever more destructive nuclear weapons became a spiral upward that threatened to escape the control of Eastern and Western policymakers. Typically, the nuclear arms race became the quintessential child of this Cold War dynamic.

In addition to the bilateral U.S.-Soviet quantitative and qualitative nuclear arms race, lasting throughout the middle and later 1960s, the Cold War continued its expansion into the third world. The superpowers' mutual acceptance of the territorial and nuclear status quo for Europe was also responsible for a revitalized spillover of the Cold War in other regions. Due to the extreme risk of a nuclear confrontation over Europe, which demanded, and was provided with, a measure of stability by 1963, systems competition was confined to the periphery of the Cold War in the third world. Given the fact that the antagonists had availed themselves of a substitute battlefield, superpower tensions in the wake of the little détente were on the rise again. In a progression parallel to the development of the Vietnam War, East-West tensions escalated again.

The developments of the 1960s seemed to indicate that the international system had yet again become subject to a reinforced bipolar structure.

Instead, bipolarity was no longer the single defining factor of international politics. In reality, the international system had undergone dramatic change since the beginning of the Cold War. But this was not readily apparent, as the bipolar structure of the Cold War had for a long time controlled and disciplined the various new forces working toward change. Moreover, the very fact that these so-called structural changes were effected over the long term hid them from the view of most observers.

The first symptoms for the transition into a new phase of the Cold War became evident toward the close of the 1960s, as the superpowers made progress in controlling the proliferation of nuclear arms and disarmament. The Vietnam War, which had captivated and dominated the perspective of the superpowers since the mid-1960s, no longer took center stage in international politics. Instead, arms control became prominent. In other words, a conflictive phenomenon of the Cold War was marginalized on account of potential bilateral cooperation.

The achievements of this new tendency in international relations were tangible, indeed. In the context of the **Strategic Arms Limitation Talks (SALT)**, the superpowers agreed on the establishment of a ceiling for the production of ICBMs. The altered nature of U.S.-Soviet relations was thus symptomatic of structural changes in the international system. These structural changes also had the effect of reinforcing the dilution of superpower antagonism in the early 1970s. Forces other than East-West antagonism began shaping the international system and contributed to the undermining of the bipolar system: economic ties in the international system proliferated and intensified.

The sudden easing of tensions following the highly charged 1950s and 1960s paved the way toward the most curious phenomenon of the Cold War at the end of the decade: détente (literally, "relaxation"). In the late 1960s and early 1970s, at the height of the Vietnam War, détente constituted a sea change in the frosty climate of the Cold War in that it created the foundation for limited communication and cooperation. As opposed to the little détente of 1963, the process of the 1970s was not limited to bilateral relations between Moscow and Washington. The high tide of détente witnessed the breakthrough of the process of relaxation on a multilateral level in Europe. The multilateral arms control negotiations and the **Conference on Security and Cooperation in Europe (CSCE)** that culminated in the Helsinki Accords in 1975 proved a formative experience in international relations: not only the United States and the Soviet Union but also their respective allies—and even neutral and nonaligned states—were able to make themselves heard in a newly constituted dialog on European security.

But places other than Europe, especially Asia, were affected by change. In contrast to Europe, however, Asia lacked the multilateral institutions that could have mitigated insecurities in a transition period.

Invariably, power politics proved dominant: due to the surprising opening of China, President Richard Nixon and his foreign political alter ego, Henry Kissinger, were able to retain the regional balance of power in Asia while also paving the way to reduce U.S. involvement in Vietnam. Meanwhile, competition between Moscow and Beijing for regional hegemony became more pronounced. It is therefore not surprising that the Soviet incursion into and eventual invasion of Afghanistan was a harbinger for the decline of regional stability in Asia. At the end of the 1970s, détente became yet another casualty to Cold War dynamics.

Subverting Bipolarity: The Impact of Structural Change on the International Political System

Détente resulted from a set of circumstances and a convergence of the interests of key players. Détente was the culmination of long-term developments that had an impact on the shape and dynamics of the Cold War international system. The following six trends illustrate the extent to which the international political system had changed after World War II.

1. Since the beginning of the Cold War, military power assumed a position of preeminence. After Moscow successfully consolidated a **second-strike capability**, in the early 1970s, the Soviet Union achieved a quantitative military parity with the United States. On the one hand, the achievement of Soviet military parity was pursued with a view toward the quantity of nuclear warheads, which stabilized at more than 25,000 on each side. On the other hand, both sides possessed three similar types of delivery systems. With a tradition of naval power, the United States had robust seaborne and airborne delivery systems. As a predominantly landlocked power, the Soviet Union fielded a great many land-based delivery systems.

2. The rise of economic powers in Europe and Japan during this period blunted the undisputed primacy of military power in the international system as they became influential political players.

3. The emergence of economic power as an important factor in international politics was compounded by the advent of growing economic interdependence and the rapid internationalization of economic relations from the late 1960s onward.

4. The number of actors in international relations increased for a variety of reasons, not the least of which was the appearance of international economic actors and the conclusion of the process of decolonization. This increase in the number of international actors resulted in a diffusion of political power.

5. Growing tensions within the blocs prompted each superpower to

seek an adequate response. Whereas the West weathered the crisis by adapting to the new heterogeneity within the Western alliance, the East turned into a rigid political edifice suppressing any kind of dissent. Moreover, in this period the Sino-Soviet split reached its apex in a rivalry for supremacy within the communist bloc. Nationalism as a political force increasingly neutralized ideology as a significant factor of politics.

6. The superpowers reached the limit of their respective power in the period between 1968 and 1979. As we have seen, the United States was mired in a crippling war in Vietnam, whereas the Soviet Union repeated the U.S. experience in Afghanistan. By that time, both superpowers had committed the grave error of imperial overextension, which exhausted their economic and military resources.

Overall, then, this period witnessed the relative decline of the superpowers and the weakening of bipolarity. The relaxation of the rigid, Manichean division of the world into East and West resulted in a more heterogeneous international system, which to some extent undermined the pervasive influence of the global political chasm created by the Cold War.

The Arms Race and Strategic Parity

In the early 1960s, the United States again succeeded in prolonging its military superiority over the Soviet Union. The little détente of 1963 did not prove stable enough to effect a lasting settlement between the Cold War antagonists. The acceleration of the U.S. nuclear arms program under President John F. Kennedy exacerbated Soviet fears. Ironically, just when the U.S. government pursued a course of limiting its nuclear arsenal, Soviet hard-liners comprehended that the United States sought no less than the creation of a first-strike capability. Indeed, the Soviets feared that the United States intended to create a nuclear capability that could reduce the Soviet armed forces to utter impotence in one concerted attack. This would leave the Soviet Union defenseless. To many observers, the political consequences of U.S. nuclear superiority were amply demonstrated in the outcome of the Cuban missile crisis. Nikita Khrushchev, the argument ran, was compelled to yield because the Soviets proved unable to match U.S. nuclear capabilities. Factually, it had been Khrushchev's fear of an escalation of the crisis, not a sense of Soviet nuclear inferiority, that had determined his decision to give in. Nevertheless, it was the reality of Soviet quantitative nuclear inferiority—quite insignificant in itself—that drove the Soviet Union to great efforts at attaining quantitative nuclear parity with the United States. Indeed, Soviet nuclear capabilities expanded during the second half of the 1960s; in the early 1970s, the Soviet Union achieved numerical strategic parity with the United States.

What was the significance of strategic parity for the international system? Toward the late 1960s, both sides had the capability to eradicate the other's society *following* a nuclear first strike. In fact, a situation of mutual vulnerability had emerged as a consequence of the recent buildup in nuclear weaponry: the superpowers were facing a balance of terror. One consequence was the relative decline of military might as the symbol of power in superpower competition. In other words, as the nuclear age advanced, the balance of military power lost some of its meaning. Instead, the interpretation of threats made by the opposing side became decisive. Superpower conflict was therefore no longer a test of arms but a test of wills fought before the use of force became an extension of policy. On the one hand, military capability lost its prestige as a unique symbol of power on the global stage. On the other hand, the significance of economic power rose at least commensurately to the decline of military power. In regard to the rise of economic potential as a new key element in international relations, the United States and the Soviet Union became subject to increased pressure by new economic powers in Europe and Japan.

Arms control: the Non-Proliferation Treaty and the Strategic Arms Limitation Talks, 1968–1972.   Once quantitative strategic parity had been achieved, the political significance of military power gradually declined. At the same time, Moscow and Washington faced exorbitant costs from the nuclear arms buildup in addition to the threat and risks emanating from unfettered proliferation of nuclear weapons technology. Against this backdrop, questions concerning **nonproliferation** and strategic arms control were addressed with increasing urgency between the late 1960s and the early 1970s.

In the wake of the Cuban missile crisis, during which Kennedy and Khrushchev drove to the edge of nuclear war, the superpowers were bound by a mutual interest in constraining the proliferation of nuclear weapons systems—especially in regard to China and West Germany. The superpowers worked together to bring about the Limited Nuclear Test Ban Treaty, according to which no nuclear testing was to be conducted in the open seas, the atmosphere, or in space. With the exception of France and China, almost 100 states acceded to this treaty. Another treaty followed in 1968. The terms of the Nuclear Non-Proliferation Treaty set forth the necessity of limiting the spread of nuclear capability to countries not already in possession thereof. Again, the superpowers were in the vanguard of this achievement. The Seabed Pact banned the testing of nuclear devices on the bottom of the world's oceans in 1971, and a year later the Biological Warfare Treaty addressed the production of biological agents for purposes of war.

Since the 1950s, the arms race was fueled by problems of either a perceptual or an actual kind. The concept of the missile gap is an example of the former, whereas the Soviet effort to achieve nuclear parity after 1963 illustrates the latter. Mutual fears encouraged a massive buildup of nuclear arsenals. And despite the various curbs on the arms race, the U.S. and Soviet nuclear arsenals were growing at an alarming rate during the 1960s. Advances in technology resulted in the production of more destructive warheads with higher payloads, as well as increasingly sophisticated delivery systems. By the end of the 1960s, the combined U.S.-Soviet megatonnage of nuclear materials was more than enough to render the entire planet uninhabitable for centuries to come: an escalation of hostilities to the breaking point could lead to the end of human civilization. When the Soviet Union achieved strategic parity with the United States by the early 1970s, the pressure for arms control mounted. The constant fiscal drain caused by defense expenditures compelled the superpowers to neglect other national interests, such as the fact that new economic power centers were on the rise. A partial solution to the dangers of unfettered nuclear stockpiling presented itself in the Strategic Arms Limitation Talks. Following preliminary negotiations on a treaty to control nuclear arsenals in the late 1960s, U.S. President Richard Nixon and Soviet leader Leonid Brezhnev concluded the SALT I Treaty in May 1972.

SALT I set limits for ICBMs; the superpowers also agreed to construct and maintain no more than two antiballistic missile defense systems. The logic behind the second term was that if both sides remained vulnerable to each other's first strike capabilities, then the consequent balance of terror would act as a deterrent to the deployment of nuclear weapons. SALT I limited Soviet ICBMs to 1,398, those of the United States to 1,052. At first sight, the Soviet Union gained more under SALT I than did the United States. Effectively, the U.S. nuclear potential was still greater than that of the Soviet Union, for SALT did not include SLBMs or aircraft delivery systems such as strategic bombers. The United States also possessed more strategic warheads, as well as a delivery system, that could transport several warheads at once: MIRVs, which revolutionized the arms race. MIRVs rendered SALT I nearly obsolete, because they shifted the nature of the nuclear buildup from the quantity to the quality of delivery systems. Nevertheless, SALT I was the first significant step toward a gradual relaxation of superpower relations. East and West could finally hope for an eventual end to the permanency of the spiraling arms race. This was especially true for the entirety of Europe, with its high concentration of nuclear weapons and the questionable honor of being located at the heart of the Cold War.

The rise of economic powers and economic interdependence.   The shifts in the international system of the 1960s and 1970s corresponded to a growing limit on the power of the principal Cold War antagonists. Although it was true that the superpowers maintained the potential to project power around the globe, other states had improved increasingly important dimensions of their own power in international relations, including economic potential. By way of comparison, in 1945 the United States had been the only power with the ability to use its economic and military resources on a global scale. In the 1970s, this no longer held true.

The situation for the economic recuperation of Europe and Japan changed dramatically with the onset of the Cold War. The Marshall Plan enabled the rapid reconstruction of European economies in the 1950s and 1960s. Following the conclusion of World War II, Japan was in receipt of similar economic aid. As a consequence, European and Japanese economies saw unparalleled growth for two decades. In the course of the 1960s, Western Europe and Japan became great economic powers. The economic miracle that led to the establishment of the two new economic power centers was also the result of the low defense spending of these states. Europe, as well as Japan, profited from the nuclear deterrent provided for by the United States without having to make any significant financial contribution.

What were the effects on the international system? The new economic strength of Europe and Japan allowed more independence in relations with the United States. The economic potential of Europe and Japan also gained significance as to the Soviet Union, especially because it paralleled the developing nuclear stalemate. In this context, economic power was able to counterbalance military power.

Not only did the United States, Europe, and Japan become serious economic competitors; the character of international economic relations had fundamentally changed. In the three decades following World War II, the U.S., European, and Japanese economies had undergone massive growth. Simultaneously, their economies became increasingly dependent upon one another. In part, the progressing interdependence of the international economic system was caused by the information and technology revolution. Distances between continents no longer posed an obstacle to business and trade, whereas information and know-how became accessible and cheap commodities. Accordingly, the exchange of the economic actors increased dramatically.

The international economy could no longer be understood in terms of multiple national economies. The reverberations of developments at the stock exchange in Tokyo could be felt as far away as New York. A good example of the growing **complex interdependence** of the international economic system is the oil crisis of 1973–1974. The increase in the price of crude oil at that time created a panic in the United States, Europe, and Japan. Therefore, the rising complexity of international economic and financial relations spanning the globe was an important trend in the international system during the 1970s. In an interdependent international system, the unfettered use of force was no longer an attractive option, as the consequences would affect many, if not most, actors.

The proliferation of actors in the international system. In light of this rising complexity in international relations, the effects of another structural change could be felt: the number of actors in the international system had increased. In 1945, some forty-five states shared the globe; today, we count no less than four times as many. The process of decolonization is accountable for this marked rise in state actors since World War II. The process of national emancipation steadily progressed throughout the 1950s and 1960s. Notably, the third world contributed many new states as former colonies obtained independence. The Non-Aligned Movement sought to create a third bloc between East and West, and its agenda contributed to the complexity of the international system. The proliferation of states had a lasting effect on the United Nations, where it created a new majority in the UN General Assembly favorable to the developing states.

Nonstate actors, such as international organizations, transnational corporations, and nongovernmental organizations (NGOs), also proliferated during this period. What was the consequence of this increase in the quantity and quality of actors in the international system? Principally, the rising number and types of international actors effected the diffusion of political forces. Even though the possibilities and capabilities of the superpowers had not decreased, the new powers gained on them in various dimensions—militarily, economically, and scientifically. The distribution of power remained unequal, but the superiority of the United States and the Soviet Union was no longer as pronounced as it had been during the apex of the Cold War in the 1950s and 1960s.

The Pentagonal International System and Regionalism

Nevertheless, by the early 1970s there were still only two superpowers. The United States and the Soviet Union were the only nations with the ability to defeat any foe with conventional and/or nuclear weapons. Although Britain, France, and China had also developed nuclear weapons, their arsenals paled compared to those of the superpowers. Equally, in the realm of conventional warfare both superpowers had at their disposal the necessary surveillance and logistical means, as well as a well-trained cadre of military leaders, to project power anywhere around the globe. Thus, even though militarily the international system remained bipolar, politically speaking it was tending toward multipolarity, that is, toward a diffusion of political power. And with respect to economic power in the early 1970s, three examples can be identified: the United States, Western Europe, and Japan.

China proved unable to achieve either military or economic parity with the leading states. On the basis of its large population, however, China exhibited a potential power that could no longer be ignored. If China ever developed its full military and economic potential in the future, it would have to be admitted to the concert of Great Powers. As a consequence of structural changes in the international system, the five power centers—the United States, the Soviet Union, China, Western Europe, and Japan—had emerged as the leading elements of international politics. For this reason, we can describe the new landscape as a **pentagonal international system**. No other state in the world could match the influence of these five powers. Conversely, power was unevenly distributed among the five powers. Unique among them was the United States in that it was both militarily and economically potent. The United States was at the center of a politico-strategic triangle, consisting of itself, the Soviet Union, and China. At the same time, the United States also constituted the core of a triangular economic relationship with Western Europe and Japan.

The pentagonal illustration of structural change in the international system no longer exclusively reflects the Cold War dichotomy of East versus West. Instead, this depiction makes allowance for the increasing tensions *within the blocs* and the growing diffusion of power in the international system (i.e., five "poles," or multipolarity, as opposed to the two of the Cold War's bipolar system). In the West, relations between the United States, Japan, and Western Europe evidenced rising economic competition, whereas in the East the brewing Sino-Soviet split indicated possible political and military confrontation. In the final analysis, the pentagonal perspective demonstrates that international relations had become *more complex* during the 1970s. Moreover, the advent of the pentagonal system presaged that future conflict could only be partially understood within the confines of the old bipolar international system.

The pentagonal model is a perspective on the global level of analysis. Therefore, it does not pretend to take a closer look at the lower levels of analysis, such as the state and the individual. The increasing prominence of economic power marks one of the latest developments in international relations and is closely connected to regional integration and, ultimately, to the emergence of globalization. From the early 1970s onward, the international system received much of its dynamic from regional political and economic developments. Conversely, the multipolarization of the international system during that period also fueled regionalism, that is, the formation of political and economic systems at regional levels. Throughout the 1970s, the trend toward regional specification/diversification stood out as a new phenomenon.

As a consequence, four units emerged: the Euroatlantic, Asia, the Middle East, and Latin America. Each region faced different challenges

that tended to develop in different ways. The divergence of regional interests manifested itself in asynchronous dynamics in individual regions,
which not only contrasted with each other but also proved incompatible
with the nature of superpower relations and therefore with the interests of
the superpowers themselves. This observation is especially applicable to
U.S.-European disagreements in the Euroatlantic and to the Soviet-Chinese
competition for hegemony in Asia. The frequent divergence between the
development of bipolar (i.e., U.S.-Soviet) relations and multipolar (i.e.,
pentagonal and regional) relations thus constituted an amalgamated diffu-
sive force in the international system that undermined the hitherto preponderant bipolar system of the Cold War. Having established the framework
for structural change in the international system in the present section, we
will take a look at events in each of these integrating regions in those below
and follow up with an analysis at the end of this chapter.

The Euroatlantic

NATO reforms during 1966–1969 culminated in a more evenhanded, multilateral dialogue between the United States and its European allies concerning strategic issues, such as nuclear power-sharing and deployment. Due to
this process of consensus-seeking, Western Europe gained an increasingly
self-confident and even independent position vis-à-vis the United States.
The European tendency toward political emancipation within the transatlantic framework was further enabled by the fact that U.S. priorities at that
stage rested with the pursuit of the Vietnam War. In this constellation,
European political leaders were able to thaw relations with the East. In the
event, the Europeans proved instrumental in initiating and directing the
process of détente on a multilateral level. The East-West dialogue was
henceforth no longer the exclusive preserve of the bilateral Soviet-U.S.
level, which helps to illustrate the attenuation of U.S. influence in Europe
during this period.

Toward Détente: Ostpolitik and the Helsinki Accords

Illustrating this regional dynamic was Willy Brandt's deftly implemented
rapprochement with the communist-dominated states of Eastern Europe at
the end of the 1960s. West Germany's Ostpolitik—a policy to achieve
improved relations with the Eastern bloc—led to a lessening of tensions
between the Soviet Union and an economically and politically integrated
West Germany and, by extension, the entire Western bloc. Brandt's
achievement was that he improved dialogue over formalizing German border issues—a legacy of World War II—without foregoing the possible
reunification of Germany. The conclusion of the Ost Treaties ("ost" in

German meaning, literally, "east") between East and West Germany, as well as the so-called Four Powers Treaty, effectively amounted to a settlement of postwar boundaries in Central Europe.

In this series of treaties, signed between 1970 and 1973, West Germany recognized the postwar boundaries with its neighbors to the east. As a quid pro quo, the Soviet Union granted the West unhindered access to Berlin. On the one hand, this understanding finally eliminated Berlin as a recurring potential hotspot of the Cold War (for decades, the Soviet Union had expediently used Berlin for a bargaining chip); therefore, the resolution of the Berlin issue constituted a significant achievement for the West. On the other hand, the reciprocal recognition of the German postwar frontiers decreased the probability of future West German claims on territories, which at that time belonged to East Germany or to Poland and could threaten the Soviet sphere of influence in Eastern and Central Europe.

Brandt's conciliatory policy of limited cooperation with the East came to fruition, whereas bilateral superpower negotiations had time and again been frustrated: Ostpolitik generated a sense of goodwill between East and West Germany, both of which were quintessentially representative of the bipolar dichotomy at the geographic heart of the Cold War. The definition of the postwar boundaries for Central Europe achieved through these negotiations had been a long-standing demand of the Soviet Union and its allies in Eastern Europe. Concurrently, the initiation of multilateral talks regarding Mutual and Balanced Force Reductions, as well as the superpowers' breakthrough on the reciprocal imposition of constraints on strategic arms development in the SALT negotiations, also met Western demands for substantial progress in disarmament. Therefore, by mid-1973 the graduated concurrence of the superpowers on previously contentious issues laid the foundation for exploratory negotiations concerning a European security conference, leading into a phase of multilateral preparatory talks.

With the sole exception of Albania, every European country as well as the United States and Canada took part in the Conference on Security and Cooperation in Europe held in 1975 at Helsinki. Between September 1973 and July 1975, the participants had hammered out a formulation for the final debate of the CSCE in long discussions held at Geneva. By and large, the opposing interests of the Eastern and Western blocs had shaped the talks. Eastern demands for recognition of a post–World War II settlement and more economic exchange were confronted by Western requirements for anchoring human and basic rights, as well as for an attenuation of the governmental stringency toward citizens of the Eastern bloc countries—ideas, and the (relatively) free movement of people, and the flow of information. By suggesting several proposals for compromise, the loosely organized group of neutral and nonaligned states had factually assumed the role of mediator between the two blocs.

In review, the highlights of the conference were the formal recognition of postwar borders, West Germany's renunciation of its claim to sole representation of all Germans, and a mutual agreement on the maintenance of human rights by East and West. The latter constituted one of the more significant results of the CSCE: the Helsinki Accords affirmed and codified a list of critical human rights. In relation to the former, the participants of the Helsinki conference (with the superpowers in the vanguard) had finally achieved the partial resolution of the old German border grievance with Poland, for the delegates had agreed to abide by a resolution stipulating that the established boundaries were to be changed only by peaceful means. Moreover, the Soviet Union and the United States agreed to admit observers to military maneuvers to increase transparency.

The CSCE was the closest that the Cold War antagonists came to official cooperation. In retrospect, the Helsinki conference constituted the high tide of the multilateral policy of relaxation in Europe. Thirty years after the end of World War II, the CSCE Final Act constituted a consensus on the shape and substance of détente policy that satisfied both East and West. Significantly, the impact of the spirit of multilaterally engineered détente on the bilateral level was not negligible either. The evident commitment with which Brandt and other European leaders sought to improve ties with the Eastern bloc had a signal effect on the Soviet leadership. To take only one example, Ostpolitik certainly proved conducive to a softening of attitudes in the Kremlin, which in turn had a benign effect on bilateral talks leading up to the SALT negotiations concluded in 1972.

The Rise of the European New Left
and the Resurgence of Political Terrorism

If détente and SALT symbolized the achievements of high politics in the late 1960s and early 1970s, the rise of the **New Left**, and the emergence of political **terrorism** closely associated with it, expressed a generational conflict, a protest culture directed against postwar capitalist achievement and consumerism in Western Europe. The Prague Spring and the eruption of student riots in France, Italy, and West Germany all occurred in 1968–1969. In France, student protests were aimed at Charles de Gaulle's autocratic and conservative rule and initiated a chain of events that led to his resignation; in Italy during the so-called Hot Summer of 1969 they constituted an expression of social dissent and a reaction to the weakness of trade unions; and in Germany they were directed against the cynicism of an establishment seemingly dedicated to forget the Nazi legacy by allying with the militant and interventionist United States and, in the process, allowing Germany to become the potential battleground of the Cold War.

Across Europe, student protest movements aired discontent at the social and political postwar status quo. The rejection of the war in Vietnam, which to many in Europe and the United States constituted a symbol of the failed postwar order, provided for a common denominator for the protesters. With the exception of Italy, dissent remained confined to the universities. Nevertheless, from among the mainstream of the student protesters rose a radical fringe. What the protest movements of 1968 all shared at some stage, albeit to varying degrees, was their rejection of Western capitalist and, by extension, material values. Contemporaries referred to the phenomenon as the rise of the New Left. Marxist-Leninist ideology played a key role in the radicalization of student and youth protest movements after 1968. A significant development within the New Left was the idea of direct action to bring about social change and revolution. But a minor segment of the university-based radical fringe did not content itself with conducting sit-ins or organizing rallies and protest marches: a small number was prepared to use force to bring about revolutionary change.

The evolution of student-inspired social discontent, which began with a justified need for reform at the universities, underwent a process of radicalization that finally led to a multiplicity of political violence movements steeped in the trappings of Marxist-Leninist ideology. By tapping into various social and political grievances and harnessing the inadvertent cooperation of the media to disseminate their activities among the public, small terrorist groups garnered sympathies from the discontented and maximized their impact on established government authorities across Europe. In Great Britain, where radical political protests had for the most part constituted an isolated phenomenon, a long-standing nationalist and religious rivalry between Protestants and Catholics in Northern Ireland erupted into warlike conditions at the end of the 1960s. A civil rights campaign to attain equal rights for members of all denominations afforded the new, radical, and socialist Irish Republican Army (IRA) an opportunity to gain prominence and to renew its war against Britain. Uncharacteristic of the hitherto traditional tenets of the Republican struggle, the political objectives of the IRA between 1968 and 1972 were founded on an admixture of nationalist and socialist tenets: an end to partition, and the proclamation of a socialist republic. Following a split in the nationalist movement in 1972, the more conservative Provisional IRA took the lead in the nationalist war against the British presence in Northern Ireland.

In northern Italy, the leftist Red Brigades spread fear throughout cities. Although the Red Brigades were the direct result the New Left's radical fringe, they were also the most recent and extreme manifestation of a leftist tradition of social discontent. Aside from bombings against various installations of logistical, cultural, and political import, their spectacular abduction of Aldo Moro, who was the leader of the Italian Christian Democrats, in March 1978 marked the high tide of terror in Italy. Although they may not have been responsible for the detonation of a bomb at the Bologna railway station in 1980—neofascist forces have since come under suspicion—the incident cost the Red Brigades much sympathy among their less extreme advocates. The Red Brigades and their splinter groups continued their activities into the late 1980s.

Unlike those terrorist movements able to utilize existing or even historical divisions and grudges, the Rote Armee Fraktion (RAF) in Germany, alternatively known as the Baader-Meinhof group, was a purely ideological phenomenon. The RAF stood out due to its extreme Marxist-Leninism, its emphasis on anti-imperialism, the tiny size of the group, and its members' extraordinary ruthlessness. Throughout the 1970s, prominent German industrialists were kidnapped and murdered when RAF demands for the liberation of their fellow members detained in West German prisons were not heeded by the authorities. Political assassinations, arson attacks on shopping centers, and multiple bombings typified the RAF's campaign to overthrow the state and government of West Germany. An alliance with the Palestinian Liberation Organization kept the RAF well-armed, informed, and potent enough to endure into the early 1990s. As the antimaterialism and radicalism of 1968 gave way to the economic bounty and new conservatism of the 1980s, however, the dynamic fueled by socialist ideologies petered out, and radicals returned to work within the constitutional framework and were supplanted by right-wing terrorist groups.

The Western Economic Crisis of the Early 1970s

As the scourge of terrorism beset Europe, Western Europe, the United States, and Canada were hit by an economic crisis when oil prices soared in 1973. The Yom Kippur War in the Middle East had prompted the **Organization for Petroleum Exporting Countries (OPEC)** to initiate an embargo against all states supporting Israel in its struggle against the Arab attackers. OPEC had been founded in 1960 by the major oil-exporting nations in the Arab world to gain leverage against the most powerful multinational oil corporations, most of which were of Western origin. These predominantly Western companies largely controlled the production, refining, and sale of oil. Together they formed an unassailable cartel—until the advent of OPEC. OPEC's influence was based on the reliance of the industrialized North for a cheap source of energy. After World War II, the resuscitation of industry and, hence, dependency on foreign oil supplies rose as demand in the West outpaced oil production in the global market. Oil consumption in the North (the United States, Western Europe, and Japan) more than doubled until the early 1970s. The rising demand for cheap imported oil from the Middle East rendered the economies of the West vulnerable to outside manipulation.

The growth of Arab nationalism and the concomitant series of conflicts with Israel between 1948 and the early 1970s finally led the Arab-dominated OPEC to make use of oil as a weapon of sorts. When the United States and West European states began to supply Israel huge quantities of arms, OPEC launched an oil embargo in 1973 that waylaid the Western economies. And though the United States was able to mitigate the worst effects of the OPEC oil embargo with domestic resources, Western Europe and Japan badly suffered. In order to counteract OPEC, the United States initiated efforts to coordinate Japanese and Western European measures in early 1974, which proved to be a complete failure. OPEC quickly realized the potency of its oil weapon and increased the price per barrel by more than 400 percent. For the remainder of the 1970s, OPEC continued to manipulate prices.

In the mid- to long term, price levels were normalized due to the influence exerted by the richest member of OPEC: Saudi Arabia. The Saudis had a vested interest in protecting investment opportunities in the North and were characterized by a moderate political position as well as a pro-Western alignment. Although Saudi Arabia was in a position to alleviate the impact of the 1973 oil embargo, the West had learned a painful lesson from developing countries. In the process, some of the North's arrogance toward the South underwent a reappraisal: dependency, in the end, worked both ways. In the final analysis, the devastating effects of the oil embargo highlighted structural changes in the international system, the attendant rise of economic power in international politics, and the spread of complex interdependence in the international economy of the early 1970s.

Asia

In the period between 1968 and 1979, both superpowers had engaged in a confrontation that threatened to sap their resources. Essentially, they had permitted such growth in their empires that they had unwittingly exceeded the fiscal means required to support them, a classic example of imperial overextension. Moreover, the superpowers had determined foreign policy according to the ideological threat perception of one another. In other words, ideological factors determined which threats were identified in the first place. In light of the bipolar division, Washington and Moscow inferred a permanent threat to their national interests. This zero-sum perspective, in turn, led the superpowers to global commitments to forestall the potential expansion of the other side. This ideologized foreign and security policy agenda led the superpowers into a worldwide engagement beyond their resources and power.

Before imperial overextension was fully understood, the United States and the Soviet Union had to undergo a painful experience. In the event, the

Vietnam War demonstrated the limits of U.S. power. Only a few years later, the Soviets embarked on a military adventure in Afghanistan that would ultimately topple the communist empire. Notably, both conflicts were fought in Asia, and it was in Asia where the great reversal of the Cold War alliance system occurred.

Sino-Soviet Rivalry and the Success of Triangular Diplomacy

Just as the war in Vietnam was ending, the United States made a decisive reversal in relations between East and West. The architect of this dramatic turnabout in international relations was President Nixon's secretary of state, Henry Kissinger. Ever since the Communists won the Chinese civil war, the United States pursued an openly adversarial policy toward China. Under Presidents Harry Truman, Dwight Eisenhower, and John F. Kennedy, the United States fought China in Korea and Vietnam. Conversely, China opposed every U.S. effort to interfere in East Asia and Southeast Asia by supporting fellow communist states (Vietnam) or by directly attacking U.S. forces (Korea). Throughout the 1950s and 1960s, the United States had no official relations with Maoist China. To Washington, China was firmly in the communist camp and, along with the Soviet Union, came to be seen in the West as an integral part of a monolithic communist bloc held together by international socialist solidarity. Following the Cuban missile crisis and more emphatically in the late 1960s and early 1970s, East and West drew closer to détente. The Chinese reaction was not to seek support from the West but to denounce the Soviet policy of improving relations with the West as an outright betrayal of world revolution. The superpowers criticized Maoist policy for being detrimental to global stability.

Following several skirmishes along the Soviet-Chinese border, Henry Kissinger persuaded the fervently anticommunist Richard Nixon to leverage the worsening relations between China and the Soviets to U.S. advantage. A student of nineteenth-century statesman and pragmatist Prince Klemens von Metternich and a proponent of the concept of balance of power, Kissinger was able to identify the Sino-Soviet split as a way to weaken the Soviet position by seeking China's friendship. The United States took the initiative, and Nixon openly acknowledged Mao's regime as the rightful government of China in early 1971. The next step was entirely informal but in the end won over the Chinese. A U.S. table tennis team was touring Southeast Asia when it was invited to Beijing. Chinese prime minister Zhou Enlai responded positively to the visit of the U.S. team—a hint not lost on Kissinger and Nixon. The U.S. government thereupon improved economic relations with China, and in July 1971 Kissinger himself secretly traveled to Beijing for the purpose of exploring the possibility of positive diplomatic relations with China. Within only six months, Nixon flew to

China to meet Mao. Why did this dramatic reversal in East-West diplomacy take place?

The question of *why* the Sino-U.S. rapprochement had taken place was closely tied to the far more important question of *when* it came to pass. This change almost certainly could have been effected before 1972. But having accepted the perceived reality of international socialist solidarity since the early 1950s, successive U.S. administrations did not discern the Sino-Soviet split for what it was; it never occurred to them to use the split to advance U.S. interests. Chinese-Soviet antagonism centered on two issues fueled by an ideological schism and geopolitics: the Soviet challenge of Chinese hegemony in Southeast Asia, and the contested border. In the context of the Vietnam War, the Soviet Union challenged China in its immediate sphere of influence by offering Hanoi patronage with the concomitant military and financial benefits. During the gradual U.S. withdrawal from Vietnam, the situation was exacerbated by a power vacuum that would be filled by one of the two principals in the communist bloc. The race for influence in Southeast Asia thus exacerbated the Sino-Soviet rift during the first stages of U.S.-China rapprochement. In effect, tensions over Vietnam opened up the possibility of Chinese military intervention against any Soviet client in the area. In the 1970s, this persistent possibility was transformed into a probability.

By the time Kissinger spotted the crack in the monolith, the two communist countries were on the verge of escalating their border conflict on the Ussuri River into a major war, with the Soviets panicking over the Chinese threat and the Chinese denouncing Soviet socialist imperialism. The speed of the U.S.-China rapprochement suggests that anti-U.S. rhetoric in China was not representative of geostrategic realities. The Chinese were isolated within the communist bloc. The Ussuri River conflict demonstrated that when it came to the defense of national boundaries, international socialist solidarity took a backseat to nationalist considerations. China was seriously threatened by a massive concentration of Soviet conventional forces equipped with tactical nuclear weapons along the Siberian border. As Kissinger had properly divined, the Chinese could hope to break out of meaningless isolation only if they established relations with the United States, which was to act as a counterweight to the Soviet threat.

Although the Chinese had denounced Soviet leader Nikita Khrushchev as a traitor for his policy of relaxation in the 1960s, the Chinese leadership was pragmatic enough to realize that they shared interests with the United States. Kissinger's own analysis was framed in terms of a change in the balance of power. Ultimately, it was his understanding and perspective of geopolitics that allowed him to look beyond the confines of bipolarity and dispel the illusion of a monolithic communist bloc. As opposed to politicians of a purely U.S. cast of mind, Kissinger—who was informed by a

European cultural heritage—had no compunctions about breaking with Washington's orthodox division of the world into East and West. By playing off China against the Soviet Union while the United States fostered good relations with both communist giants, Kissinger transformed the bipolar world of the Cold War into a more diffuse structure: this was an achievement in **triangular diplomacy**.

Indochina After the Vietnam War and the Sino-Soviet Struggle for Regional Hegemony

The Vietnam War's costs included human life, political instability in Southeast Asia, and deteriorating national economies. Two million civilians had perished in the Vietnam War by 1975. To this figure must be added 1.1 million North Vietnamese and Vietcong fatalities and some 600,000 wounded in action. The U.S. Air Force had dropped a staggering 7 million tons of explosives—three times as much as had been used during World War II—and defoliated, or otherwise impaired, an estimated 24,000 square kilometers of Vietnamese territory. Following the withdrawal of U.S. troops, South Vietnamese military leaders fell to a North Vietnamese invasion. In 1976, north and south were reunited as the Socialist Republic of Vietnam.

The war had driven away the peasants responsible for agricultural production, and the incipient northern industry had been much reduced during sustained U.S. bombing raids. A Vietnamese economic recovery was further hampered by the country's interdiction through the application of U.S. pressure on Southeast Asian nations. Efforts on the part of the Vietnamese government to be admitted to the **Association of Southeast Asian Nations (ASEAN)** were repeatedly frustrated. Finally, Vietnam was forced to seek support from Moscow, which in turn decreased potential good relations with pro-Western countries in the region. In the context of the Sino-Soviet split, a closer association with Moscow would in all likelihood provoke Chinese retaliation. This is exactly what happened in the wake of the Vietnamese invasion of Cambodia in 1979. The Vietnamese offensive against the extremist communist government of Pol Pot was an overdue response to repeated Cambodian raids across the border into Vietnam.

Pol Pot had overthrown the pro-Western Lon Nol regime when the United States pulled out of Vietnam in 1975. The Khmer Rouge, the Cambodian communist guerrilla force, then seized Phnom Penh. The opposition was subsequently persecuted and slaughtered in so-called reeducation camps. Between Pol Pot's accession to power in 1975 and 1978, the Khmer Rouge murdered some 1.5 million Cambodians. Cambodia's Killing Fields have come to mean mass murder. Pol Pot regarded Vietnam as a dangerous rival, and during a campaign to destroy a rebel force ostensibly of

Vietnamese origin and operating from territory adjoining the Vietnamese border, he struck deep into enemy territory. The Cambodian attack was only thinly veiled as a police action; it was, in fact, an overt hostile act of aggression by one state against another. As a consequence, Vietnamese troops conquered Cambodia and installed a pliant government in Phnom Penh. Cambodian troops continued to resist along the Thai border. Meanwhile, the international community denounced Vietnam's intervention. Western criticism was to be expected, but the Chinese vociferously attacked the Vietnamese and threatened to teach them a lesson. In February 1979, Chinese troops marched across the border into Vietnam and met Vietnamese troops in open battle. A month later, the invaders left. Their object lesson failed to achieve the desired results, however, for it drove the Vietnamese deeper into the Soviet orbit.

The result of Chinese intervention was an expanding Soviet presence in Vietnam and a mutual defense treaty. Meanwhile, the situation in Cambodia had been exacerbated by the appearance of supporters of Lon Nol and the conservative Prince Norodom Sihanouk. They cooperated with the Khmer Rouge against the Vietnamese presence in Cambodia. The Cambodian civil war dragged on until a multilateral truce and peace agreement resolved the conflict in 1991. While the war lasted, 360,000 refugees were dislocated, and many of them ended up in Thai camps. Tragically, many Cambodians (as well as Laotians and ethnic Chinese from Vietnam) perished off the shores of Indochina in the exodus of the boatpeople. It was only following the resolution of the Cold War in 1991 and the concomitant waning of Soviet influence in Southeast Asia that the region again had any hope for peace. Only recently the international community—especially the West—freed the communist countries of Indochina from the hardships of a sustained economic embargo. Ever since, countries in the area have experienced a moderate economic upturn.

The Soviet Invasion of Afghanistan

Toward the end of 1979, the Soviet Union invaded Afghanistan in northeastern Asia, repeating the same mistake that the United States made in Vietnam. Soviet divisions crossed the border in response to Afghanistan's internal strife, which threatened to overthrow the leftist government in Kabul. The suddenness of Soviet military intervention caused surprise and consternation in the West. Except for oil, Afghanistan had no natural resources to speak of; strategically speaking, the country was a nonentity; and economically, it was among the most underdeveloped nations in the world. Moreover, Afghanistan lay beyond the Soviet orbit. Unlike the communist client states of Eastern Europe, Afghanistan was not located in the Western or in the Eastern sphere of influence. So why had the Soviets deployed an army of 80,000 troops to maintain a corrupt, albeit socialist, government in power?

Until 1973, the two superpowers were competing for influence in the region. In 1973, the traditional Afghan monarchy was overthrown and succeeded by a leftist clique under Prince Muhammed Daoud. The Soviet Union became a natural ally. Following the initial coup, Afghanistan faced two more violent changes in government. The new rulers had in common only their socialist leanings. Prior to the Soviet invasion, the government in Kabul was split between the established supporters of a pro-Eastern policy and a new faction under the leadership of Hafizullah Amin, advocating a reversal of alignments in favor of the West. The socialist Afghan governments in Kabul faced open resistance in the outlying rural areas. There, feudal warlords guided by the word of the Prophet in all things held sway. Attempts by the central government to impose new laws designed to change the conservative social order and to develop rural economies were met with stiff resistance by the mujahideen, the resistance fighters.

It is very likely that fears of an Afghan defection to the West inclined the Soviets to consider direct measures. Although the Politburo under Leonid Brezhnev had repeatedly refused to support communist governments in Afghanistan in their attempts to quell rebellions, it was Brezhnev and his advisers who in 1979 perceived that Amin's progressively heavy-handed rule had provoked the wrath of many Afghan warlords in the countryside—and that the Afghan Communists were about to face an open revolt that could drive the country into the Western orbit. Even more important, the Soviets were concerned that a fundamentalist Islamic regime would establish rule in Kabul. (The Soviet invasion also has to be understood against the backdrop of the Iranian revolution; see below.) Should the religiously motivated rebel forces in Afghanistan succeed in destroying the socialist government, Moscow feared the consequence of spillover into Soviet territory. Some 50 million Soviets were Muslims, three-fourths of whom practiced religion despite state atheism. Ethnically speaking, Soviet Muslims belonged to peoples only recently subjugated by czarist Russia. For the most part they inhabited the Central Asia republics of the Soviet Union, some of which bordered Afghanistan.

As the mujahideėn converged on Kabul, the Soviets invaded Afghanistan and justified the military intervention on the grounds of the Brezhnev Doctrine. According to the Soviet perspective, religious and reactionary forces threatened the socialist government. Soviet forces in Afghanistan fought against an indigenous warrior culture reared to survive in a harsh environment. Reminiscent of the U.S. experience in Vietnam, the Soviet military was bogged down and drawn into costly skirmishes with mujahideen forces. Troubles were exacerbated by a steady flow of arms financed by revolutionary Iran, Libya, and the U.S. administration under

Ronald Reagan. Initially, President Jimmy Carter had imposed a grain embargo on the Soviet Union and boycotted the 1980 Summer Olympics in Moscow, two futile measures with little impact. U.S. support for the mujahideen resistance groups was Reagan's answer to the Soviet invasion. Using allied Pakistan as a base of operations, U.S. arms supplies reached the mujahideen. The United States had experienced the limits of its own power in Vietnam; in Afghanistan, the Soviets were about to learn the high price of imperial overextension. The major difference between Vietnam and Afghanistan was the nature of the resisting forces. Whereas the Vietnamese national liberation movement under Ho Chi Minh conformed to the bipolar structure of the Cold War by throwing its lot in with the Communists, Afghanistan's mujahideen were driven by the religious tenets of Islam.

The Rise of Japanese Economic Power

Elsewhere in Asia, especially Japan, national economies were on the rise in a largely stable political climate. In the decade after World War II, the Japanese economy had been reconstructed under the auspices of the United States: nearly U.S.$2 billion went to Japan as direct aid; the United States provided for the entire Japanese defense establishment and made the U.S. market available to Japanese manufacturers while allowing tariffs protecting the Japanese economy to stand. To begin, U.S. support was not idealist philanthropy or boundless altruism; it was geared toward the creation and maintenance of a reliable Asian ally during the Cold War. Japan proved its worth as a base for U.S. troops acting under a UN mandate during the Korean War. Conversely, Japan obtained the financial wherewithal to boost its foundering economy through the sales of manufactured goods to U.S. armed forces in the early 1950s. Japan's success story lasted into the 1973 oil crisis and beyond. Until 1973, Japan maintained the largest growth rate of any industrialized country in the world (an incredible 11 percent annually). After 1973, the growth rate averaged 4.5 percent annually but still exceeded that of Europe by 1.5 percent.

A combination of hard work, initial low wages, and a series of successful investment and production strategies propelled Japan's economy to become the second largest behind the United States. After 1964, however, growing economic imparity strained relations between the United States and Japan. By the late 1970s, the U.S. bilateral trade deficit—the difference between commodity imports and exports—had reached U.S.$12 billion. By 1987, the U.S. trade deficit had grown sevenfold. Discontent in the United States at the growing indebtedness with Japan, and the beginnings of a recession at home, increased in the early 1980s. Calls for tightening trade policy with Japan grew in Washington at a time when superior and cheaper Japanese commodities competed with indigenous products of a lesser quality on the U.S. market. U.S. politicians began to accuse Japan of allowing its defense to be paid by the U.S. government while maintaining trade barriers that kept U.S. products out. The United States alleged economic expediency and opportunism.

The true issue was the trade barriers, and the possibility of a trade war suddenly loomed. The Reagan administration, however, realized that neither the United States nor Japan would gain by that. Over the next few years, then, successive U.S. governments have pressured Japan to lower its protective tariff and nontariff measures. In response, Japanese government officials blamed the United States for a bad economic management, low productivity, and poor quality of its products. In the event, U.S.-Japanese relations weathered the tensions, helping to lower the U.S. trade deficit to approximately U.S.$55 billion in 1988. In that same year, U.S. imports to Japan rose 34 percent. In the late 1980s, U.S. and Japanese bilateral efforts achieved a significant relaxation in trade relations.

The Middle East

The nations of the Middle East—including the Islamic world—often proved less pliant as superpower clients. Arab states such as Egypt just as easily discarded Soviet support and instead invited U.S. military advisers following the accession of Anwar Sadat, as they were willing to act as independent power brokers. The principal U.S. outlier in the Middle East, Israel, time and again accepted Western aid while conducting independent-minded foreign policy. Regarding Arab nations, their control of large oil reserves gave them leverage with the superpowers.

Oil, however, would become a controversial issue as the Arab oil exporters' control of fuel affected the national interests in the North. In order to protect such a vital interest as oil, Western coalitions headed by the United States repeatedly intervened in the region, be it to grant naval protection on the major shipping lanes or to instrumentally support belligerents. Conflict in the Middle East, however, was not confined to the old enmity between Israeli and Arab. Iraq and Iran waged a war over predominance in the Persian Gulf region. Direct and indirect superpower involvement in any one of these localized conflicts ensured that the region would remain unstable. In this sense, the Cold War dynamic reinforced the conflictual tendencies of the Middle East.

The Road to Camp David

The Yom Kippur War of 1973 ended with another Israeli victory. As opposed to the earlier Arab-Israeli conflicts, the Egyptian offensive in the first phase of the war had actually forced the Israelis to give ground.

Encouraged by this development, Egyptian President Sadat felt that his country's success set it on an equal footing with Israel. Negotiations with the Israelis became a viable prospect. Sadat was prepared to extend diplomatic recognition to Israel. Bilateral visits by Israeli Prime Minister Menachem Begin and Sadat in 1977 laid the foundations for a Middle East peace process culminating in the conclusion of the Camp David Accords a year later. The Egyptian leap of faith proved worthwhile, ending almost thirty years of war with Israel. On the Israeli side, offers to return the Sinai Desert ensured further Egyptian cooperation. The Camp David Accords, however, did not resolve the Palestine question, which continued to haunt any settlement in the Middle East. Sadat had broken the united front of Arab hostility toward Israel. He paid for his courage with his life when an Islamist extremist assassinated him in 1981.

The Iranian Revolution and
the Birth of Modern Islamic Fundamentalism

A new dynamic in international relations, **Islamic fundamentalism** surfaced toward the end of the 1970s. Its birth in Iran sent tremors throughout the Middle East. Iran had a rich cultural history stretching back to ancient Persia. Following the overthrow of the socialist government after World War II, Shah Mohammed Reza Pahlavi returned, facilitated by a CIA-engineered coup, in August 1953. Iran was a bastion of pro-Western stability. Oil revenues financed the influx of Western capital, consumer goods, military advisers, expert personnel, and arms. Conversely, the strengthening of ties with the West, especially the United States, led to social stratification and popular dissent with the shah's regime, perceived as a threat to traditional Islamic values. Historically, Iranian Islam was predominantly Shiite (as opposed to the prevalent Sunni denomination), which looked upon secular government and opulence with hostility. Between the early 1950s and late 1970s, the shah's autocratic regime served the United States in containing communism and retaining stability in the region. During the 1970s, however, the shah encountered more and more domestic opposition to his foreign policy.

A repressive government aimed at modernization in Iranian society, as well as an erosion of traditional Islamic values, provoked a broad popular resistance centered on Shiite religious leaders. The secret police and army crushed dissent to no avail. The greatest of the Iranian imams—Islamic religious teachers—was Ayatollah Ruhollah Khomeini. He had been exiled in 1964 but had continued to preach against the shah from a new home in Paris. At first, Khomeini's dissenting voice was scarcely heard. But with the onset of renewed popular unrest in 1978, and the resurgence of Islamic values as a focal point of opposition to the shah's pro-Western regime,

Khomeini and his disciples became the engine that fueled and militarized Islamic resistance. Rising tensions spilled into the streets as demonstrators gathered in Tehran. The shah lost his nerve, not knowing whether he could rely on the army to put down an open revolt. In January 1979, the Pahlavi family fled the country, creating a vacuum for Khomeini and his followers to fill.

Remembering the fate of the socialist government, the insurgents—religious and secular—took steps to prevent outside intervention in support of the shah. Thousands of royalists were killed in a purge that cleared the administration, army, judiciary, and economy of Pahlavi supporters. As Iranian demands for the shah's extradition went unheeded, a militant faction of Islamic fundamentalists stormed the U.S. embassy in Tehran in November 1979 and kidnapped the diplomatic staff. The move was received with popular acclaim in Iran. In order to entrench his own position, Khomeini's party, which had come out on top in the revolution, openly supported the embassy kidnappers; more than fifty hostages were held in Tehran for 444 days.

Events in Iran struck a deep chord in the United States. A few short years separated the collapse of the U.S.-supported South Vietnamese government and the panicky flight of U.S. personnel from Saigon from the Iranian revolution and the hostage crisis. Like the Soviets in Afghanistan, Jimmy Carter's administration failed to respond decisively against Islamic militants, which seemed to highlight a diminution in U.S. power. Not until Reagan took office were the hostages finally set free; the United States implemented a trade embargo against Iran. But Khomeini consolidated the gains of revolution by demonizing the United States as the principal enemy of Islam. He and the hard-line clergy rebuilt the state on the basis of Islamic values: *shari'a* (Islamic religious law) courts became the highest judicial authority in the country and followed the draconian codes outlined in the law. A militia composed of Islamic fundamentalists, styled as the Revolutionary Guards, rounded up and destroyed the vestiges of troops loyal to the shah as well as any internal opposition.

The revolution in Iran challenged the mighty West and wrested power from its client, the shah. Shiites in Muslim countries began to turn toward Khomeini for guidance and leadership. The final victory of the Shiite clergy in Iran, and the foundation of a religious state in accordance with the teachings of the Koran, proclaimed the advent of a new political force in international relations: Islamic fundamentalism. Neither East nor West had in the end gained influence in Iran. Khomeini challenged East and West, denouncing both as the unholy enemies of the one true religion. Out of this challenge grew an understanding between the United States and the Soviet Union that under no circumstances could the superpowers permit the Iranian revolution to move beyond national borders. Otherwise, Islamic fundamentalism would galvanize millions of Shiites throughout the Middle East and destabilize the entire region. Events, however, embroiled Iran in a deadly war with its Arab neighbor, Iraq.

The Iran-Iraq War

Khomeini's rise to leadership in the Shiite community did go beyond the boundaries of Iran and thus posed a direct threat to any other ruler governing over a Shiite minority or, even worse, a Shiite majority. Iran's powerful contender in the area was Iraq. Ruled by a socialist party under Baathists, Iraq always looked across the Persian Gulf with suspicion. Iran was the ancient enemy of all Arabs, even though both peoples shared the same religion after the seventh century. Circumstances decreed that a number of Shiites had settled in modern Iraq, which confronted Saddam Hussein, the undisputed leader of the Baathists, with the unpalatable prospect of facing eventual religious opposition in his own ranks masterminded from Tehran.

The upheaval in Iran furnished Hussein with the perfect opportunity to improve the position of Iraq. As in Iran, one of the major Iraqi exports was oil. The main thoroughfare for oil exports was controlled by whoever was in possession of the Shatt el Arab, a strategically important site located near the confluence of the Euphrates and Tigris Rivers. A long-standing dispute over the exact border between Iran and Iraq erupted anew as the Baathists claimed that the last treaty, which dated from 1975 and granted Iran extensive rights over the Shatt, had been forced upon the Iraqis. Hussein was determined to rectify what he believed to be a blatant injustice and accordingly used the question of legitimacy regarding the Shatt dispute as a pretext to attack Iran's source of wealth: the nearby oil fields and the ports of Abadan and Khorramshar.

Hussein's principal objective in war was the destruction of the religious hegemony established by the Iranian revolution. He wanted to assume a position of leadership in the Arab world and felt threatened by the rise of Khomeini. To the Iraqis, undisputed possession of the Shatt was a matter of political prestige, as well as economic gain. In September 1980, Iraqi troops invaded Iran. The first month of the advance was the only Iraqi success during the entire war. Masses of poorly armed Iranian soldiers forced the numerically inferior but better-equipped Iraqi army to a standstill. Significant numbers had flocked to the Iranian banner, as Khomeini proclaimed a *jihad*—a religious war—against the Iraqi infidels. In 1982, the Iranians launched an offensive that resulted in the capture of some 60,000 Iraqi combatants and the recovery of territory previously conquered by Iraq. Following the Iranian initiative, the war dragged on, culminating in a bilateral cessation of hostilities under the aegis of the United Nations in 1988.

The Iran-Iraq War was attended by several extraordinary circumstances. A multiplicity of states peddled arms to either or both sides during the war, artificially prolonging the conflict. In addition, hostilities were conducted with excessive brutality, including massive suicide attacks by the numerically superior Iranians and the use of poison gas on the part of the Iraqis. In the wake of the war, a rebellion by Kurds in northern Iraq was suppressed in a ruthless campaign of terror, reaching a tragic climax in the gassing of an entire town by Saddam. In the aftermath of the Iran-Iraq War, the high death toll became apparent. Each side had lost approximately 1 million dead. Iran's and Iraq's economies had suffered crippling damage. The survivors of the war were Saddam Hussein and his Baathist regime, and Khomeini's Islamic revolution. By the late 1970s, the Middle East had become one of the most unstable regions in the world.

Latin America

In contrast to other regions affected by structural changes in the international system, divisions established by the Cold War during the 1950s and 1960s in Latin America over indigenous conflicts—especially the struggle for social justice and evenhanded distribution of land—largely persisted into the 1970s. By and large, the same mechanism designed to safeguard U.S. interests in the Western Hemisphere was still in place: anticommunist governing elites inclined to maintain the political status quo were eligible for U.S. support. Any attempt to change the social and political order in favor of a socialist or communist government in a Latin American state was treated with suspicion by the United States and was likely to be nipped in the bud.

The Civil War in El Salvador

As in most other Latin American states, a clique of wealthy landowners dominated El Salvador, the smallest and most densely populated Latin American state. Although the Salvadoran economy was well placed to expand due to its large workforce, it did not generate the wealth necessary to increase prosperity and political stability. Many workers were forced to migrate into adjacent states. Historically, El Salvador had been governed by a long succession of *juntas* that acted in alliance with the landowning oligarchs to retain control over the country. Since El Salvador's inception, 100 governments have ruled, lasting an average of about eighteen months. A communist peasant uprising in 1931 was brutally repressed; a year later, thousands of insurrectionists were murdered. Since that rebellion and until 1980, Salvadoran presidents were selected from among the ranks of the army. The 1931 rebellion furnished a blueprint for future generations in the struggle against social injustice and reinforced the tradition of agrarian violence. This is not surprising given the economic and political demography of El Salvador: approximately 90 percent of the peasants do not own any land, and about half of all arable land remains in the possession of the *latifundistas*.

El Salvador shares with neighbors a geographic proximity to the United States. As such, El Salvador was considered to be in the backyard of the United States, especially during the Cold War. Apprehensions of a communist-inspired takeover shaped U.S. perceptions of Salvadoran politics. Thus, the United States supported successive coalitions of oligarchs and the military. In 1969, government troops won a victory over neighboring Honduras. There, hostilities had broken out as Salvadoran guest workers began rioting following the defeat of their team in a game of soccer against the host country. A second match stirred more civil unrest, which compelled the Honduran government to deploy regular forces to quell the spreading riots. Salvadoran armed forces successfully retaliated after Honduran units crossed the border into El Salvador. The Hondurans claimed that the Salvadoran air force had attacked several cities. Victory in the so-called Soccer War galvanized the Salvadoran *junta* and strengthened its stranglehold on government.

Following the Soccer War with Honduras, the governing Salvadoran right-wing party was challenged by a reformist segment of the middle class under the leadership of Jose Napoleon Duarte. During the 1972 elections, Duarte beat the *junta* candidate but never gained the reins of power. The *latifundistas* and the military were loath to allow Duarte the possibility of instituting land reforms. Duarte was arrested, tortured, and finally banished. The worldwide economic crisis brought about by OPEC's 1973 oil embargo, the resulting rise in the price of oil, and an escalation of government terror fanned the flames of revolution. The appearance of right-wing death squads heightened social tensions. Guerrilla activity spread across the country and assumed the proportions of a civil war. An offshoot of the wider civil war was the so-called Dirty War conducted by the death squads against political opposition. With the murder of archbishop Oscar Romero in 1980, it reached a high tide.

Duarte's return from his Venezuelan exile in late 1979, through a coup that placed him alongside a reformist *junta* in power, did little to ameliorate civil strife. Despite some U.S.$55 million in aid from the United States, Duarte proved unable to broker a settlement with a new and unified guerrilla opposition, the Frente Farabundo Martí para la Liberación Nacional (FMLN). The steady stream of arms, funds, and military advisers from the United States offset significant gains made by the FMLN. After 1984, when Duarte was reelected under chaotic circumstances, talks with the armed opposition on the left and the right were reopened but soon stagnated.

Duarte's most powerful constitutional opponent, the conservative party, the Alianza Republicana Nacionalista (ARENA), won the elections of 1988 amid continued skirmishes among government troops, the FMLN, and the death squads. The new president, Alfredo Cristiani, proved no more successful than his predecessor in ending the protracted civil war, which had cost more than 70,000 lives by 1990.

Under Ronald Reagan, the United States pressured Salvadoran governments to democratize the country's political system and institute land reforms. Reagan's government spent U.S.$6 billion throughout the 1980s to achieve this. The U.S. investment finally paid dividends when the Salvadoran army was subordinated to civilian control in 1992. On 1 February 1992, an armistice ended hostilities between the two sides and was followed up by a decommissioning of the guerrilla forces. Another ARENA candidate, Armando Calderon Sol, succeeded Cristiani in 1994. Meanwhile, the death squads continued to eliminate exponents of the political left. Sol, despite promises to the contrary, has not included any candidates of the opposition in his government. Only time will tell if the tensions of the conflict between the haves and have-nots in El Salvador will divide the country in yet another round of civil war.

Military Rule in Argentina

In many ways, the political histories of Chile and Argentina are mirror images. The principal difference is the marked absence of continued or direct U.S. intervention. After 1945, Britain was the principal foreign power and investor in Argentina. Covering an enormous amount of territory, Argentina was parceled into many ranches owned by a *latifundista* elite. In the early twentieth century, this oligarchy enjoyed almost all the privileges and was kept in power by way of an unholy alliance with the military. Growing discontent did not manifest in the countryside, as in many other Latin American states, but rather in urban centers, where workers demanded a share in the national wealth. The principal threat to the ruling elite emanated from recently risen middle classes, which were hostile to the objectives of workers in the cities. Elections placed the middle-class Radical Party in power in 1916. A military coup in 1930 signaled a return to dictatorship.

By 1943, the army had assumed power. Colonel Juan Peron, who was entranced with the achievements of national socialism, headed the ruling *junta*. By bringing the military and disenfranchised urban workers to establish a new interest group, Peron gained popular acclaim and support. He also stifled the only potential opposition in the country. In 1955, Peron's fortune suffered a downturn, as the economy was in the grip of a crisis that had begun six years earlier, and his appeal lost much of its strength with the death of his wife, Evita. In September 1955, Peron was forced to leave the country following a military coup. Until his return to government in 1973, Argentina was ostensibly ruled by a succession of democratically elected presidents who in reality harkened to the sinister forces of the military, which remained in the background. In 1974, a few months into his second tenure, Peron passed away. Despite the popular appeal that the deceased president's second wife, Isabel Martinez de Peron, could harness, the Peronists did not last long in office, and the government was toppled by the military in 1976.

The Falklands War.   Again, the *junta* struck Argentina's feeble democratic system a heavy blow: in March 1976, the most repressive and brutal of all Argentine military cliques seized power. Over the next few years, thousands of civilians were seized, tortured, and "disappeared." Argentina's own Dirty War may have killed 30,000; exact figures remain unavailable. Beset by serious economic problems, the leader of the *junta*, General Leopoldo Galtieri, turned to adventurism in foreign policy to distract domestic discontent. Since the early nineteenth century, Argentina had claimed possession of a number of otherwise insignificant offshore islands known as the Falkland, or Malvinas, Islands. The Falklands, however, were a British possession, and their inhabitants refused to contemplate a change of government—especially if the new government was that of Argentina.

In April 1982, Argentine troops occupied the Falklands. Had Galtieri read the British government correctly, he probably would have avoided an invasion of British territory. Margaret Thatcher, the British prime minister, had a confrontational style in British domestic politics and was known for her determination. A hawkish British parliament rendered the nature of British countermeasures a foregone conclusion. U.S. attempts to settle the Argentinean-British conflict peacefully were in vain. In May, a British submarine sank an Argentine battle cruiser on its way back to the mainland: 386 sailors died in the attack. British vessels were destroyed with European high-tech weapons of the latest design. The best-known case was the Argentine attack on the British destroyer *Sheffield* with French-made Exocet missiles. By mid-June, it was all over, as the professional soldiers of the British army overran Argentine positions on the Falklands and recaptured Port Stanley. The Galtieri *junta* subsequently paid a heavy price for evoking nationalist sentiments and failing popular expectations. Argentina's defeat in the Falklands War reopened opportunities for a return to civilian government.

Raúl Alfonsín of the middle-class Radical Party was at the helm after winning the 1983 elections. Although the economy went from bad to worse under Alfonsín, the new president prosecuted the perpetrators of the Galtieri regime, three members of which were incarcerated. Continuing economic hardship led to the defeat of the Radical Party at the polls in 1988 and the ascendancy of Peronist candidate Carlos Saul Menem. Alfonsín's accomplishments in the courts were diluted by Menem's willingness to make concessions to the military. He issued an amnesty for the convicted members of the former military government. Officers who evidently had persecuted their political adversaries during the Dirty War of 1976–1982 were released. In an unprecedented move, Menem sought to curb the activities of trade unions, which hitherto had constituted one of the main pillars of the Peronist compact in Argentina's politics. This was only a first step in a general overhaul of the economy that culminated in the privatization of state-owned industries and the pursuit of a market economy.

The New Cold War International System

In this section we consolidate the thesis of the structural changes of the later 1960s and 1970s while also reviewing the new distribution of power in the international system. The shifts in the Cold War international system indicated that the superpowers increasingly came to experience limits to their power. Even though the superpowers retained the capability to influence international politics, secondary powers had closed the gap. This diffusion of power was responsible for a new configuration in the distribution of political power, as evidenced in the pentagonal international system. In other words, the international system by and large remained bipolar in terms of militarily power, whereas politically it tended toward multipolarity.

The conclusion one can draw is that the analysis of the international system as expressed in the pentagonal international system establishes a geopolitical redistribution of power effected by structural change and is illustrative of increasingly complex international relations.

The Impact of Structural Changes
on International Politics During the 1970s

How did U.S.-Soviet relations develop in the changing international system? First, the significance of military might was diminished. This was the result of the progressing strategic parity: neither superpower could hope for victory over the other in a military confrontation. Second, the resulting strategic stalemate led to a transition from standoff to détente, expressed through the successes in arms control. The conclusion of SALT I in May 1972 limited the number of nuclear delivery systems on both sides. In an international environment of competitive economics, Washington and Moscow were interested in cutting defense expenditures.

Third, domestic political factors tended to support improved and stable relations between the superpowers. Although domestic political compulsions were expressed in a variety of ways, they still corroborated an inclination for cooperation. For the Soviet Union, improved economic relations with the United States were desirable not only because of repeated crop failures but also because the Soviets required access to U.S. technology. In the absence of economic relations with the West, the Soviet Union faced the prospect of becoming utterly disconnected from the burgeoning market economy in the West. Soviet emphasis on defense spending impaired its competitiveness in all other sectors. A hiatus in the ongoing systems competition with the United States was critical for the implementation of agrarian and economic reforms in the Soviet Union: it was the only conceivable means by which the Soviet economy stood a chance to recuperate.

The case of the United States differed from that of the Soviet Union only in degree, as the U.S. Treasury could not bear the burden of exorbitant defense spending indefinitely. Domestic opposition to the war in Vietnam witnessed a dramatic surge in the early 1970s. Furthermore, the protest movement went hand-in-glove with growing congressional skepticism toward the U.S. military establishment. Tolerance for massive and unfettered military spending among U.S. constituents was waning.

Fourth, tensions within the Eastern and Western alliances grew parallel to domestic pressures. With increasing confidence, China repeatedly, if not persistently, challenged Soviet influence in Asia, and Henry Kissinger could exploit that to the U.S. advantage. Even so, the United States could no longer count on continued unqualified support from its European allies. Conflicting economic interests impaired U.S.-European relations, especially in defense. In the final analysis, superpower relations had become more complex than ever. Even though a conflict of interests persisted in relation to several policy issues in regional settings, economic and domestic pressures and incentives compelled the superpowers to seek settlement. The principal objective was no longer the expansion of a sphere of influence but rather the ensconcing of the prevailing status quo. This culminated in a variety of results in different regions.

Concerning Europe, the official recognition of the German postwar boundaries by the West, as well as guaranteed Western access to Berlin by the Soviet Union, was initiated by a succession in German government, that is, when Willy Brandt took office. Brandt policy marked a departure from the orthodoxy of German politics as practiced by his predecessors in that it reneged upon an earlier commitment to German reunification in the short term. This decisive policy shift allowed for West Germany's rapprochement with East European states and with the Soviet Union.

Overall, shifts in the distribution of power in the international system had a positive effect for Europe. The control of the superpowers over their alliances decreased so as to accelerate multilateral stabilization within the European security system. This result, however, was entirely in accordance with earlier intentions of the superpowers, which had supported this sort of approach since the early 1960s. The new distribution of power therefore created a set of circumstances in which Europe gained political leverage and maneuverability, which could be transformed into a novel potential for leadership in world politics—especially in economics. In order to maintain its internal stability, as well as to represent its interests in global politics successfully, Europe found itself confronted with the requirement of accelerating the pace of economic and political integration.

Another effect of structural change was the U.S. opening to China. President Richard Nixon surprised the world by visiting Beijing. For the first time since the communist victory of 1949, a U.S. president visited China. The impact of the meeting on the international community was tremendous. Sino-U.S. relations improved at the very moment that the Sino-Soviet rift was deepening to a degree where a military confrontation between the two communist powers seemed imminent. In the context of Sino-Soviet-U.S. triangular relations, the two communist powers were, to a degree, compelled to take their cues from the United States. Otherwise, the recalcitrant member of the Eastern bloc was faced with the prospect of isolation in Asia due to the cooperation of one communist power with the United States. In the act of opening up to China, Nixon correctly identified the means by which the United States could maintain a balance of power in Asia and render the withdrawal of U.S. troops from Vietnam politically viable.

China, in turn, was interested in improving relations with the United States to check Soviet influence in Asia following U.S. withdrawal from Vietnam. In order to curb Soviet ambitions in that area, China required an understanding with Washington. In addition, China could hope for a better standing in the international community by binding itself closer to the United States. For example, China's admission to the United Nations followed the initial stages of U.S. rapprochement in 1971. Finally, China, not unlike the Soviet Union, required access to U.S. technology. Thus, the observation that the general trend toward multipolarity also held true for Asia is validated.

Looking at the Middle East, the United States proved capable of sustained involvement there as well. Although U.S. influence in the Middle East was not comparable to that in Europe and Asia, it was significant. The Arab-Israeli peace process involving Israel, Egypt, and Syria in the aftermath of the Yom Kippur War of 1973 can serve as an example. The United

States was the nexus of peace talks. In contrast to Asia, in the Middle East—the world's greatest repository of crude oil—the superpowers' vital interests were at stake. This meant that a regional conflict could quickly lead to global confrontation. U.S. decisionmakers, however, proved capable of pursuing and maintaining their interests in the region by way of implementing a dexterous policy. This is probably also true because the United States carefully combined military and economic tools of power in the region, which accorded it a greater leverage to pursue political ends than if it had utilized unfettered military power, as the Soviets were wont to do.

Nevertheless, events moved the United States to avoid continuing its unilateral support for Israel. Until the outbreak of the Yom Kippur War, the United States had acted in accordance with the theory that the Arabs would not dare attack Israel as long as Israel's military capability outmatched that of any other state in the region. Repeated U.S. weapons deliveries to Israel ensured this military imbalance in the region. At the same time, the United States thereby enabled the Soviets to approach Arab states with offers of support, which in turn permitted the Soviets to expand weapons sales and, implicitly, Soviet influence in the Middle East. Moreover, the Egyptian attack on Israel that precipitated the Yom Kippur War proved that Arab states would initiate hostilities *even if* Israel was militarily superior. Finally, the course of the Yom Kippur War demonstrated that Arabs were capable of exerting pressure on the entire international community through their stranglehold on crude oil resources. In terms of coordinating and implementing the oil embargo, Arab solidarity was impressive and culminated in mounting tensions between Europe and the United States. At the close of the Yom Kippur War, the United States was no longer able to continue its policy of exclusive support for Israel. In light of these new circumstances, Washington faced the requirement of acting as honest broker in the region.

In summary, the structures of the international system underwent change in a variety of ways in the wake of World War II. On the one hand, change in the international system was not easily discernible because it was a long-term process. On the other hand, the bipolar system of the Cold War acted as a disciplining force against the agencies of change. In the late 1960s and early 1970s, the Vietnam War rendered change in the international system visible. With increasing clarity, observers were able to make out a move away from the bipolarity of the Cold War toward the multipolarity of a newly shaped and continuously changing international system. In the early 1970s, the harbingers of the approaching end to the Cold War were duly noted. Nevertheless, more than a decade would pass before the Cold War drew to a close.

IR Theory and Key Concepts

The Globalist Paradigm

As opposed to realist and idealist paradigms and their intellectual successors (pluralism and liberalism), a widely accepted definition of globalism highlights its different nature by emphasizing the significance of economics, in particular capitalist relations of dominance and exploitation, over politics and military power in international relations. Despite the evident Marxist and neo-Marxist heritage of globalism, not all who subscribe to this school of thought are to be understood as being Marxist in their outlook. Globalism postulates two key theses. One is known as dependency theory. Irrespective of whether dependency theory is interpreted within the frameworks of Marxist or other paradigms, it is essentially understood to comprise a critical element of the globalist perspective. The second tenet of globalism is that international relations are best interpreted within the framework of the capitalist-world-system.

North-South Relations

The terms "North" and "South" are used to describe the economic divide between the wealthy industrialized countries of the Northern Hemisphere (the first world and second world) and the global poorhouse in the Southern Hemisphere (the third world). Some who have come to use the North-South concept and nomenclature consider the former Soviet Union and the countries of the former Eastern bloc in Central and Eastern Europe to be North states. A majority, however, prefer the orthodox usage of the terminology, which exclusively designates Western Europe, Japan, and North America as the North. Key issues in the debate on North-South relations center on how the extreme divide can be ameliorated and to what extent the North is bound to aid the South.

Core-Periphery Relations

Many dependency theorists refer to the first world, or the industrialized countries in the global political economy—Japan and the countries in Europe and North America with advanced industrial or postindustrial economies—as the core. Alternatively, core is also used to describe elites in any given society. The periphery contains developing or less developed states and even regions of Africa, Asia, and Latin America. Relations between these two elements represent core-periphery relations. According to the dependency school of thought, cores dominate peripheries. Core states are economically and politically dominant. Normally, Europe, North America, and Japan are considered to be the core regions in the international system. A derivate of dependency theory, world systems theory linked the idea of periphery to the early development of capitalism in Europe. As the main supplier of cost-effective labor and raw materials, the periphery plays a significant but inferior role in the worldwide capitalist division of labor. With the spread of the capitalist system, formerly isolated countries that had previously formed a core or part of one were degraded to semiperipheral or even peripheral status. As the term *semiperiphery* implies, students of the capitalist world system believe that such states and regions have been positioned in a halfway house, being clearly part of neither a core nor a periphery. Semiperipheral states are involved in a variety of economic and other activities, some of which bear the hallmark of a core, whereas others are indicative of the periphery. Usually, semiperipheral states serve as a fallback option for investors, for example, when wages and, implicitly, production costs in the native core are on the rise. As suggested above, semiperipheral states may originally have belonged to either core or periphery, or such states may be going through the transition in either direction. Core-periphery relations are always hierarchical due to a structure of unequal exchange (the globalist priority) or unilateral dominance (the realist priority).

Critical Theory

Critical theory is a social theory linked to the German Jürgen Habermas of the Frankfurt School. At the core of this theoretical work was a paradigm of social reality rooted in the dialectic of knowledge and power. Critical theorists postulated a theory that all approaches to knowledge—in fact all knowledge—are fundamentally historical and political. Contemporary heterodox elements in the field of international relations are drawing on various works of critical theory, for example, those by Antonio Gramsci and on Ludwig Wittgenstein (linguistics and hermeneutics), as well as that of post-structuralists such as Michel Foucault. Critical theory challenges the stated and unstated assumptions and alleged objectivity of canonical social science. Critical theorists have singled out ideological and other vested interests that appear to be, or rather are presented as, theories. To critical theorists, suspect theories stand out in that they pretend to be objective perspectives of social and political reality. Basically, critical theorists do not subscribe to any belief in objective or logical positivism. To them the rigid separation of normative and empirical theory is artificial. Moreover, according to critical theorists, what we think we know is in truth a function of language and social and political context. Critical theory advocates an interpretative understanding of perceived reality, a notion originating in Max Weber's work in social science and methodology.

Key Terms
- linkage and triangular diplomacy: The concept of linkage derives from U.S. President Richard Nixon's policy of making the initiation of strategic arms negotiations dependent upon success in the bilateral discussions on political issues with the Soviet Union. But Nixon met stiff domestic resistance from two groups: the arms controllers, whose first objective was the constraining of the arms race; and the Kremlinologists, whose agenda emphasized support of Soviet moderates and the obstruction of Soviet hard-liners. Linkage policy proved successful, as the Soviets were encouraged to negotiate by the U.S. opening to China. This dramatic move in the political context of the Cold War in the late 1960s became the crucial element of U.S. strategy toward the Soviet Union. Misguided by firmly entrenched ideological precepts, U.S. policy and decisionmakers had previously overlooked the potential represented by a Sino-Soviet split. Conversely, a clear and present danger to the West was vested in Soviet fears of China, which led the Soviets to interpret any Sino-U.S. rapprochement as a serious threat to the Soviet Union. Thus, the U.S. opening toward China also held the risk of escalating tensions between the United States and the Soviet Union. The importance of reassessing the nuances of the triangular relationship between the Soviet Union, the United States, and China was at last understood. In the final analysis, China and the Soviet Union shared an increasingly hostile rivalry but were less antagonistic toward U.S. overtures. This situation gave the United States a significant opportunity to build more or less stable relations with the communist powers while also debunking the myth of a monolithic communist bloc. U.S. policy proved highly efficient in that China

reestablished relations with the West. Its motive, however, was fear of Soviet aggression rather than a genuine interest in improving relations with the United States: China sought a new ally to balance the threat represented by its old one. Triangular diplomacy eroded the rigid edifice of the bipolar political system and initiated the shift toward multipolarity in the international Cold War system.

- pentagonal system: In the 1960s and early 1970s, the international system underwent change. The proliferation of actors altered the face and the nature of international relations. The pentagonal system constitutes a model to explain this systems change. The key actors in the pentagonal system were the United States, the Soviet Union, Europe, Japan, and China. The politico-military component of the pentagonal system was vested in the Sino-Soviet-U.S. trilateral relation, whereas the United States, Japan, and Europe achieved the most powerful and advanced economic cooperation. In any event, only the United States was both economically and politically and militarily powerful enough to participate in both components of the pentagonal system. For this reason, the United States, by virtue of its nodal position at the heart of pentagonal relations, can be said to have assumed a hegemonic role in the international system.

- détente: Détente is the reduction or relaxation of existing tensions in bilateral or multilateral relations, for example, between two states in the international system. Détente especially meant the easing of superpower tensions in the Cold War international system of the late 1960s and 1970s.

- interstate war, civil war, guerrilla warfare, and terrorism: Armed conflict between two states is referred to as interstate war; intrastate war describes the condition of armed hostilities between two or more groups within a state. Since antiquity, guerrilla warfare has served insurgents against incumbents; it is the one strategy permitting a weaker party to strike against, and undermine, the powers that be. A distinct feature of guerrilla warfare is the fact that its nature is primarily political, whereas its military operations act as an adjunct tool in the overall strategy. Guerrilla movements depend on the successful rallying of popular support against unpopular governments or foreign forces of occupation. Step by step, guerrillas seek to supplant incumbent governments and their branches by setting up a countergovernment. By retaliating militarily, official governments frequently create a reservoir of resentment in the local population, which the guerrillas exploit to legitimize their political war and justify their military operations. As a military strategy, terrorism has a long and well-established tradition dating to the Roman occupation of Palestine during the first century. Its primary objective is to strike fear into the hearts of the enemy by overt acts of violence. Definitions of terrorism vary widely. Any definition of terrorism depends on the point of view of the observer. In this case, the dictum "one man's freedom fighter is another man's terrorist" holds true.[1] The following two definitions of terrorism, one issued by a foreign ministry, the other by a judicial agency, are intended to illustrate this point: (1) "Terrorism is premeditated, politically motivated violence perpetrated against noncombatant targets by subnational groups or clandestine state agents"; and (2) "Terrorism is defined as the unlawful use of force or violence against persons or property to intimidate or coerce a government, the civilian population, or any segment thereof, in furtherance of political or social objectives."[2]

- imperialism: John A. Hobson (1858–1940) and V. I. Lenin (1870–1924) articulated their own conceptions of imperialism. Hobson's theory of imperialism is based on the assumption of an international hierarchical division of labor between wealthy and poor regions of the world. Comparatively, however, the relation between these regions is not mutually beneficial or advantageous. According to Hobson, capitalist societies were confronted with three interlinked problems. First, overproduction of economies; second, underconsumption of workforces; and third, capitalists own oversavings. Due to the exploitation of the workforce, particularly through the maintenance of low wage levels, and through capitalist owners of production facilities, profits steadily increased while goods were overproduced. In order to counter the problem of overproduction and oversavings, the capitalist owners had to seek an outlet for their products. A new market was found in what is today known as the third world. The aggressive expansion of capitalist sales and investments culminated in imperialism. Lenin incorporated Hobson's twin concepts of underconsumption and overproduction as an explanation for capitalist expansion into overseas markets and unbridled colonialism. Lenin also borrowed the idea that imperialist policies were but a reflection of monopolies and finance capital, or the highest stage of capitalism, from Rudolph Hilferding (1877–1941), a German Social Democrat. Effectively, capitalism had evolved to such an extent that oligopolies and monopolies controlled the most important sectors of the economy, squeezing out or taking over smaller firms while milking domestic markets dry. The result was a compulsive requirement for capitalist expansion—a need to look elsewhere for investment and sales opportunities.

- less-developed countries, lesser-developed countries: Commonly situated in the third world, these are in most or all respects underdeveloped in comparison to Western industrialized nations.

The Second Cold War and the End of an Era, 1980–1991

THE HELSINKI CONFERENCE HELD IN 1975 MARKED THE HIGH TIDE OF DÉTENTE. After 1975, the fluid processes of détente gave way to a hardening of attitudes along the old bipolar fault lines. Relations between the superpowers deteriorated especially quickly and culminated in the Second Cold War. But gone was the relative stability of the 1950s. Instead, the pace of change accelerated in the 1980s to culminate in the dissolution of the Soviet Union, a series of Eastern European revolutions, and the reunification of Germany in the three years between 1989 and 1991.

The reasons for the resuscitation of the Cold War in the late 1970s are manifold. First, the qualitative improvement and stockpiling of a new generation of nuclear weapons continued unhindered in the years following the conclusion of the 1972 SALT I and ABM Treaties. Under SALT I the superpowers agreed to limit the number of their ICBMs. The ABM Treaty forbade the implementation of all but two defensive systems designed to neutralize incoming nuclear missiles. The subsequent SALT II Treaty introduced an even lower ceiling of 2,400 intercontinental systems for each side respectively and included limits on Soviet and U.S. strategic aircraft. However, in accordance with the stipulations of SALT II, 1,320 of the 2,400 intercontinental systems could be equipped with multiple warheads, called **multiple independently targetable reentry vehicles (MIRVs)**. Thus, the *qualitative* upgrading of nuclear arms with MIRVs opened the way to a renewed arms race.

Second, the failure of the U.S. Congress to ratify SALT II was tied to the Soviet invasion of Afghanistan in December 1979. Indeed, President Carter withdrew from the treaty and Congress postponed its ratification indefinitely. The fact that the Soviet Union had intervened in Afghanistan to prop up its socialist government reanimated old Cold War suspicions harbored by the United States. Toward the close of his tenure in office, Carter warned Leonid Brezhnev that the United States would protect its vital interests in the Middle East—by force of arms, if necessary. We now understand that the considerations that drove the Soviet Union to occupy Afghanistan—concern over the growth of Chinese influence in the Middle East; U.S. predominance in the Middle East; the rise to prominence of Islamic fundamentalism and its hold on millions of practicing Soviet Muslims—largely resulted from structural change in the international system. Soviet calculations—that the war in Afghanistan would not last long or cause detrimental effects for the Soviet Union in the wider world—badly backfired. Instead, the West, China, Iran, and Pakistan unequivocally condemned the invasion as an act of wanton Soviet aggression.

Third, the Second Cold War was fueled by intensified systems competition between East and West in the third world during the late 1970s. After Portugal divested from its African colonies in 1975, the Soviets rushed in to fill the vacuum. More often than not, the Kremlin furnished the newly independent African states with comprehensive military aid—a development reciprocated by the United States. Western fears were exacerbated by the presence of Cuban troops in Angola that were transported and supported by the Soviet Union. Increased involvement in the third world by Moscow through these new clients convinced many Westerners that the Soviets were still conducting an aggressive expansionist policy.

Finally, this chain of events led to the deepening of suspicion and estrangement between Moscow and Washington. On a personal level, relations between the superpower leaders were hampered by a lack of understanding and the turnover of incumbents. In the Soviet Union, the old guard dominated the Politburo. On the eve of the invasion of Afghanistan, Brezhnev had fallen terminally ill. His successors, Yuri Andropov and Constantine Chernenko, were both tired, superannuated men with little time left on their hands. The immediate consequence of turnover in the Soviet civilian leadership was the rise of the military's influence in foreign policy.

The West, especially the United States and Britain, reacted to the developments of the later 1970s by embracing a newly conceived and bellicose type of conservatism. In Washington, hawks decried President Jimmy Carter as a loser when he failed to substantiate earlier warnings on the Soviet invasion of Afghanistan. The protracted hostage drama in Iran following Islamic revolution there further undermined Carter's standing in domestic politics. Ineluctably, the moderation of Carter policy was presented in its worst possible light, which finally provoked a conservative backlash with far-reaching consequences for international relations in the 1980s. In 1981, President Ronald Reagan—the conservative's conservative— assumed office. Reagan's partisan rhetoric decried the Soviet Union as an "evil empire" in 1982 and called upon the West to decisively oppose Soviet expansionism.[1]

Reagan's position toward the Soviet Union was seconded by Margaret

Thatcher, the British prime minister since 1979, whose iron-fisted policies were steeped in economic deregulation and the ambitious foreign political enterprise of making Britain great again. Thatcher was the quintessential expression of British reactionary conservatism informed by the nation's imperial past. The prime minister proceeded to bring domestic opposition to heel with steely determination; she broke the power of the trade unions and attempted to bring Britain out of economic and political stagnation by the implementation of neoliberalist laissez-faire legislation and increased defense spending. Reagan and Thatcher polarized Western opinion and came to personify the reaction to détente.

The Euroatlantic
The first signs of renewed Cold War tensions and an intensification of the arms race surfaced during Jimmy Carter's term in office (1977–1981). Ronald Reagan's assumption of the presidency and the reactionary mood of the West contributed to rising tensions between the superpowers. The arms race of the 1980s came to serve as a substitute for a violent resolution of divergent positions. Military expenditures signaled the determination of each side to protect its interests. This development may also serve to signal the principal structural change in the international system: the increasing importance of economic power and the relative decline of military power. Superpower spending was a demonstration of potency.

The Renewed Arms Race
Even though SALT II was never ratified, Reagan and the Soviet leadership were careful to abide by its stipulations limiting the number of intercontinental weapons systems. Instead, the superpowers focused their competition on IRBMs. For their part, the Soviets modernized IRBMs, rapidly exchanging the older SS-4 and SS-5 missiles for the improved SS-20. With a range of 5,000 kilometers and the ability to be MIRVed, the SS-20 was in a league of its own. Significantly, the Soviets directed their efforts at producing the SS-12 and SS-23 with ranges of up to 1,000 kilometers, allowing them to target Western Europe from behind the Iron Curtain.

Soviet advances in IRBM technology posed an immediate threat to Western Europe and confounded NATO, which had no weapon to match. West European leaders also feared a unilateral abandonment by the United States given Soviet IRBM superiority. Europe was again facing a crisis of confidence. The only possible countermeasure left to the United States in the event of a Soviet attack with IRBMs on Western Europe was an escalation on the strategic level. Demanding to know whether the United States was willing to risk nuclear war for the sake of Paris and Berlin following the Sputnik shock in 1957, heads of state clamored for a credible nuclear guarantee.

The U.S. response was voiced through NATO, which enacted the **double-track decision** in November 1979, proposing negotiations with the Soviets concerning arms reductions while threatening to station some 572 theater missiles in Western Europe in the event the Soviets refused. NATO sought to tackle the problem with a carrot-and-stick approach: either way, the West would regain parity with the East by the decommissioning of Soviet IRBMs or the commissioning of U.S. IRBMs. At first, the Soviet Union balked, hoping that a vigorous peace movement, which sprang up in Western Europe in the late 1970s, would create sufficient opposition to the deployment of U.S. theater missiles in Europe. Soviet designs, however, were thwarted by German Chancellor Helmut Kohl's determined campaign for the stationing of U.S. Pershing II and cruise missiles on German soil.

The shock of suddenly facing a militarily superior Soviet Union propelled the Western alliance into action. In 1983, Reagan presented the **Strategic Defense Initiative (SDI; also known as "Star Wars")**, an ambitious project to construct a protective shield capable of defending U.S. military installations, as well as civilian targets, from Soviet ICBM attack. According to Reagan, SDI would render nuclear weapons obsolete and open the way to disarmament. The reality behind SDI was quite different: in terms of the extant technology, SDI was not viable. This was not lost on the Soviet military. Conversely, SDI was also a tool of psychological warfare, as it intimidated the Soviets. The more practical aspects of Soviet apprehensions were trained on the convergence of U.S. financial and industrial potential united by the greater vision of SDI. In Washington, the prospect of a grand solution culminating in a peaceful world rendered accessible immense financial resources that would not have been available otherwise. In the eyes of many contemporaries, the escalation of the arms race in the early 1980s pointed to a new intensification of the Cold War. The decline of détente added to the impression that bipolarity again defined the structure of the international system. As is often the case, the future turned out to be different than expected.

The Success and Pain of European Integration
Throughout the 1970s and 1980s, Europe continued its economic integration. The emergence of the European Coal and Steel Community in 1951 and the establishment of the European Economic Community in 1957–1958 were early examples. The parallel development of the European Free Trade Association after 1960 was the partial result of Britain's reluctance to be drawn into the EEC dominated by France and Germany and Charles de Gaulle's refusal of British membership later in the decade. In

1972, Britain left EFTA, joining the EEC a year later. Henceforth, the importance of EFTA as a vehicle for European integration was on the decline.

The rise of the EEC.   As détente wound down to its ignominious conclusion beginning in the mid-1980s, the growth of the European Common Market and progressing regional integration became the success stories of the decade. Since 1957 and the signing of the Rome Treaties, European economic integration overcame Anglo-French rivalry in 1969 to expand its membership from the original six to include three new members—Britain, Denmark, and Ireland—by 1973. Though Norway remained aloof, the European Community added Greece (1981), Spain, and Portugal (both 1986) to its ranks, thus bringing membership to twelve. In March 1985, the heads of state of the EC projected the establishment of a single market until 1992, whereby all customs boundaries within the territory it covered would be eliminated. The Single European Act of 1987 stipulated an end to the unanimity proviso, or national veto, which had, for example, allowed de Gaulle to keep Britain out of the EEC in 1963 and 1969 and also hampered the EC's decisionmaking capability since. The EC's objective was beyond the scope of economic collaboration. The EC sought to promote the integration of Europe by gradually eroding boundaries that kept Europeans apart. The integrative policy enacted by the EC in the mid-1980s was an ambitious project, for it sought to subordinate national regulations governing finance and banking, national boundaries, transportation, and trade to supranational legislation. How had this dramatic change come about?

In part, a new generation of European leaders—no longer steeped in the traditional mores of nationalism and trade protectionism—was accountable for this progressive vision. As opposed to de Gaulle, and following a spell in the office of president of the EC Council of Ministers, François Mitterrand believed in the necessity of European integration. The German economy was the most productive on the Continent, and Chancellor Helmut Kohl realized that the single market would also be in the national interest. As the archcapitalist promulgator of deregulation, Margaret Thatcher advocated the scheme. Adding to this drive to deregulate was that many moderate European socialists had come to accept the utility of a free-market economy and by the 1980s even professed the belief that planned state economies were intrinsically problematic. In light of increasing competition against the U.S. and Japanese markets, the continuing integration of Europe—and its eventual transformation into a trade bloc—seemed appropriate.

In its quest for unity during the 1980s, the EC experienced several difficulties. Two issues became bones of contention, one financial, the other legal. The EC budget, paid for by members, caused much wrangling, especially in relation to the Common Agricultural Policy (CAP). CAP subsidies paid to European farmers reduced the annual budget by two-thirds. Moreover, the farming community produced what was known as butter mountains and wine lakes, that is, massive surpluses paid for by taxpayer money but lacking a market outlet. At the same time, food prices across Europe were higher than average prices set for non-EC economies.

Another problem was members' resistance to delegate sovereign power to EC headquarters in Brussels. To give but one example, Britain was divided over the question of democratic institutions within the EC. From the British point of view, the Brussels bureaucracy governed the EC, not any democratic institution. The Conservative British government was split over monetary union in the context of a single market. In general, Britain was reluctant as to European integration beyond closer economic cooperation.

Finally, a confluence of French and British apprehensions developed due to the dramatic expansion of Germany's economy. Since the first two postwar decades, when France sought to tie West Germany to a European strategic and economic framework, West Germany had developed into a self-confident, assertive, and expanding economic power, well on the way to assuming preponderance in Europe. In terms of economic output generated annually, Germany surpassed France and Britain by the mid-1980s and was approaching Japan and the United States. Would Germany's burgeoning economy place it in a position of leadership within the EC, and in the event of a closer political association, would Germany again come to dominate the Continent by virtue of its economic power? These questions and insecurities were shared by many EC member states and spilled into the next decade when economic integration would be superseded by the vision of political union.

The Beginning of the End: The Soviet Union in Crisis

At the center of events that changed the face of international relations at the end of the 1980s was a deep-seated economic crisis in the Soviet Union. Although it continued to assume the position of a superpower militarily, the Soviet economy had been gradually, but substantially, weakened. Structural changes and the pentagonal system had changed the face of international relations. And the new prominence of economic power as a defining characteristic in international relations put the Soviet Union out of business in a literal sense.

The Root Cause for the Decline of the Soviet Union

The collapse of the Soviet Union was economic in nature. At the heart of the problem was the Soviet Union's command economy. Put simply, Soviet economic policy since its inception had been to increase inputs (e.g., labor, capital, raw materials, and energy) to bolster production. Up to the 1960s, this formula resulted in an impressive growth rate, because Soviet planners before then were still en route to mobilizing the full potential of all available inputs. The problem with input-induced economic growth is that it is wasteful. By contrast, capitalist economies carefully consider the extent and type of inputs used and compensated by maximizing productivity, that is, efficient production of goods.

In the 1970s, as economic power rose to prominence, the Soviet input potential was employed to the limit; productivity stagnated. Industrial plants overdue for overhauls simply continued to produce goods of questionable quality using time-honored methods of inefficient production. Lacking the stimuli that exist in open-market economies, dependent upon a derelict traffic and transportation system, and distinguished only by pervading corruption, the Soviet Union began to fall behind the standards set by the international economy.

This long-term development resulted in budget shortages, which prompted Soviet economists to sound the alarm and the military to face defense cutbacks. The costly armaments program undertaken by the West was reciprocated by the Soviets, who had prioritized the expansion of their heavy industrial capabilities and had therefore failed to catch up with the demands set by the service and communications sectors. With increasing urgency, the Soviets required access to Western technology to cope with impending economic isolation. Finally, the maintenance of a Soviet military presence in Eastern Europe, as well as various Soviet military, economic, and consultative commitments in the third world, further sapped state finances. Thus, the Soviet outlay caused by an inefficient command economy, exacerbated by the Second Cold War, hastened the dissolution of the Soviet Union.

The War in Afghanistan

Soviet troubles in supporting a sprawling empire were first apparent throughout the third world, nowhere more so than in Afghanistan, where the Soviet army faced the consequences of imperial overextension. Since the invasion of 1979, which went ahead at the behest of Brezhnev and his closest advisers, the war against the mujahideen went from bad to worse. The Soviets spent billions of dollars annually to prosecute an increasingly futile conflict. The Islamic resistance fighters were in the main supplied by China and the United States and commanded an impressive high-tech arsenal that included devastatingly accurate ground-to-air Stinger missiles.

As a consequence, the 120,000 Soviet soldiers stationed in Afghanistan incurred heavy losses by the standards of the day. Some 15,000 men perished in fighting the mujahideen between 1979 and the

Soviet withdrawal a decade later; 37,000 were wounded during the war. The Politburo justified intervention in Afghanistan by referring to the Soviet Union's internationalist duty to support a fellow communist government and likened the conflict to that of the Red Army against the Nazi invaders during World War II. The returning soldiers, however, told a very different story to the public. Afghanistan veterans described demoralization and defection among the Soviet troops and heavy losses inflicted by the mujahideen.

Throughout the early 1980s, the war in Afghanistan was conducted with but one objective in mind: to gain control of the embattled rural areas and bring about ultimate victory. Victory, however, proved elusive. With the rise of Mikhail Gorbachev in 1985, a significant change in the conduct of the Soviet war took place. Gorbachev realized that the war was imposing an unbearable financial and human toll on the strained Soviet economy. His conclusion was simple: all Soviet troops had to be withdrawn, and the last chapter on the war in Afghanistan was to be closed as soon as possible. Moreover, Gorbachev was under pressure to satisfy the West in its bid to improve Soviet relations with the United States. Peace in Afghanistan became imperative.

At the same time, Gorbachev was not willing to countenance a dishonorable peace. The mujahideen were not willing to negotiate a compromise that would have allowed a communist regime to remain in power in Kabul. At first, Gorbachev emulated Richard Nixon's escalation of the war in Vietnam in 1972. The Soviet leader was hoping to crush the enemy before the Soviet withdrawal. The plan backfired for several reasons. First, the mujahideen were heavily armed and well-supplied. Second, the unrestricted pursuit of final victory demanded very high financial and human sacrifices, which a grumbling majority in power was no longer willing to make. Furthermore, the West would not look kindly upon a resumption of Soviet aggression.

Gorbachev finally agreed to withdraw all Soviet troops without any kind of settlement with the mujahideen. Conversely, he did seek a settlement with the United States. An agreement with Reagan—stipulating that both superpowers cease all direct or indirect support for their clients in Afghanistan—was signed in April 1988. By mid-August 1989, the last Soviet troops exited the country. In their wake, the Soviets left an Afghan communist government to its own devices. One million Afghans died as a consequence of the war; 2 million refugees were adrift within the boundaries of the state; and 5–6 million escaped into Pakistan. The country had been ravaged, and the capital had been bombarded by heavy artillery.

Hostilities in Afghanistan did not come to a close with the Soviet departure. Quite the opposite was the case: Shiites dominated the mujahideen, whereas most of the fighting men were Sunnis. In and of itself, the tense relations between the two Islamic traditions would have been sufficient to spark a major clash. What exacerbated the existing animosities was that both sides were backed by powers—Iran for the Shiites, Saudi Arabia for the Sunnis—that were themselves at loggerheads. Thus, after a decade of foreign occupation, Afghanistan was plunged into a protracted civil war.

Enter Gorbachev: The Advent of Perestroika and Glasnost

With the demise of Leonid Brezhnev in 1982, the last long reign of a communist leader came to a close. The Brezhnev era was succeeded by two short, quasi-interim tenures of former intelligence director Yuri Andropov (late 1982 to February 1984) and Konstantin Chernenko (1984 until his death a year later). Both Andropov and Chernenko were choices of convenience, satisfying the interests of the majority in the Politburo. The two men who succeeded Brezhnev also shared their advanced age. This circumstance may well have influenced the Politburo in its choice of the comparatively younger Mikhail Gorbachev as Chernenko's successor.

After Gorbachev was confirmed in his new office (general secretary of the Communist Party), he was quick to indicate that the general thrust of his policy would be directed by change in the political system of the Soviet Union. The first opportunity came in February 1985. A bewildered Central Committee and the Politburo were told that the Soviet Union stood in need of serious reform. Many members were Brezhnev's placemen and operated within the framework of the bygone era of patronage and the reward of sinecures. Resistance to reform would most likely arise from the ranks of conservative bosses, occupants of key positions, and upper echelons of the party apparatus—the *nomenklatura*—that wanted to protect privilege.

Gorbachev realized the pressing need for reforms at home. First of all, the Soviet leadership had to tackle an escalating domestic economic crisis. The prerequisite for any solution to this problem was the abandonment of Brezhnev's global politics, which had led to imperial overextension and an unbearable strain on the Soviet economy. In 1987, his ideas were published in a book entitled *Perestroika*. In the book, Gorbachev set forth his ideas on restructuring Soviet society. *Perestroika* entered the vocabulary of international relations as a byword for revolutionary change in a moribund political system whose economy was on the verge of collapsing. Indeed, this definition aptly described both the disease and the cure for the structural problems that had befallen the Soviet Union since the early 1970s. At the same time, Gorbachev fully realized that a sustainable reform of the economy would prove impossible without reforming Soviet rule. The complement for *perestroika*, also introduced by Gorbachev, was *glasnost,* that is, the need for transparency and open dialogue among the public at large about problems in the Soviet Union.

Glasnost was to take its first hurdle in 1986, when an atomic reactor in Chernobyl melted down. Even though it took Moscow almost three weeks to respond to the unfolding crisis in the Ukraine, which also affected Scandinavia and Western Europe, Gorbachev rose to the task and revealed the extent of the catastrophe, as well as the fact that it had initially been beyond the control of the authorities. His frankness, although belated, earned him the trust of large sections of the populace and an international audience. The Chernobyl incident also served Gorbachev to rid the party of conservative elements that actively sought to undermine *perestroika*. The old ways of restricting the dialogue to the *apparatchiks* was no longer acceptable, as it failed to address real and pressing problems. Gorbachev thus sought support from the people and the media and, once he obtained it, felt strong enough to oust the conservatives. During his first two years in office, Gorbachev introduced sweeping changes in the structure of the Communist Party. His reforms began to pay a small but significant dividend, allowing those who had hitherto been excluded a measure of participation in the political dialogue.

Economic transformation and political polarization. The major problem with Gorbachev's economic reform policies was that they were moderate approaches to problems that required decisive action. Gorbachev feared a backlash caused by the accelerated transformation of a socialist command economy into a fledgling capitalist market economy and the attendant issues affecting Soviet society and the cohesion of the Soviet Union. The consequences of an economic reform policy that was only hesitantly implemented did not take long to surface. In 1987, the restructuring of the Soviet economy, including the various initiatives to control economic input and increase productivity, resulted in a stark decline in the standard of living. Whereas staple goods had been available in some measure to the population in moderate quantities before, after Gorbachev's accession they grew scarce.

The political reality of the Soviet Union in its last years, however, did not permit Gorbachev much leeway for his plan of gradually implementing *perestroika*. In due course, the ensuing polarization over Gorbachev's reforms assumed a face or, rather, two faces. On the one hand, the second secretary, Yegor Ligachev, headed the conservatives in a bid to mitigate the impact of *perestroika* and was ultimately opposed to *glasnost*. Ligachev and his supporters represented the status quo ante. On the other hand, Gorbachev faced radical reformers under the leadership of the Muscovite head of party, Boris Yeltsin. To radical reformers, Gorbachev's handling of the reforms was neither effective nor far-reaching enough to be of any consequence in finding a workable solution for the Soviet Union's ailments.

The miscarriage of the 1987 attempt to institute some measure of economic independence (by introducing legislation curtailing the power of the central planning authorities) culminated in a disheartening setback for radical reformers. The failure of the Law of State Enterprises in 1987, however, convinced the radicals to push ahead. Essentially, much of Gorbachev's energy was taken up by maneuvering between the two sides. Ironically, it was Gorbachev who, quite inadvertently, blunted the reforms he sought to introduce.

The polarization within the Communist Party escalated in October 1987, when Yeltsin told an assembled Central Committee of the party that he would tender his resignation from the Politburo. Repeated accusations by Yeltsin against the powerful in the party prompted Ligachev to bring about his rival's downfall. By threatening to step down, Yeltsin placed Gorbachev in an impossible position by openly compromising the integrity of the Soviet Union's most important political decisionmaking body. Though he considered Yeltsin an ally, Gorbachev was left with no other choice than to put the radical in his place. Yeltsin was recalled from a hospital, where he was being treated for a heart ailment, and demoted in front of his native Muscovite party committee. Initially intending to placate the conservatives under Ligachev, Gorbachev had badly miscalculated in his attack on Yeltsin. Although Yeltsin disappeared from the political stage for a number of years, his return brought the Soviet Union crashing down.

The breakthrough at the arms control negotiations: domestic political stalemate.   Although Gorbachev faced stiff resistance domestically, in his foreign policy he outshined all his predecessors. His foreign policy triumph occurred in 1987, when he met U.S. President Ronald Reagan at Reykjavik, Iceland (an initial summit in November 1985 had gone awry over disarmament). The Reykjavik summit ended with a mutual agreement—the **Intermediate-Range Nuclear Forces (INF) Treaty** signed in 1987—to abolish two entire classes of nuclear missiles: short-range and intermediate-range. Both sides agreed to reduce approximately 30 percent of their respective nuclear warheads. The INF Treaty was a stabilizing force in superpower relations and became a symbol of mutual trust.

Liked in the West for his frank appearance and indefatigable advocacy for the need to create understanding between the Cold War antagonists, Gorbachev even elicited praise from British Prime Minister Margaret Thatcher: "I like Mr. Gorbachev—we can do business together."[2] Indeed, Gorbachev differed from his dour predecessors in that he seemed less restrained and more approachable. In that sense, he was the product of the Khrushchev era, unlike Brezhnev, Andropov, and Chernenko, who had been around during the Stalinist climate of fear. Yet it is important to understand that even though Gorbachev was a reformer, at heart he remained a socialist and never wavered in his conviction that the Soviet Union remain communist.

In the end, affability did not save Gorbachev from presiding over the final days of the Soviet Union. At the center of Soviet political structures, the Nineteenth Party Conference—the point of departure that would lead to revolutionary changes and break apart the Soviet Union into constituent republics—convened in Moscow in June 1988. There, Gorbachev made known his intention to initiate the separation of the party from the state. Furthermore, the Supreme Soviet was to be abolished and supplanted by a Congress of People's Deputies, its members to be elected in a moderately democratic fashion. These constitutional reforms might not appear to convey the fundamental changes in the Soviet political system, but in reality they ended the undisputed hegemony of the Communist Party in the state. This, however, was a midterm development and not immediately apparent. The confrontation between Ligachev and Yeltsin, in fact, overshadowed Gorbachev's announcements. Yeltsin, in an unprecedented oratory, criticized the slow pace of *perestroika* and denounced corrupt practices among the party hierarchy. Ligachev's rebuttal sounded hollow. Yeltsin's otherwise futile stand against the party apparatus was televised in the spirit of *glasnost* and had a significant impact on public opinion. Hitherto, public opinion had not counted for much in the decisionmaking processes of the Soviet Union. The dissemination of Yeltsin's attack returned him to center stage in politics, for it afforded him unparalleled public exposure and widespread popularity.

The East European Revolutions
and the Reunification of Germany

Gorbachev's top-down approach to reforming Soviet rule did have an impact on the member states of the Warsaw Pact. The introduction of *perestroika* and *glasnost* resulted in rapid delegitimization of communism in Eastern Europe. Gorbachev's reform policy was interpreted as an abnegation of traditional Soviet imperial claims. Between 1989 and 1991, there followed a chain reaction that resulted in the disengagement of communist Eastern Europe from Soviet domination.

Poland was the first Soviet satellite to break away. Discontent with the communist leadership and the declining standard of living in Poland gave rise to *solidarnosc* (solidarity) during the 1980s, a movement that had its roots in the heavy industry unions. In April 1989, *solidarnosc* was legalized and free elections were negotiated with the government for June 1989. Following the elections in August 1989, Tadeusz Mazowiecki was confirmed as the first noncommunist prime minister of Poland. During the same month, the regime of Janos Kadar was overthrown in Hungary; in October the single-party system was abolished and political opposition was legalized. By the end of 1989, two East European states had successfully overthrown communist rule. Shortly, East Germany, Czechoslovakia, Bulgaria, Romania, and Albania forced communist governments out of power. Meanwhile, the disintegration of communist rule in the historically independent-minded Yugoslavia constituted a drawn-out process that had as much to do with the rejection of communism as with ethnic tensions in an arbitrarily erected state.

As Soviet satellite regimes in Eastern Europe toppled like so many dominos by the end of the decade, the face of international relations was forever changed. For more than four decades the Iron Curtain had divided Europe. The changes in Eastern Europe were over in a matter of three years (1989–1991). The reverberations of the dissolution of the communist bloc could be felt on distant continents and its repercussions continued to impact policymaking for a decade. The sudden end of the Cold War had a significant effect on Europe not shared by any other region. Fundamental issues that remain important concerns today suddenly topped the European political agenda: Were Europe and its regions going to supplant the national state? How large ought Europe to be? Which states would be represented in what institutions? How should Europe deal with an economically and politically more powerful and reunified Germany and the new, territorially diminished Russian Federation that had risen from the ashes of the Soviet Union? Would historic rivalries between the Great Powers be resuscitated? In the final analysis, would the United States disengage from Europe in order to focus on the Pacific?

The Resurgence of Nationalism in Yugoslavia

While Gorbachev extracted the Soviet Union from Afghanistan and battled internal opposition in the Soviet Union, events in Eastern Europe, especially in the Balkans, were coming to a head. The death of Marshal Tito precipitated the disintegration of the Federal Republic of Yugoslavia, which in turn presaged a chain-reaction revolution that would lead to the collapse of the Soviet Union between 1989 and 1991. The Balkans were populated by a multiplicity of ethnicities, each of which possessed its own historic grievances. The "powder keg of Europe" is a fitting description. In terms of religion, the peoples of the Balkans were split between Christians and Muslims and, among Christians, between the Eastern Orthodox and Western Latin traditions.

This religio-ethnic makeup, compounded by a long record of internecine strife, endured into the twentieth century. The problems were not solved with the artificial construction of a federated republic consisting of the various southern Slav peoples in 1918. Imposed against their will, the new state united Slovenes, Croats, Bosnians, Herzegovians, Albanians, and Macedonians. At best, the foundation of Yugoslavia glossed over the historical, ethnic, and nationalist divides etched in collective memories. During World War II, the peoples of Yugoslavia split over whether to support the Axis or the Allies. The two dominant factions were made up of the Serb royalist Chetniks and the Croat fascist Ustasha. In terms of numbers, Serbs constituted the preponderant power within Yugoslavia. In the brutal civil war that held Yugoslavia in its grip throughout World War II, the Chetniks and the Ustasha were themselves defeated by the forces of ideology. Ultimately, communist partisans under Marshal Tito prevailed. Tito, a Croat, endeavored to limit Serb aspirations to hegemony within the southern Slav federation by tying them into a federal state in which no group could occupy a dominant position without uniting all others against it. This ambitious scheme, closely modeled on the precepts of the balance of power, worked out to Yugoslavia's benefit.

A reform implemented in 1974 devolving limited autonomy to the constituent republics of the federation revived Serb nationalism hitherto tempered by Tito's evenhanded rule. The death of Tito six years later hastened Serbia's pursuit for predominance in the Balkans. In the 1980s, legislators sought to forestall the breakup of the federation by introducing a series of constitutional amendments and by seeking a consensus on a completely new constitution. In addition, the Yugoslav economy was taking a serious plunge, soon experiencing unprecedented hyperinflation. Slobodan Milosevic became the head of the Serb Communist Party in 1987. Within two years, he successfully fomented nationalist dissent and provided an outlet for 1 million Serbs to commemorate a historic battle against the Turks in ethnic Albanian Kosovo. The Albanians of Kosovo are Muslims, their religion being a vestige and reminder of centuries of Ottoman occupation. Historically, Serbs always saw themselves as the principal bulwark of Christianity against the tide of Islam. Moreover, Milosevic envisioned the reestablishment of Serb hegemony in his idea for Greater Serbia, of which Kosovo had been a part in the distant past.

The reassertion of Serb nationalism in the late 1980s and the concurrent dissolution of the Soviet Union into its constituent republics frightened or inspired other member states in the Yugoslav federation. Milosevic's elimination of devolved government in the province of Kosovo ignited a series of protests that led to rioting and then insurgency against the Serb presence. The Serb's old rivals, the Croats, were stirring, as well. In Croatia, Serbs were persecuted; in Slovenia, the Communists were ousted. Between late 1990 and early 1991, the Serbs' bid to establish themselves as the preponderant power within the Federal Republic of Yugoslavia was no longer at stake; the future of the federation, however, was, for Slovenia and

Croatia were edging toward secession. By June 1991, both republics declared independence unilaterally. Slovenia's proximity to the West rescued it from civil strife. Serb troops, the dominant contingent in the Yugoslavian army, withdrew quietly from Slovenia while they attacked Croatia and its ramshackle militia. Surprisingly, the Croat militia fought the advancing Serb juggernaut to a standstill, losing only a minor portion of their newly independent country to the enemy. A diplomatic offensive sponsored by the European Union and the United States bought enough time for the United Nations to dispatch a multinational peacekeeping force to Croatia. For the moment, ethnic tensions and the threat of widespread hostilities in the Balkans seemed to have been averted. The Slovenian and Croatian secessions, however, were only the first step in a process that would culminate in the dissolution of the Federal Republic of Yugoslavia.

The Dissolution of East Germany and Reunification

What occurred in Yugoslavia in the late 1980s and early 1990s indicated a trend away from communism toward nationalism in Eastern Europe and the Soviet Union. East Germany had been the communist exemplar after its inception in 1949. Economically, it was doing better than its fellow socialist states within the Soviet sphere of influence in Eastern Europe. Its principal problem—the loss of its workforce due to mass emigration—had been temporarily solved by erecting the Berlin Wall and securing the borders in the early 1960s. But as the flight of East Germans to the West should have suggested, all was not well in East Germany. The austere socialism practiced first by Walter Ulbricht and, after 1971, by Erich Honecker alienated many East Germans. Dissent was held in check by an unscrupulous secret police, the Stasi (a contraction of the German compound Staatssicherheitspolizei), which employed some 85,000 agents, administrators, and functionaries. Denunciation of and spying on neighbors became a national pastime. Almost twelve miles of files on the opposition that came to light attest to the wide-ranging and highly questionable operations of the Stasi.

Though Honecker may have believed that the national economy was sufficiently productive, such was not the case. Throughout the 1970s and 1980s, East German economic output was in fact stagnating. Troubles began for East Germany when Hungary demolished its segment of the Iron Curtain on the border with Austria. At first, Gyula Horn, Hungary's foreign minister, had been in a quandary: would he adhere to the 1968 treaty with East Germany stipulating that East German citizens attempting to defect to the West were to be returned, or was he to honor the more recent UN protocol on refugees, which obliged Hungary not to impede German emigrants? Horn elected to stand by the UN provisions. In September 1989, thousands of East Germans moved across the Hungarian-Austrian frontier. More followed as alternative escape routes opened up through Czechoslovakia and Poland.

This development exemplified the general dissatisfaction with the communist incumbents in East Germany. Honecker's reaction was to adamantly refuse any changes or avenues to reform. He relied on the constitution's first article, which positioned the Communist Party as the principal font of power in the state. Following the discovery of certain irregularities in local elections, the hitherto latent opposition grew vocal. The Protestant church and secular interest groups such as the New Forum were in the vanguard of a protest campaign against the communist government. As the popular protest gathered momentum, Honecker alluded to the recent violent response of the Chinese government against student protestors at Tiananmen Square, signaling to all the types of countermeasures he would undertake. In fact, Stasi personnel were endowed with discretionary powers to quell unrest in the cities.

The fall of the Berlin Wall.   Contrary to party expectations, the protest demonstrations did not lose momentum. Quite the opposite was the case. Gorbachev's visit to honor the commemoration and fortieth anniversary of East Germany set in motion the final process that led to the dissolution of East Germany and the fall of the Berlin Wall. The following day, 9 October 1989, a mass rally against the Honecker government in Leipzig forced the Communist Party to concede defeat. Party executives abstained from using force against the Leipzig demonstrators. A few days later, Egon Krenz, groomed to become Honecker's successor, overthrew his erstwhile patron with the connivance of the Politburo in Moscow. Krenz and his associates liberalized travel restrictions and thus rendered the Berlin Wall—and the whole length of the border with neighboring West Germany—obsolete. Hundreds of thousands took to the streets where they demolished the penultimate symbol for the partitioning of Europe—the Berlin Wall—among unbridled euphoria. On 9 November 1991, the Cold War came to an end for the citizens of Berlin.

Krenz's reforms proved too gradualist, as half a million people took to the streets in Leipzig to continue protesting against the Communists in power. Another, less moderate reformer—the Dresden communist leader Hans Modrow, led them. On the whole, the protesters remained peaceful and firm in their aim to break the Communists' hold on power, but a few resorted to violence against the most despised exponent of power: the Stasi. Secret-service headquarters and Stasi agents became the victims of popular outrage that was decades in the making. In December, public pressure brought about two significant changes. First, Article 1 of the constitution, which granted the Communist Party almost limitless powers in the state, was revoked. Second, Krenz himself was replaced by Modrow.

The Communist Party was no longer the principal decisionmaker, and Modrow was committed to reform. Despite the evident trend toward liberalization, the people were no longer content with half-measures. In East Germany, the economy was practically defunct due to the continuing exodus of the country's workforce to the West. At the same time, those who stayed back in the drab East Germany longingly looked across the border, where they saw a wealthy and powerful West Germany. Thus, the majority of East Germans and their leaders would not stop with dismantling the outward trappings of a communist state. They demanded no less than the dissolution of East Germany and reunification with West Germany. The West German government, too, was toying with the idea of incorporating its Eastern pendant, after four decades, to unify the two Germanies under its aegis. There were problems with such an agenda.

Toward reunification.   To begin, two World War II Allies—France and Britain—were not eager to see Germany reunited. The addition of some 17 million Germans would, in the mid- to long term, almost certainly lead to an increase in economic power. Under Chancellor Helmut Kohl, the German government had also reverted to a policy of not unequivocally abrogating its claims based on pre–World War II borders. As no peace treaty had been signed with Germany following the conclusion of the war, the effective German boundaries were those of the status quo ante bellum. The prospect of reunification called to mind that East Germany shared a border with Poland. Against that backdrop, the Soviet Union's reluctance to welcome a reinvigorated, united German state becomes evident.

Conversely, the forces in Bonn supporting reunification became more vocal. The crisis in East Germany and the mass exodus of East Germans to the West confronted West Germany with problems that could be solved only if East Germany agreed to participate in the task. Kohl realized that the time for reunification had arrived and presented a ten-point plan for this purpose as early as the end of November 1989. The fact that a similar perspective had gained prominence in Washington, however, proved decisive. President George H.W. Bush's support for Kohl and his conservative Christian Democratic Party tipped the balance in favor of reunification.

The abolition of Article 1 of East Germany's constitution permitted free elections, which were held in due course. On 18 March 1990, the Christian Democratic Party chairman, Lothar de Maiziere, won an overwhelming victory. During his brief tenure, a monetary union between East and West was implemented. It guaranteed a one-to-one conversion of East German and West German currencies and East German savings of up to

4,000 deutsche marks. The monetary union and conversion schemes were designed to encourage East Germans to remain in East Germany. Despite the successful outcome of these schemes, de Maiziere's incremental approach to unification with West Germany prompted the public to set its own pace. By August, the East German parliamentary assembly abolished East Germany after forty years.

Following the strong U.S. backing of Kohl's reunification plan, and the concurrent overruling of Franco-British concerns, only the Soviet Union remained as a serious objector. For once, events moved on while negotiations stalled. The United States was left with the task of having to formulate a mechanism that would render German reunification acceptable to the Soviet Union. The product of Washington's labors was the so-called 2+4 process, whereby the four former Allied countries of World War II—the United States, the Soviet Union, Great Britain, and France—were asked to participate in the discussion revolving around external aspects of German reunification, such as the confirmation of the post–World War II boundaries and the termination of the wartime Allies' occupation of Germany. The decisive element of the U.S. proposal, however, was that the two German states would have to settle all internal issues bilaterally while having say on the external issues.

Gorbachev's perspective was that it was one thing to approve reunification; it was far more difficult to allow a reunited Germany to integrate into the Western alliance. A reunited Germany would become a powerful addition to NATO and, implicitly, would destabilize Soviet-U.S. relations. Kohl deflated Gorbachev's fears when he agreed to reduce the number of troops in the German armed forces by 220,000 men and reiterated the historic West German renunciation of all **weapons of mass destruction (WMD)**. Moreover, the Germans agreed to compensate the Soviet Union for the relocation of troops stationed in the former East Germany. The German government was also at pains to publicize its official retraction of all previous claims on the pre–World War II territories held by the Third Reich. Nevertheless, the decision to reestablish the German capital in Berlin resurrected many bad memories in adjoining states.

The reunification of Germany on 3 October 1990 certainly was one of the most significant events in the history of post–Cold War Europe. Any illusions of a smooth transition for people living in the former East Germany were soon dispelled. The derelict economy of the new *bundesländer*—the subfederal territorial units—had to be resuscitated with massive financial infusions. The money sent to the East had to be provided for by increased taxation in the old *bundesländer*. In the former West Germany, disgruntlement over the financial burdens of bringing the former East Germany's economy up to par was compounded by the steady influx of East Germans during the next two years. Between 1990 and 1991, some

440,000 former East Germans migrated over to the former West Germany. In addition, the provisions made by the government for foreign refugees seeking asylum in Germany had the effect of stoking the flames of racism in the new *bundesländer*, where up to 3 million remained unemployed. Since then, Germany has managed to deal with the most serious difficulties resulting from reunification. Conversely, and by way of comparison to other former Soviet satellite states in Eastern Europe, the people of the new *bundesländer* could count themselves lucky for having been absorbed into the economic giant of Europe.

The Velvet Revolution

Although Czechoslovakia was not as privileged by Soviet economic support compared to the former East Germany, its transition from communist rule and a command economy to a pluralistic political system and a market economy was smoother than elsewhere in the former Soviet sphere of influence in Eastern Europe. In the wake of the Prague Spring, Brezhnev's appointee, Gustav Husak, directed a hard-line communist government with a strong hand. Throughout the 1970s, the Czechoslovak economy went through a period of growth, improving the lot of workers and peasants alike. This development took a sudden turn in the following decade, when the economy teetered on the brink of catastrophe. The problem bedeviling the economy was endemic to the entire Eastern bloc: inefficient means of production and low productivity combined to bog down economic development and took a toll on the environment. As dissatisfaction mounted in light of the economic crisis, the government relied on Moscow to back it up. Like Honecker in East Germany, Husak, to his detriment, found that the Soviets would not uphold a moribund regime.

Opposition in Czechoslovakia gathered momentum in 1977, when a number of key members of the primarily Czech intelligentsia founded the Charta 77 organization. Initially, the mission of Charta 77 was to lobby for basic human and civil rights as stipulated in the Helsinki Final Act of 1975. The situation in the late 1980s, with many other socialist neighbors in a state of political and economic turmoil, allowed the continually persecuted members of Charta 77 to make their comeback and take a leading role in the overthrow of the Communists. During the early stages of the dissolution of communist rule in Eastern Europe, between late 1988 and early 1989, Czechoslovakia remained under the rule of Husak and his associates. Husak left office in December 1987, but he appointed fellow Communist Milos Jakes as successor; Jakes maintained power into 1989. An escalation of tensions occurred on 17 November 1989 when a multitude of students staged a protest rally in Prague. Security forces deployed to stifle the demonstrations used excessive force—a fact that galvanized the opposition.

At this stage, members of Charta 77 became the nuclei for civic resistance groups. Notable were the playwright Vaclav Havel and Jiri Hajek, Alexander Dubcek's foreign minister during the Prague Spring. Dubcek himself was called upon to rally the people against the communist incumbents. The opposition movement gradually grew in strength, with large crowds supporting claims made by exponents of Charta 77 for more freedom and an end to communist rule. Only when the workers joined a strike were Jakes and members of his cabinet compelled to hand over the reins of power to the leaders of the Civic Forum, as the organized Czechoslovak opposition was called. Not unlike the English Glorious Revolution of 1688, the Czechoslovak Velvet Revolution earned its name by virtue of constituting one of those rare landmark events: social transition without significant bloodshed. Havel was elected president on 29 December 1989.

The breakup of Czechoslovakia.   The government's record under Vaclav Havel was marked by brevity and successes in advancing an incremental transition from a command economy to a competitive free-market economy. But Havel and colleagues failed to solve the Slovak question, which threatened the cohesion of the state. The Slovaks' penchant for independence was advanced in early 1992 and was similar in ways to the internal tensions experienced in the Federal Republic of Yugoslavia. Both states faced nationalist-secessionist forces as principal actors. Both states were founded as artificial constructs at the end of World War I. In the case of Czechoslovakia, the Slovaks were alienated by the Czechs' preponderance within the federation. The Czechs also reneged on promises to grant Slovaks a measure of autonomy. Another reoccurring problem that fueled resentment was questions over use of the Slovak language, which hitherto had not been recognized as the official first language in Slovakia.

Thus, following the decline of communism, the Slovak Prime Minister Vladimir Meciar seized the first possible opportunity to break away from the federation. The absence of violence during the difficult transition from multinational federation to nation-state attests to the unusually high sagacity and foresight among the leaders of the two peoples. The separation occurred toward the end of 1992. Significant differences in economic potential, however, led to divergent developments in the two successor states. Most of the heavy industry and tourism were located in the Czech Republic, and the agricultural Slovaks lagged behind. The differences were staggering. Since separation in 1992, the Czechs have come a long way. Their application for NATO membership has been well received, and economic recovery was brought about in a comparatively short period. At the time of this writing, the Czech government is preparing to bring its country up to par with standards stipulated by the European Union, with EU membership expected in the near future.

The Overthrow of the Ceausescu Regime in Romania

As opposed to the transitions in East Germany and Czechoslovakia, and with the notable exception of Yugoslavia, Romania experienced greater bloodshed during its transition. Since 1965, Nicolae Ceausescu had directed the fate of Romania. His foreign policy was largely independent of that of Moscow. Although Romania remained within the Warsaw Pact, Ceausescu refused Brezhnev's call for aid in the invasion of Czechoslovakia in 1968. His record of disagreements with Moscow was long and gave him the appearance of being better disposed toward the West during the Cold War. In fact, Ceausescu's regime was not dissimilar to that of Stalin in the 1930s. The state was essentially run by the secret police—the Securitate—itself subject to the whims of the Ceausescu clan. Finally, Ceausescu assumed the title of *conductor* (leader). His heavy-handed rule included the relocation of ethnic minorities, even the forced migration of Romanians, who were compelled to make space for Ceausescu's grandiose construction projects. Extreme poverty was the result of an ambitious plan to pay off the entire foreign debt: workers slaved six days per week, subsisted on the goods remaining in the country (most foodstuffs were exported abroad), and lived in the constant shadow of the Securitate.

As changes swept through neighboring communist states, the Romanians' situation worsened, and the political climate grew increasingly charged. A minor incident set off a chain of events that would lead to the overthrow of the *conductor* and the ruling clique associated with him. When Ceausescu ordered the deportation of a dissident Hungarian Protestant clergyman, he provoked local resistance in the town of Timisoara, which soon spilled over into a nationwide protest. An orchestrated rally organized by members of the *nomenklatura*—the ruling elite within the Communist Party—backfired when the audience began to scream abuse at Ceausescu, who had sought to use the opportunity to impugn the recalcitrant Timisoarans. This debacle marked the end of Ceausescu's rule. He and his wife were arraigned, sentenced in a military court, and executed in late December 1989.

The new regime, headed by the prominent critic of Ceausescu's excesses, Ion Illiescu, was composed of some of the *conductor*'s oldest comrades, who proceeded to purge the party as well as the police apparatus. And though the new government gave the outward appearance of democratic leadership, it continued to rule autocratically. Illiescu missed his opportunity to reform the Romanian political system and economy, thereby condemning his country to continued social misery and instability. His brief flirt with a watered-down fascist revival did little to improve his tenure. At present, Romania remains a poverty-stricken country, its democratic institutions only beginning to tackle the host of problems that bedevil its government and people.

Asia

Standing in stark contrast to the economically declining Eastern bloc, the Pacific Rim was a success story and brought forth the so-called Four Tigers of Asia. After the economic miracle that boosted the Japanese to the heights of productivity and wealth, South Korea, Taiwan, Hong Kong, and Singapore joined the ranks of Asian countries that produced startling growth rates during the Cold War and after. Most attempts to explain the successes of the Four Tigers point to commonalities, ranging from shared cultural Chinese roots, a paternalistic value system that promoted a sense of duty and diligence, authoritarian rule, and an infrastructure left behind by the Japanese after World War II. The Tigers' adoption of Japan's economic model proved conducive to double-digit annual growth rates.

South Korea and Taiwan were at the head of the class. Again, their success stories are marked by a parallel development: both were threatened by communist powers. In the case of South Korea, the communist North Korea, with its powerful armed forces, endangered security; as for Taiwan, it was confronted by the Asian juggernaut of communism—the People's Republic of China. The palpable danger emanating from the nearby communist states helped instill a popular sense of direction and necessity, eagerly streamlined by the government in the furtherance of stability at home. And the two pillars of that stability were strong militaries supported by burgeoning economies. Economic development thus became a prerequisite for national security and social stability. The regimes in Hong Kong and in Singapore, albeit safe from threat of attack by vengeful neighbors, nevertheless ruled with a firm hand—a task made easier by a Confucian frame of mind that stressed the primacy of duty, seniority, and hard work.

The Rise of the Asian Market Economies: The Four Tigers

The Korean War had largely left South Korea in tatters. Only a decade after the war, however, the economy picked up and expanded throughout the 1970s to peak at a growth rate of some 14 percent. With only a slight diminution in the 1980s, South Korean production and its market continued to grow steadily. A succession of military *juntas* ruled the country for most of that period. The reigning generals were opposed by increasingly violent student demonstrations. Only in 1990, two years after the Summer Olympic Games in Seoul brought attention to political conditions in South Korea, was a president democratically elected. It was during the successive tenures of military dictators that economic leapfrogging was undertaken. Massive loans provided by the United States and Japan for a dedicated pro-Western country allowed South Korean leaders to foster economic growth, which might help offset the financial burden of the military.

Taiwan. The independent state of Taiwan sprang out of the Chinese civil war, which ended with a communist victory and the withdrawal of all Nationalist forces under General Chiang Kai-shek in early 1949 to the island of Formosa off the Chinese mainland. Chiang and 2 million Nationalists occupied the island, inhabited by an indigenous population of 13 million. After suppressing local resistance, the new founders took advantage of an infrastructure left over from the Japanese occupation and preferential status from the United States. The military forces needed to be maintained, and so the need for economic expansion soon became pressing. Chiang instituted sweeping changes throughout the 1950s, reorganizing the ownership of land and laying the groundwork for the later successes while firmly holding on to power.

After this period of political and economic consolidation, the 1960s witnessed the emergence of export production, and the 1970s saw the introduction of high-tech industry, which became the most lucrative branch of Taiwan's economy in the late 1980s and 1990s. Politically, Taiwan remained under the thumb of the Nationalist establishment. After Chiang passed away in 1975, his heir, Jiang Jingguo, gradually liberalized the political system until the first free election could be held one year after his own death in 1988. The similarities with South Korea are obvious and intriguing.

Hong Kong. Hong Kong and Singapore shared a common characteristic, as both were urban centers with only marginal rural areas; their populations consisted mostly of ethnic Chinese. They differed in their styles of government. Hong Kong was a British Crown Colony until it reverted back to the People's Republic of China in 1997. Hong Kong's government was vested in the governors appointed by Her Majesty's government. Singapore had gained independence in 1964 and was ruled by a single authoritarian, Lee Kuan Yew. Both city-states exhibited a prodigious economic growth rate in the postwar period.

Since the nineteenth century, Hong Kong had been a British colonial possession kept apart from the Chinese empire by force of arms. Following the Chinese civil war between the Communists and Nationalists, Britain had been able to retain its hold on Hong Kong due to the weakened state of China. Beijing realized that Hong Kong represented no threat, and Chinese leaders were not inclined to imperil the potential gains from Hong Kong's flourishing economy by laying waste to it in a misguided attempt to maintain Chinese territorial integrity. In any event, the Communists could afford to wait until Hong Kong returned to the fold peaceably. Despite the looming reversion, Hong Kong became a regional trade capital and growing production outlet. Investments from all over Asia and beyond found their way into Hong Kong firms. Renowned for their industry, the people of Hong Kong thrived as the economic sector grew to include banking and insurance businesses, which had been attracted since the 1970s due to the politically stable climate underpinned by the sagacious administration of the governors.

British authorities realized that an absence of a clear plan for the transition of power to China would result in losses crippling to the Hong Kong economy. Accordingly, they set out to negotiate a deal with the Chinese starting in the 1970s. By 1984, the British achieved partial success, securing a guarantee that Hong Kong's capitalist economy and autonomous status would remain after reversion. The Tiananmen Square massacre impaired Sino-British relations only five years later and initiated a mass emigration from Hong Kong. The flood turned to a trickle when the Communists acquiesced to demands that Hong Kong residents should be able to leave town if they owned a British passport prior to reversion. Needless to say, British passports became a valuable commodity. The last flare-up before reversion was caused by the announcement of the last British governor, Sir Christopher Patten, that the franchise for the Legislative Council would be expanded. Beijing, in turn, announced its intention to abolish all governing bodies and run Hong Kong by its own appointees, a high-handed reaction that caused widespread insecurity in Hong Kong. Economically, however, Chinese threats seemed to have no impact, for the annual growth rate continued at around 5 percent. Since reversion, the Chinese lived up to some of their threats: the media has been muzzled, and communist functionaries hold a tight grip on Hong Kong politics. So far, though, China has not killed the proverbial goose laying the golden eggs.

Singapore.   In contrast to Hong Kong, Singapore is a relatively young state, having evolved from another British colony: Malaya. A member of the Association of South East Asian Nations, Singapore has become an economic and political asset to the region. This is partly due to its stability in the political sphere. In contrast to the other ASEAN member states, Singapore's majority consists of ethnic Chinese. And the policies of one-man government under Lee Kuan Yew are mainly responsible for the success story here. Making good use of Singapore's privileged geographic situation—it is located at a crucial intersection of maritime trade routes—Lee's autocratic government was tempered by careful policies designed to optimize conditions for economic growth. Access to, and standards for, education are among the best. The efficient implementation of skilled labor has set an example for other countries, which find it hard to match Singapore's productivity. Stringent laws are responsible for Singapore's low crime rates.

The shadier side of Lee's legal innovations is that they pay no heed to privacy and, at times, result in judicial absurdities. Singaporeans, for example, are fined for failing to flush a toilet. The death penalty is applicable for possession of illicit substances, no matter what they may be, or in what quantities. Such draconian measures are legitimized by Lee's firm belief that they possess a moral and educational value. And though the idea of optimizing economic output through regimentation in society has worked, basic civil liberties are at stake. Singapore, it would seem, has sacrificed the latter for the former.

Continuing Problems in Southeast Asia

In contrast to the Four Tigers, in several Southeast Asian states ethnic and ideological struggles undermined political stability. In these cases human rights do not count for much, and the common form of government is a dictatorship or a military *junta*. They share the common heritage of decolonization during the 1950s. The insidious influence of the Cold War could be felt in the region: North Korea invaded South Korea; France and then the United States fought a long, savage war in Indochina to stem the communist tide. To ameliorate the ill effects of war and political instability, five former colonial possessions—Indonesia, Malaysia, Thailand, Singapore, and the Philippines—that had recently gained independence combined to found the Association of South East Asian Nations in 1967.

ASEAN's basic mission is to foster a climate of peace and stability in the region. Its character can be understood to be like an informal working group and, unlike NATO and the EU, ASEAN was never intended as an integrated military, political, or economic alliance. Members had only recently become independent and were nationalist in outlook and character, which did not render membership in a regional organization easy; ASEAN was far from a cohesive force. ASEAN's policy of strict noninterference in the internal affairs of members paid homage to these strong nationalist undercurrents. Thus, it was a common enemy—communism—that fused the five states. Following U.S. withdrawal from Vietnam 1975, China and Vietnam ranked high in ASEAN's list of enemies.

Economically, ASEAN fared well throughout the 1960s and 1970s but faced recession by the mid-1980s, forcing members to implement reforms. This led to more cooperative endeavors among ASEAN member states and an increase in economic growth. In the final analysis, ASEAN has promoted peace and trade in the region. Other Southeast Asian states that were not part of ASEAN suffered by comparison. Left to their own fates, these nations experienced internal division that stifled their economies.

Military Rule in Burma

Three examples show the dark side of recent Southeast Asian history. Heading the list is Burma, renamed Myanmar in 1989. When the British withdrew from Burma in 1948, they left in place a constitutional government. For ten years, democracy survived under the aegis of U Nu. Several ethnic minorities within Burma had been in a state of conflict for some time before the country achieved independence. Communist groups, like elsewhere in Asia, repeatedly beset the U Nu government from all sides. The saving graces of U Nu's government were, on the one hand, the fact that the insurgent groups fought one another as fiercely as they did against the government in Rangoon; and on the other, the powerful military under the leadership of General Ne Win. When antigovernment forces destabilized the country to the extent it was nearly ungovernable, U Nu stepped down in favor of Ne Win. He proved able to deal with the crisis and after two years was able to return power to U Nu, having strengthened the latter's mandate in a general election. If this seems surprising, it must be understood that the Burmese military establishment by and large supported U Nu's twin policies of steering clear of the Cold War's bipolar global entanglements and seeking accommodation with China rather than India.

When rebellion and revolution again threatened to overturn the established order in 1962, Ne Win ousted U Nu from power. For the next quarter-century, Burma was ruled by a military *junta* headed by Ne Win. In this period, Burma became a one-party state in the image of the Soviet Union. The military proceeded to isolate the country from the international community, something that had disastrous consequences for the Burmese economy despite abundant natural resources and foreign investment. But by 1974, the Ne Win *junta* transformed the country into the Socialist Republic of the Union of Burma. Following a thorough program of nationalizing all sectors of the economy, the Burmese foreign debt rose from more than U.S.$230 million in the early 1970s to more than U.S.$3.5 billion by the end of the 1980s.

By 1987, popular frustration with the lagging economy and the backward-looking autocratic regime exploded in a series of riots in Rangoon. The protesters were mostly drawn from the urban and university tiers of society. Too old and erratic to guide the country, Ne Win was marginalized by his fellow generals. A year later, in 1988, the situation had ostensibly improved with free elections promised and a civilian government in power. Military intervention ended all premature hopes for an improvement of Burma's political plight. General Saw Maung launched a repressive campaign directed at all suspected members of the opposition, as well as its principal exponent, Aung San Suu Kyi. An estimated 3,000 perished in the bloodshed that inaugurated the new leaders, who did not except the ethnic minorities from their vindictiveness. Aside from the National League for Democracy (NLD) led by Aung San Suu Kyi, who was the daughter of one of Burma's national heroes, the Karen tribe led a well-organized resistance against General Maung's State Law and Restoration Council. But the government proved more successful in the case of the Rohingya—a Muslim minority inhabiting the northern portion of the country—whom they persecuted mercilessly in 1992.

In a bid to polish its tarnished image, the Burmese *junta* renamed the country Myanmar and by 1989 announced free elections for the middle of 1990. This was not to pass. The opposition, with Suu Kyi's NLD in the vanguard, won a landslide victory over the candidates fielded by the *junta*. Maung, however, was not of a mind to cede power. Suu Kyi was arrested and confined to her home until released in 1995. Her courage in the struggle against the military regime earned her the Nobel Prize in 1991. Although the unfolding drama attracted criticism and attention from the international community, multinational corporations continued to cooperate with the unconstitutional government of Myanmar to exploit the country's natural resources.

In 1997, Myanmar was admitted to ASEAN as a full member, an event that has improved the country's economic prospects and bolstered the legitimacy of the *junta*. At present, the principle of strict noninterference in the internal affairs of ASEAN member states protects the new rulers, allied around Ne Win's former intelligence chief, Khin Nyunt. In 1999, the military power brokers renamed the *junta*'s governing body into the more palatable State Peace and Development Council. Meanwhile, resistance from ethnic minorities has been crippled to the degree that it is little more than a nuisance to the government. Politically, Suu Kyi's position remains difficult, as the opposition she leads is being brutally suppressed. Change appears to be on a distant horizon.

Crisis in the Indonesian Archipelago

Indonesian independence and the initial phase of statehood is a story unto itself (see Chapter 2). After the Japanese vacated the principal islands of the Indonesian archipelago—Java, Sumatra, Borneo, and Celebes—after 1945, the former Dutch colonial masters seized power again with the instrumental support of the British. In 1949, a large body of Dutch troops was shipped home, as years of Indonesian native resistance took their toll and ended foreign rule. On 17 August 1950, Indonesian leader Achmed Sukarno changed the constitutional framework from a federation to a unitary republic. Unlike its federal predecessor, the new Indonesian republic could no longer do justice to the ethnically, religiously, and politically heterogeneous populace. Conflicting interests of various groups provided ample fuel for hostilities.

Nevertheless, Sukarno allowed a measure of democracy. Internationally, he played the bipolar game to the utmost advantage of Indonesia, accepting the support of both East and West while keeping Indonesia on a course of nonalignment. Sukarno underscored this position by hosting the Bandung Conference of the Non-Aligned Movement in 1955. But Washington and Moscow were at a complete loss as to what kind of policy Sukarno was advancing. Under mounting pressure by the various interest groups, the Communists, who represented a latent but growing power within the state in the shape of the Partai Nasional Indonesia (PNI; National Party of Indonesia), were admitted to the government. This sparked massive protests by a traditional Muslim minority who were among a more moderate majority of coreligionists. Beset by multiple uprisings staged by ethnic and religious minorities, Sukarno turned to so-called guided democracy—read: autocratic rule—in 1958.

From Sukarno to Suharto. Economic stagnation then combined with ethnic and political unrest, and the unpopularity of the Sukarno regime became more palpable in the 1960s. In the aftermath of a referendum on Borneo in 1963, during which Sarawak and Sabah were ceded to a nascent Malaysia, Sukarno challenged the outcome with military force. His anti-Malaysia policies continued into 1965. Sukarno had calculated that an external enemy would bolster Indonesian nationalism and therefore distract public attention from the domestic problems. Such was not the case. Instead, Indonesian dissenters swelled the ranks of the PNI, and a multinational force drawn from the British Commonwealth prevented further Indonesian expansion into Borneo. Sukarno's only choice was to cooperate with the PNI. The Communists then attempted to overthrow the government; the military launched a counterstrike in which it purged the government of all Communists.

This witch hunt, initiated and supervised by General Ibrahim Suharto, resulted in the death of some 760,000. By the end of the purge the army had wrested control from the shattered Communists, as well as from Sukarno, who was marginalized and then reduced to a nonentity. General Suharto, whose pro-Western policies differed markedly from those of his predecessor, directed the new regime. Speculations as to the involvement of the United States in Suharto's bid for power in 1965 abound. Presumably, the United States had a stake in seeing Indonesia freed of all communist influence. And the confluence of the increased U.S. presence in Vietnam and Suharto's accession to power implies cooperation between Washington and the anticommunist Indonesian military.

The country's economy had remained in the doldrums under Sukarno, and though it picked up after 1965, with crude oil becoming its principal export commodity, inefficient administration and widespread corruption in the bureaucracy neutralized most of the potential benefits. But the principal problem in the economy was the state's control. Only in the 1980s were liberal reforms introduced, and only because the foreign debt had assumed astronomical proportions. Suharto's rule was not disguised as a democratic presidency. Bedecked in military regalia, the new leader introduced momentous changes in his country's foreign policy. Sukarno's prior engagements with China and the Soviet Union made room for a rapprochement with the United States. Anti-Malaysia operations on Borneo were curbed. Only in one respect did Suharto continue Sukarno's policies: the suppression of ethnic and religious minorities.

Unrest in Irian Jaya, East Timor, and the province of Aceh.   Three incidents occurred in Irian Jaya (West New Guinea), East Timor, and the province of Aceh. Since 1965, the citizens of Irian Jaya fought Indonesian government troops that had annexed their territory. With the support of various indigenous Papua tribes, the Organisai Papua Merdeka continued the struggle against the Indonesian occupiers. By 1992, 100,000 had been killed as a direct consequence of this conflict.

East Timor had been a Portuguese colony for more than 400 years when it gained independence following a successful revolution in Portugal in 1974. One year later, the former Timorese independence movement had been sundered, with the left-wing Frente Revolucionária de Timor-Leste Independente/Revolutionary Front for an Independent East Timor (FRETILIN) outmatching the political right (the União Democrática Timorense/Timorese Democratic Union). A right-wing coup failed to topple the leftist government but afforded Suharto the opportunity to intervene militarily in December 1975. FRETILIN forces melted into the backcountry and commenced guerrilla operations. In reprisal for the continued resistance, Indonesian troops wantonly harassed and murdered civilians suspected of sympathizing with FRETILIN. Since 1980, FRETILIN has reorganized its ranks and confronted the occupying forces with an organized resistance. To date, almost 200,000 lives have been lost in the struggle for Timorese independence. Following massive international pressure spearheaded by the United Nations and widespread disturbances in East Timor, an election on 30 August 1999 was to allow East Timor's 800,000 people to decide on the future of their country: autonomy within Indonesia, or full independence.

The Indonesian government was responsible for creating and maintaining security within East Timor prior to the election. After May 1999, the security situation in East Timor deteriorated. Anti-independence militias were blamed for much of the violence, attacking civilians and threatening UN personnel preparing for the election. Many thousands were forced to flee their homes as a result. A week after the election was held, the United Nations announced that more than 78 percent of all enfranchised East Timorese had voted in favor of independence. In the week following the ballot's announcement, prointegration militias carried out their threats to lay waste to East Timor should the result in fact be independence. Unknown numbers of East Timorese were murdered, their homes burned, the entire infrastructure of the country razed. More than 100,000 East Timorese fled to West Timor, and unknown numbers were displaced within East Timor.

On 15 September 1999 the UN Security Council responded to the rapidly deteriorating situation by authorizing the deployment of a peace enforcement contingent acting under Chapter VII of the United Nations Charter. The International Force in East Timor (INTERFET) was authorized to deploy in East Timor; it was to be replaced as soon as possible by a UN peacekeeping operation. The UN Transitional Administration in East Timor (UNTAET) was sent to East Timor on 20 September 1999. INTERFET has been responsible for the restoration of peace and stability, to protect and support the UN Mission in East Timor (UNAMET) in carrying out its tasks and to facilitate humanitarian operations. Security Council Resolution 1264, adopted on 15 September 1999, asked the UN Secretary-General to plan and prepare for a UN transitional administration. Authority for East Timor has now passed to UNTAET. The Security Council authorized a successor mission, the United Nations Mission of Support in East Timor (UNMISET), on 17 May 2002. The mission was established for an initial period of one year, starting on 20 May 2002. Its mandate is to provide assistance to administrative structures essential to the political stability of East Timor; to provide law enforcement and public security; to support efforts to establish an East Timor police service; and, finally, to contribute to East Timor's external and internal security. UNTAET will be fully responsible for the administration of East Timor during its transition to independence, which is expected to take two to three years.

The conflict in the province of Aceh was fueled by demands for local autonomy by a traditionalist Muslim population, as well as resistance to attempts to exploit local natural resources on the part of Jakarta. Even though the government had granted Aceh limited cultural and religious autonomy as early as the 1950s, separatist forces continued their campaign, which gained renewed impetus in the 1980s. The civil rights movement in Aceh is concerned with the attainment of devolved government, whereas indigenous Muslim guerrilla forces are launching attacks on Javanese settlers and Indonesian government troops. The battle for Aceh has cost some 2,000 lives to date.

At present, Indonesia is poised for a gradual but genuine transition from decades of autocratic rule to democracy. Facing mounting pressure, Suharto (whose attempt to disguise his rule by exchanging his uniform for a suit fooled nobody) was compelled to step down in 1999. President Wahid has since sought to resist a growing movement in parliament advocating his removal from office. Wahid was censured by the Indonesian parliament in May 2001 and was ousted after an overwhelming vote against him. Megawati Sukarnoputri, who was sworn in as the fifth president of Indonesia on 23 July 2001, succeeded him. She is Sukarno's daughter (Wahid left the country on 26 July 2001). More recently, President Abdurahman Wahid had the chance to close the book on Indonesia's bloody past by bringing former dictator Suharto to justice, thereby beginning a new saga in the political history of Indonesia.

Popular Dissent and Civil War in the Philippines

The Philippines gained independence yet underwent troubled times between 1946 and 1986. Dictators had led the country up to 1965, when lawyer Ferdinand Marcos rose to power on a political platform of reform. But he soon abandoned his campaign promises, protecting instead the interests of the powerful landowning oligarchy. At that time, the Philippines' economic output exhibited growth paralleling that of the future Four Tigers of Asia. Marcos's tenure changed this success in the most drastic terms, leaving the country impoverished and debt-ridden. A succession of staged elections confirmed Marcos in his office, and when his second and last term was about to end in 1972, he declared martial law due to the communist and separatist Muslim insurgencies, which by then had become part and parcel of the problems that had bedeviled government for years.

The United States kept Marcos in power because of his public opposition to communism. Moreover, the United States sought to protect its important financial investments and military interests in the shape of two of the largest extraterritorial bases located on Filipino territory: Subic Bay Naval Base and Clark Air Base. The United States also shut its eyes to Marcos's social injustice and arbitrary government as long as he provided the political stability necessary to safeguard the U.S. economic stakes and strategic commitment in Asia during the Cold War. Meanwhile, Marcos's corrupt regime was able to embezzle public funds and redirect money from economic and humanitarian aid packages to the dictator's own pockets. Politics had become a lucrative business for the Marcoses.

Civil war raged among the 7,100 islands and islets making up the Philippines between 1968 and the end of (and beyond) Marcos's rule in 1986. As of 1972, Marcos again declared martial law; this time, however, he extended it to the entire territory belonging to the Philippines and proceeded to crush the communist New People's Army (NPA) based on Luzon and the Muslim separatists operating on Mindanao and the Sulu Archipelago. The NPA soon removed its theater of operations to Mindanao and at times made common cause with the Muslim Moro National Liberation Front (MNLF). Marcos reacted with unmitigated harshness. He deployed large military forces and launched offensives against rebel forces throughout the Philippines. The superior military hardware available to the regular troops due to U.S. financial aid proved decisive in the destruction of the resistance.

But his time was up by the early 1980s. Marcos's cardinal mistake was an overt act of violence. The principal opposition politician, Benigno Aquino, was permitted to quit the Philippines for health reasons after languishing in prison. Aquino enjoyed widespread popular support and was the most likely opposition candidate for the presidential office—that is, if free elections were ever held. In this sense, Aquino was a powerful symbol of constitutional as well as nonconstitutional resistance to the dictator. In 1983, Aquino returned to the Philippines in a bid to oust Marcos—and was promptly assassinated upon arriving in Manila. The people took to the streets. Demands for an investigation into the murder of Aquino finally compelled Marcos to acquiesce, and he ordered an inquiry. The results pointed to many dubious circumstances in the murder, including a direct link to a high-ranking military officer related to Marcos. Despite the evidence amassed by the investigative commission, the suspected perpetrators went free. Aquino's murder had far-reaching consequences. On the one hand, Aquino's symbolic value to the opposition was enhanced by his martyrdom. On the other hand, the turmoil caused by the overtly political nature of Aquino's assassination had a detrimental effect of foreign investments essential to a weakening national economy.

Marcos versus Aquino.   Things got worse for Marcos when the communist NPA escalated its struggle against government troops. Growing pressure from all sides, including from within his own ranks, left Marcos with no other option than to announce new elections for 1986. Capitalizing on the legacy of her late husband, Corazon "Cory" Aquino rallied the opposition to its cause. Though Marcos's partisans in all likelihood manipulated the ballots, the final result was not conclusive. Nevertheless, Marcos announced that he had won the elections. For the first time in Marcos's tenure, the political opposition—in the interim augmented by the church and business interests—would not play along. Church representatives acted as a focal point for dissatisfaction with the dictator. Army officers and members of the government defected, and the U.S. president refused to support a corrupt tyrant incapable of maintaining peace and stability in his own country. With his wife, Imelda, and the rest of his family in tow, Ferdinand Marcos fled the country for exile in Hawaii. Marcos did not fail to generously provide for himself and his dependents.

Conversely, Cory Aquino was left behind as the de facto victor of the elections and proceeded to implement new policies. Although she was largely responsible for the restoration of civil liberties and various reforms, she was quickly disabused of any illusions that twenty years of Marcos rule could be changed quickly. The worst among the many long-term problems was a huge foreign debt, the servicing of which cost the Philippines much of what it earned. Aquino's preferential treatment of certain segments of the officer corps earned her the distrust of more neutral and potentially hostile factions within the army. Numerous coups against Aquino illustrated the spreading discontent with her policies. By 1990, she had effectively lost her political mandate. Aquino declined to run again in 1991.

Former defense minister General Fidel Ramos, who prevailed over Marcos's widow Imelda, succeeded Aquino. In 1992, Ramos signed an amnesty setting free some 4,500 interned Communists and relegalized the Communist Party. In the same year, the United States finally pulled out of its two bases in the Philippines following protracted negotiations, which were cut short when a volcano erupted and destroyed both U.S. installations. By 1993, Ramos was able to end the twenty-five-year conflict with the Muslim MNLF on Mindanao. The reality of the Philippines' multiethnic population was acknowledged when Manila consented to the establishment of various devolved governments to run affairs in the autonomous regions. After decades of tyranny and military suppression, the Philippines were again under democratic rule.

The Middle East

Although the Camp David Accords of 1977 ended hostilities between Israel and Egypt, the Palestine problem lacked a solution. In fact, the political climate had taken a bad turn for the Palestinians, who were forced to vacate their longtime base in Jordan subsequent to a failed bid for domination. Yassir Arafat and his adherents moved to the only other place in the Middle East where they could rebuild a base of operations. And the only reason that Lebanon became the new—albeit unwilling—host country to Arafat's Palestine Liberation Organization was due to the civil war that had crippled its government since 1958. The actual fighting between the contending Lebanese factions—the Maronite Christians and the Muslim majority—had ceased, but when the Palestinians arrived in two waves between 1967 and 1970, the central government could no longer cope with the multiple divisions in the country.

The Lebanese Civil War and the Israeli Invasion

Between 1970 and 1975, Lebanon was plunged into civil war. Each of the interest groups maintained a military arm to enforce their wills in their respective spheres of influence. The infusion of Palestinian irregular troops into the existing turmoil exacerbated the prevailing instability. The ensuing conflict can be described as having taken place on two different levels. Christians fought Muslims while leftist groups within the denominational groups fought conservatives. In other words, there was no unified front of, say, Palestinians and local Muslims, or such a thing as a Christian Maronite movement. To make matters worse, the Syrians heeded the call of the Lebanese government, the majority of which was Christian, to intervene on their behalf. For their part, the Israelis supported the Christian Maronites against all and sundry. Meanwhile, the PLO used war-torn Lebanon as a staging area for raiding missions across the Israeli border and kept up the intermittent shelling of Galilee with cheap Soviet-made Katyusha shrapnel missiles. This border conflict held sway into the early 1980s, when the U.S. special envoy to the Middle East, Philip Habib, brokered an armistice taking effect in July 1981.

In Israel, the political climate had also changed, with an end to the hegemony of Social Democratic rule. Menachem Begin, well known for his involvement in the anti-British resistance in Palestine after World War II, won the election of 1977. His general outlook was, if not reactionary, then at least very conservative. Begin's principal objectives were the retention of land won in previous hostilities with neighboring Arab states, as well as the elimination of the Palestinian threat. In the pursuit of this strategy, the hawkish Ariel Sharon, the experienced general who brought about the Israeli victory during the Yom Kippur War of 1973, supported Begin. Sharon urged Begin to clean house in Lebanon. Israeli civilians in Galilee were not infrequently the targets of the PLO's Katyusha attacks, and despite the temporary cessation of hostilities, they were not of a mind to accept this in the future. Furthermore, the Syrians constituted a major security threat on Israel's northern border. U.S. Special Envoy Habib and President Ronald Reagan warned the Israeli government that a drastic change in the status quo would in all likelihood have far-reaching consequences for the volatile situation in the Middle East. Sharon, however, argued that his plan only envisioned a quick strike across the border to dislodge the Palestinians and Syrians from Lebanon.

The 1981 surgical air strike against an Iraqi nuclear facility by the Israeli air force portended subsequent events. When an Israeli diplomat was severely wounded in an assassination attempt sponsored by PLO elements not under the control of Arafat on 3 June 1982, Sharon went into action. Operation Peace for Galilee was commenced on the day after, with the Israeli air force successfully destroying multiple targets in Lebanon. The Israeli Defense Force was already advancing on Beirut on 6 June and shattered strategic Syrian positions in the Bekaa Valley seventy-two hours later. The Israeli invasion, however, did not stop with rooting out PLO activists in Beirut, which was under siege, but proceeded to eliminate all enemy strongholds that were outside its immediate theater of operations. As a military fighting force, the PLO was all but destroyed by August. Arafat's irregulars were evacuated on 21 August.

Militarily, the Israeli invasion of Lebanon was a spectacular success; politically, it turned out to be a disaster. For the first time in the history of the state, Israeli troops fought an offensive action designed to protect the national interest (as opposed to earlier wars, fought for self-preservation). This new drift in policy was not well received by the international community. When the Maronite leader, and Israel's principal ally, Bashir Gemayel was assassinated on orders from the Syrians in September 1982, all hope for achieving political stability in Lebanon had to be abandoned. It had been Begin's intention to groom a Maronite government for power that would be able to restore democratic rule but remain on friendly terms with Israel. The frustration of Begin's political designs for Lebanon robbed the Israeli invasion of any legitimacy. The subsequent massacres in the refugee camps of Sabra and Shatila by allied Christian Phalangists (right-wing militias) critically damaged Israel's claim of wanting to secure peace for Galilee. In Israel, protests by the Peace Now movement mounted as more and more defense force personnel were returned from Lebanon in body bags. Beset internally as well as externally by opponents to Israel's further involvement in Lebanon, Begin pulled out his forces, but not without first creating a security zone between the two countries. At the price of expelling the PLO from Lebanon, Israel had become a deeply divided nation.

The military campaign waged by the Israel Defense Forces dismantled the PLO's Lebanese base of operations. From Tunisia, Arafat sought to hold together the various factions of his organizations, which sought to obtain leverage within the PLO by courting various Arab states for material support. After its defeat in Lebanon, the PLO was split between the dominant and tendentiously moderate Fatah led by Arafat, and various radical splinter groups. Although Al Fatah leaned toward a compromise with Israel and sought to achieve a working relationship with moderate Arab politicians such as the Egyptian President Hosni Mubarak and King Hussein of Jordan, the radicals worked toward a closer relationship with Hafez Assad of Syria.

But the mid-1980s were a time of internecine struggle for the Israelis, too. In Israel, the electorate was deeply divided over the Palestine problem and Israeli relations with Arab neighbors. Although Begin resigned over the Lebanon debacle in 1983, another conservative drawn from the ranks of the hard-line Likud Party promptly replaced him at the helm: Yitzhak Shamir. One year and an election later, Shamir had allied with the leader of the leftist opposition, Shimon Peres. The coalition government managed to exclude elements from the radical fringe, but its composition betrayed a deepening political rift within the Israeli body politic. Worse yet, what had begun as a marriage of convenience ended in a stalemate between the coalition partners, which undermined their ability to conduct any sort of comprehensive policy.

The Intifada

This state of affairs persisted until the political deadlock in Israel was shattered in December 1987 by the **intifada**—the Palestinian uprising. The intifada spread to all the Occupied Territories (i.e., lands occupied by Israel after the Six Day War of 1967). The sporadic violence in the West Bank and Gaza Strip was stepped up by the Palestinians, which forced the Israeli government to deploy regular troops to contain it. The situation created by the intifada raised many questions among the Israeli electorate, the most important of which was how to bring about peaceful coexistence with the Palestinians. With Shamir in office, there was practically no chance to work out a compromise. After 1990, Shamir's tough policy was compounded by a steady influx of Jewish immigrants from the former Soviet Union, who frequently settled in areas claimed by the Palestinians. Politically speaking, the PLO capitalized on Israel's difficult situation with a brilliant initiative, offering to accept the state of Israel in return for the withdrawal of Israeli forces from the West Bank and Gaza Strip as set forth in UN Resolutions 242 and 338.

Although Shamir's conservative government continued its hard-line policy toward the Palestinians, the stage had been set for peace. As pressure from the international community on Israel to respond to the PLO initiative mounted, the more moderate Yitzhak Rabin replaced Shamir in June 1992, and the Israeli stance underwent a transformation. Rabin believed that in the long term only Palestinian autonomy would permit a lasting peace. With the support of the Israeli Peace Now movement, Rabin's government was able to broker an agreement with the Palestinians at Oslo, Norway, which was officially signed at the White House in September 1993. The two sides agreed to a five-year period of limited autonomy for the West Bank and Gaza and a withdrawal of Israeli forces from Gaza and a portion of the West Bank, although Jewish settlements would remain under Israeli authority. The Palestinians would elect their authorities and establish their own police force of former PLO combatants. Finally, Israel pledged to support the Palestinian effort to build an economy. This represented the endpoint of what has become known as the first intifada; a second would follow in 2000.

The Gulf War

In the early 1990s, the Israeli-Arab conflict was overshadowed by other events in the Middle East. The Persian Gulf region provided the stage for a U.S.-led confrontation with Iraq. Saddam Hussein, president-dictator of Iraq, claimed the Rumaila oilfield on the border to Kuwait. Furthermore, he accused Kuwait of producing and selling oil in excess of the quota fixed by OPEC and thereby lowering the price of crude oil on the world market. Finally, Hussein demanded that Kuwait pay reparations of U.S.$14 billion for damages caused by its transgressions, as well as to cede two islands to Iraq. U.S. diplomatic efforts and Arab mediation seemed to have averted the threat of hostilities, but the emir of Kuwait refused Iraq's demands. The West and the Arab world were surprised when Hussein's forces invaded Kuwait on 2 August 1990 and declared it to be the nineteenth province of Iraq. Nobody had anticipated a full-scale Iraqi attack only two years after the end of the Iran-Iraq War. Thus began the Gulf War.

The annexation of Kuwait and the Western response. This time, Hussein had underestimated the significance, strategic and economic ramifications, and impact of the invasion as well as the international response it would elicit. By annexing Kuwait, Hussein effectively held 24 percent of the world's production in crude oil. Iraq's neighbor and major oil-producing state, Saudi Arabia, felt threatened by the forceful acquisition of the Kuwaiti emirate. More generally, a majority of the member states of the Arab League would not permit Iraq to multiply its power at their own expense by hijacking the economic power that came with access to the combined oil fields of the Persian Gulf region. Should Hussein control the gulf, he could dictate prices to the industrial nations of the West and compel other Arab nations to follow his lead. Accordingly, Saudi Arabia called upon the United States to defend against further Iraqi pretensions in the area. Intervention on the part of the United States, however, could easily be misconstrued as an imperialist design against an Arab state and be manipulated by Hussein to gain sympathy within the Arab League. On 6 August, only four days after the attack on Kuwait, the UN Security Council imposed a trade embargo on Iraq. Shortly thereafter, it condoned the use of force to implement the original Security Council decision. In this novel context, the president of the United States, George H.W. Bush, endeavored to bring about an international coalition including Arab states to confront Iraq and force Saddam Hussein to relinquish his claim on Kuwait.

At the behest of the United States, Operation Desert Shield was commenced—a massing of Coalition troops in Saudi Arabia. Under the command of U.S. General Norman Schwarzkopf, more than 600,000 troops funded and provided by some thirty countries stood ready to force Iraq's compliance with a number of UN resolutions, which called, inter alia, for the withdrawal of Iraqi troops from Kuwait. By November 1990, the United Nations had passed Resolution 678, championed by President Bush, calling for unconditional withdrawal from Kuwait by 15 January 1991. Meanwhile, Saddam Hussein had initiated a few political maneuvers of his own. In an effort to avert an attack, some 20,000 foreigners and diplomatic staff in Iraq were held hostage—a human shield in the event of a Coalition offensive. Hussein also proceeded to court Arab nationalist sentiments by offering to withdraw from Kuwait if the Israeli government agreed to quit Gaza and the West Bank. Obviously, the Israelis refused to contemplate this quid pro quo; the Coalition, including the Arab partners, dismissed it outright. His designs frustrated, Hussein bided his time and built up his strength.

The role of the United States in the Gulf War was not entirely uncontroversial. Shortly before the invasion of Kuwait, the U.S. ambassador to Iraq had failed to appreciate the danger of the dispute over the Rumaila oilfield. Neither had Hussein been warned to expect a vehement backlash from the United States in the event of hostilities. The nature of Iraq's stormy relationship with Iran made Hussein an ideal U.S. ally in the region. During the Iran-Iraq War, Iraq had received Washington's economic and military support. In light of the earlier U.S. sponsorship of Iraq, President Bush's coalition-building against Iraq, and his declared goal of ousting Hussein, which was beyond the liberation of Kuwait as stipulated by the pertinent UN resolutions, remain highly questionable. But to Bush, the invasion of Kuwait became a cause célèbre for what he termed the "new world order." Expressed in a more mundane manner, the crisis in the Persian Gulf region was the first of its kind after the dissolution of the Soviet Union, and Bush envisioned that the United States, as the sole surviving superpower, would lead the United Nations in an effort to enforce order in the international community. To his critics, Bush's idea of a new world order smacked of U.S. imperial pretensions and occasioned the reanimation of the old charge of acting as the world's policeman—the so-called globocop. In a similar vein, detractors accused the United States of going to war because it wanted to free oil from the clutches of Saddam and ensure a continuous flow to the industrial nations. Domestic critics attacked Bush for trying to circumvent the congressional prerogative of declaring war by obtaining a mandate from the United Nations. Either way, it seems that the conduct and policy of the United States during the Gulf War was equivocal.

Operation Desert Storm.   As the deadline drew closer, Hussein released his foreign hostages as a concession, and the Coalition attempted to cow Iraq into submission by displaying its quantitative and qualitative superiority. When Hussein's attempt to create goodwill failed, he mimicked the Coalition's show of force by threatening the Mother of All Battles and daring the Coalition to do its worst.[3] Iraq, Hussein promised, would use chemical weapons of mass destruction should the Coalition attack. These bitter exchanges and miscalculations on the part of Bush and Hussein—both believed the other would blink at the last moment—initiated the transition from Operation Desert Shield to Operation Desert Storm.

On 17 January 1991, the Coalition air force struck Baghdad. In the opening hours of the offensive, thousands of sorties demolished designated targets in and around the capital. Surgical strikes carried out with sophisticated high-tech weapons were capable of locating and eliminating comparably small targets. The world viewed broadcast images of lit-up skies over Baghdad, with continuous live coverage courtesy of CNN. The darker side of the Gulf War was that it no longer only served the ideal represented by the new world order but had also become a publicly advertised spectacle, an opportunity for Western arms manufacturers to demonstrate their products.

From 17 January to 22 February 1991, the so-called shooting war was fought in the air; at noon on 23 February, the land war commenced. It lasted only 100 hours, as Iraqi troopers, including the elite Republican Guards, retreated given the overwhelming odds. On 27 February, the war was effectively over. By 3 March, the Iraqi ambassador to the United Nations, Tariq Aziz, accepted terms for cessation of hostilities. Hussein, however, had struck back during the fighting by firing Soviet-manufactured Scud missiles at Israel—a country that was not part of the Coalition against Iraq. Hussein was hoping to provoke a hostile Israeli response, which in turn would weaken the resolve of the Arab members within the Coalition. The prospect of Israel's entry into the war was, indeed, an unsavory one to the United States, as well as to Israel's militarily vulnerable Arab neighbors; in such an event, the likelihood of the conflict being continued in limited terms would be almost nil. Israel's military superiority remained unchallenged in the region: an Israeli counterattack was likely to devastate Iraq and precipitate a regional war. For these reasons, the full weight of U.S. diplomacy was mobilized to keep Israel out of the war at all costs after Scud missiles detonated in Haifa and Tel Aviv. Israel cooperated when offered the protection of defensive Patriot missile batteries from the U.S. arsenal.

The U.S.-led forces won a decisive victory against Iraq in at least one respect: Kuwait was liberated. On a different score, however, the Coalition in the Gulf failed to achieve its objective. Despite the fact that Iraq's armed forces were reduced and its military installations largely destroyed, Saddam

Hussein remained in power. Adding insult to injury, Hussein turned his military setback into a moral victory by claiming to have resisted the combined might of the West. Moreover, liberated Kuwait had been left behind in a ruinous state by the Iraqi occupiers. Several hundred oil wells were set ablaze, and retreating Iraqi troops caused a massive oil spill in the Persian Gulf. In excess of 33,000 Kuwaitis had fallen to the Iraqis. Iraq had suffered between 30,000 and 90,000 casualties as opposed to the 466 killed and 1,187 wounded on the Coalition side, but Hussein demonstrated an uncanny ability to remain in power.

While the war was being fought, President Bush actively fomented rebellions against Hussein's regime in the south among Shiites and in the north among Kurds. While the Shiites seized Basra, the Kurds asserted themselves in the northern territories. Following the Gulf War, Bush abandoned the Shiites and the Kurds to their fates. Once the cease-fire between the Coalition and Iraq went into effect, Saddam Hussein wasted no time in meting out retribution in his own country. The brutal repression of the Shiites ended in the headlong flight of approximately 1 million refugees into adjacent Iran, and the suppression of the Kurdish revolt caused the deaths of 50,000 people and a mass exodus of Kurds into Turkey and Iran. The declaration of a regularly patrolled no-fly zone by the Coalition in southern Iraq was not enough to help the Shiites in their plight. One million Kurds were caught in the mountains in the border country, and a humanitarian catastrophe threatened to unfold. A belated decision on the part of the U.S., British, Dutch, and French governments to aid the Kurds staved off the worst effects of the potential disaster: in April 1991, a multilateral contingent ensured the safety of the Kurdish refugees and provided relief until the United Nations took over two months later.

Finally, the Iraqi Sunni majority suffered the ill effects of a strictly enforced economic embargo, with little hope for the near future. Saddam Hussein's intransigence, and his repeated violations of the terms stipulated in the cease-fire agreement, ensured that the blockade would remain in place. Hussein's refusal to allow UN inspectors on the premises of plants suspected of producing biological and chemical weapons of mass destruction was in direct contravention to the terms of the cease-fire. Repeated provocative acts that could only be construed as potentially hostile, such as troop movements toward the border with Kuwait in 1994, kept the United States on its toes. By the mid-1990s, the Coalition assembled against Saddam Hussein's regime in Iraq was falling apart. In 1996, the United States demonstrably failed to protect the Kurds in northern Iraq when Hussein's troops regained portions of Iraqi Kurdistan. At present, only the United States and a few allies continue to enforce the no-fly zones over Iraq.

IR Theory and Key Concepts

Neorealism Versus Neoliberalism

The debate between the neorealist and the neoliberal schools of thought is essentially concerned with the critique of the neorealist perspective of international relations and its conclusions. At the center of the debate stands the neorealist argument concerning the restricted role of international organizations in the process of shaping international politics. The Neorealist position is grounded in a tenet that the opportunities for cooperation in the international system under conditions of anarchy are marginal at best. Conversely, neoliberalist scholars have called neorealist arguments into doubt on two counts. Attempting to demonstrate the frailty of neorealist argumentative logic, neoliberalists question the logical coherence of their opponents' position. Moreover, neoliberalists criticize the paucity of neorealist arguments in their explanatory power—especially if compared to their own conclusions. Neoliberal arguments tend to build on the institutionalist tradition in that they postulate that under certain conditions—especially when based on complementary interest—cooperation can indeed develop. In general terms, institutions have a bearing on patterns of cooperation. In other words, neoliberalists criticize neorealists for failing to see that institutions can very well act as catalysts for international cooperation. Another point of contention in the debate is whether military capabilities (as stressed by the neorealists) or economic factors (emphasized by the neoliberalists) are more important in international affairs. Although both theories differ in important ways, they have much in common: an assumption of rational and utility-maximizing actors and similar methodologies.

Key Terms

- Neorealism is a school of thought derived from the realist perspective of international relations, also known as structural realism. The landmark neorealist text is *Theory of International Politics* (1979) by Kenneth Waltz. Neorealists are especially interested in investigating and explaining the behavior of states in an anarchic international system. They tend to highlight the encompassing validity of the structured nature of the international system and how that structure influences and restricts state actors in their preferences and choices. For neorealists, states show a tendency to balance against hegemonic powers rather than bandwagoning (i.e., joining the stronger side). A contentious point among neorealists is whether states try to seek security by maximizing power or by maintaining the status quo. Neorealists have had to face many criticisms, such as that they have ignored the significance of values and norms integral to classic realist theory as developed by Hans J. Morgenthau and E. H. Carr. Charges of this kind, even the label "neorealist" itself, have been denied by those deemed to be neorealist protagonists.

- Neoliberalists believe in the importance of nonstate actors and states and are therefore critical of pluralist (or liberal) theories that denigrate the relative significance of state actors. Neoliberalism constitutes a rationalist research program mainly developed as a response to neorealism in the 1980s. It emphasizes ways of mitigating the constraints that international anarchy imposes on states and absolute gains, and gives a high priority to analyzing the international political economy.

- Pluralism (liberalism) is the argument that nonstate actors are important forces in international relations. Clearly diverging from realist theory, pluralists assume that the state comprises many different groups such as bureaucracies, interest groups, and individuals in a state of competition. To pluralists, competing interests in global politics vary greatly and are certainly not confined to security policy. Due to the emphasis on the multiplicity of relevant actors and the diversity of significant factors in international relations, research on decisionmaking and transnational phenomena rank high on the pluralist agenda. Frequently, the term *liberalism* is used interchangeably with *pluralism*.

New Developments in the Emerging International System, 1991–2002

THE HISTORIC UPHEAVALS EXPERIENCED BETWEEN 1989 AND 1991 IN EUROPE AND elsewhere brought the Cold War to a close. The bipolar antagonism between two value and social systems (East and West) no longer defined the structure of international politics. The system of international relations that had influenced the Cold War period lost its validity in only a few years. A situation not dissimilar to that prevailing after World War II rendered the search for a new world order a pressing issue. Due to the implosion of the Soviet Union, the East's superpower, it was evident that the key impulse would have to emanate from the United States. Like Woodrow Wilson after World War I and Franklin D. Roosevelt during World War II, U.S. President George H.W. Bush presented his vision of a new world order against the backdrop of the Gulf War:

> We have within our grasp an extraordinary possibility that few genera-
> tions have enjoyed—to build a new international system with our values
> and ideals, as old patterns and certainties crumble around us. . . . I hope
> history will record that the Gulf crisis was the crucible of the new world
> order.[1]

During the early 1990s, many hoped that global security and global governance would be achieved by burgeoning international organizations such as the United Nations. There was a prevailing conviction that the process of economic globalization would underpin a peaceful world order. Some within the liberal school of thought interpreted the triumph of the free-market economy and the growth of international economic interdependence as a development that would contain conflict and, ultimately, render war obsolete. More than a decade later, such is not the case. At the beginning of the twenty-first century the term *world* dis-*order* seems to better characterize the last few years. Flatly contradictory to many forecasts, the state remains the single most important actor in the international system, and military power continues to play a significant role in international conflict management. Tensions between national and international security persist, and frequently diverging state interests and values will in all likelihood endure and continue to influence international relations.

Emerging Trends

The 1990s were a time of insecurity, continuous change, and a quest for new structures for an incipient post–Cold War international system. At the time of this writing, the search for a new international system has not been concluded. Many questions remain without answers, as evidenced by the September 11 attacks on New York City and Washington, D.C. A few observations can be made in light of these and related events. In the wake of the Cold War, international politics has become more complex, with multiple layers. Below, we identify trends and new developments characteristic of this transitory period from the end of the Cold War into the twenty-first century and map out the contradictory and complex developments of the 1990s and beyond.

From a Bipolar to a Multipolar System

With the end of the Cold War, the disciplining force of a bipolar international system became invalid. Within the Western alliance, as well as within the communist bloc, the perception of a common threat was the defining principle of order. Subsequent to the demise of the bipolar system, some observers believed they saw an emerging **unipolar** system, within which the international agenda would be set by the lone remaining superpower. This perspective, however, overrated U.S. possibilities in a world characterized by the diffusion of power.

Instead, the international system has assumed the characteristics of a multipolar political system in which the United States is contending alongside five or six other powers and in which several middle powers and many small states pursue their own national interests. The principles ordering the international system, however, are distinct from the balancing system of the eighteenth and nineteenth centuries in that the centers of power are distributed on a global scale and no longer limited to a particular region. Furthermore, the international order in the Euroatlantic area is complemented by a dense institutional network and well-ensconced multilateral structures.

The democratization of the state system.   Democracy has experienced significant growth and spread following the dissolution of several multiethnic communist states. Although calls for the end of history have proven premature, the broad trend toward democratization has had a significant impact on international politics: in the past, democracies exhibited a tendency toward a peaceful resolution of conflicts among themselves. Simultaneously, the decline of authoritarian government systems created two types of states—the ethnic splinter state and the transitional countries—each bedeviled by its own distinct set of problems.

Hard and soft power. The criteria that define power and influence of a state in the international system have undergone change since the 1970s. During the nuclear age the significance of military power entered a gradual downward slide as economic power gained prominence. In information and service economies and their societies, influence is no longer primarily derived from so-called hard power factors such as territory, military power, and natural resources. Conversely, soft power, characterized by information flows, technological achievement, and flexible institutions, has gained much weight.

The revolution in information technology and globalization has, however, not affected all states equally. Proportionally, we cannot speak of a complete upheaval and comprehensive change of existing power structures. Thus, the definition of *network power* better explains the relevance of the means of power in the future: power is generated by the interaction of diverse instruments of power in the context of international networks. Soft power derives its weight through the circumstance that represented values and objectives are based on a broad international consensus, are thereby possessed of political projective force, and hence can exert political pressure. Similarly, hard power employed in support of a soft power agenda in the present can no longer be brought to bear without broad international political support.

The multiplication of international actors. In an environment typified by decentralized networks and soft power structures, much ink has been spilled over the decline of the state. Indeed, economic and political power transfused upward to an international level on which new institutions, such as the European Union, established themselves; it also evidenced a lateral, external motion, thereby infusing civil society. New networks of interconnected transnational actors underwent rapid growth, at least in the Euroatlantic. Multinational corporations, currently numbering some 60,000, are being solicited, if not wooed, by states. The competition in the arena of corporate investments has become, if anything, more pronounced. But civilian organizations also acquired, and continue to develop, the ability to efficaciously influence the political agenda of information society. In the 1990s, the number of NGOs rose from 6,000 to no less than 26,000. Obviously, this development did not take place in a political vacuum but is intricately connected to a world also consisting of nation-states. States continue to represent the principal actors in international politics, but they are compelled—more or less successfully—to adjust their functions to a new international context. Successful international politics are tied to a functional collaboration between the public, civil, and private sectors in the sense of mutual global governance.

The Globalization of International Financial and Economic Relations

In the process of increasing economic globalization, the traditional Westphalian state system underwent change. Since the sixteenth century, international politics was conceived of and practiced in a manner that delineated domestic from foreign politics. In the course of the information revolution, the boundaries of nation-states have become more porous. Economic liberalization and privatization have caused enormous growth and encouraged cross-border flows of capital, services, and goods. Success in a global economy, however, also hinges upon local conditions: the level of education, the quality of the available infrastructure, and the legal and political context. The augmented significance of international economic politics demands that international politics has to be thought of in a different framework that sets global and local factors in relation to each other. In such an event, the darker side of economic globalization is more visible: globalization not only holds the tenuous promise of its potential blessings but also renders its dangers more palpable and manifests its risks.

The rise of international complex relations of state and nonstate actors has provided a massive boost to transnational financial and commercial activities, but it has also permitted drugs, nuclear material, and so-called dual-use technologies to circulate freely on a global scale, which has made the control of such hazardous traffic far more difficult. Although the activity radius of legitimate economic actors has expanded, the same applies to organized crime and international terrorism. Globalization bears new risks to international security and has simultaneously increased the difficulty of tackling such risks. Due to the growing importance of economic issues, foreign political decisionmaking processes became subject to the vagaries of election campaigns and pander to domestic political interests and linkages. Evidently, such a trend can easily lead to a massive leadership deficit in international relations, which given the rising global challenges is a matter of concern.

The Regionalization of the International Order

Globalization does not represent a global phenomenon. In fact, globalization not only has accentuated social tensions between the haves and have-nots but also has served to further highlight regional imbalances. The significance of regions in international relations has yet again gained ground. In the economic sphere of international relations, one can observe the formation of three incipient trading blocs that center on the dollar in North and South America, on the yen in the Asia Pacific, and on the euro in Europe. At the same time, a differentiation in the nature and principle of regional security structures can also be discerned, albeit with a major difference: as compared to the Cold War era, local and regional factors have assumed a preponderant role. International politics has become multilayered: postmodern, modern, and even premodern societies coexist and are intricately interconnected. The creation of structures of global governance, which will have to stand up to the complexity of the emerging international system, therefore will constitute the single most important task of international politics in the near future.

The Age of Intrastate Conflict

The end of bipolar power relations left in its wake a power vacuum, which in turn gave rise to new tensions and necessitated a reorientation of the international community. As the force of ideology was waning after the collapse of the Soviet Union, the ancient scourges of ethnic strife, religious fanaticism, and politically motivated intimidation and murder by small interest and pressure groups resurfaced in new, and especially unsavory, guises. Adding strength and virulence to these manifestations of the post–Cold War international system was the rapid development of communications, information, and weapons technologies in the digital age, which permitted all kinds of belligerent groups accelerated logistics, cost-effective dissemination of their creeds, and, worst of all, access to cheap homemade weapons of mass destruction. The combination of a transition from an industrial to an information age and the fundamental realignment in the global distribution of power gave a unique cast to world politics in the 1990s.

A trend during the 1990s was the shift from interstate to intrastate conflict. The actual number of wars fought between states had been declining overall, a development that gained impetus with the end of the Cold War. Even so, in excess of 5 million people died as a result of wars fought during the 1990s, more than in any other decade since the end of World War II. More than 90 percent of the casualties were civilians—women, children, and the elderly. This record is due largely to a steep increase in the number of intrastate conflicts in ethnic splinter states, transitory states, and developing states. Frequently, intrastate conflicts were fought for reasons of ethnicity and identity and were thus marked by excessive violence and unfettered emotional and irrational conduct. The protagonists of these intrastate conflicts were often nonstate actors who expediently employed chaotic civil war–like conditions to build alternative systems of profit and power. As a consequence, many of these nonstate actors had little or no interest in a peaceful settlement—if only because of economic considerations.

In the context of intrastate conflicts, traditional means proved insufficient to conduct crisis management and resolution, for those means had been developed to deter and contain interstate conflict. Accordingly, the international response to the many crises of the 1990s was not satisfactory. Usually, the international community reacted belatedly with humanitarian intervention and by employing massive military resources, as in Bosnia and Kosovo, and only after tens of thousands had lost their lives and hundreds of thousands had been forced to flee. Alternatively, the international community responded halfheartedly, as in Somalia and Rwanda, despite the fact that 850,000 people in Rwanda had been butchered.

Two issues led to intensive debates on the international level. The first concerned whether intervention in an intrastate conflict had any legal basis. Did a shift of paradigms in international law occur in the 1990s, one that condoned military intervention in the name of human rights at the expense of national sovereignty and equality as enshrined in the United Nations Charter? In the event such was the case, what criteria govern the right to intervene, and what role would the United Nations assume in such a situation? The war in Kosovo gave such discussions considerable weight, facilitating the expansion of the normative agenda since the end of the Cold War. Concurrently, and in stark contrast, the West's response during the second war in Chechnya illustrated that the timing of international intervention remained dependent upon the political will of states as much as upon international legal considerations.

The second issue was new military technology. Proponents of the so-called *revolution in military affairs* believed that employing modern information and communications systems, as well as flat command-and-control structures, could overcome the fog of war, that is, intelligent ammunition and high-precision weapons systems could vanquish opponents from a safe distance without causing excessive collateral damage (read: civilian casualties). Opponents of this view argued that high-tech weapons and operational precision would be of only limited value in intrastate wars and would be easily neutralized by asymmetric types of warfare such as guerrilla warfare and terrorism. Only the future will tell whether these skeptics' criticism is justified.

Even though intrastate conflicts tended to be spatially bounded and their potential for military escalation was usually considered manageable, the international community was coming under increasing pressure to address the nonmilitary consequences. Major migration flows, transnational organized crime, and the unfettered proliferation of antipersonnel landmines and small arms—as seen in the Balkans—have the potential to destabilize regions. In the event that the international community intervenes only after the mass media brings the humanitarian catastrophe into our living rooms, the costs of military and civil stabilization efforts may be expected to skyrocket. The total cost of the efforts to resolve the seven major crises of the 1990s is estimated at some U.S.$200 billion. Once an escalation of violence has led to the mobilization of contending groups—and to the inevitable victimization and crimes on both sides—military intervention can only hope to protect civilian populations against excesses in the short term. It cannot, however, serve as a foundation for a lasting peace settlement. Accordingly, the recall of peacekeeping forces often proved a difficult task for the community of states. In the final analysis, what is required of the international community is a change of paradigms, from a culture of reaction toward a culture of prevention. Moreover, the involvement not only of states but also of international organizations, exponents of civil society, and private industry is critical for the early recognition of potential conflicts and the peaceful solution of existing disputes.

Ethnic Cleansing: The Conflicts in Bosnia and Kosovo

In the 1990s, the Balkans became the site of increasing ethnic tensions, generally resulting from the dissolution of the Federal Republic of Yugoslavia formerly under Marshal Tito and the subsequent rise of Slobodan Milosevic. Because the centrifugal tendencies in the federal republic were no longer counteracted by the stern regime under Tito, and as the tide of political and economic disintegration could no longer be contained, tensions between the diverse ethnic groups increased to such an extent that ancient enmities between the peoples of the Balkans resurfaced and aspects of ethnic tensions became ever more prominent in politics. The six constituent republics of Yugoslavia—Slovenia, Croatia, Bosnia-Herzegovina, Serbia, Montenegro, and Macedonia—had always acted autonomously under Tito. But the power vacuum supplied by the concurrent dissolution of the Soviet Union afforded nationalist extremists an opportunity to stimulate ethnic and religious tensions.

In a first step, Slovenia and Croatia seceded from the federation in 1991. Though Slovenia was spared the ravages of war, Croatia was invaded by Yugoslavian troops but was nevertheless recognized as an independent state by the international community. In March 1992, Bosnia-Herzegovina followed, but its path to independence was fraught with dangers and difficulties. Mirroring the population of the federation, the Bosnian population was mostly of Slavic origin, though almost half were Muslims, some 30 percent Orthodox Christian Serbs, and another 20 percent Catholic Croats. When Bosnian leader Alija Izetbegovic sought and found the recognition of the international community for a common state of three nations, tensions between Muslims, Serbs, and Croats rose and quickly developed into open hostilities.

The Bosnia crisis.   The Bosnian Serbs, who could count on the support of the Yugoslavian federal forces, conquered some 70 percent of Bosnia's territory in a rapid advance. Nationalist politicians such as Serb leader Radovan Karadzic pursued the establishment of a greater Serbia and announced that they considered all territory inhabited or settled by Serbs as their own. In an effort to cow the Muslims, the Bosnian capital, Sarajevo, was besieged and shelled by Serb troops. As a reaction to a number of massacres committed by Serb regulars against civilians, the UN Security Council implemented an economic embargo against Serbia and Montenegro, the two remaining federated republics of Yugoslavia. A series of diplomatic and military initiatives entailing the reinforcement of peacekeeping forces and the brokering of peace plans, such as the failed Vance-Owen Plan of early 1993, followed in due course.

In 1992, UN peacekeeping forces established a number of security zones around Tuzla, Gorazde, Zepa, Sarajevo, Bihac, and Srebrenica in Bosnia. Despite these UN efforts, the peacekeeping forces proved unable to protect the Muslim population against Serb and Croat attacks. Instead of ensuring the safety of the civilians, UN troops were themselves caught in the crossfire, alternately blackmailed and threatened by the belligerent parties. The Serbs, however, were not the solitary culprits of the war: Muslims and Croats were quick to avenge the wrongs done them whenever the opportunity for punitive action afforded itself. The most heinous crime of the entire war—the Srebrenica massacre—was committed by Serb troops against Muslim civilians during 12–18 July 1995. Some 8,000 Muslims were systematically murdered, despite the circumstance that Srebrenica was under the protection of the **United Nations Protection Force (UNPROFOR)**. The international forces left Bosnian Muslims to their fate and did not attempt to hinder Karadzic and General Radko Mladic from perpetrating the most gruesome destruction of life on European soil since World War II. The international community did not back UN Resolution 819 to the hilt by complying with its key stipulation of making "use of force" to defend the Bosnian Muslims under its protection, a fact that undermined the reputation of the United Nations.[2]

Only toward the end of 1993, and following a one-sided waiver of the weapons embargo imposed earlier, were the Bosnians able to make up for the territorial losses with the support of Western arms. While the leaders took up negotiations, their respective forces in the field continued to fight for every yard. Only because of the heavy-handed intervention by the United States, which committed several cruise missiles to Operation Deliberate Force, could the Bosnian Serbs be persuaded to return to the negotiating table. Following a cease-fire, Serb, Croat, and Muslim Bosnian leaders met for talks under the auspices of UN Ambassador Richard Holbrooke at a U.S. Air Force facility near Dayton, Ohio. All parties involved at Dayton agreed to guarantee the existing borders of the Bosnian state, an elected parliament, and a presidential council composed of nine members drawn in equal parts from the three ethnic groups. They further agreed to guarantee freedom of movement for all Bosnian citizens, to allow all those refugees to return to their homes, and mutually decided to demilitarize Sarajevo. The task of enforcing the Dayton Accords was given to the **United Nations Implementation Force**. Thus, Bosnia was partitioned: 49 percent of the territory went to the Serbs, and the remainder was distributed between the Muslims and the Croatians.

The Kosovo crisis. The war in Bosnia (1992–1995) was the precursor to the Kosovo crisis, which began in 1998. Like the Bosnians, the Kosovars were ethnically divided. On the one side, the Serbs looked upon Kosovo as the cradle of their culture; on the other side, the Albanians demanded that Kosovo be handed over to them as their homeland. As early as March 1989, the de facto local autonomy granted by Tito to Kosovo as a Serbian province was withdrawn. Since July 1990, Kosovo was forcefully administered from Belgrade. In 1990, an illegal plebiscite demonstrated that 98 percent of all Albanian Kosovars demanded independence. The Kosovar independence movement was brutally suppressed by means of illegal arrest, abuse of political dissenters, and show trials. In the course of the 1990s, Belgrade effectively instituted a two-class society, with 200,000 Serbs holding all key positions, and 1.8 million Albanians deprived of all rights and no access to public schools, administration, and health services.

While the wars in Croatia and Bosnia held the center stage of events in the Balkans, Milosevic's regime violated human rights continuously in Kosovo, and the international community persistently ignored Albanian leader Ibrahim Rugova's pursuit of independence. Finally, in 1997 the newly surfaced Kosovo Liberation Army (KLA) staged a series of attacks against Serb police and administration. The increasing violence of the KLA's campaign and the armed Serb response escalated into civil war. By mid-1998, the KLA controlled 40 percent of Kosovo. Militarily speaking, the KLA's offensive was doomed from the very beginning; the KLA was gambling for a moral and political victory.

Following the visit of a mission headed by Richard Holbrooke in October 1998, the majority of the Serb units stationed in Kosovo were withdrawn, and it was agreed that 2,000 observers from the **Organization for Security and Cooperation in Europe (OSCE)** were to be deployed in the disputed area to verify the local conditions and ascertain free elections. With the onset of winter, however, fully armed KLA fighters returned to territories previously held by the Serbs. The KLA's actions stood in direct contravention to the agreement brokered by Holbrooke with the Serbs. Because the OSCE lacked sufficiently trained personnel, armored cars, and, most of all, financial resources, the outcome of the Kosovo mission was a foregone conclusion. Meanwhile, on the diplomatic stage, politicians led by the British and French governments sought a solution to the intractable Kosovo problem in Rambouillet, France. The United States exhausted its diplomatic arsenal and applied maximum pressure to the belligerents to bring about a peaceful settlement.

Due to the discovery and media coverage of massacres and atrocities perpetrated against the Albanian population, hawks within NATO, who advocated a forceful resolution of the Kosovo Crisis, won the upper hand. Finally, on 24 March 1999 NATO commenced the bombardment of Yugoslavian military installations. For the first time in its fifty-year history, NATO was embroiled in hostile activities. As Serb regular units began their offensive against Albanians in Kosovo, which was compounded by attacks of Serb guerrillas, thousands of Albanians fled across the borders into adjacent states. The catastrophe that NATO had sought to avoid was propelled forward by the unfolding events. During the seventy-two-day aerial war waged by NATO against the Serb combatants in Kosovo, the highly mobile enemy ground troops proved impossible to destroy.

The politics of ethnic cleansing.   The Yugoslavian civil war was fought between 1991 and 1999 and cost thousands of lives, displaced millions, and reduced significant numbers to a state of homelessness. The politics of **ethnic cleansing**, by which an advantageous fait accompli of predominantly Serbian settled territory in Kosovo for the upcoming negotiations was to be brought about, was given highest priority and was pursued with the utmost ruthlessness. Milosevic's tactic of ethnic cleansing in Kosovo was identical to the one previously employed by his regime in Bosnia: he deployed the full force of the military against the civilian population while masking a campaign of terror directed against the same groups in the confusion of an armed conflict. Many non-Serbian denizens were compelled to quit the territories claimed by the Serbs in a relatively short period. Sometimes, the Serb military commanders who were involved in the war crimes during the war in Bosnia were employed to repeat the experience in Kosovo. The most notorious war criminal to emerge from the Yugoslav succession wars was Zeljko Raznatovic, a/k/a the infamous "Arkan."

In many a Kosovar village, ethnic minorities—and sometimes even the entire resident population—were forcibly expelled and interned, then subjected to organized mass rape and carefully planned wholesale executions. Businesses and houses were burned and pillaged; by destroying the municipal records of the citizenry, the refugees were systematically deprived of a verifiable identity. Subsequent to the war, more than 200 mass graves were discovered. For the duration of the hostilities and in the context of peace negotiations, the populations of Bosnia and Kosovo had been distinguished according to their respective ethnic origins. Ironically, the policy of those who had made use of ethnic cleansing was proved to be a resounding success. Before the war, some 225,000 Serbs had lived in the Muslim-Croat territory of Bosnia. By 1996, some 36,000 remained in their homes. In the areas controlled by the Serb authorities, the number of Muslim inhabitants had declined from 840,000 to 73,000.

Some of those responsible at the political level—including Karadzic and Milosevic—were indicted by a UN-led **international war crimes tribunal**, but to this day the warrant for Karadzic's arrest and arraignment has not been executed. The trial of Slobodan Milosevic was undertaken in the Hague, Netherlands, under the authority of the UN International Criminal Tribunal for the Former Yugoslavia (ICTY). The trial, which began on 12 February 2002, was expected to continue for two years. It is exemplary in that it is the first time that a head of state has been held accountable before an international court on such charges. Milosevic was charged with more than sixty counts, including genocide, for war crimes committed in Bosnia, Croatia, and Kosovo during the 1990s when he was the president of Serbia and later Yugoslavia. Some 350 witnesses were listed to testify against the former Yugoslav president. On 11 September 2002 the prosecution in the Milosevic case finished presenting its case with regard to Kosovo. The part of the Milosevic trial pertaining to Croatia and Bosnia and Herzegovina started on 26 September 2002. Moreover, the Milosevic trial no doubt will have an impact on the establishment of the permanent International Criminal Court. Many suspects sought by the ICTY remain at large.

In Bosnia as well as in Kosovo, the victims of ethnic cleansing were instrumentalized by the media as well as by the information policy of the belligerents; all sides manipulated the public. To this day, forensic experts remain in the dark as to the nature of the Racak massacre, which was the principal catalyst for NATO's intervention in Kosovo. The possibility that the bodies found on the site of the alleged massacre at Racak had been previously manipulated by the KLA remains extant. In the same vein, no conclusive evidence concerning the existence of concentration camps in Bosnia has surfaced. In any event, the tragedy of the events in the former Yugoslavia, which have been supported by the undeniable weight of incontrovertible proof, in themselves bear testimony to the terrible consequences of ethnic war.

Ethnic Tensions in Rwanda and Burundi

In the 1990s, the ravages of ethnic war were not confined to the Balkans, Eastern Europe, and the former Soviet Union. An ancient conflict in

Rwanda and Burundi in Africa flared up between 1988 and 1996. The central problem in the unfolding ethnic hostilities in Burundi, but especially in Rwanda, was an artificially reinforced distinction between the Hutu and Tutsi tribes living in the area. Historically, the Hutus, who represented the majority, had settled and cultivated the area for hundreds of years before Tutsi herdsmen arrived in the fifteenth and sixteenth centuries from the Horn of Africa. The Tutsis, who set up a monarchy, suppressed the Hutus over the next few centuries. By the time Belgian colonists finally released Burundi and Rwanda into independence, the old ethnic divisions had been magnified by the Belgian practice of issuing ethnic identity cards. Even to the practiced eye, the outward differences between Hutus and Tutsis were not readily recognizable; the colonial rulers had furthered the apartheid between the two tribes by granting the Tutsis preferential status. Thus, when both countries were released into independence in 1962, decades of colonial policies had artificially reanimated and reinforced the vestigial ethnic lines of divisions.

Since 1962, ethnic tensions in Burundi and Rwanda have led to a sadly repetitious cycle. Usually, tensions would escalate along an almost predictable course. The disadvantaged Hutu majority in Burundi, which represented some 85 percent of the total population, would rise up against the Tutsis and go on a killing spree, only to be savaged in turn by the vengeful Tutsis. In Rwanda, Hutu army officers attempted to oust the Tutsi-dominated government in 1965, but their design was thwarted by Tutsi elements in the armed forces. The aftermath to the coup saw the wholesale destruction of the entire Hutu leadership. In Burundi, where the Tutsi ascendancy was firmly established, a Hutu rebellion in 1972 resulted in a Tutsi campaign of mass murder. Some 250,000 Hutus died at the hands of the Tutsis. The following year, a coup led by a highly decorated Hutu officer, Juvénal Habyarimana, overthrew the established Rwandan government and permanently ended Tutsi supremacy. Thus, what had been a disappearing distinction between the two tribes in the immediate precolonial period had become a stark political reality by the 1980s. The repetitive cycle of death and destruction ensured that Hutus and Tutsis would find no common ground in the near future.

While tribalism burgeoned and the hostilities in Burundi continued in their usual manner, the invasion of northern Rwanda by formerly exiled Tutsis organized as the Rwandan Patriotic Front (RPF) in late 1990 began the first round of open hostilities in the country's long civil war. The conflict did not really end after the conclusion of an armistice in August 1993. Meanwhile, in Burundi, the assassination of a democratically elected Hutu president, Melchior Ndadaye, by Tutsi militants sparked a bloody confrontation in which 50,000–100,000 people were killed and more than 500,000 displaced. In 1994, civil war between the Hutus and the Tutsis again broke out in Rwanda after President Habyarimana was killed when his aircraft was shot down over the Rwandan capital of Kigali. Burundi's Hutu president, Cyprien Ntaryamira, had accompanied his Rwandan colleague on his flight to Kigali and was killed as well. The Hutus accused the Tutsis of the murder of the two presidents and embarked upon a campaign of terror. The persecuted Rwandan Tutsis joined the RPF and commenced operations against the government. The RPF's campaign was successful, and its leader, Paul Kagame, formed a new government but was careful to share his power with Hutu politicians.

Tens of thousands of Rwandans died in massacres, and many thousands fled the country. When the worst of the fighting seemed over, disease, particularly cholera, continued to ravage the population. After the end of the April 1994 massacres, in which as many as 500,000 people died—more than 90 percent of them Tutsis—the exiled Tutsis began returning to Rwanda. The death toll rose to more than 1 million. Relief for the refugees—both Hutu and Tutsi—came too late for many despite the fact that almost a fourth of the combined global relief resources were sent to Rwanda and Burundi. Despite the successful conclusion of an agreement between Rwandan authorities and the relevant UN institution, the Hutu refugees feared returning to their homes because of potential Tutsi reprisals. Worse, they were afraid to be attacked by the remnants of the defeated Hutu military. Finally, the return of large numbers of Tutsis, some of whom had been living in neighboring countries since 1959, raised fears of a return of minority domination. In any event, the refugee camps straddling the borders with Zaire and Tanzania, as well as the continuing deaths in the camps due to exposure and the lack of food and water, remained a fact of life in 1996, by which time the Hutu-Tutsi conflict engulfed the borderlands with Zaire.

Bands of armed Hutus crossed the border into Zaire, where they linked up with Zairian regulars to drive off the Tutsis inhabiting the area. In response to the Hutu attacks, the Rwandan Tutsis collaborated with their Zairian brethren in an effort to dislodge the Hutus there. The marauding Hutu and Tutsi bands frequently targeted refugee camps in the border area around the city of Goma. Numerous Hutus were compelled to abandon their camps and return to the Rwandan heartland. In Zaire, the armed uprising of the Tutsis erupted into a full-scale conflict. Tutsi troops under the command of Laurent Kabila conquered the country's capital of Kinshasa and overthrew Zairian President Mobuto Sese Seko. The consequence of the ongoing Hutu-Tutsi strife was a general destabilization of the region. Several African states began the arduous and mostly fruitless task of restoring a semblance of order by straining their diplomatic resources in an attempt to bring about a settlement between Kabila and Mobuto. After tribal strife in Rwanda and Burundi had abated, the United Nations endeavored to launch a gargantuan inquiry into the genocides committed by Hutu and Tutsi extremists. An international war crimes tribunal faced the prospect of investigating close to 100,000 individuals suspected of war crimes during the massacres committed on both sides during the period 1994–1995. Nevertheless, tit-for-tat killings continue in Rwanda and Burundi, albeit below the threshold of open warfare. At the time of this writing, there was no end in sight to the feud between the Hutus and Tutsis.

The Struggle for Kurdistan

The oldest and among the most tragic of ethnic conflicts relates to the Kurds. In an area bounded by the Caucasus, Anatolia, and Iran, which is known historically as Kurdistan, one of the oldest cultures and peoples of this world ekes out an existence in a political climate utterly inimical to their national aspirations. Kurds have played a significant role in the history of the region currently occupied by the states of Iran, Iraq, and Turkey. The Kurds founded several important states during the Islamic epoch between the tenth and thirteenth centuries, as well as in the distant past. The Turks, whose roots are in Middle Asia, migrated to Anatolia via Iran after the eleventh century and founded the Seljuk state and subsequently the Ottoman state. For a long time, Kurdistan was the site of military clashes between the Ottoman and Persian Empires. During this period, Kurdish princes sided first with one and then the other state, thus maintaining their autonomy. But in the year 1638, Kurdistan was officially divided between these two powers in the Treaty of Kasri Shirin. From that time until the mid–nineteenth century, Ottomans and Persians made armed attacks on the Kurdish princedoms to destroy them.

The Kurds' struggle against their enemies took on a nationalistic character at the beginning of the nineteenth century. Kurdish princes fought for the unity and independence of Kurdistan, but they were ultimately defeated. After World War I, the Ottoman Empire became history: new states arose on its former territory. According to the Treaty of Sèvres of 1920, the state of Kurdistan was also to be established in the region. But this was not implemented. In the Treaty of Lausanne, signed in 1923, that part of Kurdistan that had been controlled by the Ottoman Empire was carved up again. Part of it was included in British and French mandates, whereby Syria and Iraq later came into being. The largest part of Kurdistan remained within the state borders of the Republic of Turkey, which had been founded on the ruins of the Ottoman Empire.

The case of Turkey. The old Ottoman and the Persian Empires did not question the existence of the Kurdish people at any time. The Republic of Turkey also initially defined its new borders as encompassing territories settled by Turks and Kurds. However, after the signing of the Treaty of Lausanne, Ankara's policy rapidly changed. The structures of the new state were designed wholly in accordance with Turkish interests. The Kurds' existence was denied. The Kurdish language, the practice of Kurdish culture, even the concepts of Kurdish and Kurdistan were forbidden. The leadership of the modern Turkish state paid no attention to the multicultural structure of Anatolia, which was in fact a mosaic of different ethnic groups. A key element of their policy was the forced integration of other languages and cultures into the mainstream of Turkish language and culture, thus creating a unified nation under duress. Article 39 of the Treaty of Lausanne, according to which the citizens of Turkey have the right to freely use their respective languages in all areas of life, was trampled upon, and the use of the Kurdish language was forbidden in the educational system and the printed media. Speaking about the Kurds and criticizing the oppression of them was held to be a crime and was severely punished.

In 1925, Kurds led by Shaikh Said Piran rose up against their oppressors. But the uprising was brutally suppressed; tens of thousands of Kurds were killed and driven into exile. There were more Kurdish insurgencies in subsequent years, the major ones taking place in Ararat in 1930 and in Dersim in 1938. After 1938, there was a relatively peaceful hiatus that lasted about twenty years. However, it is not surprising that the Kurds—who had no national rights and were being subjected to oppression and persecution, who were forced into poverty and ignorance, and who saw all peaceful and legal avenues of political struggle closed off—once again began to arm themselves against the oppression of the Turkish state. Since 1979, Turkey has ruled its Kurd minority through military law, a state of emergency, and its own dirty war.

The emergence of the Kurdistan Workers Party (PKK) in 1978 altered the rules of engagement in the conflict between Ankara and Kurds living in Turkey. Under the leadership of Abdullah Öcalan, the PKK has waged a protracted and costly guerrilla war against the Turkish state. In recent years, PKK activists have also staged spectacular protests in many major European capitals, including mass demonstrations, occupation of press bureaus, and voluntary self-incinerations. Negotiations for a settlement and devolved government in Turkish Kurdistan have failed to solve the conflict, as the insurgents demand at least autonomy and, at most, independence. A massive Turkish offensive in 1991 resulted in the destruction of Kurd strongholds in Anatolia and northern Iraq. As a consequence, the PKK has intensified and broadened its campaign to include terrorist attacks against Turkish businesses abroad—especially in Europe. Ankara launched a second campaign against Kurdish rebels in Anatolia in 1995 and has repeatedly pursued Kurdish resistance fighters into Iraqi territory. In January 1999, the PKK suffered its worst political setback when a Turkish special unit—

allegedly with the collusion of U.S. and Israeli intelligence services—pinpointed and abducted Öcalan from the Greek embassy in Nairobi and put him on trial. The outcome of Öcalan's trial, in which the defendant was accused of high treason, was at best a political farce: he was to be executed. Massive protests by Kurdish expatriates in Europe succeeded in galvanizing international sympathy for Öcalan and his cause. Due to great pressure exerted by the European Union and the international community at large, Ankara has deferred the sentence.

The case of Iraq.   The Kurds living within the borders of Iraq, in a region considered by some as "southern Kurdistan," have also been resisting oppression since World War I. They, too, staged uprisings against repressive regimes, uprisings that also ended in defeat. In Iraq, however, a certain measure of toleration and autonomy was extended to the Kurds. Moreover, as a result of the uprisings, Kurds were granted certain cultural rights. They were given access to schools, universities, and the media. The most serious Kurdish uprising in northern Iraq began in 1961 under Mustafa Barzani and lasted until 1970. In 1970, Kurds reached an agreement with the central government concerning an autonomous region. However, the government in Baghdad stalled the Kurds and ignored the conditions of the agreement. For this reason, war broke out again in 1975. With several pauses, this struggle lasted until 1991.

The war against the Kurds has been expensive for Iraq. In order to halt Iran's support of the Kurds, the regime of Saddam Hussein initially made territorial concessions to Iran, then under the rule of Shah Reza Pahlavi. Then, for a variety of reasons but also to win back these areas, Iraq started the destructive eight-year war against revolutionary Iran, which devastated Kurdistan. Iraq even used poison gas in its attacks on the Kurds. After the Iran-Iraq War ended, Iraq invaded Kuwait and started the Gulf War, and Saddam Hussein suffered a massive defeat by the Coalition forces. Goaded into rebellion by the Coalition, Kurds rose against the Hussein regime, only to be abandoned by their Western confederates. The Kurds were initially subjected to mass expulsion, but later a UN declaration created a security zone for them. The refugees returned to their homeland. In northern Iraq, the Kurds created a parliament and a national government. But to this day the problem has still not been solved. Iraq is subject to a continuing UN embargo, and Iraqi Kurds are in an extremely difficult situation: they do not support the central government in Baghdad yet suffer from the effects of the embargo.

The case of Iran.   Iran has practiced a policy of oppression against the Kurds similar to that of Turkey. After World War II, when Iran was occupied in the north by the Soviet Union and in the south by Great Britain,

Kurds were able to pause for breath and quickly organized themselves. The Democratic Party of Kurdistan was founded, and subsequently the Kurdish Republic of Mahabad was proclaimed. But soon thereafter the government in Tehran, with the political support of Great Britain and the United States, annihilated the Republic of Mahabad. But the Kurdish people's resistance has not ceased. When the shah's regime was overthrown in 1978, this part of Kurdistan could once again enjoy freedom. Yet this phase did not last long, either, as the new regime of mullahs attacked. The armed resistance to this regime, which began in 1979, continues today. In general, the Kurds have and are still being persecuted and oppressed by the governments of Turkey, Iraq, and Iran, each of which claims parts of the historic Kurdistan territory. The Kurdish quest for a home state continues without a solution in sight. Meanwhile, Kurds continue to fight a war on several fronts that they cannot win.

Displacement and the Refugee Problem During the 1990s

The displacement of hundreds of thousands of civilians from their homes in Iraq, Turkey, and Iran due to civil and ethnic conflict is not a phenomenon confined to the Kurds. The growth of intrastate conflicts in the 1990s witnessed a marked upsurge in the numbers of refugees and **asylum-seekers** worldwide. The problem of migration stimulated by hostilities has become one of the most important concerns of the United Nations. In its report for the year 2000, the **United Nations High Commissioner for Refugees (UNHCR)**, the relevant UN agency, estimates that some 22 million people are to be considered displaced for various reasons. In 1990, the UNHCR was extending aid to some 17 million; by 1995, the number of "concerned persons" skyrocketed to an unprecedented 27 million. The reasons for this upsurge are manifold. One can begin by enumerating the principal events responsible for the sharp rise in the number of **displaced persons**, such as the dissolution of the Soviet Union as well as inter- and intrastate war in the Balkans, Afghanistan, Indonesia, the Great Lakes and Horn of Africa, and the Persian Gulf. This list is far from comprehensive; it recalls only some of the most severe crises resulting in the uprooting of peoples.

There are various types of displaced persons. According to the UNHCR, no less than 11.6 million have been classed as refugees, that is, persons who are outside their country and cannot return "owing to a well-founded fear of being persecuted for reasons of race, religion, nationality, membership of a particular social group or political opinion."[3] The Cartagena Declaration of 1984 went so far as to include those who have been forced to flee because of war or civil war. In 2000, some 2.5 million refugees agreed to return to their country of origin. These **returnees** often require special assistance on the part of the United Nations, national authorities, and NGOs in order to restart their lives. More often than not, conditions in the country of origin remain too destabilized for refugees to return in safety.

The second category concerns asylum-seekers, a term that describes refugees who have applied for sanctuary in a state other than their own. Currently, there are some 1.2 million applications for asylum in countries around the world. Their status remains unresolved, largely due to complex bureaucratic procedures in the sanctuary states. Procedures governing admission and/or refusal of asylum-seekers adopted by most of these destination states are more often than not too cumbersome and prevent rapid handling of many cases. Improved travel opportunities have resulted in greater mobility, which in turn has compelled wealthy nations in the West to implement stringent immigration and asylum legislation to render their countries less attractive to asylum-seekers. In the 1990s, this led to an enormous backlog of asylum applications. The European states especially have faced a host of problems caused by refugees from the former Federal Republic of Yugoslavia, where the hardships of the war caused many people to flee their homes.

Fears among indigenous populations in Western and Central European countries regarding job losses and financial outlays for asylum-seekers have often led to xenophobia and ugly excesses. Finally, the recent upheavals around the globe have also increased the number of **internally displaced persons (IDPs)**. The prime catalyst for the growing number of IDPs, which do not fall within the UNHCR's mandate, was the dissolution of the Soviet Union. IDPs living in the former Soviet Union usually forfeited citizenship because none of the Soviet successor states would extend the privileges of citizenship to them. In many cases, the Soviet problem originated in the mass resettlement programs of the communist era, during which one ethnic group was frequently foisted upon another to suit the agenda of the central planners or the state's security interests. Globally, the total number of IDPs is currently estimated at 5.4 million.

Since 1995, the number of displaced persons has decreased to approximately 22 million. But many problems wait to be tackled, one of which— the integration of refugees and asylum-seekers—can threaten to overtax a host country. The lot of the asylum-seekers is frequently harsh: barely tolerated by their host societies due to their foreign, even alien-seeming cultures, asylum-seekers seek safety in the familiar surroundings of expatriate communities, which often leads to more recriminations, misunderstandings, and a mutually perceived segregation from indigenous populations. In a more general sense, the UNHCR's constraints in effectively helping displaced persons have been hampering its efficacy. On the one hand, the UN agency operates on an annual budget of roughly U.S.$1 billion—not nearly enough to tackle the gargantuan task stipulated by its mandate; on the other hand, UNHCR manpower—some 5,000 agents—are not nearly enough to coordinate relief work and to distribute the food, shelter, and medicines to the needy. Thus, the threat of a humanitarian disaster in any of the affected areas continues to linger within sight.

The Resurgence of Political Polarization

The close of the Cold War brought an increase in the number of intrastate conflicts in postcommunist transition countries and in developing states. And to a lesser or greater extent, major shifts in politics could be observed in other regions. Such trends are intricately linked to a general resurgence of local and national political forces in the wake of the century of ideologies and are partly the result of a steep increase in migration, intrastate conflict, and the concomitant xenophobia building in the host countries. Two of these shifts in regional politics stand out: the first in Europe (because it was a full turnabout), the second in South America (because of its resilience and escalation).

The decline of the New Left and the reemergence of political rightwing extremism in Europe after the Cold War constitute a new trend that continues today. As we have seen, the most radical and violent exponents of the New Left in Europe—the Marxist terrorist groups—declined throughout the 1980s and moved toward extinction in the 1990s. The waning of their power to intimidate was a sign of the times. Concurrently, the mainstream of the constitutional left-wing parties became more moderate, merged with the peace and Green movements in the 1980s, and was firmly established as a legitimate left-of-center parliamentary actor in the 1990s. The European political right, by contrast, grew in strength after 1980. In fact, the rise of right-wing parties all over Europe awakened fears of a new political extremism.

The rise of Europe's New Right.   The list of protagonists on the far right is impressive, but some examples should suffice. In France, Jean-Marie Le Pen founded the Front National in 1972 and gained a substantial mandate in elections throughout the 1980s. Preunification Germany sported the ultraconservative Republikaner Party, which at one point carried about 10 percent of the vote in local elections. German reunification resulted in a dramatic upsurge of voters on the far right; continuing unemployment in the former East Germany ensures that the reservoir of frustration will remain at dangerously high levels for years. Despite the federal government's strict practice of outlawing any form of organization suspected of propagating fascist ideology, the German right wing also has its own radical fringe, composed of various neo–National Socialist groups responsible for many racist and anti-Semitic hate crimes.

The Lega Nord of Umberto Bossi is probably the most notorious of the ultra-right Italian parties for having (ineffectually) declared an independent state—Padania—in northern Italy. Established in 1991, the Lega has campaigned for secession of the wealthy north from the poverty-ridden south and has, not infrequently, employed an intrinsically racist vocabulary in the pursuit of its goals. More recently, the electoral advances of conservative parties in Switzerland and Austria have caused some consternation. While the Swiss People's Party is essentially conservative and sometimes even reactionary, the history and rhetoric of Jörg Haider and his Austrian Freedom Party gave rise to apprehensions; the Freedom Party's accession to a coalition government in 1999 prompted the European Union to formally suspend Austrian membership in several EU bodies.

In light of the darker chapters in European history, the simultaneous rise of right-wing constitutional parties throughout the Continent can be understood as a significant new development in post–Cold War international relations. As opposed to the fascist parties of the period between World War I and World War II, the New Right invariably seeks to pass xenophobic legislation and to retain idealized nationalistic values. But the recurrence of the right-wing extremist movement is linked in part to the steady influx of foreigners since the 1960s—whether guest workers, asylum-seekers, or refugees. The radical fringe of the New Right may from time to time employ fascist rhetoric and publicly espouse its principles, but at heart it is a reactionary movement. Nevertheless, European political extremism differs from comparable phenomena elsewhere in that it has a well-established record of excess. It is the burden of that past that renders the rise of the European New Right such a sensitive and potentially dangerous phenomenon. Significantly, as the recent Austrian example demonstrated, the fear of an ascendant New Right may also pose a serious challenge to the fragile European integration process.

The persistence of revolutionary movements in Peru and Colombia. In some South American states, the radical left has proven indomitable despite government persecution and has even intensified its war against the incumbent powers. Historic, deep-rooted, and blatant social injustice has led to agrarian violence in most of Latin America over the years. In international relations, the persistence of a revolutionary movement in South America— especially in Peru and Colombia—is diametrically opposed to the recrudescence of the extreme right in Europe. It also stands out as a unique feature since 1990.

Largely rural, a significant segment of Peru's peasant population (*los campesinos*) consists of the indigenous Indios, who have traditionally been subjected to exploitation by the landowners. Economic stagnation and decline have forced many *campesinos* to migrate into the large urban centers, the greatest of which is Lima. The influx of Indio peasants from the countryside has contributed to the establishment of sprawling slums, not unlike Brazil's infamous *favelas*. A constellation of bad government, economic recession, and massive inflation in the 1970s and 1980s gave rise to widespread dissatisfaction in general and outright dissent in Peru's disadvantaged rural provinces. With poverty levels rising, two revolutionary organizations established during that period made war on the central government in Lima: the Maoist Shining Path (Sendero Luminoso) and the Movimento Revolucionario Tupac Amaru (MRTA, named for a famous Peruvian rebel leader of the eighteenth century). Shining Path was founded by a left-leaning philosophy professor, Abimael Guzman Reynoso, who proceeded to inculcate the *campesinos* with Maoist values, strategies, and tactics—the assumption being that underprivileged rural Indios would rise against the hated central government as the Chinese rose under Mao after World War II.

The accession of Alberto Fujimori to the presidency in 1990, and the subsequent liberalization of the Peruvian economy, worsened the situation for the masses. Some 40 percent of all Peruvians are malnourished and lack access to medical aid. Fujimori's autocratic style of government drove many more into the arms of the revolutionary left. Although Guzman succeeded in escalating the conflict in the early 1990s and even controlled large tracts of territory for extended periods, the brutality of his campaign eroded the very support he required to launch a popular uprising. He was captured in 1992, and the government proceeded to extend amnesty to members of the Shining Path as well as MRTA; as many as 6,300 of an estimated 8,000 resistance fighters accepted. This dealt the Shining Path a crippling blow, albeit without destroying the organization root and branch. Some 700 guerrillas continue to struggle against the government troops to this day. MRTA was established in the mid-1980s and is probably best known for its spectacular occupation of the Japanese embassy in Lima between December 1996 and April 1997, which culminated in the storming of the premises by U.S.-trained antiterrorist units and the deaths of all the MRTA occupiers. As a movement, MRTA continues underground and is known to collaborate with the Shining Path. The threat of violence from the revolutionary left may be contained for the moment; it is, however, not ended.

The Colombian example reads like a parallel of the Peruvian case. A politically divided oligarchy has ruled the country since the nineteenth century. Liberal and conservative elites failed to provide the country a stable government and frequently proved incapable of ameliorating the worst problems faced by Colombians. Extreme social stratification, a grossly imbalanced distribution of wealth—some two dozen families own 40 percent of the gross national product—as well as long-standing suppression of opposition movements calling for social justice provoked a violent response centered around a traditional leftist underground. The most powerful organization of the radical left is Fuerzas Armadas Revolucionarias de Colombia (FARC), which since its inception in 1982 has conquered 40 percent of the country. Moreover, FARC is in control of the single largest production site of cocaine on Earth. The fact that FARC is known to have engaged in **narcoterrorism**—that is, using funds accruing from the sale of drugs to further the revolutionary cause—goes a long way to show just how cynical and depraved the conflict between the Colombian government and the guerrillas has become.

In the past, FARC collaborated with the infamous Medellín cartel, a powerful drug syndicate, which prompted the Colombian government to call on the United States for support. Throughout the 1990s, the U.S. Drug Enforcement Agency, alongside regular Colombian troops, fought a protracted war against FARC, with no end in sight. Despite several government overtures to negotiate a settlement, FARC has proven adamant in its demands and unwillingness to be cajoled into a cessation of hostilities. U.S. involvement has escalated the conflict; in the 1990s, the Colombian civil war was transformed from a struggle against social injustice into a clash of two interest groups vying for supreme power by whatever means necessary. Sadly, it is only the leftist trappings and Marxist rhetoric that distinguish one from the other.

Russia and the Former Soviet Union

Like no other event in the 1990s, the dissolution of the Soviet Union left its mark on the emerging international system. The contraction of Soviet power to a Russian core gave the forces of nationalism great force in the territories of the former Soviet Union, as well as in adjacent areas. As a result, a series of ethnic conflicts were fought in the region. Moreover, relations between the successor Russian Federation and the former Soviet republics were in need of redefinition—a task that proved difficult due to historical legacies and political and economic interdependencies. Conversely, Russia had to come to terms not only with the loss of an ideology but also with the loss of empire. At the same time, the Russian Federation was faced with the complex challenges of an economic and political transformation, a process fraught with pain and difficulty. The internal development of Russia and the shaping of its relations with former Soviet states would have a decisive influence on the formative processes of the emerging international system.

Russia, because it now possessed the former Soviet Union's nuclear arsenal and its permanent seat on the UN Security Council, held the same trappings as a Great Power. How would the relations between the Russian

Federation and the only remaining superpower, the United States, develop against such a backdrop—especially concerning nuclear capabilities? The image and rhetoric of a political giant, however, became increasingly difficult to reconcile with the possibilities of an economic dwarf. The erosion of Russian power is reflected in a 1999 gross national product of only 58 percent of the 1989 level—a GNP smaller than Austria's. In addition, Russian economic dependence on EU states became more pronounced throughout the 1990s. How would Russian relations with the European Union and NATO develop in light of the fact that those two organizations were sponsoring initiatives to expand eastward? The West could not afford to ignore the Russian Federation because of Russia's strength and the federation's frailty. Precisely because Russia frequently exhibited the characteristics of a regional power, the impact caused by its development was not limited to Europe. Would a power vacuum in Asia and the Middle East follow the dissolution of the Soviet Union? Developments in Russia were important indeed.

The Core: The Making of the Russian Federation

The accession of Mikhail Gorbachev to power in 1985 made possible the introduction to sweeping reforms under the twin aims of *glasnost* and *perestroika* (see Chapter 6). The birth of the Russian Federation occurred amid the ruins of the old Soviet Union and was masterminded by a politician out of favor with the old order. When Gorbachev introduced *perestroika* in the late 1980s, reformers and conservatives alike criticized him. Boris Yeltsin was among Gorbachev's most strident critics, and following Yeltsin's defeat in the power struggle against conservatives in 1987, Yeltsin was forced to the sidelines. His return to politics in 1990 heralded the end of the Soviet Union and led to the creation of the Russian Federation.

Frightened by the impetus *perestroika* had gained, Gorbachev veered to the right in 1990. The principal reason for this shift was the so-called Shatalin Plan, named after the Soviet economist Stanislav Shatalin, who advocated the installation of a market economy within eighteen months. Gorbachev feared the consequences of such a radical transition of the Soviet economy and therefore allied with conservative forces in the Kremlin in late 1990. Yeltsin anticipated Gorbachev's reaction and chose that moment to officially quit the Communist Party. What followed had all the trappings of a communist reaction in the face of destabilizing forces: as Eduard Shevardnaze, Gorbachev's principal supporter of *perestroika* and Soviet foreign minister, proffered his resignation on 20 December 1990, he warned of the potential danger of dictatorship.

Gorbachev saw the signs of the times for what they were and swerved to the reformist bloc again. But the centrifugal forces at work in the Soviet satellite states in Eastern Europe led to the dissolution of the Warsaw Pact, with official disbandment occurring in July 1991. At this point, Albania, Romania, and Bulgaria were the only Warsaw Pact member states with communist governments in power. The function of the Warsaw Pact as a military alliance and instrument of control in Eastern Europe became obsolete—and the point of no return had been reached. In early 1991, Gorbachev and Yeltsin hammered out a new blueprint for governance, the **9+1 formula**, which was intended to devolve powers to the individual Soviet republics. It was hoped that such a measure would defuse some of the tensions caused by national aspirations in the Soviet Union and give policymakers of all denominations time to handle the looming crisis.

In the elections of June 1991, which were the first free elections ever held in the Soviet Union, Yeltsin emerged as the victor and new head of the Russian Soviet Social Republic. The added leverage that the reformist movement gained in the Kremlin by Yeltsin's election increased the pressure on conservative old-school Communists, who by that time saw their power in the state seriously threatened. During a Gorbachev vacation in August 1991, reactionary forces in government seized the opportunity to attempt an overthrow of the new order. The coup was organized by several high-level *apparatchiks*, who declared a state of emergency in Gorbachev's absence. As tanks roamed the streets of Moscow, the conspirators held Gorbachev, who had been declared temporarily unfit, in the Crimea. The problem with the coup was that it had merely targeted the nominal head of government without taking into account political realities. Put simply, as president of Russia Yeltsin had become a power to be reckoned with. By not targeting Yeltsin, the conspirators failed to remove the second focal point of resistance. As it was, Yeltsin faced down the forces loyal to the reactionaries in Moscow. Prior to Yeltsin's showdown, played out dramatically in front of the Russian parliament building in Moscow, Yeltsin had been able to enlist the support of key military commanders and civil administrators; the plotters were compelled to stand down and release Gorbachev. Yeltsin's quick and decisive action had averted the threat of open civil war. He was the hero of the hour.

Conversely, Gorbachev's time had now passed. To begin, he never held a popular mandate and was always seen, despite his historical role in the transformation of the Soviet Union, as an integral part of the old communist order. In fact, the involvement of Communists in the attempted undermining of *perestroika* contributed to the eradication of the Communist Party in the following months. The earlier compromise policy developed mutually by Gorbachev and Yeltsin (i.e., the 9+1 formula) no longer represented a tenable option. Effectively, the botched coup had played into President Yeltsin's hands by shifting the center of power in his favor. The central government institutions of the Soviet Union had lost clout; the new centers of power were vested in the institutions of the individual Soviet republics. Yeltsin soon acted out the Communists' worst fears: dissolving the Soviet Union, then disestablishing the Communist Party. Finally, the Russian tricolors replaced the Soviet hammer-and-sickle flag. The Soviet Union was no more. After almost half a century of the Cold War, the dissolution of the Soviet Union brought it all to a close.

Russia Under Yeltsin

The Boris Yeltsin presidency (1991–2000) was a period of sweeping political and economic change—and massive corruption. This is especially true for the first few years after his accession to power. The impact of capitalism on a society governed by communist central planners for so many decades required that Yeltsin stand by his commitment to reform. However, the transition from a command economy to a market economy was painful. As the shock overcame Russia, an economic crisis threatened political stability.

Between 1991 and 1992, hyperinflation reached unprecedented proportions (no less than 2,000 percent), and an overwhelming majority of Russians lived in poverty. The government budget was in shambles. Attempts to decrease Russia's foreign debt coincided with the beginning of a global recession, and foreign loans available through the International Monetary Fund (IMF) were made dependent on Russia's progress toward a stable market economy. Stipulations by the IMF carried political weight in the sense that should the IMF withhold its loans to the former Soviet Union in general, and Russia in particular, the rapidly declining economic situation could compromise the transition from communism to democracy.

At the elections of 1992, the situation was equivocal. On the one hand, voters were more concerned about their own lot than ever before. On the other hand, Yeltsin was able to capitalize on his promise not to bend to the IMF's will. Nevertheless, Yeltsin and reformers elsewhere in the territories lost much support for failing to alleviate the economic misery that resulted from the end of communist rule and the introduction of capitalism. The apparent failure of the economic experiment led to a dismissal of proponents of capitalism in the Russian government—and their replacement with former Soviet functionaries.

By early 1993, Yeltsin faced a full-fledged mutiny in the legislative branch—the Congress of People's Deputies (CPD) over his breakneck conversion from a command to a capitalist economy. Yeltsin threatened to dissolve the CPD, as its sitting members, having been drawn from communist deputies, were never properly elected but installed by the party and therefore held no popular mandate. The CPD, in turn, announced Yeltsin's imminent impeachment. Events came to a head in April, when Yeltsin called for a plebiscite and was confirmed in office by a majority. But even in light of Yeltsin's victory, the CPD was loath to concede defeat. CPD members called for a rising against Yeltsin and then mobilized sympathizers. Demonstrations, as well as seizures of government media offices, finally forced Yeltsin to declare a state of emergency, surround the site of Russia's Federal Congress with army units loyal to the government, and finally order the bombardment of the congressional deputies and their armed retainers inside the building. Some 144 people were killed in the government's attempts to quell the unrest. Yeltsin substantiated his initial threat and disbanded the CPD and the Constitutional Court, which had upheld the latter's decision that the president could not unilaterally disestablish the legislative assembly. The new constitution accorded the presidential office vast powers and effectively enabled Yeltsin to rule by decree.

Political stagnation and the war in Chechnya.   In the next elections, set for 1996, Yeltsin's prospects for reelection were marginal at best. The intervening three years had been marked by a steady economic decline, hastened by a fall in productivity and economic output, as well as an increase in unemployment. A protracted conflict *within* the Russian Federation's boundaries against the breakaway republic of Chechnya since late 1994 seemed inconclusive in the short run, and the number of body bags sent home made the war unpopular. The Chechnya crisis deserves some attention, as the two succeeding wars between the federation and the secessionist movement in Chechnya held center stage in domestic Russian politics and continues to engage the Russian army in hostilities to this day.

The first Chechen war began toward the end of 1994, with strident calls for Chechen independence. The Chechens had a long history of resisting their Russian overlords and were subdued in the nineteenth century. Joseph Stalin resettled the Chechens, allegedly for collaborating with the Germans during World War II; Nikita Khrushchev permitted them to resettle in their Caucasus native homeland during the 1950s. Because the Soviet Union had only recently disintegrated, Yeltsin's reaction to Chechen claims of independence was to intervene militarily.

The breakup of the newly created Russian Federation was not an acceptable option. As civil war between federal loyalists and the secessionists got out of hand, Yeltsin deployed the military. Fierce Chechen resistance greeted the federal troops as they marched into Grozny, the Chechnya capital. After protracted fighting, Chechen separatists under the command of former Soviet General Dzhokhar Dudayev involved Russian troops in a costly fighting retreat. Just before the Russian elections of 1996, Yeltsin's chief negotiator, General Alexander Lebed, arranged a cease-fire, which was promptly broken by the Russians after Yeltsin gained a second term in office. Chechen guerrilla activities continued to cost many lives on both sides, and since Yeltsin left office in late 1999, the federation's operations against Chechnya's Islamic separatist rebels have escalated into a second full-scale war.

Moreover, Yeltsin's post was stiffly contested by malcontents of his rule, who were usually affiliated with the old order. Gennadi Zyuganov represented the interests of those who had lost, or failed to gain, power since 1991. He advocated the reinstitution of the Soviet Union in pronouncements discolored by ultranationalist rhetoric. Zyuganov and his proponents wanted to turn back the clock to the old days. To many voters, Zyuganov's campaign pledges held the promise of more stability in the near future. Traumatized by the abrupt introduction of capitalism, many Russians had lost their savings, which had fallen prey to inflation, or were disgruntled because the government was in arrears with the payment of pensions. At the same time, the Communists' political program promised little besides a return to the old system. It presented no vision and, for those willing to read between the lines, promised to bring back a moribund economic system that had, in the first place, been responsible for the dissolution of the Soviet Union.

In the immediate preelection period, Yeltsin used the resources of his office to mollify voters, dispensing funds through various initiatives to pay arrears to government employees, double pensions, and lavish subsidies on regional interests. Although polls indicated that Yeltsin would not be able to hold on to the presidency for a second term, he won the election against the Communists. A majority of the electorate understood that in order for Russia to have any hope to complete the transition to capitalism in a reasonable period, the country could simply not afford another tenure of communist rule. In the event of a communist victory, foreign investors and transnational organizations, such as the IMF, were likely to pull out their assets and renege on pledges for loans.

A sideshow to the political race between Zyuganov and Yeltsin was provided by the candidacy of retired General Alexander Lebed, who had acted as the government's go-between in the negotiations leading to a cease-fire with the Chechen secessionists prior to the elections. Lebed's popularity was based on his public reception as the honest broker amid a corrupt political establishment. His reputation endeared the retired general to a large segment of the disenchanted Russian voters. Lebed won about 15 percent of the votes, which rendered him an attractive partner to his former patron, Yeltsin. Accordingly, Lebed was called upon to act as the government's security adviser. As Yeltsin's health was declining—he suffered a serious heart attack during the election campaign—Lebed attempted to take the political high ground and used his soaring popularity to impugn the incumbent interior minister, Anatoly Kulikov, whom he accused of being responsible for the repeated military failures in Chechnya. Kulikov, in turn, accused Lebed of planning the overthrow of the government. As recriminations reached a climax, Yeltsin intervened and publicly released Lebed of all official duties.

The Lebed-Kulikov feud exemplified the political infighting that was to persist throughout Yeltsin's second term in office (1996–2000) and ended only when the ailing Yeltsin installed his protégé, former KGB officer Vladimir Putin, as his designated successor. The president was forced to move into the background due to his ailing health, and a succession of frontmen took hold of the reins of power, only to be dismissed by Yeltsin over diverging views on government policies. The frequent changes in the Yeltsin cabinet in those years were mainly responsible for the modest progress achieved on the political and economic fronts.

Political processes in Yeltsin's Russia were dominated by executive power and powerful personalities; they were not based on the rule of law and a system of institutionalized checks and balances. The powerful oligarchs as well as the regional governors focused on their personal enrichment and on expanding their own power rather than on achieving structural economic change. The level of corruption and the number of politicians with a criminal past will have to be reduced before further consolidation in Russian democracy can occur. This will not be easy to achieve as long as the economic crisis does not take a definitive turn for the better.

The strong hand of Vladimir Putin.   The last of a number of Yeltsin appointees was Sergei Stepashin, a former minister of justice in former Prime Minister Viktor Chernomyrdin's cabinet. Stepashin was confirmed as Russian prime minister in May 1999 but was unexpectedly relieved of his duties by presidential decree in August that same year. The relatively obscure Vladimir Putin, the fifth Yeltsin appointee in the prime minister's post, succeeded Stepashin as interim incumbent on the last day of the twentieth century, when Yeltsin finally stepped down. In March 2000, Putin polled slightly more than 50 percent of the popular mandate. Putin had been a career officer in the KGB and served the mayor of St. Petersburg. He was brought to the Kremlin by Yeltsin associates, where he was appointed head of the Federal Security Bureau, the successor to the KGB.

There is no better example for the manipulative character of Russian democracy than Putin's rise to power. His election victory was built on a newly founded party (The Bear), formed from scratch at the eleventh hour by Kremlin forces in an attempt to overcome the opposition stemming from the Fatherland–All Russia movement. Putin was not elected by virtue of a political program. On the contrary, he made a point of having no program and by making a fresh start. His ascendancy was characterized by the heavy use of the media and the carefully projected image of a strong hand against the background of the war in Chechnya. The crisis in Chechnya, however, continued after an initial intensification of hostilities on the part of Russian federal troops.

There have been signs of hope for Russian reforms since Putin's election as president. Putin successfully filled the power vacuum created by the retirement of Yeltsin. Russia's economic recovery, although heavily dependent on world energy prices, was better than expected in 1999 and 2000, and after the reform of the Federation Council and Putin's compromises with Communists in the Duma (parliament), those two organs became loyal to the president. State-building in Russia was driven by decentralization for much of the 1990s. However, this changed with the financial crisis and the beginning of the second war in Chechnya. Regional leaders lost their battle with the Kremlin during the Duma election campaign of 1999. State-building under Putin so far has been marked by a strong recentralization effort. Whether Putin's federal reforms will be a successful source of structural change remains to be seen.

Putin increased Russia's international presence and has impressed the international community with his tough, pragmatic handling of Russian politics. As for his foreign policy, Putin pursued cooperation with the international community—especially with the United States—but has also shown that he intends to maintain a balance of power by seeking a working partnership with China. It remains to be seen whether Russia is aiming at a multipolarity similar to that of the nineteenth century or a multipolarity represented by the many focal points of the economic and information technologies of the twenty-first century.

The Periphery: From Soviet Republics to the Commonwealth of Independent States

As progressive and conservative forces debated the future course of the Soviet Union, the open public discourse advocated by *glasnost* reanimated an old grievance in the constituent Soviet republics: national self-determination. The Soviet Union, not unlike Tito's Yugoslavian federation, consisted of multiple ethnicities whose relations were predominantly defined by their conflictive pasts. Historically, the powerful Muscovite state had conquered various peoples that had lived in the Soviet republics over the centuries and incorporated them into the early feudal fiefdoms and later into the czarist empire. By the time of the Russian Revolution in 1917, more than 100 different nationalities came under Soviet rule. In theory, communism acted as the great equalizer and fused the heterogeneous ethnic groups into a single unit, as had been the case in the Soviet state. Constitutionally, each group had the right to break away from the union. However, communism (at least as it was practiced in Moscow) was intrinsically antinationalist. The conspicuous absence of secessionist movements under the Soviet rulers up to Constantine Chernenko seems to have suggested the validity and legitimacy of the Soviet Union.

By providing multiple trouble spots and depriving Gorbachev's reformist government of direly needed resources, the nationalist problem, among others, accelerated the process begun with the introduction of *perestroika* and *glasnost,* pushed it beyond its intended objectives and ultimately resulted in the end of the Soviet presence in Eastern Europe after 1988 and the fracturing of the Soviet Union in 1991. Not only did the many ethnically and politically motivated conflicts in the Soviet Union and Eastern Europe resurface between 1988 and 1991; they did, in fact, survive and only fully unfolded their destructive potential during the post-Soviet period. Thus, the legacy of the dissolution of the Soviet Union was one of intermittent war and economic decline.

But the nationalist problem was not the only headache in the final days of the Soviet Union. The struggle between reformers and conservatives at the center of power and against the backdrop of an economically hamstrung empire sapped the Soviet authorities' capability to respond on the periphery. Therefore, the power struggle within the Communist Party was directly connected to the ailing economy and the nationalist conflict on the periphery. Beset by internal and external tensions, and deprived of a sufficient material basis, the Soviet Union became the casualty of centrifugal forces. What had started out as an attempt at moderate structural reforms culminated in the most significant change in the international system during the second half of the twentieth century. Where there had once been a single powerful state, after 1991 fifteen newly independent successor states emerged to take its place. Among them, the Russian Federation, containing more than half the population of the former Soviet Union, was by far the most powerful and, accordingly, began to assume the role of regional hegemon.

Even after the constitution of the Soviet Union was no longer in force, Gorbachev attempted, using all means at his disposal, to preserve the unity of the Soviet republics. The conclusion of a new treaty of union, however, failed due to Ukrainian opposition. On 21 December 1991, the Ukraine, Russia, and Byelorussia founded the **Commonwealth of Independent States (CIS)** in Alma-Ata. The CIS constitutes an association of eleven states whose integrity is maintained by only a few, sketchily defined central institutional bodies. Of the former Soviet republics, only the Baltic states remained aloof, and Georgia did not venture beyond the dispatching of observers.

National Identity and the Former Soviet Republics

As *perestroika* and *glasnost* shook the foundations of the stagnant Soviet political system, Russians were without a doubt the dominant ethnic group.

Out of a total Soviet population of some 280 million, 145 million were Russians. Moreover, a majority of the Soviet population was of Slavic stock; statistically, more than 70 percent of the entire Soviet population consisted of Slavs. Based on this ethnodemographic perspective, it was to be expected that non-Slavic peoples would be the first to call for independence. Although this assumption turned out to be true, it must also be said that non-Russian Slavic peoples had, since their conquest, developed a national identity and—following the introduction of *glasnost*—a renewed thirst for political and cultural autonomy.

As the discussion about increasing autonomy spread from Russia to the other fourteen Soviet republics, the pressure on the central authorities to accommodate nationalist expectations increased. On the one hand, Moscow could support a policy of devolved government, transferring political and economic competences to the individual Soviet republics while remaining in overall command over the union. This solution primarily appealed to moderates but not nationalists, who finally saw a chance to obtain independence on the horizon. The alternative to devolving power to the constituent republics was secession—an approach that would ultimately lead to the destruction of the Soviet Union and was therefore opposed even by the moderate Gorbachev.

The Baltic states: independence reconsidered.   The three most important trouble spots that emerged as a result of Gorbachev's reforms during the late 1980s lay in the Baltic states—Latvia, Estonia, and Lithuania—in Georgia and Ossetia and along the Azerbaijan-Armenia border. Aside from the principal clashes shortly before, during, and after the breakup of the Soviet Union, there was a host of highly charged and potentially conflictive situations throughout the fifteen constituent Soviet republics. As for the Baltic states, the problem was not so much shaped by ethnic tensions as it was the product of historical and nationalist forces. During World War II, the Baltics had been ceded to the Soviets by way of the Nazi-Soviet Nonaggression Pact of 1939. As a result of the Nonaggression Pact, Stalin annexed the Baltic states, which had gained independence following the Russian Revolution in 1917. The advent of Gorbachev's reforms ended decades of silence concerning this dark chapter of history. The subsequent critical reappraisal of the past, and the discussion that followed, took shape in Lithuanian demands for autonomy and then complete independence. Accordingly, in December 1989 Gorbachev faced a dilemma: break up the Soviet Union, or revert to the old-style communist rule that he had worked so hard to overcome.

Accordingly, Gorbachev undertook to sway the Lithuanians by paying them a visit in January 1990, to no effect. Lithuanians generally seemed disinclined to contemplate any further association with the Soviet Union.

Between January and March, the situation grew tense as Lithuanian nationalists prepared to secede from the Soviet Union. On 11 March, the Lithuanian parliament unilaterally proclaimed an independent state. The Soviet response was predictable: the long arm of Moscow was felt in Vilnius, where Soviet tanks and ground troops occupied the city. In legal terms, representatives of the Soviet Union argued that independence for Lithuania could be discussed only within the limits of the Soviet constitution—and not imposed by a secessionist movement. Gorbachev's bid to cow the Lithuanians was a failure. From military intervention, the Soviets then moved to an economic blockade that equally failed, as the other two Baltic states—Latvia and Estonia—followed Lithuania that same year. The struggle for independence in the Baltic states was over as quickly as it began, not least because the central government in Moscow was confronted with potential secessions elsewhere. Nevertheless, the debacle in the Baltic states was a serious setback and set in motion a process that would end only with the breakup of the Soviet Union. The first crack in the facade of the monolithic communist state was there for all to see.

Nagorno-Karabakh and the rise of Azeri-Armenian tensions. The essential difference between the Baltics' independence movement and the multiple conflicts in the Caucasus was that the former was inspired by anti-Russian nationalism and sentiments developed over two centuries, whereas the latter were as often as not a direct product of ancient ethnic hatreds or internecine rivalries suppressed by decades of communist rule. Following the Communists' seizure of power after the Russian Revolution, Armenia was forcefully wed to Georgia and Azerbaijan to form the Transcaucasian Federation in 1922. The problem that led to all that followed was the ethnic composition of the Transcaucasian Federation: Armenians and Georgians were predominantly Christian, whereas Azeri ancestors had been Turkish nomads. In the case of Azeri-Armenian relations, the lack of territorial integrity inhabited by either group, as well as their diametrically opposed territorial claims, added fuel to an antagonism rooted in a mutual past characterized by blood and strife.

The Armenian exclave of Nagorno-Karabakh is situated in Azerbaijan and practically adjoins the Armenia homeland. Nagorno-Karabakh contains an overwhelmingly Armenian population surrounded by a hostile Azeri majority. As of 1988, Armenians, encouraged by Gorbachev's reforms, pressed their demands for independence and for the reunification of Nagorno-Karabakh with Armenia. Tensions between the Azeri incumbents and the Armenians living within the boundaries of Azerbaijan reached fever pitch and soon resulted in repeated pogroms. The deteriorating situation in Azerbaijan was compounded by the emergence of powerful nationalist forces in Armenia, which gained an outlet in mass demonstrations held at

Yerevan for reunification with Nagorno-Karabakh. The Soviet government vetoed any such move and generally seemed to support the Azeri side in this dispute. Between 1988 and late 1989, Armenian militias mounted several attacks on Azeri areas in reprisal for the killings of Armenian civilians. The conflict grew worse when an Azeri enclave on Armenian territory, Nachitchevan, declared its independence from the Soviet Union on 15 January 1990. Azeri militias cordoned off Armenia, imposing a blockade.

In response to the peremptory Nachitchevan secession and Azeri-Armenian tensions in general, Gorbachev moved 160,000 Soviet troops into the Caucasus and imposed a cessation of hostilities by virtue of superior firepower. He declared a state of emergency for the entire region. The superior troops quickly crushed all Azeri resistance. The state of emergency continued until the end of 1991, but the real problem remained unresolved. When the Soviet Union finally collapsed in the summer of 1991, Armenia and Azerbaijan were quick to proclaim their independence, on 23 and 30 August, respectively. When Soviet troops moved out of the Caucasus, it was only a question of time until the two new states would go to war. Indeed, the Azeris again isolated the Armenians by imposing an embargo on all essential staple goods.

At the beginning of 1992, the conflict entered a new phase. When Nagorno-Karabakh was subjected to direct Azeri administration on 2 January 1991, the Armenians in the exclave in turn declared their own independence. For three years, the armed forces of Armenia and Azerbaijan and the Nagorno-Karabakh militias fought each other. Only when Armenian President Lewon Ter-Petrosyan called on the UN Security Council to intervene was a cease-fire negotiated with the support of the Conference on Security and Cooperation in Europe (the predecessor of today's Organization for Security and Cooperation in Europe [OSCE]). Since 1988, 40,000 civilians and combatants were killed and another 22,000 injured. In 1993, in excess of 1 million Azeri refugees attempted to escape the fighting. The only positive aspect is that since 1994 full-scale engagements between regulars of both sides have ceased.

Georgia and the Abkhazian struggle for independence.   Multiethnic composition and competing interests caused an eruption of hostilities in Georgia. Of the 4 million inhabitants of the Georgian Republic, approximately 30 percent are of non-Georgian stock. The most vocal minorities in Georgia are Abkhazians and Ossetes. In the Georgian context, the Abkhazian struggle for independence was the most intensely fought of all. Following a prolonged campaign against the Ossetes, Georgia—which was itself on the verge of civil war—was plunged into another military confrontation with Abkhazian separatist forces. On 26 July 1992, Abkhazia proclaimed its independence, which was opposed by the Georgian government under former Soviet Foreign Minister Eduard Shevardnaze. In connection with an abduction of Georgian hostages by loyalists of ousted President Sviad Gamsakhurdia, Georgian regulars crossed the border into Abkhazia on 14 August 1991. Subsequently, Georgian and Abkhazian units clashed in a series of skirmishes in the borderlands.

The Georgian government proceeded to issue an ultimatum, calling for the Abkhazian parliamentary President Vladimir Ardsinba to step down within seventy-two hours. The ultimatum went unheeded, which furnished Georgians the pretext to occupy the Abkhaz capital of Suchumi. Although Abkhaz troops were forced to retreat in the face of a Georgian offensive, the Abkhazians called upon and gained the support of a confederation of Caucasian mountain peoples headed by the Chechen rebel leader Dudayev. Russian troops, furnished by the recently independent Russian Federation, which had initially supported Shevardnadze's campaign against the Abkhaz secessionists, withdrew in order to maintain nominal Russian neutrality in the conflict. In the wake of the Russian retreat, Abkhazian troops made significant territorial gains. By 1993, the tally of war exceeded 3,000 fatalities. A negotiated cease-fire rendered possible by the simultaneous diplomatic initiatives of the United Nations and the CIS ended the hostilities. Intense negotiations continued into 1995 with only marginal results. A peacekeeping force furnished by the CIS arrived in the disputed area in June 1994 and acted as a guarantor for the cease-fire.

For a short time in early 1994, the situation again threatened to escalate, as approximately 350 armed Georgian nationalists attempted to cross into Abkhazia at the instigation of former Minister of Defense Tengis Kitowani. They were intercepted by Georgian police and detained. Nevertheless, the Abkhaz contingent guarding the border was put on alert and heavily reinforced. The Kitowani incident went a long way to show that the situation remained potentially unstable even after open fighting ended. Not until Abkhaz leaders suddenly abandoned their claim for an independent state—following a meeting held at Geneva in February 1995—was the danger of a renewed flare-up averted.

The Euroatlantic

More so than any other region, Europe was seriously affected by the consequences of the end of the Cold War. The rapid dissolution of the Eastern bloc and the Soviet Union created a novel set of circumstances potentially affecting the future of the Euroatlantic. The partitioning of Europe imposed by the dictates of the Cold War came to an end, symbolized by fall of the Berlin Wall. And as the power of the Soviet Union was reduced to its Russian core, Germany regained considerable weight through reunification. In Eastern and Southeastern Europe, as well as in the territories of the former Soviet Union, a group of states came into being (although in the early 1990s they had only just undertaken the formative processes toward statehood). Simultaneously, concerns about political destabilization and security in Europe due to the economic and political chaos in Eastern and Southeastern Europe had to be addressed. Such apprehensions were justified, as became apparent in the tragedy surrounding the breakup of the Yugoslavian federation; war had returned to Europe after decades of peace.

Concurrent with the expansion of conflicts and their geographic scope, as well as the security political risks they represented, the pressure on the states of the Euroatlantic for economic and social action was rising. The Gulf War served as a stern reminder that Europe's economies were dependent upon crude oil resources from the Arab region. In addition, a recession struck Europe, which had a negative impact on the European rate of consumption. Against the backdrop of progressing economic globalization, the competition between U.S. and European markets became more pronounced, which in turn increased the pressures on governments and their regulatory power. If the social and cultural challenges of the transition process of industrial states en route to becoming information societies are added to the list of problems, we can begin to grasp the complexity and dimension of the internal and external changes in the Euroatlantic.

In the 1990s the Euroatlantic experienced a generally successful, albeit slowly progressing, adjustment of its security structures to a fundamentally altered international political environment and climate. At the center of this emerging system was a quickening of the economic and political integration of Europe and, to a lesser extent, intensified Euroatlantic cooperation. Today the risk of fragmentation in the region is considerably lower. Since 1990, the extent and intensity of international cooperation in the context of five political processes, outlined below, have reached a new and deeper level:

1. A solidification of civil society on the basis of mutual values and norms could be verified. With the dissolution of multiethnic communist states and the generally simultaneous spread, as well as corroboration, of a state of law, of democracy, and of the market economy, the boundaries of the Euroatlantic grew.

2. The political and economic integration of Europe underwent major progress, as exemplified by the transition from the European Community to the European Union. By introducing a single market and a single currency, the European Union became the largest trading bloc worldwide. At the same time, enhancing the EU role in matters concerning internal state security, as well as the introduction of the **Common Foreign and Security Policy (CFSP)**, prevented the renationalization of European security policy.

3. A struggle for a new balance between European initiatives and transatlantic cooperation became an enduring feature of regional politics. U.S. leadership in matters of, and U.S. obligations for, the security of Europe could no longer be expected to the same degree as during the Cold War—not least because the economic and security political interests of the Western alliance had become more disparate. In the early years of the twenty-first century, Europeans seem to have come to terms with the prospect that they will remain dependent upon the United States for the foreseeable future in terms of hard power and the ability to lead the Western alliance. In turn, the United States has come to accept the autonomous decisionmaking of the European Union and is granting it full recognition in the area of soft power.

4. Cooperation with the incipient democratic states of Eastern and Southeastern Europe, as well as with Russia, was especially significant to the region at large. The integration of such states into the institutional structures of the West was regarded as critical to the stability of the expanded European security area. Against this backdrop, NATO and the European Union carefully sought to expand.

5. The institutional dimension of international cooperation gained prominence, and the basic structures of a new European order became apparent. Neither the functional system of collective security nor a hierarchy of institutions in the context of a clearly delineated security architecture stood in the foreground of this new European order. Instead, practical multilateral collaboration within a framework of reciprocally supporting institutions proved decisive.

Western Europe and the United States: The Rise of Institutionalism

The key question for the Euroatlantic community after the end of the Cold War was whether states were up to the challenge of formulating new structures of order in close cooperation or, conversely, whether they would opt to primarily follow their own interests. In the early 1990s, the realist school had clear ideas about this issue. By and large, they expected a weakening of institutions relevant to Europe's security, in particular a renationalization of security and defense policy and, thus, a return to a European balance-of-power system. Such predictions agreed with the theoretical precepts of realism, according to which states enter stable patterns of cooperation only in the event they face an external military threat and if cooperation is encouraged by a hegemonic state. With the disintegration of the Warsaw Pact and the Soviet Union, Western institutions lacked such an enemy. The United States reduced its complement of troops in Europe in the 1990s and seemed to turn toward the Pacific. A number of observers expected the enfeeblement, or even the breakup, of European institutions—first and foremost NATO and the European Union.

Nevertheless, we now know that cooperation is possible despite the absence of palpable threats and hegemony. In the face of realist skepticism, integrationists, functionalists, and institutionalists have long maintained that the process of European integration has developed an inexorable dynamic. In the interim, European states cooperated not only in economics but also in security policy. At the beginning of the twenty-first century, European politics seem to represent a dense framework of interwoven multilateral structures. The normatively designed instrument of the OSCE came to play a significant role in this regard—primarily in prevention and reconstruction. The crises in the Balkans, however, were a painful reminder that elements of soft power could take effect only if combined with the disciplining force of hard power.

Militarily, NATO assumed a position of leadership: apart from its core competence as the instrument of transatlantic collective defense, NATO also took on the role of crisis manager. Aside from acting as a military stabilizing force, NATO increasingly was tasked with political functions, amply illustrated by its endeavors to create a network of military cooperation through the **Partnership for Peace (PfP)** and the **Euro-Atlantic Partnership Council (EAPC)**. Even though little could be expected from the United Nations concerning security in the region, the role it fulfilled on the basis of its mandate as stipulated by international law, and in light of the progressing globalization of security issues, was important in and of itself. As compared to other institutions, the European Union incrementally developed the potential to collectively bring political, economic, and, increasingly, military instruments to bear. We will now look at this innovative institutional development process in some detail.

The Consolidation of the European Union

Concurrent with the collapse of the Soviet Union and the end of the Cold War, the European Community's plans for a closer union came to fruition in the momentous **Maastricht Treaty** signed in December 1991. It provided the framework for what was to become the European Union in 1993—one of the most powerful trade blocs on the planet. The Maastricht provisions outlined a political program that would, upon the achievement of its stipulations, weld Europe together economically and, more gradually, politically. With this program, European leaders declared their will to render the European Union a multilayered and dynamic institution that would become a central actor in global politics. In addition to its classic economic function, the European Union was also tasked with other political mandates; currently no aspect of national politics remains untouched by the common decisionmaking process in Brussels. The key areas of cooperation defined by Maastricht are:

- a single European currency (the euro);
- common European citizenship;
- common foreign and security policy, as well as closer internal EU cooperation in justice and home affairs; and
- a common labor policy

In the context of monetary union, a single European currency was to replace all national monetary systems in the territories belonging to the European Union. The euro was to replace the British pound sterling, the Italian lira, the French franc, and the German deutsche mark. Freedom of movement within the boundaries of unionist Europe would become an intrinsic right extended to all EC citizens and would, moreover, allow European workforces higher mobility. The CFSP was to establish a comprehensive European foreign policy and render the member states of the EC a single entity in international relations, speaking with a single voice. The common labor policy would ensure that all European governments in the near future would meet standards of labor law. In a moderate fashion, since 1991, Europe has been edging closer toward a "United States of Europe"— a vision presaged by Winston Churchill in the earliest days of European integration.

After the conclusion of Maastricht, the European Union was imbued with an encompassing security dimension. The Treaty of European Union expanded the traditional pillar of the supranational European Community, to which were added the economic and monetary union, to include two additional intergovernmental pillars: the CFSP and a cooperative framework in internal security and migration (Justice and Home Affairs). On the one hand, EU security policy was intended to strengthen the economic and monetary union and consolidate an internal area without boundaries; on the other hand, these measures were intended to stabilize that part of Europe that was not yet fully integrated into the European Union. The two governmental pillars were designed as complementary aspects of an overall European security strategy. Whereas the CFSP was mainly conceived of as a solution or, at the least, an attempt to contain the crises along the European periphery, the cooperation within Justice and Home Affairs was primarily directed at tackling the nonmilitary consequences of such crises for societies within the European Union.

In any event, at the time they were put forward, the objectives set forth by the Maastricht Treaty were ambitious—and remain unfulfilled. Maastricht did, however, give new momentum to the integration of Europe. Conversely, one of the major stumbling blocks to the implementation of Maastricht was the persistence of sovereignty movements in nation-states that remained apprehensive over political unification in Europe. Although

Europe had come a long way since the days when federalists were bitterly opposed by functionalists, the conflict in principle remained the same: progressing integration meant the incremental loss of national sovereignty and was, therefore, inimical to nationalist interests. The idea of a united Europe had languished for decades, and many Europeans were of a mind to let it stay that way. Enjoying the benefits of economic integration and, by extension, union was one thing; it was quite another to forsake one's sovereign political rights.

The nationalist backlash manifested itself in two distinct ways: First, Denmark refused to ratify Maastricht in a plebiscite held in 1992; second, Britain resisted the introduction of the euro. But in 1993, by becoming the European Union, the European Community took the first step in affirming its will to fulfill the provisions of Maastricht. In 1994, the European Union concluded a treaty with its regional (and in the meantime eclipsed) peer competitor, the European Free Trade Association, by offering it nonvoting member status in the European Union, which expanded the tariff-free inner-European market to include all EFTA member states. Despite protracted controversy over the introduction of legal standards—especially in labor and social legislation—in 1995, the newly constituted European Union grew from twelve to fifteen members. The accession of the three new member states (Austria, Finland, and Sweden) was not surprising. The three had not joined before then because each practiced neutrality to varying degrees. After 1991, however, the situation drastically changed, and allowed Austria, Finland, and Sweden to prepare their EC/EU membership applications.

The **Amsterdam Treaty** of 1997 consolidated the achievements of Maastricht in four separate areas: (1) freedom, security, and justice; (2) citizen rights; (3) a common commercial policy; and (4) reform of the CFSP. The aim of the Amsterdam Treaty's architects was clear. They wanted

> to create the political and institutional conditions to enable the European Union to meet the challenges of the future such as the rapid evolution of the internal situation, the globalization of the economy and its impact on jobs, the fight against terrorism, international crime and drug trafficking, ecological problems and threats to public health.[4]

The Amsterdam Treaty was ratified and came into force on 1 May 1999, and the much-anticipated day finally arrived on 1 January 2002: eleven national currencies (in Belgium, Germany, Spain, France, Ireland, Italy, Luxembourg, the Netherlands, Austria, Portugal, and Finland) were replaced by the euro. The Danish crown and the Greek drachmae remained the national currencies of their respective countries. Denmark, Sweden, and Great Britain remained aloof.

Enlargement and institutional reform.   The issue of enlarging the European Union was addressed at Maastricht. On the one hand, a number of neutral states lobbied for enlargement and their own membership. On the other hand, ten **Central and East European Countries (CEECs)** were in the process of applying, or had already applied, for membership. The three neutral states were duly admitted in 1995. In the case of the CEECs, the premise for admission was more complex in economic, political, and social terms. The Council of Europe's intention to include some CEECs is linked to concerns about the safeguarding of political and economic stability among the prospective European Union candidates. By contrast, EU enlargement is intrinsically coupled with its finances: if all ten CEECs are granted EU member status, then Europe's population would grow by 29 percent and European territory by 33 percent, but gross domestic product would increase by a mere 3 percent. Concerning the financial outlay for the fifteen existing member states, the greatest problem will be the implementation of the Common Agricultural Policy, for it will strain EU resources to the limit. Obviously, the current levels at which prices have been guaranteed in the European Union for agricultural staple goods, such as cereals, beef, and dairy products, will no longer be tenable. With CEECs visibly lagging behind EU economic, social, and political expectations, the Eurocrats in Brussels soon understood that enlargement could be accomplished at best gradually and at worst incrementally.

For purposes of screening applicant states as fairly as possible, a catalog of hurdles for CEEC accession had to be agreed, which happened in the shape of the so-called **Copenhagen criteria**. Most important, the Copenhagen criteria call for a stable democracy, a functional market economy, and access to sufficient administrative capacity to adopt the EU legal system (commonly known as the *acquis communautaire*). The process of selecting suitable new EU member states became daunting, indeed. In the first place, the question was which countries should be offered membership. The 1997 Luxembourg summit led the European Union to initiate accession negotiations with six states: Cyprus, the Czech Republic, Estonia, Hungary, Poland, and Slovenia (the so-called Luxembourg six). Officially, the European Union approached the Luxembourg six in 1998. But negotiations with these applicant states caused jealousies in other CEECs. Estonia's neighboring Baltic states, Latvia and Lithuania, were quick to stake out their own claims to EU membership. At the recent Helsinki Council, a second group of applicants was under review: Bulgaria, Latvia, Lithuania, Malta, Romania, and Slovakia. For the moment, the Balkan countries are not likely candidates for EU membership, a state of affairs expected to continue for some time. Finally, the European Union is intending to extend an invitation to Turkey, but opposition to that initiative (due to a dismal human rights record) is still vocal and is likely to impede Turkish membership in the near term.

The European Union expects to admit the first new members by the end of 2002. Institutional problems can be expected in the event that membership grows from fifteen to twenty-five. If unanimity remains a requirement in the decisionmaking processes within EU institutions, deadlocks in many matters are probable. As the European Commission will not increase the number of its members, the major countries in the European Union will loose their second seats to the new arrivals. But how do these prospective members think of EU membership? In the first place, CEECs intending to join are driven by economic incentives. More significant, however, is the CEECs' persisting need for security. Only recently freed from Soviet suzerainty, the CEECs want to safeguard their newly found independence and sovereignty—especially from the Russian Federation, which many still regard as the source of regional instability. Until it is fully operational, the CFSP cannot provide the necessary protection; NATO, by contrast, has the required conventional and, failing that, nuclear capability to defend the CEECs if necessary. Essentially, the CEECs' position is that only a two-tiered integration—economic and strategic—will serve their interests: NATO *and* EU enlargement is what they seek.

From the CFSP to the ESDP.   Efforts to steel the CFSP began with the insight that a global economic power—which would have to carry two-thirds of the global burden accruing from its engagement with humanitarian aid—would have to develop its foreign political capabilities. After achieving economic and monetary union, the CFSP constituted the next step in the logical progression of integration—especially for states such as France. The resuscitation of war in the Balkans also convinced other states—for example, Germany—that an augmentation of the European foreign and security policy was of critical importance.

One of the most important results stemming from the Amsterdam amendments to Maastricht was the enhanced character of the Common Foreign and Security Policy. The CFSP was launched in the context of Maastricht and came into force in November 1993. Since then it has progressed into a budding European institutional framework for devising a comprehensive EU foreign and security policy. The benefit is that an enhanced CSFP will empower the European Union to represent a single position in international relations, in general, and armed conflict and humanitarian issues, in particular. In light of decades-old wrangling among modern European states, this is an achievement indeed. For forty years, the very concept of a common European foreign policy was anathema to national leaders. But with the introduction of CFSP, a European foreign policy became an irrefutable fact, further corroborated by the appointment of the former secretary-general of NATO, Javier Solana, to the post of High Representative for the CFSP in June 1999. The choice of Solana was auspicious, as his professional record under NATO gave the CFSP a distinct cast.

The Maastricht and Amsterdam provisions also establish between the European Union and the Western European Union (WEU)—a defense organization founded in 1955 that became moribund but was revived from time to time to serve as the formal vessel for successive European defense ventures. Moreover, the CFSP encompassed a new role for the European Union in the field of humanitarian aid and peacekeeping through the inclusion, in the Amsterdam Treaty, of what have become known as the **Petersberg Tasks**. The Petersberg Tasks are named after the conference center near Bonn, Germany, where they were adopted in 1992. They include humanitarian, rescue, peacekeeping, and international crisis-management roles, such as peace enforcement, developed to meet new global problems since the end of the Cold War. The opportunity for constructive abstention permits member states to remain aloof of specific operations as long as they accept the affirmative commitment of decisions taken and do not hinder their implementation.

Maastricht had defined the CFSP in a comprehensive manner. In the long term, and in accordance with Maastricht's stipulations, the definition of a common security policy was intended to open avenues to the gradual formulation of a common defense policy (and capability) in the future. Until 1999, however, the development of the CFSP was focused on questions pertaining to its institutional development. Only in the run-up to the European Union summit of 3–4 June 1999 in Cologne did the discussion surrounding the **European Security and Defense Policy (ESDP)** take center stage, which in turn gave political substance to the CFSP reform debate. The assembled leaders of the European Union passed a decision to the effect that the Petersberg Tasks were to be implemented and, vitally important, would endow the European Union with the necessary instruments: "The Union must have the capacity for autonomous action, backed up by credible military forces, the means to decide to use them, and a readiness to do so, in order to respond to international crises without prejudice to actions by NATO."[5] In order to secure the immediate availability of EU operational capability, the functions of the WEU required for the implementation of the Petersberg Tasks were integrated into the European Union. Conversely, NATO was to remain the centerpiece of its member states' collective defense.

In December 1999, the European leadership instituted a permanent committee on security policy, located in Brussels. At the same time, EU member states agreed on an ambitious plan to create the **Rapid Reaction**

Force (RRF) to tackle situations like the Kosovo conflict. During early 2000, leaders of the fifteen-member EU approved plans to assemble a multinational force of up to fifteen army brigades numbering 60,000 troops. This highly mobile force is expected to be ready by the year 2003. The idea behind the RRF is not to create a European army but rather to build military capabilities that will allow the European Union to implement the full spectrum of the Petersberg Tasks. Member states are not called upon to augment the size of their respective armies. Instead, they now offer to deploy units not only for UN peacekeeping operations and NATO interventions but also as an EU intervention force.

Why did this decisive developmental boost of the ESDP, in only two years, occur? Because progress like this in the area of intergovernmental politics does not threaten the sovereignty of participating states; rather, it will have an effect in the long term. Of critical importance was the French rapprochement with NATO during the 1990s. Following the failure of floating a project to create a European security and defense policy independent of NATO under then–President François Mitterand, the successor President Jacques Chirac turned toward a policy of balancing the European Union and NATO. Conversely, once Great Britain decided to stay aloof from the monetary union, its leaders could only take recourse to substantiating its involvement in European security policy. Great Britain was compelled to follow this course of action in order to maintain its weight in Europe while also retaining its influence in Washington.

The French leadership tends to view the ESDP as constituting first and foremost a European project, its ability to globally broadcast power being based on, and substantiated by, NATO's operational resources. Great Britain, by contrast, considers the augmentation and consolidation of the ESDP a sine qua non for the maintenance of NATO's cohesion in the future. These positions show the extent to which the European sense of almost complete dependence upon U.S. military strength during the resolution of the Kosovo crisis has, in fact, become the very engine behind the endeavors to endow the ESDP with the substance it requires.

Whereas the Europeans exhibited signs of no longer accepting the status of a subcontractor within NATO, the United States feared a duplication of NATO structures, the decoupling of the European Union from the United States, and potential discrimination from NATO member states that were not part of the European Union. The question of EU NATO collaboration turned out to be one of the most controversial issues in relation to the ESDP, though its actual significance is easily overrated. First, progress in negotiations leading to preparation for permanent agreements on EU-NATO consultation and collaboration has been satisfactory. Second, in the event of a crisis, consultation would almost certainly occur simultaneously in formal and informal, bilateral, and multilateral forums. Finally, it is to be expected that the ESDP will remain a project of limited scope in the near term.

The Adaptation Processes of NATO and the OSCE

As the principal exponent of hard security, NATO underwent significant change in the aftermath of the Cold War. NATO successfully adapted its role to the challenges of the new security environment. The Western alliance remains the institutional cornerstone of the post–Cold War Euroatlantic security architecture. Established as a multifunctional body, NATO developed a complex system of norms, structures, and procedures. Its institutional flexibility laid the foundation for the quick adaptation of NATO functions vis-à-vis the changing security needs and perceptions in the Euroatlantic. At the beginning of the twenty-first century, NATO has evolved from a collective defense organization into a modern security management organization. And though collective defense remains the backbone of NATO (against a potential relapse into old confrontations and the emergence of new confrontations), the cooperative security policy functions of NATO have gained more attention in recent years.

NATO's successful adaptation to new international challenges is surprising insofar as the future of NATO was called into doubt at the beginning of the 1990s. Although NATO did demonstrate the value of its operational and institutional capacity during the Gulf War, NATO was at that time also looking for a new role. The years leading up to the successful NATO summit in 1994 bore the mark of internal tensions, which by and large hamstrung the entire organization. Four major disputed issues came to the fore. First, U.S. and European leaders disagreed on the desirability of any European security and defense policy that was independent of the United States. Second, there was no concurrence between the two sides on how to end hostilities in the Balkans. For a length of time, the French and the British, who contributed the lion's share of troops to the UN force in Bosnia, were unwilling to countenance U.S.-sponsored proposals to end the arms embargo and carry out massive reprisals against Serb positions. Third, against the backdrop of the clamor for a peace dividend, a solution to the highly touchy subject of burden-sharing became urgent. Fourth, NATO's eastern expansion split its members into factions.

Despite this unfavorable starting point, the January 1994 NATO summit held in Brussels was a success. At the end of the summit, tensions between the United States and its European allies had abated. While France drifted closer to NATO—in October, the French minister of defense had attended a meeting of NATO defense ministers for the first time since 1966—the United States moved from obstructing closer European cooperation in security to actively encouraging a separate European defense identity. In June 1995, the foreign and defense ministers decided to create the **European Security and Defense Identity (ESDI)** within NATO, thereby giving European states the ability to access NATO resources for missions in which the United States did not wish to play an active role. In the interim, however, developments in the context of the ESDP have rendered ESDI practically obsolete.

The controversy over NATO's eastern expansion was also satisfactorily addressed at the Brussels summit. The U.S. initiative—the Partnership for Peace—was able to bridge the divide over enlargement, at least in the short term. The PfP was designed to act as a waiting room of sorts for East European applicants and, as such, permitted postponement of the decision whether to expand eastward. In due course, NATO's involvement in Bosnia became a catalyst for the continuing development of the PfP with a focus on military cooperation. Alongside NATO member states, a number of partnering states endeavored to implement the military component of the Dayton Accords. This collaboration made apparent the necessity of improved interoperability of multinational coalitions. Moreover, partnering states expressed the desire for inclusion in the planning, decisionmaking, and implementation of peace-support operations at the political level.

A major breakthrough concerning many of the pending issues occurred in 1997 at the NATO summits in Sintra, Portugal, and in Madrid, Spain. There, NATO members decided to redefine and enhance cooperation with PfP states. The desire for extended political consultation culminated in the creation of the Euro-Atlantic Partnership Council. First, the EAPC functions as a political "roof" over the intensified military cooperation within PfP; its operational role in crisis management was augmented in the context of an expanded PfP. Second, NATO agreed to reconsider and improve its cooperation with the Russian Federation and Ukraine. The agreements with the two most important East European states served to mitigate negative consequences arising from NATO's eastern expansion. This enhanced cooperation, in turn, allowed NATO to extend invitations to Poland, the Czech Republic, and Hungary to join it. On the occasion of the Washington summit in the spring of 1999, convened to celebrate the fiftieth anniversary of NATO's founding, the public was presented with a new NATO, one that had successfully adapted to the changed circumstances and security challenges following the end of the Cold War. NATO expanded its territory eastward and thereby expanded its collective defense mandate, as stipulated in Article V of the North Atlantic Treaty, to include NATO's three new members. At the same time, NATO announced that it intended to assume tasks in conflict prevention and crisis management in the future that would cut across the geographic boundaries of the expanded NATO.

With this new departure, NATO established itself as the core of the

Euroatlantic security system. The process of change, however, has not been concluded. It is conceivable that NATO's political functions will continue to grow to become still more important. Moreover, the enlargement process has not yet run its course and will continue to present difficult challenges. Russia, the leading regional power in Eastern Europe, perceives NATO enlargement as a potential threat to its own security and has repeatedly expressed its concern over the recent defection of three former Warsaw Pact states. Russian grumbling over the Baltic states suggests that the apprehensions within the Russian strategic and military establishments— that NATO might actually expand to Russia's borders—may in fact come to pass.

NATO thus strains to tread delicately around the fearful Russian giant in the East. Another dimension of the same problem will surface *within* NATO, for eastward expansion would indeed enlarge NATO's area of operations and thereby enhance the Eastern European commitment to stability in the region; but expansion also hollows out NATO from within. The inclusion of the three former Warsaw Pact states increased NATO strategic responsibilities and financial commitments, as the Polish, Hungarian, and Czech economies are not up to the military and financial challenges posed by membership—a process likely to repeat itself with further expansion. The disadvantages of enlargement, however, ought to be juxtaposed with the evident benefits: by admitting additional states from Eastern and Southeastern Europe into NATO, a measure of democratization and economic progress can be maintained in those countries.

NATO's and the European Union's expansion processes give rise to insecurities and fears of new fault lines in Europe. Each round of expansion brings the potential for further tensions. In this light, the Organization for Security and Cooperation in Europe represents a viable alternative security organization to some—mostly Europeans and Asians—but not to others. The OSCE is itself a child of the institution-building that emerged from the soft security approach to European politics. The Helsinki process, which began in 1973, culminated in the Helsinki Final Act, asserting Europe's national boundaries while binding communist countries to a convention on human rights for the first time since World War II. It established the CSCE and initiated détente and disarmament and thus constituted the genesis of the OSCE. Often, the significance of the OSCE is not fully realized; it was the human rights groups that emerged from the Helsinki process that contributed to the eventual downfall of the communist regimes during 1989–1991.

After the thirty-four CSCE member states officially ended the confrontation between East and West with the Charter of Paris for a New Europe in 1990, they strove to give the CSCE new functions beyond being a forum for dialogue; they wanted the CSCE to assume leadership in the security of Europe. These endeavors resulted in an incremental process of institutionalization. Since 1 January 1995, the new entity—the Organization for Security and Cooperation in Europe—constitutes a supranational organization with permanent institutions and procedures. Equally significant was the increase in the number of participating states as a consequence of the recent upheaval in Europe: the OSCE currently has fifty-five member states. Following the collapse of the Soviet Union, the OSCE became the instrumental asset in conflict prevention and resolution in the Soviet successor states. It was uniquely placed to fulfill its role as honest broker precisely because all the conflicting protagonists were OSCE member states. The OSCE is the only institution that spans Europe in its entirety. It is also the only regional security institution or organization that is compliant with Article V of the United Nations Charter and must therefore be considered a pioneering enterprise supportive of the UN commitment to peace and security.

OSCE activities in the 1990s expanded in scope to include arms control, confidence- and security-building measures, human rights, elections monitoring, and economic and environmental security. Its services to the troubled former communist countries proved to be of great worth in the all-out effort to stabilize Eastern Europe. But could the OSCE do more? Many observers doubt it. To begin, the Helsinki Final Act, the moral basis of the OSCE, is not a treaty and thus lacks binding legal force, which may explain the great number of participating states. The OSCE has no central decision-making body with the ability to enforce any of its decisions. It does have a secretariat in Prague, an election-monitoring office in Warsaw, and a conflict-monitoring center in Vienna, but none have any decisionmaking competence. Finally, the OSCE has no enforcement mechanism and so is compelled to rely on voluntary contributions from members. There is no armed or paramilitary corps.

All these observations, however, do not preclude the possibility of the OSCE becoming an important actor in the regional security community over time. For the moment, however, the OSCE remains limited to its normative role as a valuable soft security supplement to the European Union and NATO.

The United States: Between Hegemony and Isolationism

U.S. foreign policy in the 1990s has proven somewhat erratic. In the absence of the bipolar Cold War, U.S. foreign policy under Presidents George H.W. Bush and Bill Clinton reflected at least two subcurrents: interventionism as well as isolationism. Despite the obvious contradictions, U.S. foreign policy since the collapse of the Soviet Union in 1991 has displayed the historical divergence in U.S. political thought despite occasional mentions of a new world order, which in any case was never adequately defined.

Under President Clinton, two prominent administration members used catch phrases like "enlarging democracy" and "peace preservation" (attributed to Anthony Lake and Madeleine Albright, respectively). But in reality the Clinton administration first and foremost focused on domestic, and especially economic, problems.[6] At the same time, Congress and the U.S. public viewed international commitments with skepticism. Thus, the contradictions in U.S. foreign policy during the 1990s reflect the lack of consensus among the political establishment as to the proper U.S. role in the post–Cold War international system.

Muddling through: the ambivalence of U.S. foreign policy.   U.S. leadership constituted the most clear-cut trend in the context of the emerging international system. The dominance of the United States in the post–Cold War world was based on values such as liberalism and democracy that were successfully propagated in the past and witnessed a global dissemination in the present. But following the dissolution of the Soviet Union, the United States remained the only power with the capability to project its force globally and again developed a superiority in cutting-edge technology. Washington also demonstrated superiority in soft power and exerted a far-reaching influence over the international agenda.

Despite the military and political superiority of the United States or, rather, because of it, U.S. decisionmakers were repeatedly exposed to criticism—domestically as well as abroad. And whereas some discerned the first signs of a weary hegemon, others saw increasing arrogance. The U.S. penchant to "go it alone" encouraged fears of a more unilateralist U.S. foreign policy. Indeed, the United States has of late evinced little consideration for international agreements and shown less interest for the virtue of combining preponderance with cooperation. In this regard, one might recall that the United States remained aloof from the International Criminal Court and the Ottawa Convention banning the use of antipersonnel landmines, and it consistently failed to pay off its arrears to the United Nations. Following long negotiations and partial payments, the U.S. House of Representatives voted on 25 September 2002 to pay the remaining amounts due to the United Nations.

The volatility of U.S. foreign policy in the 1990s reflected the complexities and difficulties of foreign political decisionmaking in a world in which economic issues dominated defense policy; in which domestic politics gained prominence at the expense of foreign policy; in which risks and threats had assumed a transnational character; and in which the entire international community faced similar challenges. In such a world, defining national interests and security objectives was no easy task. The days of coherent foreign policy and grand strategy, as conceived of and practiced by George F. Kennan and Henry Kissinger, were past. U.S. foreign policy in the 1990s was thus also an expression of the fact that there were only few convincing answers for coping in a world that was changing and more complex—the legacy of the Cold War.

With U.S. foreign policy being ambivalent, then as it is now, a monolithic analysis thereof would be premature. Clearly, the sudden absence of the Soviet threat deprived the United States and its Western allies of a Manichean global perspective; the nascent international system provided for unanticipated challenges in a heterogeneous, and hence complex, international environment. Sea changes in U.S. foreign policy, as such, failed to manifest since the early days of the George H.W. Bush administration; but over time significant changes in the U.S. perception of its new role as the sole surviving superpower caused a shift in its foreign relations. The most important question relating to the United States under the first George Bush and Clinton is whether the United States *behaved* like the only superpower left in the international system (the unipolar perspective) and sought to consolidate its power vis-à-vis other key players, or whether the United States sought to advance its interests in collaboration with other states, thus implicitly acknowledging them as important forces and potential partners in the new international system (the multipolar perspective). As we have seen, the record of U.S. conduct in the 1990s made the task of coming up with answers difficult but not impossible.

Generally, where vital U.S. national interests were concerned (e.g., during the Gulf War), military intervention offered the only viable solution, albeit in the shape of the multilateral Coalition force. This phenomenon equally applied to the mid- to long-term U.S. international agenda (i.e., issues where U.S. interests were not immediately at stake, such as questions of regional stability), as exemplified by the powerful U.S. backing for the campaigns in Bosnia and Kosovo. Again, U.S. involvement was not formally unilateralist but occurred within the framework of NATO. Moreover, U.S. assertiveness in these cases, which culminated in U.S.-orchestrated interventions, was prompted by Europe's reluctance to revert to military action, as well as a distinct lack of unity and initiative.

Many among the U.S. public have become increasingly frustrated with the complexity of conflicts in the post–Cold War era and the thankless tasks that come with confronting them. People have become disillusioned with the limits of the United Nations and disappointed in U.S. allies' reticence and have, furthermore, become unwilling to shoulder every responsibility alone and at all times. Nevertheless, the U.S. leadership learned an important lesson during the 1990s: in a world that is regionalized, democratized, and economized, neither isolationism nor unilateralism will work. The multilayered challenges of the future can be addressed only in cooperation with other international actors. However, the question of whether U.S. foreign policy will be hegemonic or will shift toward coordination and consensus within multilateral coalitions will remain a difficult one to answer and will become clearer only as time moves on.

From rogue state to peer competitor and back.   The end of the Cold War forced the United States to reorient its foreign policy and, therefore, find a means to identify those interests hostile to its own. The answers given by the security and foreign political establishments also existed under the changes in recent history. The 1990s brought forth a concept in international relations that was stunning in both its simplicity and its capacity for categorization: the **rogue state**, a new category of state actor that was the product of the U.S. State Department and derived from the main tenets of post–Cold War U.S. foreign policy. According to the prevalent view in U.S. policymaking circles, rogue states represented various types of threats to the international system. Rogue regimes' domestic policies usually do not correspond with the standards set by the United States in particular and the West in general. Such regimes are considered to be a regional threat to the interests of Western allies around the globe. They are also believed to undermine regional and, at worst, global stability. Some rogue states actively sponsor terrorism as an extension of foreign policy. On a strategic level, rogue regimes are involved in the development of WMD and delivery systems that—in the event of successful production and deployment—will pose a danger to world peace. The list of rogue states maintained by the U.S. State Department was never official, but throughout the 1990s Iran, Iraq, Libya, North Korea, Sudan, Yugoslavia, and Cuba were identified as rogues.

There are problems with the nomenclature as well as the perspective that brought this concept into being. The definition of *rogue state* has attracted many criticisms. It has been decried as a political tool designed to impugn such states that do not act in conformity with U.S. interests. In fact, the only meaningful observation that can be made about these states' commonalties is that all of them have at one time or another threatened U.S. national interests. The intricate relationship between the U.S. concept of the post–Cold War international system as a new world order and the concept of a rogue or renegade state shows that both are predicated on the assumption of U.S. hegemony after 1991. The U.S. position toward rogue states, rightly or wrongly, assumes that the United States and, by implication, the Western world are the arbiters and enforcers of global peace. But advocates of U.S. foreign policy targeting the rogue states maintained that for legal and moral reasons rogue regimes that ruled dictatorially; sheltered, abetted, and sponsored terrorists; or developed **atomic/biological/ chemical (ABC) weapons** needed to be isolated and shunned by the international community in order to establish universally recognized constraints on the behavior of states and, therefore, to promote stability, peace, and prosperity.

Officially, this was part of the rationale that underpinned the Coalition forged by the United States against Iraq during the Gulf War in 1991 and NATO's air raids against Yugoslavia during the Kosovo crisis eight years later. Punitive measures on a tactical level, intended to create maximum political impact, occurred from time to time. In August 1998, for example, the U.S. Air Force launched a strike against a Sudanese pharmaceutical complex just outside of Khartoum suspected of producing nerve gas; Iran, which has been accused of financing Shiite terrorist groups around the globe, has been subjected to an economic embargo since the revolution of 1978. And as early as 1986, a U.S. airborne squadron targeted Libya for its alleged support and sponsorship of various terrorist groups. Since the end of the Cold War, North Korea has received attention from several U.S. administrations attempting to curb President Kim Jong-il's ambitious nuclear weapons development program. The U.S. policy was to isolate the rogue states, maintain heavy pressure on them, and ultimately promote a domestic context wherein the rogue regime could no longer cling to power and would eventually be replaced by a government in line with U.S. interests. Nevertheless, not in a single case—from Iraq to Yugoslavia—where U.S. and Western power was brought to bear on the rogues or outlaw states in various degrees of operational intensity did this stratagem succeed. Saddam Hussein remains entrenched in Iraq, and Slobodan Milosevic was not brought to the bar of justice until 2001. At best, the United States has been able to contain rogue states and minimize the challenge they pose to U.S. regional influence.

In any event, the rogue-state designation was dropped in the middle of 2000 in favor of a new category—**states of concern**. This shift in nomenclature indicated a change in the U.S. perception of international politics and reflected recent developments in the countries on Washington's blacklist. For example, Iran's government has moved toward liberalization and democracy, and Libya has cooperated in the prosecution of the suspects in the Lockerbie airline bombing of 1988. But the adoption of the new terminology also reflected a changed threat scenario as perceived by U.S. policymakers. The confusion caused by the end of the bipolar system, in which no new power center challenged the United States, created a situation in which regional threats rose to prominence. Because regional powers, such as the Russian Federation and China, did not choose to challenge U.S. policy toward rogue states, the first Bush and early Clinton administrations enjoyed a relatively free reign in implementing their schemes against renegades. In recent years, however, regional powers advanced to become the **peer competitors** of tomorrow and, consequently, have taken the center stage in the U.S. global threat analysis. Moreover, the peer competitors—in particular China—have, by virtue of their improved power status in the eyes of Washington and its allies, also become potential future patrons of regional client powers that have gone rogue or better serve the foreign policies of their respective protectors.

With the September 11 terrorist attacks on New York and the Pentagon, the focus on threats shifted again. In his State of the Union Address delivered on 29 January 2002, President George W. Bush specifically identified Iran, Iraq, and North Korea as an "axis of evil."[7] Was the United States reverting to the concept of the rogue state? At the same time, and as a result of the September 11 attacks, the United States forged closer ties with China and the Russian Federation in the war against international terrorism (discussed further below).

International trade: NAFTA and the World Trade Organization.   In the economic sphere, Washington promoted two venues to further U.S. interests vis-à-vis the European Union and the so-called yen bloc in the Pacific region. The first Bush and Clinton administrations took exception at the emergence of what they understood to be trade blocs that to varying degrees impeded the importation of U.S.-made goods. Successive U.S. administrations considered the trade lockout on the part of the Europeans and Asians to be unfair. Viewed from the perspective of the U.S.-generated free-trade premise, trade blocs of any kind—especially if they developed an ability to restrict U.S. access to their own markets—were counterproductive. In order to counteract trade discriminations of the European and Asian regional trade blocs, therefore, the United States launched what can be interpreted as a retaliatory economic association. Implementation of the **North American Free Trade Agreement (NAFTA)** began on January 1, 1994.

The NAFTA agreement was intended to gradually remove most trade barriers between the United States, Canada, and Mexico, and it has been a success on many counts. NAFTA effectively abolished all agricultural trade tariffs between the United States and Canada, and a number of other significant impediments are to be phased out over the next decade. But Mexico has proved to be a difficult ally, as low-wage workers in the Mexican economy are more competitive in the stratum of low-paying jobs than their northern counterparts. Problems with NAFTA identified by the United States and Canada have centered on the job drain from north to south. Supporters of NAFTA have pointed out that the loss of low-wage positions had been ongoing before NAFTA was concluded and would have taken place regardless. In fact, NAFTA proponents, especially in the United States, have been asking whether Americans would prefer to produce computer chips or potato chips.[8] In other words, the U.S. pro-NAFTA lobby has been telling the U.S. workforce to concentrate on higher-paying jobs in high-tech industries, as low-paid illegal immigrants in the United States frequently fill jobs.

NAFTA and the European Union share many commonalities, such as their respective populations and gross domestic products. At the same time, there are significant differences, such as the goals established in the charters of the two trade blocs. NAFTA's objectives are limited to the elimination of trade barriers, whereas the European Union seeks the economic and, eventually, the political integration of Europe. In that respect, the European Union is the most ambitious of the three trade blocs. Moreover, the European Union has implemented the free flow of labor and capital, whereas NAFTA permits, within certain limits, only an exchange of goods and services for its members. Also, the European Union instituted external tariffs binding all its members, whereas NAFTA members are at liberty to establish any type of tariff agreements with other states not a party to NAFTA.

As mentioned before, the United States pursues a two-pronged approach to the economic aspect of its national interest. If the first is constituted by NAFTA, the second is evident in the instrumental support offered by the United States in conjunction with other leading trading partners in the global economy: the establishment of the **World Trade Organization (WTO)** in 1997. Although NAFTA's declared objectives are congruent with those of the WTO, the two organizations differ in scope. Whereas NAFTA is a regional trading bloc, much like the European Union, the WTO takes a global approach. Both NAFTA and WTO embody a will to lower trade barriers, but they diverge on questions of geography. NAFTA's agenda—like those of the European Union and the yen bloc—is the result of and affects its immediate sphere of operations—namely, its region of concern. The problem is that this is antithetical to the very premise of WTO, which maintains that trade barriers need to be eradicated around the globe. The progress of WTO heralds the decline of the regional trading blocs, as external tariffs would become a source of friction. Effectively, a successful WTO would render the European Union, NAFTA, and the yen bloc obsolete. The successful implementation of WTO regulations will progress at a much slower rate than, say, those of the European Union. The outcome of future developments will then indicate whether the international system will move toward regionalism or globalism. For the moment, and for the foreseeable future, it seems safe to say that the prevalent trend is toward regionalism.

Asia

Even during the Cold War, the Asian security system fundamentally differed from that of the Euroatlantic. The United States had been compelled to base its involvement in East Asia primarily on bilateral defensive alliances, as the recent memory of World War II made East Asian countries balk at security cooperation with Japan. As early as the 1970s, the hard frontier between the blocs became porous. While China turned its back to the Soviet Union, Sino-U.S. relations entered a phase of rapprochement— China's opening to the West. As a consequence, events in Southeast Asia were largely shaped by regional conflicts, which in turn were influenced by the competition between the United States, the Soviet Union, and China for preeminence in the region.

The dissolution of the Soviet Union curtailed its role as an Asian power. The end of the Cold War also brought a decline in the significance of the U.S. bilateral security pacts with East Asian states. Events were largely influenced by the incremental emancipation of Japan in international politics, the rise of China, as well as the appearance of middle powers in the region. Shifts in the constellation of power caused major insecurity, which could not be ameliorated by powerful institutions or cushioned by the asymmetrical growth of Asian economies. In Asia, in contrast to Europe, the transition into the post–Cold War era did not parallel a course of arms reduction. Instead, the transition became a catalyst for tension and thus fueled an arms race. In the 1990s, the emerging Asian security order stood under the shadow of massive armament by a number of regional powers that resulted in instability.

Feelings of insecurity remained unchecked and were not channeled by functional multilateral structures. Thanks to the existence of ASEAN since 1967, Asia did have a functionally oriented organization that was supportive of loose economic cooperation without political finality. With the foundation of the Asia Pacific Economic Cooperation forum (APEC) in 1989, a loosely organized forum for cooperation was created and today includes all the states of the Pacific Rim. However, due to its size, APEC is unlikely to become the foundation of a security system in the Pacific area. The most promising initiative so far was the ASEAN Regional Forum (ARF) established in 1994, which, aside from the original ASEAN member states, also included the United States, Canada, Japan, Australia, New Zealand, South Korea, and the European Union. China and the Russian Federation have been granted guest status, and Vietnam and Laos are observing the proceedings. Significantly, the ARF constituted a comprehensive forum for discussing security policy, comparable to the CSCE in its objective to encourage dialogue.

Integration Problems
Despite the fact that Pacific Rim states indicated their willingness to cooperate, the actual potential of the integration process was marginal at best.

Moreover, the leading powers in the region—the United States, Japan, and China—were disinclined or incapable of encouraging an effective integration process. An overview of the five obstacles to further integrative development demonstrates that the forces of integration are walking a long and difficult road:

1. One of the most difficult problems for integration is represented by the geographic fragmentation and spatial expanse of the Pacific region. With the exception of Southeast Asia, there are few points of contact between Asian states, and many states in the region are confined to islands and have, therefore, exhibited a tendency for parochialism in regional relations. The physical distances in the Pacific are enormous, which renders integration difficult.

2. The fundamentally different cultures of the region—Confucian-communist, Confucian-capitalist, market economy–oriented, and democratic-economic—continued to clash. Such contrasts were further exacerbated by the deep chasm between the rich and the poor.

3. Japan was hard put to face and address its recent history. Indeed, resentment against the Japanese surfaced time and again. An integration of Northeast Asia, however, was predicated on a sincere engagement with the past and a genuine reconciliation of the parties affected. A comparable sense of distrust could be discerned in the case of China, which did little to build trust by upholding its claim to the former territory of Indochina and the South Chinese Sea as part of its traditional sphere of influence.

4. Growth in Asian markets was based on a mode of production that was geared toward exporting goods. Exports, however, were not extended to other countries in the region, something that would have supported economic integration; instead, products were destined for Europe and the United States. Asian states were competing against one another for foreign markets.

5. The relatively young East Asian states lacked the experience and opportunity to cooperate within multilateral structures and institutions.

The Proliferation of Nuclear Weapons:
North Korea, India, and Pakistan

On 12 March 1993, North Korea announced that it would withdraw from the Nuclear Non-Proliferation Treaty (NPT). At the same time, the North Korean economy went into a slump, and the country's population faced a crisis due to food shortages. Pyongyang responded to the domestic crisis by exerting more foreign political pressure. Almost a year later, on 1 March 1994, the inspectors of the International Atomic Energy Agency were prevented from accessing North Korean nuclear installations, and Pyongyang stated that the plutonium required for the construction of nuclear weapons could be produced in their own nuclear test reactors. Put on guard by the North Korean threats, the United States for the first time directly negotiated with Pyongyang and initiated the Korean Peninsula Energy Development Organization (KEDO) to dissuade the North Koreans from continuing their nuclear weapons program. With the aid of the West—financed by South Korea and Japan—two lightwater reactors were to be built in North Korea; deriving from nuclear fission, their by-products would not be suitable for the construction of nuclear weapons. In return, North Korea agreed to abandon its nuclear weapons program. The KEDO project started operations in 1997 but soon ran into problems.

Another crisis involving North Korea came to a head on 31 August 1998 when Pyongyang launched a ballistic missile that violated Japanese airspace. Shocked, leaders in Tokyo immediately terminated all financial aid to North Korea and ceased all diplomatic relations. The South Korean reaction proved more moderate. Seoul decided to continue working toward improved cultural and economic contact with North Korea despite the provocation. Despite its badly tottering economy, exacerbated by a nation-wide famine and natural catastrophes, North Korea persisted in wanting to dictate the terms of the game. All efforts on the part of South Korea, Japan, and the United States to involve Pyongyang in a continuous dialogue have failed. The more difficult it becomes to negotiate with North Korea, the stronger the Chinese position grows. China seems to be the only power that is taken seriously by the North Koreans. At the same time, the danger of polarization—between a South Korean state allied to the United States and a North Korean state allied to China—looms large.

In another region of Asia—that is, South Asia—India and Pakistan have in recent times fought three major wars and are on the verge of a fourth. Following a brief thaw in the otherwise frosty relationship of these two archenemies, relations between Delhi and Islamabad rapidly deteriorated in the second half of the 1990s. The climax was a nuclear arms race between the two states. India's successful testing of a nuclear device in May 1998 took the U.S. intelligence community by surprise and caused much consternation in the international community—not least because of the de facto moratorium instituted by the 1996 ban on nuclear testing, as well as the underlying assumption of prevalent opinions and trends supportive of nonproliferation.

Predictably, Pakistan's response was to condemn the Indian test and to accuse the Indian government of compelling Pakistan to reciprocate in kind. That same month, Pakistan achieved a successful nuclear test of its own. Both states justified their actions by arguing that the major nuclear powers (the United States, Great Britain, Russia, China, and France) engaged in discriminatory practices against nonnuclear states. Conversely, protracted clashes over the disputed territory of Kashmir between Pakistan and India undermined any rhetoric reminiscent of the Non-Aligned Movement on their part and presaged a nuclearization of the border dispute. Beyond threatening the region, such an outcome would have global implications. Finally, the Pakistani-Indian tensions may very well have instigated an arms race in Asia.

The motives for increasing Pakistani and Indian nuclear capabilities are manifold and multidimensional. To begin with, India feels slighted for being ignored as a potential major power. India's population numbers some 975 million and is expected to exceed that of China within the next twenty-five years. India's ambitions will be thwarted only at the expense of regional stability. India's current position on nonproliferation is based on the belief that the entire nonproliferation regime is intrinsically insincere. Delhi's reaction was based on its perception of strategic encirclement, which was determined by three factors. First, the Indian Ocean was patrolled and hence controlled by forces of the U.S. Navy and U.S. Air Force. Second, Pakistan was arming its forces. Third, China, which was developing into one of the most significant, if not the preponderant, power in the region, was actively supporting Pakistan's efforts at nuclear armament. In addition to these strategic challenges, India also faced stiff economic competition from Japan. As compared to other Asian economies, that of India was possibly even falling behind. Nevertheless, the question of whether the nuclear tests constituted a suitable or effective means to address these challenges as yet remains without an answer.

In the case of Pakistan, political, strategic, as well as religio-political considerations may well have had a decisive influence on the decision to develop its nuclear capability, for Pakistan felt that its credibility as a leader in the Islamic world was at stake. Indeed, its acquisition of the so-called Islamic bomb assumes an important role in the collective consciousness of the Islamic world, for it symbolizes unity, determination, and self-confidence. From Algeria to Iraq, the Islamic bomb is widely held to constitute a guarantee against further humiliating defeats inflicted by the West and is also seen as a symbol of the resurgent power of Islam. Pakistan's transition from peripheral power to nuclear power brought with it benefits in the shape of financial pledges from the wealthy oil-producing Arab states, and the fathers of the Islamic bomb were honored as national heroes. However, in the wake of the terrorist attacks of 11 September 2001, tensions between the Pakistani government and the fundamentalist segments of Pakistani society have become more pronounced. Civil disturbances even suggest a significant divergence between the governed and the government in terms of foreign political preferences. In the eyes of the fundamentalists—in and beyond Pakistan—the Pakistani government has appeared supine in its willingness to collaborate with the United States and its allies. As a consequence of this recent development, the capacity of the Pakistani nuclear program as a safeguard against Western meddling has been called into question.

The End of a Singular Economic Boom?

The economic and social development of Northeast Asia and Southeast Asia were unique in the history of the global economy. Former developing states with hopeless prospects suddenly flourished due to the continuous structural change to break through the industrial threshold and ultimately compete with established industrial and commercial powers. We have already recounted the rise of the Four Tigers (see Chapter 6). The Asian economic boom resulted in a process of urbanization of formerly agrarian societies as the number of wage recipients rapidly increased. As a consequence, poverty declined. In Indonesia, for example, 60 percent of the population lived in poverty in the 1960s; by 1997, only some 10 percent did. Furthermore, the difference in income levels during the 1990s was less accentuated in Asia than in Latin America.

By 1950, only 17 percent of the global gross product was made in Asia; in 1997, Asia was responsible for 40 percent. Based on the extraordinary economic success, the idea spread in the region that the center of the world, after a European intermezzo of a few centuries, would in the future again shift to East Asia. Proponents described an Asian model of civilization that was at least equal with, though not superior to, that of Europe. Values such as diligence, higher education, frugality, and especially the prioritization of the community over the individual were understood to constitute genuine Asian virtues and were identified as the very foundation of the Asian economic miracle. The exertion of political power was shaped by such factors as the personification of leadership through charismatic individuals, an intricate interrelationship between power and morally legitimate rule, a powerful state, and a single dominant political party.

However, as a consequence of the economic miracle, such social and political distinguishing marks came under tremendous pressure by the concurrent trend toward modernization. In Japan, for example, the hegemony of the Liberal Democratic Party was abruptly terminated by the political opposition after an uninterrupted tenure of three decades. Taiwan and South Korea also were in the process of becoming functioning democracies. At the same time, ruling in Asia was still subject to high normative expectations, which helps explain the beginning of the currency crisis of 1997.

In terms of its severity, the financial crisis that rocked the Asian economies and markets in the late 1990s was a singular event in the post–Cold War world. The high tide of the crisis lasted from mid-1997 to mid-1998. Beginning in Thailand, the crisis expanded in concentric circles and affected, albeit unequally, most Asian currencies and markets and even had a significant impact on the global economy. Experts likened its spread to a contagion. The world has not fully recovered from the aftershocks.

Opinions differ as to the causes, but it can be said to have begun with the announcement by the Thai government in early July 1997 that it would support the baht by a managed float. At the same time, the Thai government requested technical assistance from the International Monetary Fund. On the same day, the value of the baht fell by 20 percent. The intervention of the Thai government was the catalyst for a regional currency that threatened to spiral out of control. In only a few weeks, symptoms surfaced in the Philippines and Indonesia. Both governments were compelled to take measures in defense of their respective currencies. At the end of July, the prime minister of Malaysia, Mahatir Mohamad, went so far as to accuse rogue speculators—some by name—as the culprits in the crashing of the ringgit. In due course, financial crisis struck the national economies of Taiwan, Hong Kong, Singapore, and elsewhere. Although they evinced some stability, property and stock markets were by then on a downward spiral. Toward the end of October 1997, the crisis had engulfed the global economy. In New York on 27 October 1997, the Dow Jones industrial average suffered the worst point fall since its inception. Trading operations were immediately suspended on Wall Street.

What were the reasons for the crisis? Generally, Asian currencies, or rather their respective values and appreciation in the international economy, at that time stood in no relation to the economies underpinning and sustaining them. Considerable amounts of speculative capital were invested in property and real estate development, only to fuel further speculation culminating in a bursting bubble caused by asset price inflation. This is exactly what occurred in Thailand in early July 1997. First and foremost, the affected economies suffered from financial-sector weaknesses that left them at the mercy of the crisis once it struck.

During the 1990s, several Asian economies witnessed growth in credit to the private sector. This mushrooming of credit vastly exceeded real economic growth, the consequence of which was that the respective national economies became vulnerable to changes in credit conditions. The value of property fell, and nonperforming bank loans were on the rise. Banks and their corporate clientele, whose borrowing abroad was done in foreign currencies and at short maturities, exacerbated the vulnerability of these economies. These borrowing conditions were supposed to keep the servicing expenses of the loans taken out at a low level; but such actions opened the gate to risky speculation and curtailed the governments' options for timely intervention. Notably, such a state of affairs would have been unlikely if governments had imposed controls on the financial sector as a matter of course.

Moreover, economies that bore the brunt of the crisis had run up substantial current-account deficits; some countries, such as Thailand, had accumulated external deficits that fell just below 10 percent of gross domestic product. These external deficits, considered harmless for some years prior to the crisis, as they caused no turbulence in the public sectors and were primarily used to expand investment, had to be reviewed in 1996 and 1997. Investments were either high-risk, misdirected into overextended sectors, eaten up by gargantuan infrastructure plans, or channeled into inefficient government monopolies. Furthermore, overproduction in certain key sectors, and the mounting export competition of regional states, called into doubt the sustainability of the accumulated external deficits.

Thus, the Asian financial crisis spread throughout the region and beyond like a contagious disease, rapidly plunging state after state into economic turmoil. Although the crisis originated in an economic dwarf, it soon engulfed some of the major economic players in the global market. Like a chain reaction, the Asian financial crisis became an inexorable force. Some economists believe that the events in Thailand in July 1997 were a wake-up call to investors worldwide. As a consequence, the rating of Thai credit was scrutinized, as was that of most Asian borrowers. Investing parties realized that most Asian states suffered from economic weaknesses not unlike those exhibited by Thailand. The second major force that extended the crisis was found in the dynamics of currency devaluation. In the wake of currency depreciation by several states, all those who did not follow suit (by effecting a commensurate devaluation) found that their competitiveness was lacking, which again rendered their currencies vulnerable to attack by speculators.

In the final analysis, Asian economies will require time and effort to recuperate from the negative effects and aftershocks of the Asian financial crisis. The most important lesson of the Asian financial crisis, however, was the insight that the global economy has become genuinely and irreversibly interlinked—and not always for the best, as frequently claimed by the proponents of liberalism. Economic growth in one corner of the world will have an effect on other regions. Equally, the failure of even a national economy may—at least potentially—freeze global markets.

China and the Post–Cold War World:
Between Isolation and Integration

In early June 1989, as the Cold War came to a close, the Chinese communist government crushed a domestic prodemocracy movement—with the world watching—in Tiananmen Square. The international outcry against what was certainly a highly repressive policy by a government that seemed unaffected by the winds of change had a significant, negative impact on

Sino-U.S. relations. A five-year freeze in relations followed: the United States offered political asylum to the Chinese democracy movement's leadership and stalled all security- and military-related bilateral negotiations with China. Beijing, in turn, responded by turning down all applications by U.S. companies for trade operations on mainland China.

By 1992, U.S. President George H.W. Bush broke with the established foreign political practice of not openly supporting Taiwanese defensive capabilities by approving the sale of advanced military hardware to Taipei. In 1993, Bush's successor, Bill Clinton, linked China's most-favored-nation trading status with the United States to the country's human rights record. Chinese noncooperation and the further deterioration of relations compelled Clinton to abandon this linkage policy of constructive engagement with Beijing by May 1994. When the U.S. government approved a visa for Taiwan's President Lee Teng-hui a year later, the Chinese immediately recalled their ambassador. In 1996, the Chinese Peoples' Liberation Army conducted a show of strength by conducting missile tests and maneuvers off the mainland coast, which called for a U.S. presence in the Taiwan Strait.

The second half of the 1990s saw a tenuous improvement between the United States and China. Sino-U.S. relations thawed after a meeting between Clinton and Chinese President Jiang Zemin at an APEC forum held in Manila in 1996. Two years later, U.S. Defense Secretary William Cohen visited China to discuss closer military cooperation in the region. Congressional allegations of Chinese espionage against the United States again soured relations in June 1998, only to be patched up by President Clinton at the Sino-U.S. summit, which concluded with the mutual decision to detarget their respective nuclear warheads. Although critics argued that the warheads could be easily retargeted, improved relations between the United States and China lasted into 1999, when NATO's campaign in Kosovo and the inadvertent bombing of the Chinese embassy in Belgrade sparked violent anti-U.S. protests in Beijing. A U.S. invitation to Taiwan to participate in a theater missile defense system increased Chinese insecurity. More recently, the announcement of the **National Missile Defense (NMD)** program under President Clinton, as well as the follow-up actions on missile defense under his successor, George W. Bush, further burdened Sino-U.S. ties.

In light of tensions between the only remaining superpower and the principal Asian regional power, the future of the post–Cold War world looks uncertain. The question in the mid-1990s—how to avert a potential escalation between the West and China—is directly linked to China's feeling of insecurity in the context of contemporary international relations, its historically instilled, deep distrust of Western powers, and a perpetuation of the Cold War mind-set among policymakers on both sides. No answer is readily apparent in the early twenty-first century.

The Chinese leadership believes that a post–Cold War international system should be based on a multipolar order, as expressed in its endeavor to create a Sino-Russian axis in order to balance U.S. unilateralism in the late 1990s, as well as peaceful economic and political coexistence. Thus, Chinese analysts frequently look upon U.S. foreign policy as being meddlesome and disrespectful of Chinese sovereignty. Moreover, China charges the United States with interference in the pursuit of vital national interests in the region. It is obvious that China and the United States are vying for the place of regional hegemon in Asia.

On the other side of the fence, U.S. policymakers are trying to make up their minds on whether China represents a new evil empire (invoking the thesis of the China threat), or whether China simply represents a lumbering giant taking its time to fall into step with the global economy and the international community. Although some incidents—like China's saber rattling directed at Taiwan and its brutal suppression of Tibetans, the prodemocracy movement, and even sects such as Falun Gong—suggest a bellicose aspirant for regional supremacy, others—such as China's efforts at social and economic reform and its accession to the WTO on 11 December 2001—indicate that China is indeed interested in further international and regional integration. Mutual perceptions are of critical importance in shaping future Sino-U.S. relations, and many problems between the regional key players in the Pacific area remain unresolved, the greatest of which is represented by the pace and extent of Chinese economic, social, political, and military development, as well as its integration into a growing regional and global economy and a multilateral security framework.

Post-Tiananmen China is a paradox. On the one hand, communist China is a fast-growing regional military power in pursuit of multiple irredentist claims; the country also constitutes the single greatest potential market on the world. On the other hand, China's military potential and its demands to revise territorial boundaries may lead it to adventurism in the region, which would almost certainly trigger a head-on confrontation with the other great Pacific power—the United States. And domestically, the rapid growth of its economy renders the country more interdependent upon regional and international trading partners and requires the Chinese government to implement economic reforms that do not fit easily within the tenets of communism.

China is a country that desperately seeks to radiate the strength of a world power, but it is preoccupied with processing fast-paced changes at home by attempting to control the dynamics of the modern information society and economy. Whether a course of incremental reform will indeed bear the dividends hoped for by the Chinese leadership is unclear; it remains to be seen whether China opts for further integration into the international community by pursuing a course of accelerated reform, or whether a confrontation over regional hegemony with the United States will force it into deeper isolation.

The Middle East

The end of the Cold War brought fundamental changes to the security system of the Middle East. Competition between the superpowers had come to an end, and it was difficult to anticipate how the great powers of the world (the United States, Russia, China, Britain, France, and Germany) would react to future crises in the region. The test case was not long in making an appearance: paralleling the dissolution of the Soviet Union, the Gulf War took its course. President George H.W. Bush used the confluence of the two events to make the crisis a precedent for his concept of a new world order.

The defeat of Iraq at the end of the Gulf War altered the political landscape in the Persian Gulf region. The single most distinctive mark was that the dominance of the West—represented by the United States—became highly visible at the expense of the contracting influence of the Russian Federation. On the one hand, the conclusion of the Gulf War had changed the strategic environment to the extent that the prerequisites for an Israeli-Arab peace process had improved. Israel, Syria, and Egypt together had opposed Iraq; a resuscitation of an Arab eastern front consisting of Jordan, Syria, and Iraq against Israel therefore seemed unlikely. The credibility of the United States in the region had considerably improved, and the Gulf states (traditionally, Bahrain, Iran, Iraq, Kuwait, Oman, Qatar, Saudi Arabia, United Arab Emirates, and Yemen) and Egypt had agreed to reduce their support for the Palestine Liberation Organization, as Yassir Arafat had supported Saddam Hussein during the war. On the other hand, the palpable presence of the United States caused tensions in internal Arab relations, which in turn led to a sharp decline in the acceptance of the West among the Arab population at large. At the same time that Arab governments tried to find an understanding with the United States for purely pragmatic reasons, the chasm between Western culture and the Islamic world became more pronounced. The countermovement to Western dominance made itself felt under the label of Islamic fundamentalism.

Western Security Guarantees Versus Regional Hegemony

Immediately after the conclusion of the Gulf War, Arab states harbored hopes of realizing a regional order in which the actors would cooperate for security and stability in the region. In March 1991, the foreign ministers of Syria, Egypt, and the member states of the Gulf Cooperation Council

(Saudi Arabia, Qatar, Oman, Bahrain, the United Arab Emirates, and Kuwait) met in Damascus to assume mutual responsibility for the security of the Gulf region. The ministers intended to form the core of a military force out of Egyptian and Syrian contingents. In return, the two principal providers of troops would receive financial support for development in their respective states. The Arab motto for guaranteeing and securing stability in the region was therefore "cash for security." This vision of a regional security system was, however, never realized. Neither Iran nor Turkey would countenance an exclusively Arab arrangement. The Arab states, in turn, proved incapable of resolving the funding issue. As a consequence, tensions between Egypt, Saudi Arabia, and Kuwait heightened. The withdrawal of the last Egyptian units from the Gulf region in September 1991 marked the end of the project.

The vision of a regional security system was replaced in due course by Western security guarantees for individual Arab states. The Gulf states reacted to internal Arab dissension by initiating massive armament programs and by simultaneously concluding bilateral defensive pacts with major Western powers. Kuwait announced that it would acquire arms for the value of some U.S.$10 billion over the next decade. At the same time, Kuwait concluded a defense treaty with the United States, its duration also limited to ten years. An analogous agreement was reached between Bahrain and the United States; Great Britain and France also participated in negotiations with a number of Arab states to the same effect.

On a fundamental level, the failure of the envisioned regional security system and the significance of U.S. security guarantees had much to do with the two remaining insecurities in the Gulf region. Iran and Iraq had both claimed the position of regional hegemon at different times. But even after the conclusion of the Gulf War, the future of those two states remained unclear. Iran accepted the consequences of its political isolation following the Iran-Iraq War and shifted to a more moderate policy. Even though the bloody days of the Iranian revolution seemed far in the past, Iran continued to pursue hegemonic aspirations in the region. The West observed the massive armament of Iran with concern, and a number of territorial disputes between Iran and the Gulf states required solutions. Iraq, by contrast, would remain a source of instability for as long as Saddam Hussein remained in power. During the 1990s, Western apprehensions concerning the successful revival of Saddam Hussein's programs for the development of WMD grew.

Islamic Revivalism

The spread of Islamic fundamentalism, a phenomenon of the post–Cold War international system, had its roots in the **Islamic revivalism** of the late

1970s. The Iranian revolution of 1978–1979 called attention to a reassertion of Islam in Muslim personal and public life. The unexpected ouster of the shah of Iran by the charismatic Ayatollah Khomeini and the creation of an Islamic republic under his mullahs stunned the world. Fears that Iran would export its Islamic revolution to other countries in the Middle East became the lens through which events in the Muslim world were viewed. The 1979 takeover of the U.S. embassy in Tehran and Khomeini's expansionist designs, Libyan leader Muammar Qaddafi's posturing and promotion of a third world revolution, and Egyptian President Anwar Sadat's 1981 assassination by Muslim extremists supported the idea of a growing and more militant Islamic fundamentalism. The struggle of the Afghan mujahideen against a superior Soviet occupying force, kidnappings, hijackings, and attacks on foreign and government installations by various Islamic violent political groups, such as the Islamic Resistance Movement (Hamas) and the Iran-funded Hezbollah and Islamic Jihad in Lebanon and Israel, received enormous publicity. In the late 1970s and throughout the 1980s, the prevailing picture of the Islamic world in the West was of militants bent on undermining non-Islamic revivalist countries' stability, overthrowing governments, and imposing their own version of an Islamic state.

One possible explanation for Islamic revivalism is the profound loss of self-esteem among Muslims during the postcolonial era. Political and military failures, such as the devastating defeat inflicted on the Arab world and burgeoning Arab nationalism by the Israelis in 1967, the secession of Bangladesh from Pakistan, and the Lebanese civil war were demoralizing. The effects on Islamic societies were compounded by a widespread conviction that the Western world was insensitive and even ill-disposed toward Islam. This condition was remedied only by the Arabs' success during the Yom Kippur War against Israel in 1973 and the economic power demonstrated by the oil embargo under OPEC. Khomeini's overthrow of the shah's secular order and return to the religious values of Islam cast the Islamic recovery in devotional terms; the turn for the better boosted the self-confidence of the Islamic world.

For the vast majority of Muslims, the resurgence of Islam is a reassertion of cultural identity, formal religious observance, family values, and morality. The establishment of an Islamic society is seen as requiring a personal and social transformation that is a prerequisite for true Islamic government. Effective change is to come from below through a gradual social transformation brought about by implementation of Islamic law—the *shari'a*. Yet a significant minority views the societies and governments in Muslim countries as hopelessly corrupt. They believe that un-Islamic societies and their leaders are no better than infidels and that the religious establishment has been co-opted by the government. Such critics believe that established political and religious elites must be overthrown and that a new, committed leadership be chosen, and Islamic law imposed. These radical revolutionary groups, though relatively small in membership, have proved effective in political agitation, disruption, and assassination. Although Islamic extremist tendencies have been observed in a number of states, such as the former Soviet republics in Central Asia and the Caucasus, Algeria, and Sudan, they have not (with the notable exceptions of Afghanistan and Iran) successfully mobilized the masses. It is important not to condemn an entire social system because of a fanatical minority prone to use violence.

Nevertheless, the emergence of a significant number of Islamic extremist groups supported by various Islamic states—either as the latter's political stooges, or in order to forcibly export the Islamic revolution—has created a perceived threat to large parts of the non-Islamic world. The Western reaction to Islamic revivalism and extremism—a distinction almost never made—has borne the imprint of a visceral, occidental backlash, probably prompted by its unexpectedness in the West and compounded by a feeling that the reactionary fervor exhibited by Islamic revivalism has no place in the modern secular international community. Though prominent in the Western threat assessment of global politics, Islamic extremism and the creation of Islamic theocracies in Iran and Afghanistan merely constitute elements of a larger mosaic.

The Middle East Peace Process After Oslo

Despite a comprehensive peace process taking shape after the negotiations conducted at Oslo in 1993, extremists on both sides continued to undermine the efforts of Yassir Arafat and Yitzhak Rabin. The Palestinian militant group Hamas charged Arafat with betraying the Palestinian cause and threatened violence. In 1994, an American-Jewish settler murdered several Palestinians at prayer in a mosque. A few months later, a suicide attack on a public bus in Tel Aviv caused numerous civilian casualties. But if the extremists had hoped to derail the peace process, they were sorely disappointed, as Rabin and Arafat, the latter of whom had been elected president of the Palestinian Authority, moved to implement the next stage of their agreement. The road to peace, however, remained deeply problematic. Many issues, such as the controversial status of Jerusalem, continued to threaten the achievement of a final peace agreement. Moreover, in 1995 Hamas intensified its bombing campaign against Israeli civilian targets in a bid to weaken Arafat. Rabin, however, continued to support peace talks with Arafat, which resulted in a further accord setting forth a schedule for the orderly withdrawal of Israeli troops from roughly a third of the West Bank. Furthermore, Rabin agreed to release a significant number of Palestinian prisoners.

The unexpected assassination of Rabin by a Jewish extremist in late November 1995 seemed to indicate that the Israeli leader had moved too far, too fast in seeking a lasting peace. Shimon Peres, who had been Rabin's foreign minister, became acting prime minister. Peres pursued the policies of his predecessor and completed the withdrawal of Israeli forces from the designated areas in the West Bank. During the next election, Peres lost his mandate to a candidate of the Conservative Party, Benjamin Netanyahu, who refused to parley with Arafat specifically and all Palestinians in general. Essentially, Netanyahu set out to reverse the political legacies of Rabin and Peres. He supported building new Jewish settlements at the expense of Palestinian territorial aspirations. Netanyahu also stalled the withdrawal of Israeli troops from the West Bank. A number of incidents involving stone-throwing Palestinian youths gave Netanyahu a pretext to pursue a tougher policy. Withstanding external pressure by the United States to return to the negotiating table, Netanyahu, whose actions became highly controversial among Israeli voters, continued to implement his policies and undermined the peace process. Not until his second term did Netanyahu become more tractable; and then, he only grudgingly agreed to continue the removal of Israeli forces from the Occupied Territories. Until May 1999, the next election date, the peace process became a protracted and desultory affair.

But the landslide victory of Labor candidate Ehud Barak vastly improved chances for a lasting peace. To Arafat, Barak's victory signified a return to a constructive dialogue. The peace process had remained on track for more than eighteen months when a meeting at Camp David between Arafat, Barak, and U.S. President Bill Clinton resulted in great disappointment in July 2000. The frustration and resentment felt by the Palestinians was matched only by the weariness and disgruntlement of the Israelis. Hopes for a comprehensive solution between Israelis and Palestinians remain remote; three weeks of violence in late September 2000 marked the beginning of the second Palestinian intifada (uprising; also, the so-called Al-Aqsa intifada), which continued as this book went to press in late 2002.

On 28 September 2000, the leader of the Israeli parliamentary opposition, Ariel Sharon, visited the Temple Mount in Jerusalem. This event was given considerable attention by the mass media. In the wake of Sharon's visit, Palestinian activists attacked Israeli police at the site. In the following days and weeks, Palestinian unrest spread to Gaza and the West Bank, where Israeli security forces were repeatedly harassed or assaulted by crowds of angry Palestinians. The Palestinians laid the blame squarely on Sharon's doorstep, arguing that his visit to the shrine sacred to both Jews and Arabs had in fact sparked the latest round of hostilities. Sharon and leading Israeli politicians retorted by stating that the violence that initiated the second intifada (as distinct from the intifada of the late 1980s) in

September 2000 had been organized and guided by the Palestinian Authority.

The violence in the Middle East continued into the next year. When Israel elected Ariel Sharon prime minister over Ehud Barak in February 2001, the new government immediately implemented more stringent security measures. As a consequence, the second intifada escalated beyond civil unrest. Tit-for-tat attacks grew in size and scale: Palestinian militants attacked Israeli police, military personnel, and civilians; and Israeli forces conducted counterinsurgency operations against suspected terrorists deep inside Palestinian Authority territory.

Since that time, violence in the Middle East has only intensified. A spate of Palestinian suicide bombings carried out by terrorist organizations such as Islamic Jihad, Hamas, and Al-Aqsa (the latter spawned by a radical fringe within Yassir Arafat's Fatah movement) prompted the Israeli military to intervene more vigorously. Mediation attempts by a series of U.S. special envoys to the Middle East were frustrated time and again by the refusal of both sides to move off their entrenched positions. The Israelis no longer trusted Arafat as a negotiating partner, even accusing him of condoning suicide terrorism against Israeli citizens, and Arafat and his supporters were at times barely holding on to power. The militant Palestinian factions, which were beginning to represent the mainstream of a more radicalized public opinion, were challenging Arafat's leadership internally. Beset on all sides, Arafat stalled for time. His strategy did not achieve its intended objective: internal friction continued to plague the Palestinians as Israeli political and military pressure grew. The situation in the Middle East declined even further.

The impact of the terrorist attacks of 11 September 2001 on the latest Middle East crisis demonstrated an ambivalence within the West. The Israeli government has argued that it is also waging a war on terrorism and that nothing less than the country's survival is at stake. This position gained credence after some Palestinians were shown dancing in the streets after the attacks were broadcast. Yet Israel was excluded from the U.S.-led antiterrorism coalition in order to retain some measure of goodwill among all of the West's Arab allies. The exclusion of Israel was, politically speaking, crucial to the credibility of the coalition and the U.S. war effort in Afghanistan. This stance has earned the United States criticism from Israel and its supporters, as well as praise from forces supporting George W. Bush administration's refusal to be drawn into a partisan conflict.

The European Union's recent interest in the Middle East, as well as its efforts to contribute to the peace process, have borne no fruit. In response to Palestinian suicide terrorism, and despite vociferous protests by the European Union and other global players, Israeli forces time and again invaded territories under the jurisdiction of the Palestinian Authority. One

Palestinian-led suicide attack on 8 March 2002 killed forty-five civilians of all denominations; this impelled the Israeli government to expand military operations in Gaza and the West Bank. Palestinian resistance to Israeli incursions is stiffening, and it remains to be seen how much longer the two sides are willing to escalate the conflict. The mounting death tolls and growing disillusionment on all sides—including that of the outside mediators such as the United States and the European Union—bear witness to the urgency of finding a lasting solution acceptable to all.

The Global Perspective

With the demise of the bipolar system of the Cold War, the consensus on how best to ensure global stability also disintegrated. The world has become more complex, and the dynamics of regional development are on a diverging path. Three questions have moved to the center stage in efforts to maintain international stability in the wake of the dissolution of the old order. First, how can the spate of problems arising from the nuclear legacy of the Cold War be managed? Second, how should states approach the deadly amalgamation of terrorism, globalization, and WMD (yet the resuscitation of low-intensity political violence constitutes a fundamental challenge in itself). And third, how ought the international community tackle escalating intrastate conflicts? In the early 1990s, there was hope that recent changes would overcome the risks arising in the context of the nuclear legacy and intrastate conflicts. More than a decade later, the international community has sobered up: maintaining international stability and security will continue to be a daunting task in the future.

Nuclear Arms Control and Nuclear Nonproliferation

With the close of the Cold War, it was generally believed that the role of nuclear weapons in shaping international relations might become less relevant. Indeed, in the early 1990s indications were that the U.S. and Soviet arsenals could be whittled down and even eliminated through mutual arms reduction efforts. There was also hope that the looming threat of nuclear proliferation—that is, the dissemination of critical information on the construction of nuclear weapons and the materials required to assemble them—could be contained. On both counts, such hopes were misplaced: more than ten years after the end of the Cold War, nuclear weapons continue to play a decisive role in international politics. Although the United States and Russia have reduced their respective nuclear arsenals yet again, both powers still possess enough to destroy the U.S. and Russian societies. At the same time, new states armed with nuclear weapons capabilities appeared on the world stage: Israel, India, and Pakistan. The threat of regional and even global destabilization due to unchecked nuclear proliferation cannot be ignored.

During the Cold War, nuclear stability was based on an international framework that regulated the possession and proliferation of nuclear weapons. The Nuclear Non-Proliferation Treaty of 1968 limited the possession and control of nuclear weapons to fives states (the United States, the Soviet Union, Great Britain, France, and China). Through the NPT, the five nuclear powers committed to actively support and accelerate the process of nuclear arms reduction with the ultimate goal of eliminating such weapons altogether. The ABM Treaty of 1972 stipulated that neither the United States nor the Soviet Union was permitted to devise and implement comprehensive national nuclear missile defense systems. The ABM Treaty also established the principle of mutually assured destruction as the basis for stable strategic relations between the superpowers; it also increased and sustained crisis stability while preventing a possible arms race between offensive and defensive systems. Parallel to this development, the superpowers attempted to decelerate the arms race in offensive nuclear weapons systems by introducing the SALT I, SALT II, and the INF Treaties.

Since the dissolution of the Cold War international system, arms reduction policy has achieved significant successes in various categories. Defense expenditures around the globe have decreased by approximately a third. Arms stockpiles have been reduced by 13 percent and the various armed service branches by 12 percent. A treaty on chemical weapons was concluded in 1993 that banned chemical weapons and demanded their destruction within a specified period. By 1997, a treaty on antipersonnel landmines was signed in Ottawa, Canada, which forbade the deployment, production, stockpiling, and exchange of antipersonnel landmines.

Hopeful progress: START, the NPT, and the CTBT. In relation to nuclear weapons, the end of the Cold War also paralleled the renewed efforts by the United States and the Soviet Union to reduce their oversized nuclear weapons arsenals. On 31 July 1991, the United States and the Soviet Union concluded the **Strategic Arms Reduction Treaty (START I)**. By consenting to the stipulations of START I, the United States and the Soviet Union committed themselves to reducing their strategic nuclear delivery vehicles to 1,600 each. The number of warheads on deployed ICBMs, SCBMs, and heavy bombers was limited to a ceiling of 6,000. START I constituted the first arms control agreement that reduced the number of strategic nuclear forces. The negotiations leading to START I, however, lagged behind the ambitious objective of reducing the strategic forces of both sides by 50 percent.

In this situation, U.S. President George H.W. Bush and the new president of the Russian Federation, Boris Yeltsin, in June 1992 decided to decrease existing nuclear arsenals by 60–70 percent. As early as January 1993, the START II Treaty was ready for signature. In the treaty's initial phase, the total number of deployed strategic nuclear warheads was to be reduced on both sides to an upper limit of no more than 3,800–4,250 in order to further restrict the actual ceiling to the number of 3,000–3,500. Significantly, all MIRVed ICBMs were to be eliminated, and henceforth ICBMs would be permitted to bear only a single warhead. The START II Treaty constituted a dramatic reduction of the superpowers' nuclear inventories. Despite the fact that both sides continued to possess more than enough nuclear firepower to destroy the other side—and a number of other states besides—the agreement increased crisis stability. The ratification process was postponed time and again over the next few years because the Russian Duma did not give START II undivided attention against the backdrop of NATO's eastward enlargement, renewed tensions in the Persian Gulf region, and the war in Kosovo. After President George W. Bush announced strategic reductions outside the START framework in November 2001, it seems unlikely that START II will ever enter into force.

In the first half of the 1990s, arms reduction negotiations between Washington and Moscow resulted in significant progress. Simultaneously, the risk of a rapid proliferation of nuclear technology was quickly growing. The dissolution of the Soviet Union negatively affected the physical condition and the previously centralized control mechanisms of the Soviet nuclear arsenal. In the early 1990s, a new trend among the Soviet successor states became discernible, which indicated that the new governments were disinclined to spend their scarce financial resources on such a strategically unattractive venture as costly arms reduction. The Soviet nuclear arsenal did not change hands under the most auspicious circumstances; neither was its legacy in safer hands than before the collapse of the Soviet Union. Accordingly, there was a sudden realization in the West that the situation concerning the proliferation of nuclear weapons formerly under the control of the Soviets had become alarming; Russia, Ukraine, Byelorussia, and Kazakhstan had all acquired nuclear capabilities as a consequence of the political upheavals of 1989–1991. Two scenarios were offered: First, the degradation of inactive weapons systems became a long-term concern; and second, the struggling governments of the Soviet successor states were, it was believed by the West, prone to sell nuclear weapons, or even only radioactive material, to questionable customers to make money.

According to intelligence available to Western observers, illicit weapons sales had indeed occurred due to a distinct lack of up-to-date security and control mechanisms. Against this backdrop, the United States decided to support the Russian Federation, Ukraine, Belarus, and Kazakhstan in the field of nuclear weapons safety and security with the comprehensive Cooperative Threat Reduction Program (so-called Nunn-

Lugar—programs to safeguard, dismantle, and destroy nuclear weapons in the former Soviet Union). This was the most important nonproliferation effort during the 1990s. Nunn-Lugar constituted the central element of international cooperation to prevent and combat illicit trafficking in nuclear materials.

During the second half of the 1990s, the immediacy of the proliferation threat in the Soviet successor states further abated as Byelorussia, Kazakhstan, and Ukraine acceded to the NPT (all agreed to subordinate themselves to the control of the International Atomic Energy Agency). By 1996, the Soviet successor states returned the last of their strategic nuclear warheads to the Russian Federation. Thus, the withdrawal of more than 1,900 strategic and 2,500 tactical warheads from Ukraine, more than 100 SS-18 ICBMs and 40 strategic bombers from Kazakhstan, and more than 500 strategic and tactical warheads and 81 SS-25 ICBMs from Byelorussia came to a conclusion. Since then, the Soviet successor states are no longer in autonomous control of the former Soviet weapons independently of Moscow.

The nuclear nonproliferation regime was further augmented with the indefinite extension of the NPT in 1995 and the conclusion of the **Comprehensive Test Ban Treaty (CTBT)** in 1996. The NPT is the most widely adhered to and the most successful multilateral arms control treaty in history. Only Cuba, India, Israel, and Pakistan have refused to be bound by its terms. The signatories are usually subdivided into two categories: the five original nuclear weapons states and the nonnuclear weapons states. The latter have agreed to forgo developing or acquiring nuclear weapons, and the former have committed themselves to pursuing nuclear disarmament. An important step in this regard was the accomplishment of the CTBT, which outlaws all nuclear testing. The treaty will formally enter into force after forty-four designated nuclear-capable states have signed and ratified it. As of this writing, 166 states have signed the CTBT; ninety-four states have ratified the treaty, and only thirty-one of forty-four states listed in Annex 2 of the treaty have ratified it to date. Forty-four signatures of Annex 2 states are required for the CTBT to enter into force. The CTBT suffered a serious setback on 13 October 1999, when the U.S. Senate voted against its ratification, prompting harsh international criticism and raising fears that some states might resume nuclear testing.

The crisis of the nuclear proliferation regime and NMD. The hopes of the early 1990s, however, dissipated even earlier. Continuing tensions in the Middle East, South Asia, and East Asia have demonstrated that regional security balances in crucial areas of the world remain precarious due to renewed proliferation and increasing instability. The nonproliferation regime visibly failed to prevent Israel, India, and Pakistan from developing and even testing nuclear weapons. In addition, North Korea, Iran, Iraq, and Libya remain states of immediate proliferation concern. Indeed, the goal of nuclear abolition is not actually shared by many regional actors. But it would be too simple to shift the blame to a few recalcitrant nonnuclear weapons states, which are not prepared to abandon nuclear weaponry. The nuclear weapons states have, for their part, been able to show very few tangible successes concerning their commitments to work toward the elimination of nuclear weapons.

The prevailing sense of crisis in nuclear nonproliferation has prompted a response from the United States that so far seems to have aggravated the situation. When the United States announced plans to deploy missile defense, the situation in nuclear disarmament fundamentally changed. Should the United States go ahead with NMD, it would do so against the explicit will of its European allies and the Russian Federation and be in violation of the ABM Treaty. The U.S. plan therefore would jeopardize the overall START process, because the Russian Duma made the ratification of START II contingent upon the U.S. ratification of the ABM Treaty. Although U.S. President George W. Bush suggested continuing the Russian-U.S. arms reduction process outside the START framework, it is highly unlikely that other nuclear weapons states will engage in a multilateral disarmament process on this footing. In turn, this development further curtails the chances that nations such as India, Pakistan, and North Korea will sign the CTBT in the near future. The U.S. plan for missile defense threatens the already precarious balance in nuclear disarmament for the foreseeable future. The old Cold War notion of stability based on MAD is slowly being substituted with the notion of stability organized around deep cuts and limited mutual defense. For the time being, the consequences of such a development on the multilateral nuclear nonproliferation regime remain unclear. The response of the international community to the proliferation of ABC WMD will, in any event, remain of towering significance for international peace and security.

From Classical Peacekeeping to Robust Peace Support Operations

In the wake of the Cold War, UN conflict resolution tools were expanded to contain the Agenda for Peace formulated by former UN Secretary-General Boutros Boutros-Ghali in 1999. Priority was given to conflict prevention measures and peacekeeping operations, the number and duties of which increased drastically. Since 1990, public opinion tolerated military intervention, multinational peace support operations, and economic and diplomatic sanctions by institutions—not least because of the extensive media coverage in crisis spots. With more frequency, the international community condones the protection of, and humanitarian support for, populations affected by civil strife. Accordingly, the United Nations sponsored resolutions against sovereign states in a condition of internal military conflict.

The concept of external armed intervention is not new and was practiced during the Cold War. As a rule, peacekeeping was based on clearly delineated mandates, the central objective being to maintain an armistice. The essential function of such operations was to interpose a buffer between the parties. Thus, the main purpose of peacekeeping operations was not to resolve conflict but to prevent or preempt the escalation of a conflict—predominantly in the context of interstate wars. On the one hand, the consent of the parties was decisive; on the other, peacekeeping forces were under the strict obligation to exercise their mandate neutrally, without partisanship. In such a situation, the military fulfilled a symbolic role. Accordingly, peacekeeping forces were equipped only for self-defense.

With the end of the Cold War and the escalation of numerous intrastate conflicts, the demand for peace support operations grew. Former UN Secretary-General Boutros Boutros-Ghali called upon the international community to expand its involvement in, and commitment to, UN peacekeeping operations. A positive response appeared to be possible, as the United Nations might also be able to break the deadlock in the Security Council. As a consequence, the number of troops involved in peacekeeping operations rose to 80,000 men and women. By way of comparison, only some 10,000 peacekeeping troops were deployed at any given time during the Cold War. In the second half of the 1990s, the number of UN peacekeeping troops decreased again. Instead, more peace support operations were carried out, especially in the framework of regional security organizations, such as NATO, or loose coalitions.

How can the decline of UN-sponsored peacekeeping operations and UN freedom of action be explained? The peace support operations of the 1990s differed fundamentally from the peacekeeping operations of the Cold War. In an intrastate conflict environment distinguished by ethnic rivalries, weak institutions, and humanitarian catastrophes, the imposition of an armistice frequently proved unable to end the cycle of violence. In addition, on-site developments were commensurately dynamic. Effecting stabilization in such a conflict environment could therefore be realistically achieved only if all involved also worked toward a resolution of the conflict. Beyond fulfilling their principal mandate of implementing and safeguarding the terms of an armistice, peacekeepers faced civilian tasks such as policing duties, humanitarian aid, the repatriation of refugees, disarmament, and the reintegration of former combatants into war-torn societies. Even though the United Nations could claim a few successes for its operations in Namibia, Central America, and Mozambique, its failure to adjust to the new circumstances resulted in major problems for UN missions everywhere. The abject failure of UN missions to Somalia, to Rwanda, and to Bosnia demonstrated that the effectiveness of lightly armed troops in the new, confused conflict situation was limited.

The setbacks in Somalia, Rwanda, and Bosnia led to growing skepticism over the UN capacity to be a global enforcer and a guarantor of peace. In general, UN humanitarian interventions have been faced with a number of problems. To begin, the United Nations has no troops at its disposal. At the beginning of every UN mission, the organizers have to begin from scratch, as there is no administrative or personnel continuity. Frequently, the objectives of the missions were not clearly or realistically defined; the members' willingness to contribute financially evaporated; and the bureaucratic red tape ended up paralyzing the entire enterprise. Furthermore, the danger of instrumentalizing the United Nations to further the interests of national states, or of retaining it in keeping with Great Power geostrategic concerns, was present because the United Nations, due to its financial dependency, could not act independently of preponderant states' interests.

Somalia. Between 1992 and 1995, the United Nations attempted to restore peace, stability, order, and the rule of law in Somalia by deploying the UN Operation in Somalia (UNOSOM I), the Unified Task Force (UNITAF), and UNOSOM II. The operations in Somalia were not carried out under a direct UN mandate but were instead delegated to a group of states entrusted with the implementation of a peace plan by the United Nations. The major challenges faced by UNOSOM were, on the one hand, the sheer complexity of the situation in Somalia; and on the other, its involvement in the ongoing cycle of blackmail and violence, which had come to dominate the conflict during 1991. The equipment of UNOSOM was not adequate to the task, as local warlords had access to heavy weapons. Put simply, UNOSOM was outgunned. Under the leadership of the United States, a time-limited military expedition of 30,000 troops was deployed in order to mitigate the worst effects of the famine in Somalia. The critical problem of Operation Restore Hope was that the mission objective as stated in UN Resolution 794—to establish a secure area by using all necessary means—was not clearly defined and that UN troops inadvertently became part and parcel of intertribal warfare in the course of implementing the mission's disarmament provisions.

On 4 May 1993, UNITAF was officially relieved of its duties and replaced by UNOSOM II. This latest UN mission was given the task of repatriating refugees, the clearing of landmines, and the reconstruction of the country's infrastructure and administration. As the situation continued to deteriorate following a mounting number of armed clashes with local belligerents, the United States withdrew its task force. Media coverage—especially the graphic images of UN troops being abused and dragged through the streets of Mogadishu—and the unusually high number of casualties on the part of the UN troops (some 150)—led to the abandonment of the entire undertaking. In the long run, the Somali debacle led to a general disinclination among the principal contributors of multinational peacekeeping operations to participate in future ventures. At the time, it seemed almost as if the governments concerned were no longer willing to risk the lives of their soldiers and their political fortunes in a place that was neither economically nor geostrategically vital to their own interests.

Rwanda.　The major criticisms directed against the United Nations Assistance Mission for Rwanda (UNAMIR) stemmed from mass murder. Indications of a premeditated genocide, exacerbated by the UN reaction during the early stages, which cost more than 1 million Tutsis and moderate Hutus their lives, had, according to critics, been ignored, as UN troops had refused to intervene once the killings had begun. Members of the UN Security Council were accused of refusing to set up a task force adequate to prevent the tragedy. The Somali experience probably played a major role in the Security Council decision to withhold vital aid, especially in the case of the United States. At the same time, UNAMIR was not properly equipped for the task at hand. Even new UN Secretary-General Kofi Annan admitted the failure of the United Nations to respond forcefully and promptly, adding that he was deeply ashamed by the debacle.

The principal failure on the part of the United Nations seems to have been lack of resources and determination to address the unfolding Rwandan disaster in an adequate fashion. In the first place, UNAMIR was not planned, dimensioned, established, or instructed to confront a problem of such magnitude or to respond actively in the deadlocked and seriously endangered Rwandan peace process. Against the advice of local reconnaissance, UNAMIR's strength was set at a smaller number than standard in comparable situations. The initial phases of UNAMIR bore the imprint of bureaucratic tardiness. There was a general shortage of well-trained troops and operational materials. Moreover, the mandate was not based on a well-founded understanding of the Rwandan peace process and was never corrected once the erroneous foundations were understood—despite repeated and insistent warnings from the front. The mission thus failed to function as an integrated, coordinated structure. Conclusive evidence provided by numerous eyewitnesses went a long way to show that UNAMIR, at the stage when the crisis was actually peaking, lacked political leadership and military capacity, which also indicated substandard coordination and discipline and command as well as control problems.

Bosnia.　UNPROFOR, the United Nations Protection Force in Bosnia during 1992–1995, was directed by the UN Secretary-General, but the tactical and operational commands were vested in local command headquarters.

This UN operation was intended to protect civilians in so-called safe areas from Serb excesses, to maintain no-fly zones, and to secure demilitarization and the implementation of a cease-fire. UNPROFOR was incapable of realizing all these objectives, not least because it lacked the manpower. The massacre perpetrated against the citizens of Srebrenica—which lay in one of the five safe areas—came to symbolize the failure of the United Nations in the Balkans. The replacement of the helpless UNPROFOR by the heavily armed NATO-led Implementation Force was the turning point in the employment of peacekeeping instruments. Only because of the massive on-site military presence was there any progress made in terms of implementing the political settlement of the conflict agreed to in the Dayton Accords of December 1995.

Thus, the idea of "robust" peace support operations became common in the second half of the 1990s. Robust peace support operations could be distinguished by three traits. First, based on the understanding that an escalating cycle of violence could be prevented from spinning out of control only by a massive military presence, the international community began to ensure armistices and peace settlements with mandates that in turn were derived from Chapter VII of the United Nations Charter. Because a clear delineation between peacekeeping and peace enforcement is difficult in practice, the presence and power of military force constitutes a means for conflict prevention and thus is a prerequisite to the success of stabilization measures.

Second, a trend toward the expansion of peacekeeping mandates could be discerned. Upon the assumption of political and administrative responsibilities, operations such as the Kosovo Force (KFOR) went far beyond the standard practiced only a few years earlier. In the context of executive mandates, then, the representatives of the international community organized elections, issued passports, and even dismissed local mayors. In practice, international responsibility for security and order at the local level highlighted the scarcity of internationally available police forces. For this reason, KFOR was compelled to assume policing duties in order to cope with civil unrest and criminality.

Third, the operational implementation of peace support operations was frequently delegated to regional security organizations such as NATO or, alternatively, to international coalitions of states. The often diffuse mandates called for a clear interpretation by authorities tasked with a specific mission. The principle of basing peace support operations on broad multinational platforms is intended to imbue them with political legitimacy and moral credibility. With the end of the Cold War, mandated peacekeeping based on a calculable consensus and a clear identification and responsibility of conflicting parties reached its limits. Dynamic peace support on site presupposes the employment of robust and assertive peacekeeping troops.

Each peace support operation is possessed of a unique character. Therefore, the decision to participate in such operations will always have to be made on a case-by-case basis.

The Rise of the New Terrorism

As opposed to rogue-state and peer-competitor threats, terrorism is not a novel apparition but a time-honored tool of forceful political, religious, and social agitation. But the face of terrorism began to change after roughly 1968. The terrorist groups of that age, which derived from the New Left and were inspired by the socialist rhetoric of Marxism in the 1960s and 1970s, were essentially ideological. In line with other contemporary political developments, recent manifestations of terrorism have, for the most part, been driven by ethnic, separatist, as well as religious motives.

Ethnic and separatist political violence is an ancient but, historically speaking, highly volatile phenomenon. For example, one might argue that organizations such as the Irish Republican Army (IRA) and the Euzkadi Ta Askatasuna/Basque Fatherland and Liberty (ETA) were formed long before the more recent wave of terrorist groups surfaced. Such an observation would be correct if one discounted the truth of the aforementioned groups' operational intermittency. During the 1990s, both the IRA and ETA intensified their respective campaigns against the British and Spanish governments after lying in the doldrums for years, whereas the various Red armies (the Brigate Rosse, or Red Brigades, in Italy; the Rote Armee Fraktion [the Baader-Meinhof gang] in Germany; Action Directe in France; and Cellules Communistes Combattantes in Belgium) have suffered decline and eventual extinction. In the meantime, the Kosovo Liberation Army, the Chechen resistance, and various other political violence movements prepared to use terrorism in furtherance of their goals have swelled the ranks of ethnic separatist groups. These latter groups stand out because of their longevity, a resilience explained by the fact that they draw on a greater reservoir of support than their ideological brethren. However, we also need to address the issue of the resurgence of religiously motivated terrorism. And when addressing religious terrorism, it is important to consider its variety, for religious terrorism is certainly not the exclusive preserve of a single religion or denomination.

Religious fanaticism as motivation.   The sudden emergence of religious extremism developed parallel to the resurgence of ethnic strife at the end of the twentieth century. The 1990s witnessed a marked increase of terrorist incidents perpetrated by such organizations as Hamas, Hezbollah, Islamic Jihad, and notably the Algerian Armed Islamic Group; the previously ideologically and politically driven PLO was replaced by a new leadership focusing on the politico-ethnic Palestinian-Israeli conflict.

The potential of religious fanaticism as a motivator for the use of terrorist tactics by various groups and individuals is not negligible. But it is important to note that Judaism and Christianity have spawned their own fundamentalist sects seeking to attain their goals by force of arms. In the 1980s, Rabbi Meir Kahane and his acolytes fought hard to expand settlements in the West Bank and Gaza to establish and ensure for future generations the god-given preeminence of a Jewish presence in a biblical Israel at the expense of the Arab population. They, too, were prepared to kill and maim in pursuit of their objective. The Kach group (Hebrew for "only thus") was founded by Kahane. The stated goal of Kach and its offshoot, Kahane Chai (which means "Kahane lives," founded by Meir Kahane's son Binyamin following his father's assassination in the United States), is to restore the biblical state of Israel. Both organizations were declared to be terrorist organizations by the Israeli cabinet in March 1994. This followed the groups' statements in support of Dr. Baruch Goldstein's attack in February 1994 on the al-Ibrahimi mosque (Goldstein was affiliated with Kach) and their verbal attacks against the Israeli government. Finally, Israeli Prime Minister Yitzhak Rabin, notable for his achievements in the Israeli-Palestinian peace process, was assassinated in 1995 by Yigal Amir, who was allegedly associated with the Jewish radical religious fringe.

During the Cold War, various Christian fundamentalist groups appeared in the United States, especially in the Bible Belt and Farm Belt. More often than not, they were the descendants of the religious right and white supremacist organizations such as Aryan Nations and the Ku Klux Klan. In the 1970s and 1980s, far-right Christian identity and constitutionalist groups interacted with apocalyptic survivalists to spawn a number of militant, quasiunderground formations, including some that called themselves patriots and militias. During the height of the rural farm crisis in the early 1980s, one of these groups, the Posse Comitatus—a loose-knit network that spread conspiracy theory, white supremacist ideas, and anti-Semitism throughout the Farm Belt—captured a small but significant number of sympathizers among farmers and ranchers. They coalesced to become the leader of the so-called patriot movement. The patriot movement and its armed wing, the citizen militias, were revivals of these and earlier right-wing populist movements, emerging in the 1990s after the collapse of European communism and the launching of the Gulf War. Patriot adherents who formed armed units became known as the armed militia movement.

During the mid-1990s, armed militias were sporadically active in all fifty states, with membership estimated to be 20,000–60,000. In anticipation of government coercion, economic collapse, and social unrest, or simply because of the coming "tribulations," a significant segment of the patriot and armed militia movements embraces survivalism—an apocalyptic

view of life. Because the patriot movement, militias, and survivalists propagate the constitutionally protected right to bear arms, and thus are well-
armed, federal agencies are hard-pressed to execute warrants against adherents. This problem is compounded by the fact that militias usually do not
acknowledge federal authority. In the past, the ensuing violence between
federal agents and militias has led to grotesque situations. In a 1992
shootout in Idaho, survivalist Randy Weaver was wounded and members of
his family killed by federal agents. In 1993, a Christian fundamentalist sect
holed up in Waco, Texas—the Branch Davidians—withstood a protracted
siege conducted by the Federal Bureau of Investigation and the Bureau of
Alcohol, Tobacco, and Firearms. Eighty Davidians, including leader David
Koresh, were killed in a self-lit fire following the federal attempt to storm
the compound. In April 1995, a federal building in Oklahoma City,
Oklahoma, became the target of a terrorist attack. One hundred sixty-eight
people died as a direct result of the explosion that destroyed the building.
The suspect, Timothy McVeigh, had ties with the patriot movement and
white-supremacist fringe. Although Jewish and Christian religious fundamentalist groups may not have the numbers of their Islamic brethren, the
danger of terrorist attacks at the hands of religious radicals of any denomination is not to be underestimated.

Terrorism and WMD.   New terrorism is connected to the global phenomena
in international relations: the proliferation of information about WMD and
the rise of intrastate conflicts in failing states. What is truly new about the
recent terrorist threat—whether it emanates from the religious fundamentalist fringe, ethnic separatists, or a combination thereof—is the political
use of modern WMD. Similar to rogue states in this sense, modern-day terrorists have access to information on the production of WMD via the
Internet.

The possibility of a nuclear suicide bomb anywhere in the world is
thought to be relatively small due to the difficulties involved in constructing a working nuclear device. A limited supply of the necessary fissile
nuclear material is available and is closely monitored by national governments and supranational agencies such as the International Atomic Energy
Agency. Fissile material is traceable; nonfissile radioactive material is more
difficult to track, but it would require a thorough understanding of physics
to be used in the construction of a bomb. Delivery systems demand an
advanced knowledge of propulsion technology, and the necessary components are very hard to come by.

The terrorist use of chemical and biological agents is no longer a
remote possibility. The use of chemical weapons by terrorists is only slightly more probable, as the chemical components required are highly reactive
and must be stored in the proper environment, but a determined group of

individuals could conceivably assemble a chemical weapon. In fact, the Japanese sect Aum Shinrikyo launched a sarin gas attack in the Tokyo subway in March 1995, killing ten and injuring some 5,000 commuters. In terms of their destructivity, biological weapons rank even higher. A terrorist attack using biological agents could decimate entire populations. Storage is also a problem, as bacteria and spores usually do not thrive under conditions that do not meet specific requirements. In conclusion, it can be said that the potential terrorist application of WMD constitutes the most extreme form of asymmetric warfare (in which states and substate actors, like the young David with his slingshot, employ cheap weaponry to maximum effect against more powerful opponents). Mention must also be made of crude radiological devices (so-called dirty bombs). Some maintain that the psychological impact in the wake of deploying a radiological device is of greater consequence than its actual physical impact. As suggested by some, crude nuclear devices employing highly enriched uranium may pose the greater threat.

Although the danger of terrorist WMD attacks should not be belittled, inhibiting factors should be taken into account. WMD require extensive know-how on the part of their users. Under the best of circumstances, the necessary information can be obtained; its application poses nearly insurmountable obstacles for the layman. Based on the precedents, the use of WMD is mostly counterproductive to the goals pursued by terrorists in that the use of WMD would render large areas uninhabitable for extended periods of time. Who wants to rule or live in a place thoroughly contaminated by the effects of ABC weapons? The intimate connection between cost and effect for terrorists also requires consideration. Terrorists usually seek public exposure by the media. A WMD attack would certainly guarantee global media coverage—but at too high a cost. The causes espoused by terrorists require that the incumbent leader/administration and the public be constantly reminded of terrorist demands. This purpose is better served by using the traditional tools of the trade: the automatic rifle and the bomb. Despite all the impediments in the assembly and deployment of sophisticated weaponry, the probability of a future WMD attack by terrorist fanatics must be countenanced and understood to represent a danger that should not be neglected.

The challenge of global terrorism.   Beyond the potential terrorist use of modern WMD, the more recent manifestation of terrorism, as evidenced by the attacks on New York and the Pentagon on 11 September 2001, is characterized by a number of novel attributes. The distinct features of the new terrorism demonstrate the degree to which terrorism has been shaped by globalization and has, consequently, become a product thereof: amorphous motive, diffuse responsibility for terrorist acts, a decentralized and networked model of organization, and a complex financial support structure. But the strategies and tactics differ from those of earlier types of political and religious violence movements only by degrees.

The objectives of the new terrorism are not as limited; the distinct lack of a clear ideology and authorship is a new feature. Goals have become highly diffuse, vague, or very general. In the landscape of terrorist motivations, we find disparate issues: *jihad* to cleanse hallowed ground, rid the Holy Land of U.S. or Zionist forces, and/or aid the establishment of a Palestinian state; as well as the militant opposition against globalization and anti-U.S. sentiments. The new terrorist organizations, especially Islamic radicals, have become more decentralized, with numerous branches located around the globe. Moreover, terrorist networks in Western Europe have been the beneficiaries of an open, democratic society: with practically no immediate threat of persecution, such actors can, and do, pursue their objectives unhampered by the repression they would otherwise face, for example, in the Middle East and in Arab states at large. The territorial expansion of terrorist networks beyond the boundaries of any given traditional area of interest to any particular group (e.g., Hezbollah in southern Lebanon) has also vastly increased the terrorists' recruiting pool. Group profiles indicate greater heterogeneity among the actors themselves: this ranges from a greater social and educational stratification of the actors to increasing national diversification. This development, in turn, implies more willingness than ever to cut across lines of social, national, cultural, and linguistic divisions in the service of a greater cause.

The growing diffusion of objectives and the diversification of the actors are also reflected in the increasingly sophisticated and complex internal and external financial support structures for terrorist and insurgent organizations. Although terrorist groups have for decades financed their operations from the proceeds of illegal activities, such as protection rackets among expatriate communities, a perceptible trend of cooperation, or cross-fertilization, among transnational terrorist networks and global organized crime has taken place. The FARC in Colombia has employed the drug trade as an effective means to raise funds, and other groups have become expert arms dealers and even used the vagaries of global financial markets to their own advantage. It is important to understand that terrorist groups have always used licit and illicit fundraising operations in the furtherance of their cause: the labyrinthine quality of the global financial markets and networks just makes it more difficult to identify the terrorists' brokers and the funds destined for their coffers.

In the wake of September 11, many experts and laypersons have assumed that the strategy and tactics of terrorist organizations have undergone fundamental change. Such a point of view is based on a misunderstanding of terrorism. Even if we reduce terrorism to a purely functional tool of controversial military strategy, the basic idea behind it is scalability and asymmetry. To put it simply, terrorism is predicated upon the modus operandi of lowest cost and maximum effect. Furthermore, terrorism is a form of communication, by the few to the masses, of fear by the conduit of directed violence; it is propaganda by the deed. If nobody perceives its effects, terrorism usually fails to fulfill the intentions of the perpetrators. Thus, the value of a terrorist target, whether people or buildings, is vested not only in its criticality (e.g., a military or telecommunications infrastructure) but also in its perceived symbolic value. In 1972, for example, the terrorist murders of eleven Israeli athletes staying in the Olympic Village in Munich, Germany, launched the Palestinian cause into the headlines; fewer than thirty years later, a comparable effect was achieved by the wanton murder of nearly 3,000 people in the U.S. homeland. Major TV networks disseminated the message of Al-Qaida far better than did the multitude of newspapers and independent TV stations—or the terrorist network itself. Meanwhile, the only discernible difference between the events of 1972 and those of September 11 was the number of victims and the size of the building chosen for a target. The nature of the mechanism behind terrorist strategy—that is, the effective communication and dissemination of the terrorists' capability to inflict directed violence in the name of, or against, a set of beliefs—still remains very much the same.

Historically, extremists take recourse to terrorism because they do not possess the strength necessary to meet their opponents on equal ground. The strategy of asymmetry is an integral, indivisible element of terrorism. In that way, Al-Qaida's application of asymmetric warfare, that is, low-cost, high-effect unconventional or irregular military tactics, is not surprising and certainly not new. In the context of conventional conflict, the United States cannot be defeated by conventional means—as recently demonstrated in the province of Kosovo and during the Gulf War. Likewise, it was assumed that the use of fuel-laden commercial airliners as suicide bombs constituted a new phenomenon—ostensibly a high-tech variant of terrorist tactics. But crashing objects into people and buildings has a long record in the annals of political violence. Similarly, the discipline required to maintain the high security of such an undertaking has established precedents in the sophisticated organizational structure of, for example, IRA elements operating in Ulster: the cell system renders it impossible for authorities to acquire intelligence beyond the operational details of the mission of the individual, whom they must catch in the act. Conversely, the degree of mobility exhibited was, indeed, unprecedented, as evidenced by the frequent relocations of Al-Qaida headquarters in accordance with the developments in international relations.

What rendered the attacks on New York and Washington truly extraordinary was their specific context: its authors were the declared enemy of the United States. Moreover, the location and significance of the targets—the World Trade Center, the Pentagon, and, potentially, the White House or U.S. Capitol—constituted symbols in the national consciousness and caused tremendous psychological trauma; it brought the idea of U.S. invulnerability to a violent close. The current problem is what to expect in the near term. As this book goes to print in late 2002, U.S. apprehensions (reflected to varying degrees among the U.S. allies) focus on the potential for state-sponsored terrorism and state-sponsored use of WMD.

IR Theory and Key Concepts

The Postmodern Paradigm and the
Debate on Epistemology, Positivism, and Postmodernism

Epistemology constitutes a branch of inquiry that is concerned with the question of how one knows or how one acquires knowledge. Positivism refers to the perspective of those who hold that law is derived from decisions and actions made by people with the authority to do so and is not the result of a divine or natural legal conception. According to positivists, especially in scientific circles, knowledge is the result of testing theories empirically, that is, against the evidence and facts. In the field of international relations, postmodernism constitutes a radical departure from mainstream thinking, not unlike critical theory. Postmodernism is inherently antipositivist. Critical theory and postmodernism came to the fore in international relations in the 1980s; both perspectives arose in a reaction to the dominant position of the neorealist and neoliberalist positions in the field. At the same time, postmodernism was a derivate of an intellectual predecessor, namely, the neo-Marxist dependency school, which had challenged international relations orthodoxy earlier in the twentieth century. Although the meager progress achieved by the dominant mainstream schools was an impetus for the exploration of radical alternatives, the paucity of previous radical analyses (i.e., Marxism) compelled progressives to look for a novel type of radicalism. To critics of the evolving debate, the limited value of the orthodox and the older radical intellectual movements was vested in their characteristic economism and, therefore, in their determinism. Because theory and interpretation are epistemological products, the framework in which the continuing debate between mainstream and postmodernist exponents takes place is provided by epistemology—the inquiry into the understanding of knowledge. Yet epistemology is not the only battleground of the third debate in international relations. Many adherents of new approaches, such as mainstream social constructivists, reject the postmodernist label as an instrument employed by rationalists to dispute the scientific credentials of alternative perspectives. Constructivism has emerged as a serious research program in international relations since the late 1980s. Its main argument is that the world is socially constructed and that cognitive structures give meaning to material factors. Constructivism criticizes rationalism for its neglect of factors such as norms, identities, and culture that shape international politics.

Neoliberal institutionalism shares certain traits with realism in that it is rational and utilitarian. States, for example, are understood to be rational actors guided by their interests. According to Robert Keohane and other neoliberal institutionalists, cooperation between states is dependent upon mutual interests. The neoliberal institutionalist agenda includes security and welfare issues, for the objective is to investigate how institutions play an important role in international relations. Neoliberal institutionalists argue that institutions act as political and economic facilitators in that they lend credibility to commitments; act as an information broker and warehouse; coordinate and support bilateral and multilateral interstate relations; and decrease transaction costs. To neoliberal institutionalists, institutions go beyond organizations, as they can also constitute customary (or otherwise established) recurrent (institutionalized) patterns of interstate interactions. The progress of multilateralism in international politics may here serve as an example.

Postmodernism is thus a perspective on knowledge critical of, even in denial of, modernist and scientific epistemological achievements. Deconstruction is the chosen approach of postmodernists in their investigation of meaning in spoken and written language. Postmodernists seek to unearth underlying meanings, the so-called subtext buried in our language. The most radical postmodernists hold that no knowledge or truth can be separated from people's incentives, motivations, interests, and purposes for acquiring or investigating either one; any truth or knowledge is constructed.

Key Terms
- unipolarity and multipolarity: Scholars disagree on whether international politics is dominated by a single power or whether a redistribution of power has occurred in the post–

Cold War period. Whereas some maintain that the dissolution of the Soviet Union in 1991 made the new post–Cold War system unipolar (i.e., with a single center of power), others point to a diffusion of power. The unipolar perspective gained credence when the United States took the lead in what President George H.W. Bush called the new world order (e.g., the United States leads the United Nations and middle-sized powers to stop aggressors). Moreover, the United States today is the only state with the capability to project massive military power overseas and the political influence to assume a leadership role. Conversely, the multipolar perspective proposes an international system featuring several centers of power, some of which are not military powers but rather trade blocs. According to this conception of the post–Cold War world, all centers of power are engaged in tough economic competition, and no single protagonist has the means to dominate all others. The multipolar model resembles the classic balance-of-power system prevalent in early and modern Europe. However, the comparison is somewhat flawed in that the blocs and alliances encompass many states, their dimensions are relatively static, and interaction between such entities usually occurs in the manner of economic competition, not armed hostilities.

- unilateralism and multilateralism: The concept of unilateralism is rooted in the idea of sovereignty and the sovereign state. In accordance with the fundamental tenets of unilateralism, a sovereign state is an autonomous, rational entity that is free to decide its actions (especially in foreign policy) notwithstanding the interests and concerns of, and consequences for, other states. Unilateralism is largely legitimized by affirming that the nature of the international system is quintessentially anarchic, that is, a self-help system. However, the past has shown time and again that unilateralism is prone to create or exacerbate conflicts and thus is fraught with risk. Multilateralism, by contrast, if understood as an organizational principle of international relations, constitutes an institutional avenue to coordinate interstate interactions within a framework consisting of norms and rules of conduct. Multilateralism upholds the principle of indivisibility, according to which hostilities commenced against one state are considered an attack on all. Collective security is a manifestation of this principle's application. Moreover, multilateralism maintains nondiscrimination as a key precept: states participating in a venture are treated equally, as, for example, in the context of a most-favored nation trade agree ment that penalizes discrimination against any country producing the same kind of product. Finally, multilateralism operates on the assumption of diffuse reciprocity, that is, the belief that states should not relate to each other on the basis of quid pro quo expectations but ought to put faith in mid- to long-term assurances for developments that will prove mutually beneficial. State actors consent to collaborate, even cooperate, and (ideally) abandon the pursuit of self-serving short-term policies. Overall, the theory and practice of multilateralism may well prove conducive to the peaceful resolution of disputes while also corroborating mutual interests. Although disagreements between state actors will not suddenly disappear, multilateralism at least offers a number of possibilities to resolve impending conflicts without taking recourse to armed hostilities.

- technology, globalization, and the revolution in information technology: Communications and transportation technologies, as well as nuclear weapons, have had a significant impact on our civilization; this is especially true today. The entire spectrum of political activities, from peace-brokering and peacekeeping to overt and covert armed conflict, has been affected by modern technology in a revolutionary manner. Furthermore, the shape and conduct of security policy is influenced by technological innovation. The defense strategies applied by state actors in the nuclear age are usually defined by the maxim of minimizing the danger of escalation; all major strategies of the Cold War—deterrence, détente, diplomacy, disarmament, and defense—have been developed as a response to specific problems but are also relative to the progressing technology that rendered them feasible for implementation in the first place. In the final analysis, technology has had, and continues to exert, a direct influence on the shaping of international relations.

Current Affairs

THE SEPTEMBER 11 TERRORIST ATTACKS AGAINST THE UNITED STATES STRUCK A deep chord in the collective consciousness of an increasingly media-sensitized public. These attacks on the economic and political symbols of Western power constitute the closure of an era of U.S. invulnerability. At the same time, the attacks were also a defining moment in the development of the international system. Immediately after the attacks, the feeling of fundamental change in the world was widespread; many a commentator described 11 September 2001 as a day that would change the world forever. And among those in the field of international politics as well, the conception of an epoch-making event had widespread acceptance.

There can be no doubt that the transitional phase after the end of the Cold War came to a close. However, it is difficult to anticipate the laws according to which international relations will be governed in the future. At first glance, the U.S.-led war on terrorism seems to have replaced the process of globalization at the top of the international political agenda. But globalization is linked with terrorism in a variety of ways, some of which are contradictory. The growing transnational flow of capital, goods, people, and ideas does not automatically lead to more security and less war. At the same time, new vulnerabilities and risks come into being. Global terrorism is, indeed, a child of this new epoch.

The Attacks of 11 September 2001
and the War on Terrorism in Afghanistan

In the early-morning hours of 11 September 2001, two commercial airliners were piloted into the twin towers of the World Trade Center in New York, closely followed by a third airliner that dove into an outer wing of the Pentagon in Washington, D.C., and a fourth that crashed in rural Pennsylvania. What at first seemed to be a catastrophic event of great magnitude was in fact a focused, premeditated attack against selected targets of symbolic value and representative of U.S. and, by implication, Western predominance. Like no other event in recent memory, images from the scene transmitted by the mass media shocked the public. On 11 September 2001 the post–Cold War era ended abruptly and introduced the world to the twenty-first century.

First Reactions: Emergency Response
and the Beginning of a Long Campaign

Even before the twin towers collapsed that day, U.S. homeland defense planning paid off, and first responders reacted with incredible speed and determination. The Federal Aviation Administration shut down all New York City airports; the Port Authority shut all ports in the immediate Hudson River area; the municipal fire department and emergency medical teams promptly arrived at the scene, where they would continue to battle for the survival of the victims for days to come; and President Bush addressed the nation from Offut Air Force Base in Nebraska with the news that New York and Washington had apparently been attacked by terrorists.

All major government centers that were considered likely targets of further attacks, such as the White House, the Department of Justice, the State Department, and United Nations Headquarters in New York—were immediately evacuated. All across the United States, authorities placed agencies and personnel on the highest security alert; the same also applied to the U.S. military around the globe. That afternoon, senior members of the U.S. Federal Bureau of Investigation (FBI) disclosed information on the parties suspected in the attacks. According to this source, the most likely perpetrators were Islamic radicals operating under the aegis of a long-standing U.S. foe: Saudi multimillionaire Osama bin Laden and his terrorist network, Al-Qaida. Since the attacks, the question of why the sizeable U.S. intelligence community failed to give adequate warning has moved to the center stage of public debate.

On the day of the attacks, President Bush vowed that the United States would hunt down and punish those responsible. Indeed, the planning of retaliatory and national security measures—including the preparation for a military campaign; the graduated restriction of certain civil liberties in the United States; and increased monitoring of air travel as well as the national borders—were soon under way. The FBI feverishly commenced the greatest manhunt since its inception.

As of 7 February 2002, the death toll of the attacks on New York and Washington was estimated to stand as follows: 266 aboard the four hijacked planes; an estimated 125 government employees and contractors at the Pentagon; and a staggering 2,654 individuals at the World Trade

Center. The economic cost of the attacks was immense, certainly in the billions; travel restrictions as a direct consequence of the attacks were, to say the least, severe enough to badly damage the airline industry. In conjunction with a general sense of insecurity and fear among the public concerning air travel, this drove airline companies on both sides of the Atlantic into bankruptcy.

Worldwide Solidarity, Coalition-Building, and Military Buildup

The international community's reaction to the events of September 11 was utter dismay and incredulity at the barbarism; multiple expressions of sympathy and support came from around the world. Notably, the first foreign public official to call President Bush was the president of the Russian Federation, Vladimir Putin. On the next day, U.S. Attorney General John Ashcroft confirmed that the four planes had indeed been hijacked. In each case, only a few individuals armed with knives and box cutters had seized control of the aircraft. That same day, the White House spokesmen announced that the European, Chinese, and Russian heads of state had indicated their consent to form a broad coalition against terrorism.

At exactly the same time, NATO ambassadors in Brussels had invoked Article V, containing NATO's mutual self-defense clause. Never in the long history of the Cold War had NATO activated this clause. It should be pointed out that the invocation of Article V did not, by definition, pledge the support of NATO members' military resources; each member state would have to decide on the nature and extent of the support given to the United States in its war on terror. Again, reactions from around the world condemned the attacks and expressed support and sympathy for the victims. Momentum and support for retaliatory measures in the United States were mounting by the hour. In fact, domestic political pressure for immediate military strikes against the suspected perpetrators became overwhelming. The Bush administration, however, very early on decided on a course of patience and determination in its endeavor to identify and punish the culprits.

As the evidence against Al-Qaida mounted—the investigation begun by the FBI had at that stage expanded into a cooperative effort spanning most European, Arab, and even some African countries—U.S. government pressure on the Taliban government in Afghanistan, which was then believed to be Al-Qaida's mainstay of support, markedly increased. The Taliban government, largely under the control of clerics supportive of a radically militant Islamic school of thought, was accused of not only harboring Osama bin Laden but also of actively supporting Al-Qaida.

The military buildup in the United States and in allied countries was in full swing when a wave of attacks involving the biological warfare agent anthrax swept through the Western world. Many of the alleged anthrax letters were hoaxes, but amid the many copycats were some determined individuals. In the United States, some of the parcels and letters used in this spate of attacks indeed carried anthrax spores of sufficient quality to harm and even kill their recipients, but those were the exceptions to confirm the rule.

On the diplomatic front, the U.S. coalition-building efforts focused on generating consensus for a military response to the attacks of September 11. The heterogeneity of the coalition members rendered such a task a true challenge: the Europeans were reluctant to give the United States unqualified support to a military intervention, demonstrated by the soul-searching debates in the German Bundestag. Only Britain proved to be ardent, even eager, to support the military component of the U.S.-directed war on terrorism. Despite assertions of loyalty and support for the United States, Arab allies were sitting on the fence and waiting to see how the United States would respond to Israeli overtures. Arab governments willing to ally themselves with the coalition were in a difficult position, facing domestic pressure to break their ties with the West from a population that was more inclined to Islamic fundamentalist precepts and preferences than Arab leadership.

The case of Pakistan, on which much of the U.S. diplomatic activities centered, illustrates the tensions between the governed and the government: while Pakistani supporters of the neighboring Taliban regime rioted in the streets of Islamabad, U.S. Secretary of State Colin Powell and the Pakistani leader, General Pervez Musharraf, were negotiating the terms of using Pakistani military installations and military assistance; defining the staging areas for coalition assault troops; and discussing the terms of exchanging intelligence between Pakistani intelligence and U.S. military and civilian intelligence. Ironically, Pakistan had been the principal supporter of the Taliban regime before September 11 and one of the few states to officially recognize the Afghan government. U.S. diplomatic efforts, however, were also directed at closer cooperation with the Central Asia republics such as Uzbekistan and Kazakhstan. Like Pakistan, these states adjoin Afghanistan and were thus of critical importance in coordinating a ground war in the area.

From Air War to Ground War to Manhunt

Following the evident noncompliance of the Taliban regime to hand over Osama bin Laden and key members of Al-Qaida, the loose coalition against terrorism, which only thinly veiled U.S. preponderance in the undertaking, began an aerial war against strategic enemy targets. Missiles fired from air and sea rained on Afghanistan as a consequence of the Taliban's defiance.

In Kabul, the Taliban leadership had told the U.S. government in no uncertain terms that it would not countenance giving up bin Laden, who was considered their guest, and that their forces were committed to fighting a protracted guerrilla war against the United States and its allies in case of an invasion. The Taliban was quick to warn President Bush of the Soviet Union's failure against the mujahideen in the 1980s.

It soon became clear that massive military pressure on the ground would be a prerequisite to the overthrow of the Taliban government. Support for close coordination of the ground war with the forces of the indigenous Northern Alliance grew by the day because the air war proved inconclusive in the beginning. The Northern Alliance represented the military wing of Afghanistan's pre-Taliban government and was still recognized by most states as legally representing the country. The Northern Alliance was made up of 10,000–12,000 troops from various Afghan ethnic groups; it was believed to have been supported by the Russian Federation and Iran, both of which opposed the Taliban. Until 9 September 2001, the Northern Alliance was under the command of the charismatic Uzbek-Afghan leader Ahmed Shah Massoud. The Taliban assassinated Massoud. The influx of coalition support galvanized the previously beleaguered army of the Northern Alliance, whose territorial control within Afghanistan at that time had shrunk to no more than 5–10 percent along the northern border with Uzbekistan and Tajikistan.

Aside from the military preparations and the diplomatic maneuverings, Afghanistan was facing a humanitarian crisis on a massive scale. Droughts and years of war (since before the Soviet invasion in 1979) had devastated the country to such an extent that it could no longer support its population. Large migration flows moved through Pakistan, Iran, and other neighboring countries. They were usually not well-received. According to Human Rights Watch, the total number of displaced persons from Afghanistan is estimated at some 3.7 million. A particularly grotesque situation of the coalition's war in Afghanistan occurred, and repeated itself, during the aerial war as forces dropped scatter bombs and relief goods—often in similar locations. The Taliban was not squeamish in discouraging fellow Afghans from accepting coalition support—especially humanitarian relief goods.

The offensive of the Northern Alliance gathered force in November 2001 and, once under way with coalition air support, was mainly directed against the northern city of Mazar-e Sharif, which fell after six weeks of constant bombardment since 9 November 2001. Following a few setbacks, the Taliban was successively pushed out of most urban centers by a combination of a coordinated offensive in the air, by special forces, and by Northern Alliance troops on the ground. By mid-November, Kabul fell to the Northern Alliance. After the Northern Alliance captured the city of

Konduz in the north on 26 November, Kandahar remained the only Taliban stronghold.

By early December 2001, coalition forces with Northern Alliance, U.S., and British troops in the vanguard, maneuvered the Taliban and Al-Qaida troops into the northeastern part of the country. The Tora Bora region is located just south of the city of Jalalabad and is riddled with an intricate system of caves, which had been further enhanced during the Soviet occupation with bunkerlike structures being built into the natural cave formations for defensive purposes; it became the site of Al-Qaida's last stand against the coalition. It was believed that Al-Qaida had assembled some 1,000 troops to meet the vastly superior coalition troops. The siege of Tora Bora witnessed the withdrawal of a sizable portion of the defenders on 11 December 2001. U.S. special operations forces remained in the area for weeks, scouring the area for weapons and the greatest prize of the campaign—Osama bin Laden himself.

As this book goes to print in late 2002, bin Laden and the spiritual leader of the Taliban, Mullah Mohammed Omar, have not been found; neither were intelligence services aware of their whereabouts. The war in Afghanistan against the remnants of Al-Qaida had not come to a conclusion, and the U.S.-led coalition may continue its presence for the foreseeable future.

A New Era: Continuity and Change

The effects and consequences of the terrorist attacks on the variegated transnational fields of activity were anything but homogenous. The international financial system recovered rapidly from the shock of September 11. The same does not apply to the international system of transportation. The successful handling of the new insecurities of a global environment requires the formulation of new policies and the adaptation of international institutions and regimes. Politics is experiencing a comeback, and the community of states is facing new challenges that will preoccupy us all for years to come. So far, four themes have dominated the international debate.

The Future of the Coalition Against Terrorism

First and foremost, our attention ought to focus on the international coalition combating terrorism. The tragic events in New York and Washington also generated hopes that the effects of the attacks on international relations would be fundamentally positive. Moreover, the attacks demonstrated a risk of intimidating magnitude to which all and sundry were exposed; all nations were affected, and the terror would not halt at any borders. Advocates of the coalition argued that states, given such a risk, would forego their differences and team up to fight international terrorism. Augmented cooperation among civilized states could have been a result. But can the antiterrorism coalition meet such exacting demands in the long term?

At first glance, the recent past appeared to vindicate the position of those advocating such a position. Many an international observer was surprised by the tenacity and patience exhibited by the Bush administration in its efforts to garner broad international support for its counterterrorism policy. In this context, the United States canvassed its closest and traditional allies and made a concerted effort to secure at least minimal support from Russia, Pakistan, and Saudi Arabia. The cohesion of the antiterrorism coalition, however, is not comparable to that of the comprehensive alliance systems of the Cold War. Most states have not assumed military responsibilities or tasks in the war on terrorism. To many states, supporting the United States signified first and foremost their approbation for the forces of civilization in reaction to terrorism on an unprecedented scale. The question as to if, and to what extent, the coalition partners concurred on how best to tackle terrorism was wide open. The sustaining of the coalition will become more difficult with every day that prolongs the war on terrorism.

The challenges to a successful management of the coalition are of a comprehensive nature. First, in Washington the war on terrorism is being viewed as a battle between good and evil. President George W. Bush narrowed the U.S. expectations in the international community to a succinct warning: "You're either with us or against us in the fight against terror."[1] Second, the United States assumed that other states would not challenge U.S. leadership in formulating antiterrorism strategy. Third, Washington has made it clear to its allies—with the notable exception of Great Britain—that it did not expect or desire military contributions in the war on terrorism. The difficulties encountered in Kosovo, where all decisions had to be reached in the ponderous NATO bodies, was too recent.

The global manifestations of solidarity with the U.S. victims in the hours following the attacks were impressive. In part, they may well have expressed genuine dismay and an authentic sense of having witnessed an attack against all open societies and civilization. Sympathy extended to the point that military strikes against the Taliban regime in Afghanistan and against Al-Qaida became acceptable. In the interim, the planning process in Washington moved on to consider a preemptive military strike against Iraq. For this reason, coalition partners are circumscribing their support for U.S. policy: although they continue to believe in the necessity of containing terrorism, they are no longer willing to extend carte blanche to the United States.

In a few areas, the United States was dependent upon support from coalition partners. Overflight rights through foreign airspace; access to military installations; information about the enemy—all required some degree of foreign help. The U.S. interest in intelligence analysis cooperation was commensurate. However, relations between the United States and states such as Iran, Libya, and Syria—three important sources of information about terrorist activities in the Middle East—are marked by tension, if not hostility. This highlights the disparate nature of the loose coalition as to long-term partnership and cooperation with the United States. A small group of states (including Russia, Pakistan, some nations in Central Asia, and China) proved of especial political and logistic importance to the U.S. response. For these states, support for Washington went hand-in-glove with a more or less redefined relationship vis-à-vis the leading global power and included chances as well as obstacles.

The sympathetic response of Russian President Vladimir Putin suggests that he is willing to set aside disputed strategic issues in order to enter a new and cooperative relationship with the West, especially the United States. By taking this step, Putin risked his political credibility. Significant segments of Russian society do not seem convinced that the West will properly acknowledge a reorientation of Russian foreign policy. At the same time, Putin's political course since September 11 has also put a strain on the strategic partnership between Russia and China, as well as between Russia and India, and called into question Russia's military cooperation with Iran. Concerning vital Russian strategic interests, the Bush administration has to date made two important political gestures. First, Bush was willing to further reduce strategic weapons systems to a significant extent and was also prepared to codify the results of the negotiations in a treaty. Second, Bush accepted the Russian desire for closer cooperation with NATO and supported the creation of a Russia-NATO council to meet twice a month. The Russian Federation hopes that such an institution will develop into a body of substantive consultation; this remains to be seen.

Even more surprising than the Russian support was the decision made by Pakistani President Musharraf to permit U.S. forces the use of Pakistani airspace and territory. Islamabad was hoping that improved relations with the West would culminate in a rescission of economic sanctions in place since the Pakistani nuclear tests of 1998. Moreover, the threat emanating from extremist forces in Pakistan could be contained only if Afghanistan became stabilized. The U.S. reward: only ten days after the attacks on New York and Washington, President Bush terminated the economic sanctions against Pakistan. Shortly thereafter, Washington announced the preparation of a comprehensive aid package for Pakistan.

Support from the Central Asian states could not be taken for granted. Uzbekistan indicated its pliability and allowed U.S. troops to use its territory as a staging area. Not unlike Pakistan, Uzbekistan shared an interest in containing the fundamentalist forces in Afghanistan. At the same time, U.S. rapprochement increased Uzbekistan's room to maneuver with China and the Russian Federation. Washington's compensation came in the shape of military and economic support. The interest of the Central Asian states for a long-term U.S. military presence in the region has served Putin's domestic critics well; also, in Beijing, there are serious concerns about the growth of U.S. influence in the region.

China's tacit approval of the U.S.-led war on terrorism is decisive to the success of the campaign as a whole. China is interested in good relations with the United States, as well as stability in Central Asia. Against this backdrop, Sino-U.S. relations have improved. However, the war on terrorism is no basis for increasing cooperation between the two most powerful states in the Pacific region. Neither the United States nor China has indicated a readiness to reconsider their respective positions on human rights, proliferation, missile defense, and Taiwan. Taking the long view, it seems more likely that the rivalry between Washington and Beijing will increase.

The antiterrorism coalition is based on bilateral agreements and transactions between the United States and the coalition partners. The coalition does not possess a common normative basis; neither do the coalition partners agree in their appraisals of the terrorist threat. The coalition is oddly reminiscent of the Concert of Europe in the nineteenth century. Whether it will survive the potential second phase of the war on terrorism remains to be seen.

A Fundamental Reorientation of U.S. Foreign Policy?

According to some U.S. observers, a tendency could be identified in the immediate aftermath of the September 11 attacks, prompting a fundamental reappraisal and reorientation of U.S. foreign policy. President George W. Bush identified the focus of his presidency and assumes that his success in office will be measured against his success or failure in the war on terrorism. It is argued that the frequent comparison to Pearl Harbor has signaled the end of U.S. unilateralism in foreign policy. Although the first few months of the George W. Bush administration were marked by unilateralism, George Bush Sr. himself was more recently quoted as saying:

> Just as Pearl Harbor awakened this country from the notion that we could somehow avoid the call of duty and defend freedom in Europe and Asia in World War II, so, too, should this most recent surprise attack erase the concept in some quarters that America can somehow go it alone in the fight against terrorism or in anything else for that matter.[2]

Have the priorities of U.S. foreign policy really undergone such fundamental change?

This brings us to another question: whether the events of September 11 have indeed initiated a revolution of paradigms in U.S. foreign policy—a shift from unilateralism to multilateralism; from a largely critical view of international institutions to active participation in institutions; and from doubting the efficiency of international regimes to directly supporting them. It seems to be thus, especially if we recall Secretary of State Powell's statement that was published in the *New York Times* of 19 October 2001: "Nobody is calling us unilateral anymore. That's kind of gone away for the time being; we're so multilateral it keeps me up 24 hours a day checking on everybody."[3] Even so, many disagree if, and under what conditions, the United States ought to pursue its national interests by employing unilateral or multilateral tactics. For that reason alone, it is realistic to expect a contradictory mixture of multilateralism and unilateralism in Washington.

The Bush administration will keep open its option to go it alone, if necessary, for the foreseeable future. Washington will likely support the UN General Assembly if it passes one or more resolutions against international terrorism. At the same time, the United States will point to the fact that in excess of ten international treaties and conventions on terrorism did not prevent the attacks. The U.S. government will not make its freedom to act dependent upon UN authorization—which is not necessarily a disadvantage in light of that body's limited global leadership capability.

Yet the war on terrorism earned the United States the image of an arrogant and powerful actor on the international stage. For all intents and purposes, the Bush administration has not changed its stance on the Kyoto Protocol, the Comprehensive Test Ban Treaty, the Biological Weapons Convention, and the creation of an International Criminal Court. Furthermore, the United States will not make future moves in the war on terrorism dependent upon the concurrence of allies. Washington will again employ unilateral tactics if it can thereby break an impasse and if there is a reasonable chance for a quick success. But the United States will not elevate unilateralism to the position of a guiding strategic principle. U.S. foreign policy will continue to be guided by multilateralist preferences in the near future. Little will change in this way because the major unresolved problems today possess a transnational character. Sustainable solutions can be achieved only if the interest and capacity of a broad group of public, civil, and private actors can be harnessed to a long-term development process. Against this background, the United States will have to carefully balance the potential gains of hard power against its potential costs to the current and future utility and credibility of Washington's soft power in international relations.

A U.S. Focus: How to Win an Asymmetric War

The asymmetric nature of the war on terrorism has been realized in Washington. The military campaigns against the Taliban regime and Al-Qaida in Afghanistan confirmed the earlier insights gained during the war in Kosovo and in the Persian Gulf. Fully exploiting the revolution in military affairs, U.S. forces have developed into a military instrument that cannot be challenged or defeated by any opponent. This is exactly where forces opposed to the United States begin to develop their countermeasures.

The U.S. military potential displayed in Afghanistan was impressive. The U.S military mobilized and deployed forces in a short period, with only limited access to local bases, in one of the most hostile environments known to man. U.S. casualties were negligible. Laser-guided precision missiles, manned and unmanned drones, special forces, as well as information systems and command-and-control systems—all were deployed against enemy targets without delay and in an integrated manner.

An irony is obvious in the fact that the United States has simultaneously become even *more* vulnerable to new risks. As early as 1997, the report of the Quadrennial Defense Review warned of just such a development: "US dominance in the conventional military arena may encourage adversaries to use . . . asymmetrical means to attack our interests overseas and Americans at home."[4] The events of September 11 have confirmed this warning with the greatest single-day body count since the Civil War. The modern information society in the United States has proven highly vulnerable to well-executed low-tech attacks.

Today, the United States is fighting the kind of war it has tried hard to avoid. The opponent has the properties of a phantom: the enemy cleverly blends into global society, defies almost any means of detection, and carries the war to the doorstep of U.S. civil society with lightning-fast strikes. Al-Qaida can be described as a nonstate network that has established headquarters in Afghanistan and spread its branches across many states—some in the Western world. The relationship between Al-Qaida and the Taliban regime in Afghanistan ought to be characterized as one of a state supported by terrorists rather than state-sponsored terrorism. The U.S. attack in Afghanistan liberated the state from the scourge of terrorism—at least for the time being. The success of the fight against the Al-Qaida network, however, is more difficult to assess and will require a long-term endeavor.

With considerable help from the mass media, the anthrax cases in the United States moved a novel kind of terrorism that is equipped with a spectrum of biological, chemical, nuclear, and radiological weapons to the center stage of U.S. threat perception. What is potentially new about this type of terrorism—if it became reality—would be its choice instrument of destruction and all that such a decision would imply. On the one hand,

European allies have been pointing out that the attacks on New York and Washington proved that too much attention has been given to the so-called superterrorism while other threats were neglected. On the other hand, the possibility can no longer be excluded that states hostile to the United States will ally themselves with terrorist groups and actors in the context of a crisis in order to achieve their objectives despite overwhelming U.S. conventional superiority. The warning of an axis of evil made by President Bush in his State of the Union address on 29 January 2002 is to be understood in this wider context.[5]

Technology and special operations forces have ostensibly led to a success independent of geographic distance—in the same place where the Soviet military faced despair and, eventually, ignominious defeat. The progress of U.S. military forces in implementing the revolution in military affairs since Kosovo is impressive, indeed. In conventional military forces, the U.S. military machine seems peerless: no other great power can hope to resist the United States in a conventional conflict. However, in recent decades Washington faced the challenge of spatially limited intrastate wars. This situation begs the question of whether the U.S. high-tech military strategy is the right response to asymmetric threats that have moved to the center stage of the international attention since the end of the Cold War.

A European Focus: Comprehensive Conflict Prevention

The events of September 11 conveyed a principle message to the West— that the Western world could not afford to ignore the problem of failing and failed states in Africa and Asia—and drove it home with a vengeance. How the West is to tackle this problem, however, remains controversial. In Washington, the perspective had shifted: failed and failing states were no longer understood to be only humanitarian catastrophes but were increasingly perceived as national security risks. It remains unclear, however, whether such a perspective goes hand-in-glove with a readiness to participate in peace support operations as well as an increasing responsibility for rebuilding state and civil structures. In fact, the United States seems to be proposing a division of labor with its allies.

The solidarity of the European allies with the United States was a prominent feature of the first phase of the U.S. war on terrorism. However, the closer the potential second phase of Washington's military campaign came, the more arguments were raised as to how to best combat terrorism. Increasingly, Europeans warned of moving military aspects to the center of the international strategy against terrorism. In the long run, and according to the preponderant position in Europe, terrorism can be successfully fought only if social and economic causes and grievances are addressed and redressed within the framework of a comprehensive preventive strategy.

The military response is to be limited to the war in Afghanistan and to clearly defined terrorist targets.

Against this backdrop, discussion on the security role of NATO and the European Union continued. It seems as if the trend pointed to a division of labor between the United States and its European allies, as well as between NATO and the European Union. The United States will focus on the global military challenges; the Europeans will expand their involvement in the context of limited peace support operations, especially on the European periphery. NATO will retain its unique military structure and will augment its political function in the expanded Euroatlantic area. The European Union, in turn, will concentrate on a comprehensive preventive and stabilizing strategy, in which both military and civil tools will be used.

In the months before September 11, transatlantic relations were pervaded by divergent positions on threat perceptions, basic strategic assumptions, and military capabilities on both sides of the Atlantic; the two sides were drifting apart. Events since then lead to a paradoxical appraisal of the situation: even though a rapprochement between the United States and the Europeans has taken place in matters of the overall threat perception, opinions and capabilities regarding the means of fighting the war on terrorism are beginning to split yet again. Will the United States and Europe arrive at a new division of labor in this context without jeopardizing political solidarity?

A Globalized World

The transitional period in the wake of the Cold War came to a sudden close with the attacks of September 11. This event was seen by many as a turning point in the development of the international system. With the advantage of hindsight, however, one can say that the world did not fundamentally change on, or because of, the events of September 11. Indubitably, the timing of the terrorist attacks, the chosen instruments of death, the number of casualties, as well as the scale of the physical damage are, indeed, astounding. At the same time, some trends—which had by and large left their imprint on international relations of the 1990s—were generally confirmed. The events of September 11 burned the insecurities of a globalized environment into the consciousness of a public sensitized and shaped by the mass media; galvanized the quest for new answers in the process of formulating policy; and accelerated the adaptation process of international institutions and regimes.

The challenge posed by international terrorism will not effect a sea change among the existing alliance structures and the establishment of meaningful new partnerships in the middle to long terms. If only because the war on terrorism will not result in a basic reorientation of U.S. foreign political priorities, such change is not likely to happen. U.S. foreign policy will continue to exist in a tense political spectrum, the two polarities of which are unilateralism and multilateralism. Asymmetric threats such as terrorism supported by weak states cannot be tackled by a single state—not even the United States. The successful resolution of complex intrastate conflicts requires international leadership and the ability to act militarily, as well as institutional avenues to solutions and civilian crisis-reaction capabilities. The quest of the near future will have to be one of international burden-sharing without fundamentally questioning the legitimacy of existing political, legal, and institutional structures.

The events of September 11 demonstrated how multileveled and complex international politics has become in the early twenty-first century. At the beginning of the U.S. war on terrorism, the prevalent focus was the direct threat against the United States and its global interests by an amorphous network of nonstate actors and guided by diffuse objectives. The recent past has shown that the United States can hope to cope with this new type of transnational risk only if it is prepared to collaborate with the five or six remaining world powers, a series of middle powers, as well as small states in the regions of concern. In order to achieve success, the United States has to carefully weigh the advantages of employing hard power against the costs of doing so in terms of utilizing its soft power. The difficulties arising as a result of globalization, the changing international economic system, and the regionalization of security structures can be surmounted only in cooperation with other international actors.

Notes

Chapter 2

1. The full text of President Truman's address to Congress of 12 March 1947 is available at http://www.fordham.edu/halsall/mod/1947TRUMAN.html.

2. "X" (George F. Kennan), "The Sources of Soviet Conduct," *Foreign Affairs* 25, no. 4 (July 1947): 575.

3. The full text of the North Atlantic Treaty, including the text quoted from Article V, is available at http://www.nato.int/docu/basictxt/treaty.htm.

4. Paul H. Nitze with Ann M. Smith and Steven L. Rearden, *From Hiroshima to Glasnost: At the Center of Decision, a Memoir* (New York: Grove Weidenfeld, 1989), p. 7.

5. The text of the Atlantic Charter is available at http://www.yale.edu/lawweb/avalon/wwii/atlantic.htm.

6. The full text of the interview conducted by Merriman Smith of United Press and President Dwight D. Eisenhower on 7 April 1954 is available at http://coursesa.matrix.msu.edu/~hst306/documents/domino.html.

Chapter 3

1. Quoted as an epigraph in Andreas Wenger, *Living With Peril: Eisenhower, Kennedy, and Nuclear Weapons* (Lanham, MD: Rowman and Littlefield, 1997). Report by the Panel of Consultants of the Department of State to the Secretary of State, January 1953, *Foreign Relations of the United States* (FRUS), 1952–1954, 2 (part 2): 1056–1091.

2. The text of Kennedy's speech is available at http://www.cs.umb.edu/jfklibrary/jfk_newspaper_editors.html.

3. Joint Resolution of Congress on Cuba, 20/26 September 1962, in David L. Larson, *The "Cuban Crisis" of 1962: Selected Documents, Chronology, and Bibliography*, 2nd ed. (Lanham, MD: University Press of America, 1986), p. 33. The vote in the House of Representatives was 386-7 and in the Senate 86-1 in favor of the resolution.

4. Dean Rusk, *As I Saw It, by Dean Rusk as Told to Richard Rusk*, edited by Daniel S. Papp (New York: Penguin Books, 1990), p. 237.

5. Letter, Khrushchev to Kennedy, 26 October 1962, National Security

Archive, Washington, D.C., Cuban Missile Crisis, 1962, microfiche collection, No. 01388.

6. Arthur M. Schlesinger Jr., *A Thousand Days: John F. Kennedy in the White House* (Cambridge, MA: Riverside, 1965), p. 841.

7. McGeorge Bundy, *Danger and Survival: Choices About the Bomb in the First Fifty Years* (New York: Vintage Books, 1988), p. 392.

8. Nikita Khrushchev, *Khrushchev Remembers*, translated and edited by Strobe Talbott (Boston: Little Brown, 1970), p. 494.

9. John F. Kennedy, *Address Before the General Assembly of the United Nations*, 25 September 1961, Papers of the Presidents of the United States, 1961, pp. 618–626. Alternatively, the full text of Kennedy's address is available at http://www.cs.umb.edu/jfklibrary/j092561.htm.

Chapter 4

1. Motto ascribed to Lord Ismay, NATO secretary-general (1952–1957).

2. Remarks by Robert McNamara, NATO Ministerial Meeting, 5 May 1962, Restricted Session, "May 1962 Folder," National Security Archive, Washington D.C., Nuclear History Box 14.

3. The full text of the Harmel Report is available at http://www.nato.int/docu/comm/49-95/c671213b.htm.

4. White House Memorandum for Mr. Rostow, Subject: The NATO "Harmel" Exercise, Confidential, Issue Date: 10/02/67, Date Declassified: 12/02/96, Declassified Documents Reference System Microfilm Collection, Fiche No. 300, Document No. 3570, 1998, p. 2.

5. Schlesinger, *A Thousand Days*, p. 769.

Chapter 5

1. This adage is frequently attributed to PLO Chairman Yassir Arafat, whose address to the UN General Assembly on 13 November 1974 established the Palestinian issue as a significant topic in the United Nations; it probably constitutes a paraphrase. The essence of Arafat's speech was that "the difference between the revolutionary and the terrorist lies in the reason for which each fights. Whoever stands by a just cause and fights for liberation from invaders and colonialists cannot be called terrorist. Those who wage war to occupy, colonize and oppress other people are the terrorists. . . . I have come bearing an olive branch and a freedom fighter's gun. Do not let the olive branch fall from my hand." The full text of Arafat's speech is available in *Journal of Palestine Studies*, "Palestine at the United Nations" (Winter 1975): 181–192.

2. The U.S. Department of State in 1983 and the U.S. Federal Bureau of Investigation in 1980 issued these two definitions of terrorism, respectively. Both definitions are quoted in Alex P. Schmid et al., *Political Terrorism* (New Brunswick, NJ: Transaction Books, 1988), pp. 32–33.

Chapter 6

1. The full text of U.S. President Ronald Reagan's "Evil Empire" speech of 8 June 1982 is available at http://www.fordham.edu/halsall/mod/1982reagan1.html.

2. As quoted in CNN's profile of Lady Thatcher, available at http://www.cnn.com/SPECIALS/cold.war/kbank/profiles/thatcher.

3. As quoted in the BBC profile of Iraqi President Saddam Hussein, available at http://news.bbc.co.uk/hi/english/world/middle_east/newsid_1100000/1100529.stm.

Chapter 7

1. George Bush, *National Security Strategy of the United States, 1991–1992* (Washington: U.S. Government Printing Office, 1991).

2. The full text of the United Nations Resolution 819 is available at http://www.nato.int/ifor/un/u930416a.htm.

3. Quoted from Article 1, section 2 of the United Nations Convention and Protocol Relating to the Status of Refugees. The full text of the Final Act of the United Nations Conference of Plenipotentiaries on the Status of Refugees and Stateless Persons of March 1996 is available at http://www.unhcr.ch/cgi-bin/texis/vtx/home?page=publ.

4. See the section entitled "Objectives of the Amsterdam Treaty" at http://europa.eu.int/scadplus/leg/en/lvb/a09000.htm.

5. Stated in the Presidency Conclusions to the Cologne European Council of 3 and 4 June 1999, available at http://ue.eu.int/Newsroom/loadDoc.asp?max=1&bid=76&did=57886&grp=1799&lang=1.

6. Antony Lake's term "enlarging democracy" was used in a paper entitled "From Containment to Enlargement" dated 21 September 1993. The full text is available at http://www.fas.org/news/usa/1993/usa-930921.htm. For Madeleine Albright's statement concerning the preservation of global peace, see http://usinfo.state.gov/regional/ea/uschina/alb0224.htm.

7. George W. Bush's State of the Union address of 29 January 2002 is available at http://www.whitehouse.gov/news/releases/2002/01/20020129-11.html.

8. A phrase attributed to Ross Perot in 1992 and quoted, for example, in a paper by John Page of the World Bank; see http://www.worldbank.org/mdf/mdf1/learn.htm.

Chapter 8

1. As quoted in the article of 6 November 2001 by CNN, available at http://www.cnn.com/2001/US/11/06/gen.attack.on.terror.

2. Cited in Patrick E. Tyler and Jane Perlez, "World Leaders List Conditions on Cooperation," *New York Times*, 19 September 2001.

3. Cited in Patrick E. Tyler, "Russia and U.S. Optimistic on Defense Issues," *New York Times*, 19 October 2001.

4. Secretary of Defense William S. Cohen, *Report of the Quadrennial Defense Review* (Washington, D.C.: U.S. Department of Defense, May 1997), sec. 2.

5. The full text of President George W. Bush's 2002 State of the Union address is available at http://www.whitehouse.gov/news/releases/2002/01/20020129-11.html.

GLOSSARY

alliance system: An international system shaped by an alliance and/or multiple alliances.

alliance-Axis system: Descriptive term applied to the shape of the international system during World War II.

Amsterdam Treaty: Ratified in 1999, the Amsterdam Treaty consolidated the objectives pursued by the signatories of the Maastricht Treaty, which governed the transition from the European Economic Community to the European Union. Aside from reforms and innovations achieved in freedom, security, justice, the European Union, and its citizens and institutional questions, the Amsterdam Treaty boosted the significance of an effective and coherent external policy.

antiballistic missile (ABM): Primary ground-to-air defense against incoming long-range weapons such as intercontinental ballistic missiles. No ABM system has even come close to working. The U.S. Strategic Defense Initiative, or "Star Wars," was little more than an expensive exercise in science fiction and never got off the ground. Also, it was later admitted that the U.S. Patriot missiles fired at Iraqi Scud missiles during the 1991 Gulf War almost invariably missed their targets. However, concerned by a rapid proliferation of missile technology, many U.S. politicians have been campaigning for the United States to develop nationwide missile defense capabilities. The ABM Treaty of 1972 limited the establishment of ABM systems. Russia complained that a U.S. nationwide missile defense system would break the ABM Treaty. Recently, there has been continuing pressure from the U.S. Congress to go ahead with more advanced projects. On 13 June 2002, George W. Bush's administration unilaterally withdrew from the ABM treaty, without a vote from Congress and against the express wishes of the Russian Federation and U.S. European allies.

appeasement: A concessionary policy toward a hostile state. The policy of appeasement as practiced by then–British Prime Minister Neville

343

Chamberlain achieved infamy after the 1938 Munich conference between the British and Nazi heads of state. Appeasing Hitler turned out to be a serious mistake.

arms control: Efforts to limit weapons system capabilities; different than disarmament.

arms race: During the Cold War, the superpowers produced ever more destructive weapons systems because one or the other side upgraded its arsenal. This resulted in a ceilingless spiral that increased the destructive potential of existing weapons to the degree that the world could have been rendered uninhabitable.

Association of Southeast Asian Nations (ASEAN): Trading bloc consisting of Brunei, Indonesia, Malaysia, the Philippines, Singapore, Thailand, and Vietnam. ASEAN became a force in global trade after its transition from a loose association to a formal trade bloc in 1992.

asylum-seeker: A refugee who has applied for sanctuary in a state other than their own. Currently, some 1.2 million have applied for asylum in countries around the world. Their status remains unresolved, largely due to complex bureaucratic procedures in sanctuary states.

atomic/biological/chemical (ABC) weapons: ABC agents are all weapons of mass destruction.

Axis: Established in 1936, the Axis was a coalition of countries in World War II including as its principal members Germany, Italy, and Japan. They were opposed, and ultimately defeated by, the Allies in 1945, which was headed by the United States, Great Britain, the Soviet Union, and France.

balance of power: Theory that states ally themselves with other states to balance the power of threatening states.

Bandung Conference: Historic meeting of diplomats from twenty-nine African and Asian countries held in 1955 in Bandung, Indonesia. It promoted economic and cultural cooperation and opposed colonialism. The conference set the stage for the Non-Aligned Movement as a third way outside the superpowers.

bipolar: A world divided into two power centers, as during the Cold War.

Brezhnev Doctrine: The policy of employing Warsaw Pact troops in limited interventions against states belonging to the Soviet sphere of influence in Eastern Europe and attempting to break with Moscow's suzerainty. In response to efforts in early 1968 by the Czechoslovakian Communist Party, led by Alexander Dubcek, to introduce a number of reforms, the Soviet Union adopted a policy of combating antisocialist forces.

Central and East European Countries: The group of present-day successor states to the communist-dominated states of Eastern Europe.

Central Intelligence Agency (CIA): The CIA emerged as the successor to the Office of Strategic Services established by U.S. President Franklin Delano Roosevelt in June 1942. After World War II, President Harry Truman founded the CIA by presidential directive. In 1947, the National Security Council and the CIA replaced the National Intelligence Authority and the Central Intelligence Group. Ever since, the CIA has been responsible for gathering and analysis of intelligence. The more sinister aspect of its activities is best captured by undercover operations, such as its alleged link to the assassination of Chilean President Salvador Allende in 1973.

Central Powers: The coalition of Germany, Austria-Hungary, Bulgaria, and the Ottoman Empire during World War I.

coalition war: Generically, the situation in which a number of states coalesce to confront one or more states with a conflicting agenda. Specifically applied to the major conflicts of the eighteenth and early nineteenth centuries, such as the War of the League of Augsburg, alternatively known as the War of the Grand Alliance (1689–1697); the War of Spanish Succession (1701/1702–1713/1714); the War of Austrian Succession (1740–1748); the Seven Years' War (1756–1763); and especially the French Revolutionary and Napoleonic Wars (1792–1815).

Cold War: The period between the conclusion of World War II and the fall of the Soviet Union in 1991. The period was marked by hostility between the United States and the Soviet Union, but with the absence of direct confrontation between the two superpowers.

collective security: Agreement by a number of countries to act in concert against an aggressor.

colonialism: The conquest, occupation, and exploitation of other states; predominantly undertaken by the European powers.

COMINFORM: The Communist Information Bureau; the chief agency of international communism founded under Soviet auspices in 1947 and dissolved in 1956. The COMINFORM's activities consisted mainly of publishing propaganda to encourage international communist solidarity. The chief task assigned to COMINFORM—to obstruct the implementation of the Marshall Plan and the Truman Doctrine—utterly failed.

Common Foreign and Security Policy (CFSP): The CFSP was established by the Maastricht Treaty and came into force on 1 November 1993. The provisions of the CFSP were augmented when the Amsterdam Treaty came into force on 1 May 1999. For almost forty years of recent European history, the very idea of a common foreign policy was anathema. Now the European Union has at its disposal a defined set of foreign policy instruments and decisionmaking mechanisms; it can make its voice heard in the international community and express its position on armed conflicts, human rights, and any other issue of interest in international relations.

Commonwealth of Independent States: Loosely organized body of a majority of the former Soviet republics; its status and relevance remains indeterminable.

complex interdependence: The multiple transnational channels that connect societies, including interstate, transgovernmental, and transnational relations. The resulting relations are highly complex; economic interests assume a far greater importance than in classic realism.

Comprehensive Test Ban Treaty (CTBT): A treaty that outlaws nuclear weapons testing, as well as any other nuclear explosion, anywhere on the planet. Drafted at the Conference on Disarmament in Geneva, the CTBT was adopted by the UN General Assembly on 10 September 1996. It was opened for signature on 24 September 1996 at United Nations Headquarters. By December 2000, some 160 states had signed the CTBT.

Concert of Europe: An association of European monarchies in the post-Napoleonic period dedicated to the maintenance of the political and territorial status quo. It intervened in the internal affairs of various European states on several occasions to preserve the system it advocated, notably in Italy in 1820 and in Spain in 1822; favored Belgian independence in 1830. The revolutions of 1830 and 1848 and the unifications of Italy and Germany undermined the association but could not topple its consultative aspect among the Great Powers, which continued to confer within this context for most of the nineteenth century.

Conference on Security and Cooperation in Europe (CSCE): A series of meetings attended by virtually all European nations, Canada, and the United States beginning in the 1970s. The first conference was held from 1973 to 1975; NATO as well as Warsaw Pact nations were represented, and thirty-three European countries participated. The CSCE culminated in the signing of the Helsinki Accords. Later conferences were held in Belgrade (1977–1978), Madrid (1980–1983), and Ottawa (1985). After the collapse of East European communist governments, a major summit was held in Paris in 1990 to formally end Cold War divisions. By 1992, membership had risen to forty-eight, including the former Soviet republics.

Copenhagen criteria: In 1993 at the Copenhagen European Council, the member states of the European Union took a decisive step toward enlargement, agreeing that "the associated countries in central and eastern Europe that so desire shall become members of the European Union."[1] Accession would take place when the applicant state had satisfied a number of prerequisites—the Copenhagen criteria. According to these criteria, applicant states had to demonstrate that they achieved stability of institutions guaranteeing democracy, the rule of law, human rights, and respect for—and protection of—minorities; the existence of a functioning market economy; capacity to cope with competitive pressure and market forces within the European Union; and the ability to take on the obligations of membership, including adherence to the aims of political, economic, and monetary union.

decolonization: The political process of extending independence to colonial holdings; decolonization peaked in the 1960s in Africa and Asia.

détente: Relaxation of tense relations between hostile states.

deterrence: Policy geared toward dissuading a contending state from taking undesired action by demonstrating the potentially high cost thereof.

development of underdevelopment (dependency theory): Radical theory in political science originally applied to Latin America and advocated by the dependency school since the late 1960s. It states that U.S. foreign policy and economic vested interests are geared toward controlling the Western Hemisphere by keeping it poor. Dependency scholars hold that underdevelopment is a historical process. It is not necessarily intrinsic to the third world or developing states. The dominant and dependent countries together form a capitalist system; underdevelopment is an immediate consequence of the functioning of the world capitalist system in that the periphery is plundered of its surplus, which leads to a concentration of development in the core and commensurate underdevelopment in the periphery.

Dien Bien Phu: Heavily reinforced French bridgehead in Vietnam overrun by Vietminh forces in 1954.

Diplomatic Revolution: Major reversal in the eighteenth-century European alliance system in 1756 when France allied with its traditional rival, the Hapsburgs, against Britain and Prussia. The Diplomatic Revolution sparked off the Seven Years' War (1756–1763), the first truly global conflict.

displaced persons: There are various types of displaced persons. Refugees are persons who are outside their country and cannot return "owing to a well-founded fear of being persecuted for reasons of race, religion, nationality, membership of a particular social group or political opinion."[2] Returnees are refugees attempting to resettle in their original homes. More often than not, conditions in the country of origin remain too destabilized for refugees to return in safety. Asylum-seekers are refugees who have applied for sanctuary in a state other than their own. Finally, the recent upheavals around the globe have also increased the number of internally displaced persons (IDPs). The prime catalyst for the growing number of IDPs, which do not fall into the UNHCR mandate, is another category created in the aftermath of the dissolution of the Soviet Union.

Domino Theory: The notion that if one country becomes communist, then other states in the region will probably follow, like falling dominos. The analogy, first applied in 1954 to Southeast Asia by U.S. President Dwight D. Eisenhower, was adopted in the 1960s by supporters of the U.S.

role in the Vietnam War. The theory was revived in the 1980s to characterize the threat perceived from leftist unrest in Central America.

double-track decision: In the 1970s, Soviet advances in IRBM technology posed an immediate threat to Western Europe. Western European leaders also feared a unilateral abandonment by the United States in light of Soviet intermediate-range ballistic missile superiority. Accordingly, NATO enacted the double-track decision in November 1979, proposing negotiations with the Soviets concerning arms reductions while threatening to station some 572 theater missiles in Western Europe in the event that the Soviets should refuse to comply.

Eisenhower Doctrine: U.S. foreign policy pronouncement made by President Dwight D. Eisenhower on 5 January 1957 promising military and/or economic aid to any Middle East country requiring assistance in fending off communist encroachment. The Eisenhower Doctrine was intended to check increased Soviet influence in the Middle East, which had resulted from the supply of arms to Egypt by communist countries, as well as from substantial communist support of Arab states against an Israeli, French, and British attack on Egypt in October 1956.

entanglement of alliances: The foreign policies of the European powers in the first and early second decades of the twentieth century that created an alliance system with attendant treaty obligations that in fact facilitated escalation. In the decade before the outbreak of World War I, a dualistic alliance system manifested itself in the shape of the Triple Entente, led by France and Britain, and the Central Powers, headed by Germany and allied with Austria-Hungary. The threat of German hegemony was at the hub of the nascent international system. German expansionism in Europe and abroad prompted the traditional colonial powers of the West—France and Britain—to curb further German advances. Within the Triple Entente and the Central Powers respectively, an entanglement of alliances paved the road to war; according to the treaties concluded on the eve of World War I, mobilization and war plans were designed to come into force on the basis of third-party intervention.

ethnic cleansing: The forceful removal of an undesirable ethnic group from a specific area via deportation, intimidation, mass murder, and genocide.

Euro-Atlantic Partnership Council (EAPC): A forum for extended political consultation. The function of the EAPC is that of a political "roof" over the intensified military cooperation within the Partnership for Peace (PfP); its operational role in crisis management was augmented in the context of an expanded PfP.

European Coal and Steel Community (ECSC): Administrative agency established by a treaty ratified in 1952 designed to integrate the coal and steel industries of France, West Germany, Belgium, the Netherlands, and Luxembourg. It subsequently has come to include all members of the European Union. In that sense, the ECSC acted as a precursor to European integration, which culminated in the current European Union.

European Defense Community: An abortive project sponsored by West European powers and the United States to offset the conventional military superiority of the Soviet Union in Europe by embodying a supranational European army, including a rearmed West Germany. The idea was originally shelved at the Hague Conference of 1948. Prompted by hostilities in Korea, the French politician René Pleven submitted a plan that was subsequently presented by Robert Schuman, the French foreign minister, at a 1951 meeting of the Council of Europe. Although a treaty was actually concluded in Paris in 1952, the project failed due to the French parliament's refusal to ratify it.

European Economic Community: Economic federation of West European states established in 1958 and based on the principles of the Treaty of Rome (1957) to promote European economic cooperation. Politically, it sought to promote a rapprochement between France and Germany; to interconnect the economies of the member states into one large common market; and to work toward the ultimate objective of political union in Western Europe, which would serve to forestall future conflict within Europe. The trade policies pursued by the European Community resulted in increasing trade and economic expansion in Western Europe.

European Security and Defense Identity (ESDI): A debate internal to NATO representing the continuation of efforts to strengthen Europe's role. ESDI emerged as a coherent concept after the Helsinki summit of 1994. The objective was to offer European states access to NATO resources for missions in which the United States did not wish to take on a lead role. In the interim, the debate on closer European cooperation in security matters has shifted from the confines of NATO to the European Union.

European Security and Defense Policy: Gathered support in the second half of the 1990s in the wake of the evident European military dependency upon the United States, as exemplified by the Kosovo conflict in 1999. This fiasco paved the way for a closer defense collaboration between Britain and France. At a summit on 3–4 June 1999 in Cologne, the European Union decided that it "must have the capacity for autonomous action, backed up by credible military forces, the means to decide to use them, and a readiness to do so in order to respond to crises without prejudice to actions by NATO."[3] In order to secure the immediate availability of their own operational capability, the functions of the Western European Union required for the implementation of the Petersberg Tasks were integrated in the European Union. In December 1999, European leaders agreed on an ambitious plan to create the Rapid Reaction Force of 60,000 combat troops.

European Union: Economic and political federation of West European states formally established in November 1993. Constitutes the next stage in a bid to unite Europe that began with the Treaty of Rome (1957) and the establishment of the European Economic Community a year later.

federalist, federalism: The distribution of power in an organization between the center and its constituent elements. Federation, when applied to various unit levels (i.e., state, region), has different implications. In the European context, federalism has taken on a specific meaning concerning political forces at work in the wake of World War II that attempted and continue to promote the political unification of Europe under a single government. These proponents are opposed by interest groups within the European countries that refuse to yield sovereign rights vested in the state. Federalism is a highly functional and beneficial power-sharing agreement on the state level.

first- and second-strike capability: A devastating attack by either one of the two superpowers that renders retaliation impossible—the first strike—would be strategically decisive. If, however, the nation attacked possessed sufficient forces to survive an attempted first strike with retaliatory weapons intact, then it would have second-strike capability.

first world: Term for the industrialized states of the West.

fiscal conservatism: Policy recommendation as stated in NSC-68 (1950) to describe the decrease in military spending in the wake of World War II. NSC-68 explicitly advocated an end to fiscal conservatism, as evidenced in the following quote, which formulates the suggested policy response to growing Soviet pressure and the defensive disposition of U.S. troops: "It is imperative that this trend be reversed by a much more rapid and concerted build-up of the actual strength of both the United States and the other nations of the free world. The analysis shows that this will be costly and will involve significant domestic financial and economic adjustments."[4]

Five Year Plan: Compulsory industrialization of the Soviet Union in 1930 under Joseph Stalin.

functionalist, functionalism: The acquisition of state support on specific issues that culminates in a more general, cooperative behavior among the states concerned. In the case of Europe, functionalists advocated an incremental path to federation and/or unification but remained skeptical over the necessity of such objectives.

globalization: The process by which economic liberalization and information technologies eroded the Westphalian state system and led to an enormous growth of transborder flows of capital, services, goods, ideas, and people.

Great Depression: Economic depression that affected North America, Europe, and other industrialized areas of the world; began in 1929 and lasted until about 1939. It was the longest and most severe depression ever experienced by the industrialized Western world.

Gulf of Tonkin Resolution: Congressional carte blanche for U.S. President Lyndon B. Johnson to go to war against North Vietnam in 1964 following an alleged North Vietnamese attack on a U.S. Navy vessel in the Gulf of Tonkin.

Hallstein Doctrine: Named after a German foreign policy aide, Walter Hallstein, whereby West German authorities refused to establish and maintain diplomatic relations with any of the East European states, other than the Soviet Union, and threatened to break off diplomatic contact with any state that recognized East Germany.

hegemony, hegemon: The state of being militarily and/or economically preponderant in relation to one or more states. The entity that is in that position.

idealist, idealism: Policy based on moral, ethical, and legal principles.

ideology: The idea that social change for the better can be effected by following a system of principles and/or doctrines.

imperialist, imperialism: Imperialism is the acquisition of empire; the expansion by an ethnic group beyond the historic boundaries of its own territory; the assimilation of such subject peoples into one's own cultural and political mainstream. Historically, the Romans set the landmark precedent for the formation of empire. Several key European powers, notably Spain, Britain, and France, established colonial empires overseas during the early modern period (1500–1900). In the Leninist-Marxist paradigm, imperialism constitutes the highest stage of capitalism, as capitalism is inherently expansive due to its need to find new market outlets. It is important to distinguish between empire in the ancient world, colonial imperialism of the early modern period, and the Leninist-Marxist definition.

intercontinental ballistic missile (ICBM): A ballistic missile with a range of 3,000–8,000 nautical miles. The development of the ICBM in the late 1950s and 1960s constituted a revolution in nuclear weapons delivery systems and, over time, largely supplanted strategic bombers as the primary intercontinental delivery system for nuclear warheads.

intermediate-range ballistic missile (IRBM): Land-based missile with a range of 500–5,500 kilometers. Soviet advances in IRBM technology in the late 1970s culminated in NATO's double-track decision in 1979 to compel the Soviets to withdraw their IRBMs from Warsaw Pact states or face the stationing of 572 theater nuclear missiles in Western Europe, especially in West Germany.

Intermediate-Range Nuclear Forces (INF) Treaty: In 1987, U.S. President Ronald Reagan and Soviet leader Mikhail Gorbachev signed the INF Treaty to eliminate intermediate-range nuclear forces. The superpowers agreed to abolish two entire classes of nuclear missiles: short-range and intermediate-range. Both sides were to reduce their respective nuclear warheads by approximately 30 percent.

internally displaced persons: Citizens or denizens of a country displaced within the borders of a state by natural or man-made upheavals.

international system: The global constellation of states. Commonly applied to the international systems of the twentieth century; can equally be applied to preindustrial international state systems.

international war crimes tribunal: Special courts with jurisdiction to indict and try suspected war criminals. A number have been set up by the United Nations, including in Rwanda and the former Yugoslavia. The International War Crimes Tribunal for the former Yugoslavia (ICTY) was established by UN Security Council Resolution 827 on 25 May 1993, modeled on the Nuremberg tribunal following World War II. The ICTY is located in the Hague, Netherlands, and is mandated to prosecute and try persons responsible for serious violations of international humanitarian law committed in the former Yugoslavia since 1991.

interstate conflict: Conflict between state actors in the international system.

interventionist, interventionism: Tendency in U.S. foreign policy to take recourse to military force abroad in order to interfere in another country's internal affairs.

interwar international system: The structure of the international system during the period between World War I and World War II (1919–1939).

intifada: Palestinian uprising against Israeli control of the Occupied Territories in the early 1990s; the second intifada, which is ongoing as this book goes to print in late 2002, began in September 2000.

intrastate conflict: Conflict among different groups within a state.

Iron Curtain: Phrase coined by British Prime Minister Winston Churchill to describe the division of Europe in the earliest phase of the bipolar system at a speech delivered at Westminster College in Fulton, Missouri, on 5 March 1946. Probably the most defining quote from Churchill's oration is: "From Stettin in the Baltic to Trieste in the Adriatic, an iron curtain has descended across the Continent."[5]

Islamic fundamentalism: Islamic revivalism; meaning has been overshadowed by pejorative Western connotations of political extremism and religious fanaticism.

Islamic revivalism: The politicization of the Islamic faith and its concomitant value system.

isolationist, isolationism: The reluctance in U.S. foreign policy to support military intervention abroad and to avoid entanglement in alliances of any kind.

junta: Latin American military regime and/or dictatorship that came to power by violently overthrowing its predecessor in a coup.

League of Nations: Short-lived international organization established by peace treaties ending World War I. Like its successor, the United Nations, its purpose was to promote international peace and security. The league was a product of World War I, as that conflict convinced most persons of the necessity of averting another worldwide cataclysm. But its background lay in the visions of men like the Duc de Sully and Immanuel Kant and in the later growth of formal international organizations like the International Telegraphic Union (1865) and the Universal Postal Union (1874). The Red Cross, the Hague Conferences, and the Permanent Court of Arbitration (the Hague Tribunal) were also important stepping stones toward international cooperation.

lend/lease agreement: Arrangement for the transfer of war supplies, including food, machinery, and services, to nations whose defense was considered vital to the defense of the United States in World War II. The Lend-Lease Act, passed in 1941 by the U.S. Congress, gave the president the power to sell, transfer, lend, and lease materials. The president was to set the terms for aid; repayment was to be "in kind or property, or any other direct or indirect benefit which the President deems satisfactory."[6]

limited war: A war conducted with less than a nation's total resources and restricted in aim to less than total defeat of the enemy. Alternatively, a war restricted to a relatively small area of the world and involving few warring nations.

long peace: Term coined by U.S. Cold War historian John Gaddis to describe a different perspective of the Cold War. According to Gaddis, the Cold War was a peaceful period. The superpower standoff created a relatively stable international system (bipolarity) in which a number of minor conflicts did occur without setting off a major confrontation escalating into World War III.

Maastricht Treaty: International agreement approved by the heads of government of the states of the European Community (EC) in Maastricht, Netherlands, in December 1991. Also known as the Treaty on the European Union. It was ratified by all EC member states before 1 November 1993, when it came into force. The treaty established the European Union (EU), with EU citizenship for every person holding the citizenship of a member state. It also expanded the supranational pillar with a common market and a common currency, and it committed the EC to implement two intergovernmental pillars (a common foreign and security policy, and justice and home affairs).

Marshall Plan: Plan initiated by U.S. Secretary of State George C. Marshall to support the war-torn countries of Europe in the wake of World War II, as well as to contain the spread of communism by expediting a return to material prosperity.

missile gap: A lag in one country's missile production relative to that of another country. More specifically, the term is applicable to John F. Kennedy's warnings during the 1960 campaign that the Soviets held an advantage in terms of nuclear delivery systems. The missile gap was debunked for the myth it was by Deputy Secretary of State Roswell Gilpatric in October 1961.

monopoly: Economic environment in which a single entity exercises significant control over the production and/or distribution of goods and/or services.

Monroe Doctrine: U.S. claim to preponderance in the Western Hemisphere; primarily directed at the European powers, it was proclaimed by U.S. President James Monroe in 1823.

multiple independently targetable reentry vehicle (MIRV): A reentry vehicle that breaks up into several nuclear warheads, each capable of reaching a different target. The development of the MIRV constituted a qualitative enhancement of nuclear weapons technology that secured the U.S. nuclear edge in the late 1960s and early 1970s.

multipolar: A world divided into many power centers.

Mutual and Balanced Force Reductions (MBFR): The Talks on Mutual and Balanced Force Reductions were conducted in Vienna, and began on 30 October 1973. The MBFR talks also helped set the stage for an increasingly multilateral dialogue between East and West, which culminated in the Conference on Security and Cooperation in Europe.

mutually assured destruction (MAD): U.S. doctrine of reciprocal deterrence resting on the United States and Soviet Union each being able to inflict unacceptable damage on the other in retaliation for a nuclear attack.

narcoterrorism: The financing of organizations employing terrorist tactics from the proceeds of the drug trade.

nation-state: A nation (and in the event of multiple ethnic groups, the country) that is sovereign. Alternatively, territory bounded by the distribution of a national group and where that nation has its own state.

national interest: That which is advantageous for a state within the international system.

National Liberation Front: The South Vietnamese guerrilla force that sought to topple the U.S.-supported regime of Ngo Dinh Diem during the mid-1960s; received substantial support from Hanoi.

National Missile Defense (NMD): Generically, a system to protect the U.S. homeland against a limited attack by long-range ballistic missiles; specifically, the system considered under President Bill Clinton now known as nationwide missile defense or something similar. There is widespread international opposition against an implementation of NMD, as it would void the provisions of the 1968 Anti-Ballistic Missile Treaty and render the sensitive nuclear balance among the great powers obsolete and thereby open the gate to a new arms race.

National Security Council (NSC): Highest U.S. decisionmaking body on national security and foreign policy; partially integrated into the White House staff.

National Security Council Executive Committee (ExComm): ExComm was established in the autumn of 1962 under President John F. Kennedy to manage the emerging Cuban missile crisis. A much smaller group than the National Security Council, it consisted of the president as chairman, the vice president, the secretaries of state, defense, and treasury, the attorney general, the Director of Central Intelligence, the chairman of the Joint Chiefs of Staff, as well as the National Security Advisor. After the missile crisis was successfully overcome, the ExComm continued to meet (forty-two meetings between October 1962 and March 1963, many on Cuba).

national self-determination: The inviolable right of any people to decide their own destiny; the idealist theory sponsored by U.S. President Woodrow Wilson in his Fourteen Point Program.

Nazi-Soviet Non-Aggression Pact: Soviet-German agreement on the eve of World War II. In 1939, Hitler was preparing for war. Though he was hoping to acquire Poland without force (he had annexed Austria the year before), Hitler was planning for the possibility of a two-front war (fighting two fronts during World War I had split Germany's forces and weakened and undermined their offensive; it had played a large role in Germany losing World War I). Hitler was determined not to repeat the same mistake. He thus entered the Nazi-Soviet Non-Aggression Pact. On 14 August 1939, German Foreign Minister Joachim von Ribbentrop contacted the Soviets to arrange a deal. Von Ribbentrop met with Soviet Foreign Minister Vyacheslav Molotov in Moscow, and together they arranged two pacts: an economic agreement and the nonaggression pact. Hitler eventually made the fateful decision to invade the Soviet Union—guaranteeing that Germany would have to fight two fronts.

New Left: As with any sociological terminology, the definition of the New Left varied and evolved prior to 1968. It began as an intellectual theory developed mainly by the existentialist philosopher Jean-Paul Sartre. Whereas Sartre laid solid theoretical foundations, his ideas gained momentum and were eventually transformed into a movement that essentially involved three main concepts regarding bureaucracy, alienation, and self-management. The prime attributes of the New Left, from its existentialist roots to the disillusion with Stalinism, are the rejection of classical Marxism and most other leftist movements at the time, as well as popularity among student leaders and eventually among the student body.

new world order: A term employed by U.S. President George H. W. Bush to define the post–Cold War organization of power in which nations tend to cooperate rather than foster conflict.

9+1 formula: Plan sponsored by Mikhail Gorbachev and Boris Yeltsin to devolve the government of the Soviet Union upon the heads of those republics that had not made moves for secession. A 9+1 roundtable with representatives of the Soviet republics was called in 1991.

Non-Aligned Movement: An organization of developing states that prefer to maintain solidarity and independence in international relations; its future members met at Bandung, Indonesia, in 1955, where the movement was conceived; formally created at the 1961 Belgrade summit. The Non-Aligned Movement has become the main forum representing the interests and aspirations of the developing world. Its membership has more than quadrupled, from twenty-five original members to 113 members today, from Africa, Asia, Europe, Latin America, and the Caribbean.

nonproliferation: Efforts to contain the spread of weapons technology, especially nuclear weapons technology.

nonstate actor: An agency or actor in the international system with no affiliation/association with, or allegiance to, the state other than those of its members as private citizens. Nongovernmental organizations and multinational corporations are the most common types of nonstate actors in international relations.

North, the: The industrialized states of the West (used in contrast to the developing South); according to some proponents, it includes the Eastern bloc.

North American Free Trade Agreement: Founded by the United States and Canada in 1988; Mexico joined in 1992. The second major trade bloc behind the European Union.

North Atlantic Treaty Organization (NATO): Defensive alliance founded by Western states on both sides of the Atlantic in 1949. During the Cold War, NATO was primarily intended to defend the West against the communist bloc. As early as 1991, NATO became the principal regional security management organization. Although collective defense remains the backbone of NATO, the cooperative security policy functions of the Western alliance have gained more attention in recent years.

NSC-68: A defining National Security Council report; a landmark U.S. policy document of considerable consequence to international affairs. In the fall of 1949, Western powers were shaken by the communist takeover of China and the Soviets' successful testing of an atomic bomb. As a result, U.S. President Harry Truman requested a comprehensive analysis of Soviet and U.S. capabilities. The result was an extensive document by the National Security Council examining the two powers from military, economic, political, and psychological perspectives. The report called for a massive buildup, an increase in funding, and an end to fiscal conservatism for the armed forces in an effort to contain the Soviets. Only three months after the report was written, its assessment appeared vindicated by events: North Korea attacked South Korea on 25 June 1950, and the military buildup began.

nuclear edge: The quantitative and/or qualitative nuclear power of one of the bipolar contenders over the other.

Nuclear Non-Proliferation Treaty: Treaty signed in 1968 by most states restricting access to and/or transfer of nuclear weapons technology from nuclear to nonnuclear powers and, among nonnuclear powers, to defer acquisition of nuclear capability.

nuclear proliferation: The unbridled and rapid spread of nuclear weapons technology to nonnuclear states.

Organization for Petroleum Exporting Countries: International cartel of oil-rich countries striving to control crude oil prices.

Organization for Security and Cooperation in Europe (OSCE): Originated with the Helsinki Final Act and the Conference on Security and Cooperation in Europe process, which resulted in incremental institutionalization after the Cold War. Since 1 January 1993, the OSCE constitutes a supranational organization with permanent institutions and procedures.

Ostpolitik: After twenty years of Christian Democrat domination in West Germany, the Social Democrats captured the chancellorship for Willy Brandt (1969) in a coalition with the Free Democrats, whose leader, Walter Scheel, became foreign minister. This social-liberal coalition carried through a number of domestic reforms, but its principal impact was on West Germany's relations with East Germany and the communist countries of Eastern Europe. While confirming West Germany's commitment to the Western alliance, the new government embarked upon a bold new eastern policy (Ostpolitik). Previously, West Germany had refused to recognize the existence of the East German government. And by the terms of the Hallstein Doctrine, authorities had refused to maintain diplomatic relations with all those countries (other than the Soviet Union) that recognized East Germany. Now, the Brandt-Scheel cabinet reversed course by opening direct negotiations with East Germany in 1970 for the purpose of normalizing relations between the two states.

Pact of Brussels: Precursor to the North Atlantic Treaty of 1949; a European defensive alliance that was concluded in response to the mounting Soviet threat in 1948. The pact directed signatories to extend military assistance to any member state in the event of a German attack, or any third party in Europe committing warlike acts. A closer look at this remarkable document, specifically article 4, reveals that the defensive alliance was aimed at the Soviet Union, not Germany.

Partnership for Peace (PfP): The basis for practical security cooperation between NATO and individual PfP countries. Activities include defense planning and budgeting, military exercises, and civil emergency operations. There are now twenty-six members of PfP, all of which are members of the Euro-Atlantic Partnership Council.

peer competitors: U.S. term to describe regional hegemons who are already or soon will be a world power. The peer competitor (China, in this case) also begins to fill the role of potential future patron of regional client powers, including rogue states and states of concern.

pentagonal international system: The restructured international system succeeding the bipolar system. Structural changes in the international system in the early 1970s led to an undermining of bipolarity and resulted in a new constellation of relationships among leading powers. China and the Soviet Union came to political and military prominence in comparison to the United States, which was also holding parity toward the economic powers of Europe and Japan. The United States acted as the hub within the pentagonal international system, being militarily, politically, and economically dominant.

Petersberg Tasks: Named after the conference center near Bonn, Germany, where they were adopted in 1992. They include humanitarian, rescue, and peacekeeping roles; crisis management, including peace enforcement; and international crisis management, all roles developed to meet the new global problems since the end of the Cold War. Participation in the Petersberg Tasks will be on a voluntary and case-by-case basis. It was originally intended that the Petersberg Tasks were to be implemented by the Western European Union (WEU). In 1999, the functions of the WEU required for the implementation of the Petersberg Tasks were integrated into the European Union.

Pleven Plan: In October 1950, France floated a proposal for a supranational European defense community. The Pleven Plan envisioned the integration of West German forces at the level of battalions and regiments, which would allow for easier control of its troops. Furthermore, Germany was to be denied any voice in the supreme command of the European forces. Predictably, the Germans refused to contemplate the proposal.

Prague Spring: The popular uprising against Soviet power in Czechoslovakia centered in Prague following an introduction of reforms ("socialism with a human face") under Alexander Dubcek in the spring of 1968. Dubcek's reforms were geared toward the furtherance of democratic rights such as free speech and freedom of the press. Popular support for Dubcek frightened the Politburo in Moscow and prompted a Soviet invasion in August 1968. The Prague Spring was nipped in the bud; Dubcek and his adherents were forced out of power. A lasting legacy of the Prague Spring was the ensuing mass emigration of Czech citizens, as well as the creation of several Czech expatriate communities abroad.

Rapid Reaction Force (RRF): Based on the provision of the Treaties of Maastricht and Amsterdam, and on the occasion of the Helsinki Summit in 1999, the European Union has taken the decision of realizing the Rapid Reaction Force of 60,000 combat troops until 2003, deployable in sixty days and sustainable for one year, to implement any of the Petersberg Tasks. The RRF constitutes the first visible manifestation of the European Security and Defense Policy.

realism: A perspective of international relations that focuses on the state as a unitary and rational actor and on the actions and interactions of states. Realists attempt to understand patterns of conflict and collaboration under conditions of anarchy (lack of common government). To realists, security issues are usually the most important. National interests and/or objectives, power, and balance of power are key concepts for most realists. Realists tend to view the world as it is, whereas idealists base their outlook on how it ought to be.

realpolitik: A political outlook ascribed to the Prussian prime minister and first German chancellor, Otto von Bismarck (1815–1898). Realpolitik is generally characterized as a policy of adapting to existing facts, pursuing plain objectives, and admitting no obligation to ideals. In terms of its theoretical antecedents, realpolitik derives from Machiavellian and Hobbesian political thought.

refugees: Citizens or denizens who are compelled to flee their homes due to natural disasters or political, social, or economic upheavals.

regime: In its international context, voluntary sets of principles, norms, rules, and procedures around which actor expectations converge in a given area of international relations. An example: the nuclear nonproliferation regime.

regional integration: The economic or political convergence of separate states in relative geographic proximity (region). Integration, whether regional or international, can be viewed as process or outcome that reflects and encourages cooperation among states against the backdrop of an otherwise anarchic international system.

relative power: A concept employed by realists who hold that power, as the sum of military, economic, technological, diplomatic, and other capabilities, does not represent an absolute value. Instead, many realists subscribe to the idea that the power of one state is to be measured relative to that of others, that is, the capabilities of one state must be understood in relation to those of a second state.

returnees: Refugees attempting to resettle in their original homes. More often than not, conditions in the country of origin remain too destabilized for refugees to return in safety.

rogue state: An intrinsically partisan and highly politicized term, originating in U.S. foreign policy, describing states beyond the pale of international standards and usages of international relations in general and law in particular. States frequently blacklisted are North Korea, Libya, Iraq, and Iran. Only recently, in June 2000, did the U.S. State Department revise the nomenclature. At present, the term "rogue state" has been replaced by "state of concern."

rollback: Rhetorical term used by U.S. Secretary of State John Foster Dulles (1888–1959) under President Dwight Eisenhower. Used to describe the Eisenhower administration's determination to not only contain communism but also to push it back. Such a proactive policy proved moot in light of events, as evidenced during the Hungarian uprising of 1956.

Roosevelt Corollary: Proclaimed by U.S. President Theodore Roosevelt in 1905; a policy expansion to the Monroe Doctrine of 1823. Roosevelt warned Europe not to make use of Latin American states' debts to circumvent the Monroe Doctrine.

Second Cold War: The events after the Helsinki conference in 1975, when détente came to a grinding halt. Several factors account for the outbreak of the Second Cold War in the late 1970s. First, continued qualitative improvement of nuclear weapons systems continued unabated, as only the quantitative restriction was subject to control with the introduction of the Strategic Arms Limitation Talks. Increased systems competition between East and West in the third world affected Africa and the Middle East while continuing in Asia. On a personal level, the coming to power of a conservative leadership in the West (Ronald Reagan in the United States, Margaret Thatcher in Britain) deepened the bipolar fault line. Relaxation ensued only after the political ascendancy of Soviet leader Mikhail Gorbachev in 1985.

second world: The East European states dominated by the Soviet Union during the Cold War.

South, the: Collectively, the impoverished states in Asia, Latin America, and Africa; see **third world.**

South Vietnamese Army (ARVN): U.S.-backed anticommunist South Vietnamese forces. Defeated by North Vietnamese regular forces after the U.S. withdrawal from Vietnam.

Southeast Asia Treaty Organization (SEATO): Alliance organized in 1954 (and no longer in existence) under the Southeast Asia Collective Defense Treaty by representatives of Australia, France, Great Britain, New Zealand, Pakistan, the Philippines, Thailand, and the United States. Established under Western auspices after France's withdrawal from Indochina, SEATO was created to oppose further communist gains in Southeast Asia. The civil and military organizations established under the treaty had their headquarters in Bangkok, Thailand. SEATO relied on the military forces of member nations; joint maneuvers were held annually. SEATO's principal role was to sanction the U.S. presence in Vietnam, although France and Pakistan withheld their support. Unable to intervene in

Laos or Vietnam due to its rule of unanimity, the future of the organization was in doubt by 1973. SEATO was disbanded in 1977.

sovereignty: Concept in the political sciences and in political theory that each state constitutes the highest (executive, legislative, and judicial) authority in its own territory.

sphere of influence: Dominant political, military, and/or economic influence exercised by a major power in a given area.

Sputnik shock: Western world's rude awakening in 1957 following the first satellite launched into space, by the Soviet Union. The Soviets had won the race to develop ICBMs, causing scientists and engineers in the West to experience so-called Sputnik shock. The event spurred Western efforts to close the perceived missile gap, culminating in a massive buildup of nuclear weapons programs under U.S. President John F. Kennedy.

states of concern: See **rogue state.**

Strategic Arms Limitation Talks (SALT): The Soviet Union and the United States had begun the Strategic Arms Limitation Talks in the late 1960s and, in 1972, agreed to limit antiballistic missiles and reached an interim accord limiting intercontinental ballistic missiles. Another interim SALT agreement was reached in November 1974 that limited ballistic missile launchers. SALT II, which banned new intercontinental ballistic missiles and limited other delivery vehicles, was signed in 1979. It was never ratified, but both countries announced they would adhere to its terms.

Strategic Arms Reduction Talks/Treaties (START): In 1982, the United States and the Soviet Union began a new set of negotiations—the Strategic Arms Reduction Talks. The START I Treaty, signed by President George H.W. Bush and Soviet leader Mikhail Gorbachev in 1991, called for reductions in U.S. and Soviet nuclear arsenals and for on-site inspections. In response to increasing Soviet political instability, Bush announced in 1991 the elimination of most U.S. tactical nuclear arms; took strategic bombers off alert status; and called for further reductions in ballistic missiles. With the Soviet Union's disintegration, its nuclear arms passed to Belarus, Kazakhstan, Russia, and Ukraine. Those former Soviet republics pledged to abide by existing treaties and remove outlying weapons to Russia for destruction. In 1993, Bush and Russian President Boris Yeltsin signed the START II Treaty, which called for cutting nuclear warheads by two-thirds by 2003 (and probably sooner under modifications agreed to in 1994), as well as the elimination of weapons most likely to be used in a first strike. Ukraine, fearing Russian domination, did not ratify START and the 1970 Nuclear Non-Proliferation Treaty until 1994, but by 1996 the nuclear arsenals of Belarus, Kazakhstan, and Ukraine had been dismantled.

Strategic Defense Initiative (SDI): Ballistic missile defense program announced by U.S. President Ronald Reagan in 1983. The proposal envisioned the implementation of a protective shield in space to defend the U.S. homeland from missile attack. Reagan's vision was never realized, although a similar program (generically, nationwide missile defense) continues to be pursued.

strategy of containment: Policy of impeding the expansion of Soviet power around the globe; conceived by George F. Kennan in 1947.

submarine-launched ballistic missiles (SLBMs): An integral part of the strategic deterrent for six generations, starting in 1956 with the U.S. Navy's Polaris program. Since then, the SLBM has evolved through Polaris, Poseidon, and today's force of Trident Is and Trident IIs. Each generation has been continuously deployed at sea as a survivable retaliatory force and has been routinely operationally tested and evaluated to maintain confidence and credibility in the deterrent.

superpower: A state imbued with the capability to wage conventional and/or nuclear war and the capacity to project its power globally.

supranational government: Power beyond and above the state, as in the United Nations.

system: A structure in which any element effecting change affects all other components, thereby changing the whole structure.

terrorism: Generally, the politically motivated use of violence to weaken and/or eliminate the incumbent and/or bring about social change. The debate over definitions continues to this day. No conclusive solution to the problem has been arrived at.

Tet Offensive: Massive military offensive by the North Vietnamese Army and its allies in the south that was launched during Tet 1968—the Vietnamese New Year.

third world: Collectively, the impoverished states of Asia, Latin America, and Africa; see **the South.**

38th parallel: At the end of World War II, Korea was divided at the 38th parallel into Soviet and U.S. zones of occupation (North Korea and South Korea, respectively). In 1948, rival governments were established: the Republic of Korea was proclaimed in the south, the People's Democratic Republic of Korea in the north.

totalitarian regime: A modern autocratic government in which the state involves itself in all facets of society, including the daily life of citizens. A totalitarian government seeks to control not only all economic and political matters but also the attitudes, values, and beliefs of its populations, erasing the distinction between state and society. The citizen's duty to the state becomes the primary concern of the community, and the goal of the state is the replacement of existing society with a perfect society.

triangular diplomacy: A diplomatic maneuver involving three powers in which every actor faces the potential alliance of the other two. Specifically applied to the great diplomatic feat of the Cold War in the early 1970s when Henry Kissinger, acting as U.S. plenipotentiary, arranged a meeting between Chinese Prime Minister Zhou Enlai and U.S. President Richard Nixon (Beijing, 1972) that resulted in a fundamental realignment of forces by initiating a rapprochement between the United States and China. Kissinger skillfully employed the rupture between the Soviet Union and China, which had escalated during the Ussuri crisis four years earlier, to maximum effect. In doing so, Kissinger took recourse to his profound understanding of European history to bring about the second Diplomatic Revolution—the first being the Renversement des Alliances of 1756.

Triple Entente: Alliance between the Russian, British, and French governments against the Central Powers (Germany and Austria) during World War I.

Truman Doctrine: Policy axiom defined by U.S. President Harry Truman in March 1947 to the effect that countries assailed by communism would receive U.S. support to combat it.

unilateralism: The tendency of nations to conduct foreign affairs individualistically, characterized by minimal consultation and involvement with other nations, even with allies.

unipolar: A world with a single power center.

United Nations (UN): International organization established immediately after World War II. It replaced the League of Nations. In 1945, when the United Nations was founded, there were fifty-one members; today, there are more than 190 UN member states. The United Nations Charter comprises a preamble and nineteen chapters divided into 111 articles. The United Nations Charter sets forth the purposes of the United Nations: the maintenance of international peace and security; the development of friendly relations among states; and the achievement of cooperation in solving international economic, social, cultural, and humanitarian problems—expressing the strong hope for the equality of all people and the expansion of basic freedoms.

United Nations High Commissioner for Refugees: According to the United Nations:

> The United Nations High Commissioner for Refugees, acting under the authority of the General Assembly, shall assume the function of providing international protection, under the auspices of the United Nations, to refugees who fall within the scope of the present Statute and of seeking permanent solutions for the problem of refugees by assisting Governments and, subject to the approval of the Governments concerned, private organizations to facilitate the voluntary repatriation of such refugees, or their assimilation within new national communities. In the exercise of his functions, more particularly when difficulties arise, and for instance with regard to any controversy concerning the international status of these persons, the High Commissioner shall request the opinion of the advisory committee on refugees if it is created.[7]

United Nations Implementation Force: Multinational military contingent mostly composed of North Atlantic Treaty Organization troops deployed to oversee the realization of the 1995 Dayton Accords to end hostilities in the Balkans.

United Nations Protection Force: United Nations contingent deployed in the Balkans from 1992 to 1996 and instructed to contain fighting in the former Yugoslavia. Ineffective, it was withdrawn and then replaced by the United Nations Implementation Force.

United Nations Security Council: The UN organ with primary responsibility for preserving the peace. Unlike the UN General Assembly, it was given power to enforce measures and was organized as a compact executive organ. Also unlike the General Assembly, the Security Council in theory functions continuously at the seat of the United Nations. The council has fifteen members. Five members are permanent: China (until 1971, the Republic of China [Taiwan]), France, Great Britain, the United States, and Russia (until 1991, the Soviet Union). The ten (originally six) nonpermanent members are elected for two-year terms by the General Assembly; equitable geographic distribution is required. Customarily, there are five nonpermanent members from African and Asian states, one from Eastern Europe, two from Latin America, and two from Western Europe and elsewhere. In the Security Council, the presidency is revolving (for one-month terms according to alphabetical order).

Vietcong: Generally, the communist South Vietnamese liberation movement in the 1960s; members of the Vietcong.

Vietminh: The original communist Vietnamese liberation movement against France's occupation of Indochina in the 1940s and early 1950s; directed by Ho Chi Minh.

Warsaw Pact: Formally, the Warsaw Treaty of Friendship, Cooperation, and Mutual Assistance (14 May 1955–1 July 1991). The Warsaw Pact established a mutual defense organization—the Warsaw Treaty Organization—composed originally of the Soviet Union, Albania, Bulgaria, Czechoslovakia, East Germany, Hungary, Poland, and Romania. Albania withdrew in 1968, and East Germany did so in 1990. The immediate occasion for the Warsaw Pact was the Paris Agreement among the Western powers admitting West Germany to the North Atlantic Treaty Organization. In the course of the Cold War, the Warsaw Pact provided for a unified military command and for the maintenance of Soviet military units on the territories of the other participating states.

weapons of mass destruction: Modern weapons systems capable of widespread destruction; see **atomic/biological/chemical (ABC) weapons.**

Western bloc: An association of states located in Western Europe and North America tied by cultural, social, and political affinities and opposed to the spread of communism during the Cold War. The leading force in the

Western bloc was the United States. The most visible manifestation of this association was, and remains, the North Atlantic Treaty Organization.

Woodrow Wilson's Fourteen Point Program: Landmark policy program advocated by U.S. President Woodrow Wilson in the aftermath of World War I. Central issues to Wilson's program were, inter alia, national self-determination, "open covenants, openly arrived at," "a general association of nations" (i.e., the League of Nations), and freedom of the seas and of trade.[8] It was derided as being too idealist and was ignored by most elder statesmen in the victorious European powers, which imposed stringent terms on the defeated Germany.

World Trade Organization (WTO): Founded in 1995, the WTO's principal objective is to open the world to free trade.

zero-sum game: A decisionmaking approach based on the assumption of actor rationality in a situation of competition. Each actor tries to maximize gains, or minimize losses, often under conditions of uncertainty and incomplete information, which requires each actor to rank order preferences, estimate probabilities, and try to discern what the other actor is going to do. In a two-player zero-sum game, what one loses, the other one gains.

Notes

1. Cf. http://europa.eu.int/comm/enlargement/intro/criteria.htm. This website discusses the criteria for accession to the European Union in the context of the Union's endeavors to expand eastward.

2. The full text of the Final Act of the United Nations Conference on Plenipotentiaries on the Status of Refugees and Stateless Persons of March 1996 is available at http://www.unhcr.ch/cgi-bin/texis/vtx/home?page=publ.

3. Cf. http://www.eurunion.org/legislat/Defense/esdpweb.htm. This website gives a broad overview about the European Security and Defense Policy, as well as providing important background materials.

4. As quoted in NSC-68, "Conclusions and Recommendations," available at http://www.mtholyoke.edu/acad/intrel/nsc-68/nsc68-4.htm.

5. The full text of Sir Winston Churchill's "Iron Curtain" speech is available at http://www.fordham.edu/halsall/mod/churchill-iron.html.

6. The full text of the Lend-Lease Act of 11 March 1941 is available at http://www.nelson.com/nelson/school/discovery/cantext/wwii/1941usle.htm.

7. The full text of the "Statute of the Office of the United Nations High Commissioner for Refugees" is available at http://www1.umn.edu/humanrts/instree/v3sunhcr.htm.

8. The full text of President Woodrow Wilson's Fourteen Point Program is available at http://www.lib.byu.edu/~rdh/wwi/1918/14points.html.

SELECTED BIBLIOGRAPHY

General Resources

Armstrong, David. *Revolution and World Order: The Revolutionary State in International Society.* Oxford, UK: Oxford University Press, 1993.

Baldwin, David A., ed. *Neorealism and Neoliberalism: The Contemporary Debate.* New York: Columbia University Press, 1993.

Beitz, Charles R. *Political Theory and International Relations.* Princeton, NJ: Princeton University Press, 1999.

Boucher, David. *Political Theories of International Relations: From Thucydides to the Present.* Oxford, UK: Oxford University Press, 1998.

Brewer, Anthony. *Marxist Theories of Imperialism: A Critical Survey.* New York: Routledge and Keegan Paul, 1991.

Brower, Daniel R. *The World in the Twentieth Century: From Empires to Nations.* Upper Saddle River, NJ: Prentice Hall, 1998.

———. *The World Since 1945: A Brief History.* Upper Saddle River, NJ: Prentice Hall, 1999.

Brown, Chris. *Understanding International Relations.* Basingstoke, UK: Macmillan, 1997.

Brown, Michael E. *Ethnic Conflict and International Security.* Princeton, NJ: Princeton University Press, 1993.

Brown, Michael E., Owen R. Cote, Jr., Sean M. Lynn-Jones, and Steven E. Miller, eds. *Rational Choice and Security Studies: Stephen Walt and His Critics.* Cambridge: MIT Press, 2000.

Brown, Michael E., Sean M. Lynn-Jones, and Steven E. Miller, eds. *The Perils of Anarchy: Contemporary Realism and International Security.* Cambridge: MIT Press, 1995.

Bull, Hedley. *The Anarchical Society: A Study of Order in World Politics.* New York: Columbia University Press, 1995.

Burchill, Scott, Andrew Linklater, Richard Devetak, Mathew Paterson, and Jacqui True. *Theories of International Relations.* Basingstoke, UK: Palgrave Macmillan, 1996.

Buzan, Barry, and Richard Little. *International Systems in World History.* Oxford, UK: Oxford University Press, 2000.

Cammack, Paul, David Pool, and William Tordoff. *Third World Politics: A Comparative Introduction.* Baltimore: Johns Hopkins University Press, 1993.

Clark, Ian. *Globalization and International Relations Theory*. Oxford, UK: Oxford University Press, 1999.

Couloumbis, Theodore A. *Introduction to International Relations: Power and Justice*. Upper Saddle River, NJ: Prentice Hall, 1990.

Der Derian, James, and Michael J. Shapiro, eds. *International/Intertextual Relations: Postmodern Reading of World Politics*. Lanham, MD: Lexington Books, 1989.

Dougherty, James E., and Robert L. Pfaltzgraff Jr. *Contending Theories of International Relations*. New York: Longman, 1997.

Dyer, Hugh C., and Leon Mangasarian. *The Study of International Relations: The State of the Art*. Basingstoke, UK: Palgrave Macmillan, 1989.

Findley, Carter Vaughn, and John Alexander Murray Rothney. *The Twentieth-Century World*. New York: Houghton and Mifflin, 1998.

Gabriel, Jürg Martin. *Worldviews and Theories of International Relations*. Basingstoke, UK: Macmillan, 1994.

Gaddis, John Lewis. *Cold War Statesmen Confront the Bomb: Nuclear Diplomacy Since 1945*. Oxford, UK: Oxford University Press, 1999.

Goodin, Robert E., and Hans-Dieter Klingemann. *A New Handbook of Political Science*. New York: Oxford University Press, 1998.

Grenville, John Ashley Soames. *History of the World in the Twentieth Century, Volume 2: Conflict and Liberation, 1945–1996*. Cambridge: Harvard University Press, 1994.

Halliday, Fred. *Rethinking International Relations*. Houndmills, UK: Macmillan, 1994.

Hardin, R., John J. Mearsheimer, Gerald Dwarkin, and Robert E. Goodin, eds. *Nuclear Deterrence: Ethics and Strategy*. Chicago: University of Chicago Press, 1985.

Hobsbawm, Eric J. *The Age of Extremes: A History of the World, 1914–1991*. New York: Pantheon Books, 1994.

Hollis, Martin, and Steve Smith. *Explaining and Understanding International Relations*. Oxford, UK: Clarendon, 1991.

Jackson, Robert, and Georg Sorensen. *Introduction to International Relations*. Oxford, UK: Oxford University Press, 1999.

Judge, Edward H., and John W. Langdon. *A Hard and Bitter Peace: A Global History of the Cold War*. New York: Prentice Hall, 1996.

———. *The Cold War: A History Through Documents*. Upper Saddle River, NJ: Prentice Hall, 1999.

Kegley, Charles W., Jr. *Controversies in International Relations Theory: Realism and the Neo-Liberal Challenge*. Basingstoke, UK: Macmillan, 1995.

Kegley, Charles W., Jr., and Eugene R. Wittkopf. *World Politics: Trend and Transformation*. Basingstoke, UK: Macmillan, 1998.

Keohane, Robert O. *Neorealism and Its Critics*. New York: Columbia University Press, 1986.

Keohane, Robert O., and Joseph S. Nye. *Power and Interdependence*. New York: Addison-Wesley, 1989.

Keylor, William R. *The Twentieth Century World: An International History*. New York: Oxford University Press, 1996.

Kissinger, Henry. *Diplomacy*. New York: Simon and Schuster, 1994.

Larson, Deborah. *Anatomy of Mistrust: U.S.-Soviet Relations During the Cold War*. Ithaca: Cornell University Press, 1997.

Loth, Wilfried. *Die Teilung der Welt: Geschichte des Kalten Krieges, 1941–1955*

(The Division of the World: The History of the Cold War, 1941–1955). Munich, Germany: Deutscher Taschenbuch Verlag, 1990.

Luard, Evan, ed. *Basic Texts in International Relations: The Evolution of Ideas About International Society.* Basingstoke, UK: Palgrave Macmillan, 1992.

Lundestad, Geir. *East, West, North, South: Major Developments in International Politics, 1945–1986.* Oslo, Norway: Universitetsforlaget, 1986.

MacWilliams, Wayne C., and Harry Piotrowski. *The World Since 1945: A History of International Relations.* Boulder: Lynne Rienner Publishers, 1993.

Mansbach, Richard W. *The Global Puzzle: Issues and Actors in World Politics.* Boston: Houghton and Mifflin, 2000.

Mansfield, Edward D., Friedrich V. Kratochwil, and Carmella E. Mansfield. *International Organization: A Reader.* New York: Addison-Wesley, 1994.

Morgan, Patrick M. *Theories and Approaches to International Relations.* Somerset, NJ: Transaction, 1987.

Morgenthau, Hans Joachim. *Politics Among Nations: The Struggle for Power and Peace.* New York: McGraw-Hill, 1978.

Neuman, Stephanie, ed. *International Relations Theory and the Third World.* Basingstoke, UK: Macmillan, 1998.

Nicholson, Michael. *International Relations: A Concise Introduction.* New York: New York University Press, 1998.

Osiander, Andreas. *The State System of Europe, 1660–1990: Peacemaking and the Conditions of International Stability.* Oxford, UK: Oxford University Press, 1994.

Paterson, Thomas G., and Robert McMahon, eds. *The Origins of the Cold War.* Lexington, MA: D. C. Heath, 1991.

Rosenau, James N. *Turbulence in World Politics: A Theory of Change and Continuity.* Princeton, NJ: Princeton University Press, 1990.

Roskin, Michael G., and Nicholas O. Berry. *IR: The New World of International Relations.* Upper Saddle River, NJ: Prentice Hall, 1998.

de Senarclens, Pierre. *From Yalta to the Iron Curtain: The Great Powers and the Origins of the Cold War.* Oxford, UK: Berg, 1995.

Viotti, Paul R., and Mark V. Kauppi. *International Relations Theory: Realism, Pluralism, Globalism, and Beyond.* Upper Saddle River, NJ: Prentice Hall, 1998.

Waltz, Kenneth N. *Man, the State, and War.* New York: Columbia University Press, 1965.

———. *Theory of International Politics.* New York: McGraw-Hill, 1979.

Woods, Ngaire. *Explaining International Relations Since 1945.* New York: Oxford University Press, 1996.

Africa

Abdulai, David N. *African Renaissance: Challenges, Solutions, and the Road Ahead.* London: Asean Academic, 2001.

Alméras, Philippe. *Journal noir de l'Algérie indépendante* (Black Journal of Independent Algeria). Paris: Dualpha, 2001.

Anstee, Margaret Joan. *Orphan of the Cold War: The Inside Story of the Collapse of the Angolan Peace Process, 1992–1993.* New York: St. Martin's, 1996.

Beinart, William, and Saul DuBow, eds. *Segregation and Apartheid in Twentieth-Century South Africa.* New York: Routledge, 1995.

Borstelmann, Thomas. *Apartheid's Reluctant Uncle: The United States and Southern Africa in the Early Cold War*. Oxford, UK: Oxford University Press, 1993.

Birmingham, David. *The Decolonization of Africa*. Athens, OH: Ohio University Press, 1995.

Cointet, Michèle. *De Gaulle et l'Algérie française, 1958–1962* (DeGaulle and French Algeria, 1958–1962). Paris: Perrin, 1995.

Connell, Dan. *Against All Odds: A Chronicle of the Eritrean Revolution*. Lawrenceville, NJ: Red Sea, 1997.

Davidson, Basil. *Modern Africa: A Social and Political History*. New York: Longman, 1994.

De Witte, Ludo. *The Assassination of Lumumba*. London: Verso Books, 2001.

Fage, John Donelly, and William Tordoff. *A History of Africa*. New York: Routledge, 2001.

Hargreaves, John D. *Decolonization in Africa*. London: Longman, 1996.

Hopwood, Derek. *Egypt, Politics, and Society, 1945–1990*. New York: Routledge, 1993.

Iliffe, John. *Africans: The History of a Continent*. New York: Cambridge University Press, 1995.

Kalb, Madeleine. *The Congo Cables: The Cold War in Africa—From Eisenhower to Kennedy*. New York: Macmillan, 1982.

Liebenberg, Barend Jacobus, and S. B. Spies, eds. *South Africa in the 20th Century*. Pretoria, South Africa: J. L. van Schaik, 1993.

Mazrui, Ali A., ed. *Africa Since 1935*. Berkeley: University of California Press, 1999.

Schraeder, Peter J. *United States Foreign Policy Toward Africa: Incrementalism, Crisis, and Change*. Cambridge: Harvard University Press, 1994.

Shamir, Shimon, ed. *Egypt from Monarchy to Republic: A Reassessment of Revolution and Change*. Boulder: Westview, 1995.

Stora, Benjamin. *Algeria, 1830–2000: A Short History*. Ithaca: Cornell University Press, 2001.

Asia

Allinson, Gary D. *Japan's Postwar History*. Ithaca: Cornell University Press, 1997.

Beauchamp, Edward R., ed. *History of Contemporary Japan, 1945–1998*. New York: Garland Publishing, 1998.

Bradsher, Henry S. *Afghan Communism and Soviet Intervention*. Oxford, UK: Oxford University Press, 1999.

Brentjes, Burchard. *Taliban: A Shadow over Afghanistan*. Varanasi, India: Rishi Publications, 2000.

Cayrac-Blanchard, Françoise, et al., eds. *L'Indonésie, un demi-siècle de construction nationale* (Indonesia: A Half Century of National Construction). Paris: Harmattan, 2000.

Chandra, Bipan. *India After Independence*. New Delhi and New York: Penguin Books, 1999.

Daniel, Elton L. *The History of Iran*. Westport, CT: Greenwood, 2001.

Gallicchio, Marc. *The Cold War Begins in Asia: American East Asian Policy and the Fall of the Japanese Empire*. New York: Columbia University Press, 1988.

Ganguly, Sumit. *Conflict Unending: India-Pakistan Tensions Since 1947*. New York: Columbia University Press and Woodrow Wilson Center Press, 2002.

Goodson, Larry P. *Afghanistan's Endless War: State Failure, Regional Politics, and the Rise of the Taliban.* Seattle: University of Washington Press, 2001.

Gordon, Matthew. *Ayatollah Khomeini.* New York: Chelsea House, 1988.

Karlekar, Hiranmay, ed. *Independent India: The First Fifty Years.* New York: Oxford University Press, 1998.

Kingston, Jeff. *Japan in Transformation, 1952–2000.* New York: Longman, 2001.

Maley, William, ed. *Fundamentalism Reborn? Afghanistan and the Taliban.* New York: New York University Press, 1998.

———. *The Afghanistan Wars.* New York: Palgrave, 2002.

Matray, James Irving. *Japan's Emergence as a Global Power.* Westport, CT: Greenwood, 2001.

McLeod, John. *The History of India.* Westport, CT: Greenwood, 2002.

McMahon, Robert. *The Cold War on the Periphery: The United States, India, and Pakistan.* New York: Columbia University Press, 1994.

Rotter, Andrew J. *Comrades at Odds: The United States and India, 1947–1964.* Ithaca: Cornell University Press, 2000.

Schaller, Michael. *The American Occupation of Japan: The Origins of the Cold War in Asia.* Oxford, UK: Oxford University Press, 1987.

Stueck, William W. *The Korean War: An International History.* Princeton, NJ: Princeton University Press, 1997.

Thornton, Richard. *Odd Man Out: Truman, Stalin, Mao, and the Origins of the Korean War.* Herndon, VA: Brasseys, 2000.

Yong, Tan Tai. *The Aftermath of Partition in South Asia.* New York: Routledge, 2000.

Central America and South America

Booth, John A. *Understanding Central America.* Boulder: Westview, 1999.

Chomsky, Noam. *Turning the Tide: U.S. Intervention in Central America and the Struggle for Peace.* Cambridge: South End, 1986.

Conniff, Michael. *Panama and the United States: The Forced Alliance.* Athens: University of Georgia Press, 1992.

Domínguez, Jorge I., and Abraham F. Lowenthal, eds. *Constructing Democratic Governance: South America in the 1990s.* Baltimore: Johns Hopkins University Press, 1996.

Fursenko, Aleksandr, and Timothy Naftali. *One Hell of a Gamble: Khrushchev, Castro, and Kennedy, 1958–1964.* New York: W. W. Norton, 1997.

Gambone, Michael. *Eisenhower, Somoza, and the Cold War in Nicaragua, 1953–1961.* Westport, CT: Praeger, 1997.

Gleijeses, Piero. *Shattered Hope: The Guatemalan Revolution and the United States, 1944–1954.* Princeton, NJ: Princeton University Press, 1991.

Gordon, Lincoln. *Brazil's Second Chance: En Route Toward the First World.* Washington, DC: Brookings Institution, 2001.

Graham-Yooll, Andrew. *Imperial Skirmishes: War and Gunboat Diplomacy in Latin America.* New York: Interlink Books, 2002.

Lafeber, Walter. *Inevitable Revolutions: The United States and Central America.* New York: W. W. Norton, 1993.

Lake, Anthony. *Somoza Falling: A Case Study of Washington at Work.* Amherst: University of Massachusetts Press, 1990.

Leonard, Thomas M. *Castro and the Cuban Revolution.* Westport, CT: Greenwood, 1999.

Paterson, Thomas. *Contesting Castro: The United States and the Triumph of the Cuban Revolution*. New York: Oxford University Press, 1994.

Romero, Luis Alberto. *A History of Argentina in the Twentieth Century*. University Park: Pennsylvania State University Press, 2002.

Russell, Philip L. *Mexico Under Salinas*. Austin, TX: Mexico Resource Center, 1994.

Strong, Simon. *Shining Path: Terror and Revolution in Peru*. New York: Times Books, 1992.

Trento, Angelo. *Castro and Cuba*. New York: Interlink Books, 1999.

Vazeilles, José Gabriel. *Historia argentina: etapas económicas y políticas, 1850–1983* (The History of Argentina: Economic and Political Stages, 1850–1983). Buenos Aires, Argentina: Editorial Biblos, 1997.

Vitale, Luis, et al., eds. *Para recuperar la memoria histórica: Frei, Allende y Pinochet* (To Recover the Historical Memory: Frei, Allende, and Pinochet). Santiago de Chile: Ediciones Chile América, 1999.

China

Chang, Gordon H. *Friends and Enemies: The United States, China, and the Soviet Union, 1948–1972*. Stanford: Stanford University Press, 1990.

Chen, Jian. *China's Road to the Korean War*. New York: Columbia University Press, 1996.

Christensen, Thomas J. *Useful Adversaries: Grand Strategy, Domestic Mobilization, and Sino-American Conflict, 1947–1958*. Princeton, NJ: Princeton University Press, 1996.

Edmonds, Richard Louis, ed. *The People's Republic of China After 50 Years*. New York: Oxford University Press, 2000.

Foot, Rosemary. *The Practice of Power: U.S. Relations With China Since 1949*. New York: Oxford University Press, 1995.

Meisner, Maurice J. *Mao's China and After: A History of the People's Republic*. New York: Free Press, 1999.

Mosher, Steven W. *Hegemon: China's Plan to Dominate Asia and the World*. San Francisco: Encounter Books, 2000.

Sheng, Michael M. *Battling Western Imperialism: Mao, Stalin, and the United States*. Princeton, NJ: Princeton University Press, 1997.

Tucker, Nancy B. *Taiwan, Hong Kong, and the United States, 1945–1992: Uncertain Friendships*. New York: Twayne, 1994.

Wang, Qinxing K. *Hegemonic Cooperation and Conflict: Postwar Japan's China Policy and the United States*. Westport, CT: Praeger, 2000.

Zhai, Qiang. *The Dragon, the Lion, and the Eagle: Chinese, British, American Relations, 1949–1958*. Kent, OH: Kent State University Press, 1994.

———. *China and the Vietnam Wars, 1950–1975*. Chapel Hill: University of North Carolina Press, 2000.

Zhang, Shu Guang. *Deterrence and Strategic Culture: Chinese-American Confrontations, 1949–1958*. Ithaca: Cornell University Press, 1993.

Europe

Birmingham, David. *Portugal and Africa*. New York: St. Martin's, 1999.

Bronstone, Adam. *European Union–United States Security Relations*. Basingstoke, UK: Macmillan, 1997.

Burgess, Michael. *Federalism and European Union: The Building of Europe, 1950–2000*. London: Routledge, 2000.

Gasteyger, Curt. *Europa von der Spaltung zur Einigung, 1945–1997* (Europe from Division to Unification, 1945–1997). Bonn, Germany: Bundeszentrale für Politische Bildung, 1997.

Chamberlain, Muriel Evelyn. *Decolonization: The Fall of the European Empires.* Oxford, UK: Blackwell, 1999.

Costigliola, Frank. *France and the United States: The Cold War Alliance Since World War II.* New York: Twayne, 1992.

Dietl, Ralph, and Franz Knipping, eds. *Begegnung zweier Kontinente: Die Vereinigten Staaten und Europa seit dem Ersten Weltkrieg* (Encounter of Two Continents: The United States and Europe Since the First World War). Trier, Germany: Wissenschaftlicher Verlag Trier, 1999.

Dimbleby, David, and David Reynolds. *An Ocean Apart: The Relationship Between Britain and America in the Twentieth Century.* London: Hodder and Stoughton, 1988.

Dobson, Alan P. *Anglo-American Relations in the Twentieth Century: Of Friendship, Conflict, and the Rise and Decline of Superpowers.* London: Routledge, 1995.

Garton Ash, Timothy. *In Europe's Name: Germany and the Divided Continent.* New York: Random House, 1993.

Greenwood, Sean. *Britain and the Cold War, 1945–1991.* London: Macmillan, 2000.

Hacke, Christian. *Weltmacht wider Willen: Die Aussenpolitik der Bundesrepublik Deutschland* (Unwilling Global Power: The Foreign Policy of the German Federal Republic). Frankfurt am Main, Germany: Ullstein, 1993.

Haftendorn, Helga. *NATO and the Nuclear Revolution: A Crisis of Credibility, 1966–1967.* Oxford, UK: Oxford University Press, 1996.

———. *Deutsche Aussenpolitik zwischen Selbstbeschränkung und Selbstbehauptung, 1945–2000* (German Foreign Policy Between Self-Restriction and Self-Assertion, 1945–2000). Stuttgart, Germany: Deutsche Verlags-Anstalt, 2001.

Hanrieder, Wolfram F. *Deutschland, Europa, Amerika: Die Aussenpolitik der Bundesrepublik Deutschland, 1949–1994* (Germany, Europe, America: The Foreign Policy of the German Federal Republic 1949–1994). Paderborn, Germany: Schöningh, 1995.

Heller, Francis H., and John R. Gillingham. *NATO: The Founding of the Atlantic Alliance and the Integration of Europe.* Basingstoke, UK: Macmillan, 1992.

Heuser, Beatrice, and Robert O'Neill. *Securing Peace in Europe, 1945–1962: Thoughts for the Post–Cold War Era.* Basingstoke, UK: Macmillan, 1991.

Hillgruber, Andreas. *Europa in der Weltpolitik der Nachkriegszeit, 1945–1963* (Europe in the World Politics of the Post-War Period, 1945–1963). Vienna: R. Oldenbourg, 1993.

Hogan, Michael J. *The Marshall Plan: America, Britain, and the Reconstruction of Western Europe, 1947–1952.* Cambridge, UK: Cambridge University Press, 1987.

Kaplan, Lawrence S. *NATO and the United States, Updated Edition: The Enduring Alliance.* New York: Twayne, 1994.

———. *The Long Entanglement: NATO's First Fifty Years.* Westport, CT: Praeger, 1999.

Lappenküper, Ulrich. *Die Deutsch-Französischen Beziehungen, 1949–1963: Von der "Erbfeindschaft" zur "Entente élémentair"* (Franco-German Relations,

1949–1963: From Historical Feud to "Entente Elementair"). Munich, Germany: Oldenbourg, 2001.

Lynch, Philip, et al., eds. *Reforming the European Union: From Maastricht to Amsterdam.* New York: Longman, 2000.

Maier, Klaus A., and Norbert Wiggershaus, eds. *Das Nordatlantische Bündnis, 1949–1956* (The North Atlantic Alliance, 1949–1956). Munich, Germany: R. Oldenbourg, 1993.

Mantovani, Mauro. *Schweizerische Sicherheitspolitik im Kalten Krieg (1947–1963): Zwischen angelsächsischem Containment und Neutralitäts-Doktrin* (Swiss Security Policy in the Cold War [1947–1963]: Between Anglo-Saxon Containment and the Doctrine of Neutrality). Zurich: Orell Füssli Verlag, 1999.

Mastny, Vojtech. *Reassuring NATO: Eastern Europe, Russia, and the Western Alliance.* Defence Studies 5/1997. Oslo: Norwegian Institute for Defence Studies, 1997.

McAllister, Richard. *From EC to EU: An Historical and Political Survey.* London: Routledge, 1997.

Ninkovich, Frank A. *Germany and the United States: The Transformation of the German Question Since 1945.* Boston: Twayne, 1995.

Paxton, Robert O., and Nicholas Wahl, eds. *De Gaulle and the United States: A Centennial Reappraisal.* New York: Berg, 1994.

Ramet, Sabrina P. *Balkan Babel: The Disintegration of Yugoslavia from the Death of Tito to the Fall of Milosevic.* Boulder: Westview, 2002.

Risse-Kappen, Thomas. *Cooperation Among Democracies: The European Influence on U.S. Foreign Policy.* Princeton, NJ: Princeton University Press, 1997.

Salmon, Trevor, and Sir William Nicoll, eds. *Building European Union: A Documentary History.* Manchester, UK: Manchester University Press, 1997.

Schöllgen, Gregor. *Die Aussenpolitik der Bundesrepublik Deutschland: Von den Anfängen bis zur Gegenwart* (The Foreign Policy of the German Federal Republic: From the Beginning to the Present). Munich, Germany: C. H. Beck, 1999.

Sell, Louis. *Slobodan Milosevic and the Destruction of Yugoslavia.* Durham, NC: Duke University Press, 2002.

Smyser, William R. *From Yalta to Berlin: The Cold War Struggle over Germany.* London: Macmillan, 1999.

Soutou, Georges-Henri. *L'alliance uncertaine: Les rapports politico-stratégiques franco-allemands, 1954–1996* (The Uncertain Alliance: The Franco-German Politico-Strategic Rapport, 1954–1996). Paris: Fayard, 1996.

Springhall, John. *Decolonization Since 1945: The Collapse of European Overseas Empires.* New York: St. Martin's, 2000.

Trachtenberg, Marc. *A Constructed Peace: The Making of the European Settlement, 1945–1963.* Princeton, NJ: Princeton University Press, 1999.

Tusa, Ann. *The Last Division: A History of Berlin, 1945–1989.* Reading, MA: Addison-Wesley, 1997.

Vaïsse, Maurice. *La grandeur: Politique étrangère du générale de Gaulle, 1958–1969* (The Greatness: General De Gaulle's Foreign Policy, 1958–1969). Paris: Fayard, 1998.

Middle East

Bard, Mitchell Geoffrey. *The Complete Idiot's Guide to Middle East Conflict.* Indianapolis, IN: Alpha Books, 1999.

Ben-Yehuda, Hemda, and Shmuel Sandler. *The Arab-Israeli Conflict Transformed: Fifty Years of Interstate and Ethnic Crises.* Albany: State University of New York Press, 2002.

Bialer, Uri. *Oil and the Arab-Israeli Conflict, 1948–1963.* New York: St. Martin's, 1999.

Bickerton, Ian J. *A Concise History of the Arab-Israeli Conflict.* Englewood Cliffs, NJ: Prentice Hall, 1995.

Brands, Henry W. *Into the Labyrinth: The United States and the Middle East, 1945–1993.* New York: McGraw-Hill, 1994.

Cleveland, William L. *A History of the Modern Middle East.* Boulder: Westview, 1999.

Edelheit, Hershel. *Israel and the Jewish World, 1948–1993: A Chronology.* Westport, CT: Greenwood, 1995.

Elliott, Liza. *Finding Palestine.* Pasadena, CA: Hope, 2002.

Farah, Toufeé. *The Arab-Israeli Conflict.* Woodbridge, NJ: Ken and Scatter, 1998.

Fisher, Sydney Nettleton. *The Middle East: A History.* New York: McGraw-Hill, 1997.

Freund, Wolfgang, ed. *Palestinian Perspectives.* New York: Peter Lang, 1999.

Goldscheider, Calvin. *Cultures in Conflict: The Arab-Israeli Conflict.* Westport, CT: Greenwood, 2001.

Gorst, Anthony, and Lewis Johnman. *The Suez Crisis.* London: Routledge, 1997.

Hatina, Meir. *Islam and Salvation in Palestine: The Islamic Jihad Movement.* Tel Aviv: Moshe Dayan Center for Middle Eastern and African Studies, Tel Aviv University, 2001.

Karsh, Efraim, ed. *Israel: The First Hundred Years.* London: International Specialized Book Service, 2000.

Kelly, Saul, and Anthony Gorst. *Whitehall and the Suez Crisis.* Portland: Frank Cass, 2000.

La Guardia, Anton. *Holy Land, Unholy War: Israelis and Palestinians.* London: John Murray, 2001.

Lefebvre, Denis. *L'affaire de Suez* (The Suez Affair). Paris: B. Leprince, 1996.

Lesch, Ann Mosely. *Origins and Development of the Arab-Israeli Conflict.* Westport, CT: Greenwood, 1998.

Little, Douglas. *American Orientalism: The United States and the Middle East Since 1945.* Chapel Hill: University of North Carolina Press, 2002.

Mansour, Camille. *Beyond Alliance: Israel in U.S. Foreign Policy.* New York: Columbia University Press, 1994.

Marshall, Edgar S., ed. *Israel: Current Issues and Historical Background.* New York: Nova Science, 2002.

Ovendale, Ritchie. *The Origins of the Arab-Israeli Wars.* New York: Addison Wesley Longman, 1999.

Rogan, Eugene L., and Avi Shlaim, eds. *The War for Palestine: Rewriting the History of 1948.* New York: Cambridge University Press, 2001.

Schulze, Kirsten E. *The Arab-Israeli Conflict.* New York: Longman, 1999.

Schulze, Reinhard. *A Modern History of the Islamic World.* New York: New York University Press, 2000.

Sicker, Martin. *The Middle East in the Twentieth Century.* Westport, CT: Praeger, 2001.

Smith, Charles D. *Palestine and the Arab-Israeli Conflict.* Boston: Bedford and St. Martin's, 2001.

Tal, Yi´sra'el. *National Security: The Israeli Experience.* Westport, CT: Praeger, 2000.

Thomas, Baylis. *How Israel Was Won: A Concise History of the Arab-Israeli Conflict*. Lanham, MD: Lexington Books, 1999.

Tibi, Bassam. *Conflict and War in the Middle East: From Interstate War to New Security*. New York: St. Martin's, 1998.

Wagner, Heather Lehr. *Israel and the Arab World*. Philadelphia: Chelsea House, 2002.

Wasserstein, Bernard. *Divided Jerusalem: The Struggle for the Holy City*. New Haven: Yale University Press, 2001.

Soviet Union, Russia, and Eastern Europe

Acton, Edward. *Russia: The Tsarist and Soviet Legacy*. London: Longman, 1995.

Adomeit, Hannes. *Imperial Overstretch: Germany in Soviet Policy from Stalin to Gorbachev*. Baden-Baden, Germany: Nomos Verlagsgesellschaft, 1998.

Bennett, Andrew. *Condemned to Repetition? The Rise, Fall, and Reprise of Soviet-Russian Military Interventionism*. Cambridge: MIT Press, 1999.

Beukel, Erik. *American Perceptions of the Soviet Union as a Nuclear Adversary*. London: Pinter, 1990.

Chubarov, Alexander. *Russia's Bitter Path to Modernity: A History of the Soviet and Post-Soviet Eras*. New York: Continuum, 2001.

Colton, Timothy J. *Commissars, Commanders, and Civilian Authority: The Structure of Soviet Military Politics*. Cambridge: Harvard University Press, 1979.

Crozier, Brian. *The Rise and Fall of the Soviet Empire*. Rocklin, CA: Forum, 1999.

Dukes, Paul, ed. *Russia and Europe*. London: Collins and Brown, 1991.

———. *The Superpowers: A Short History*. New York: Routledge, 2000.

Dziewanowski, Kazimierz M. *A History of Soviet Russia and Its Aftermath*. Upper Saddle River, NJ: Prentice Hall, 1993.

Garton Ash, Timothy. *We the People: The Revolution of '89 Witnessed in Warsaw, Budapest, Berlin, and Prague*. Cambridge: Granta, 1990.

Goncharov, Sergei N., John W. Lewis, and Xue Litai. *Uncertain Partners: Stalin, Mao, and the Korean War*. Palo Alto: Stanford University Press, 1993.

Holloway, David. *Stalin and the Bomb: The Soviet Union and Atomic Energy, 1939–1956*. New Haven: Yale University Press, 1994.

Kokoshin, Andrei A. *Soviet Strategic Thought, 1917–1991*. Cambridge: MIT Press, 1998.

Kenez, Peter. *A History of the Soviet Union from the Beginning to the End*. New York: Cambridge University Press, 1999.

MacKenzie, David. *A History of Russia, the Soviet Union, and Beyond*. Belmont, CA: Wadsworth/Thomson Learning, 2002.

Mastny, Vojtech. *The Cold War and Soviet Insecurity: The Stalin Years*. New York: Oxford University Press, 1996.

Lewin, Moshe. *Russia–USSR–Russia: The Drive and Drift of a Superstate*. New York: W. W. Norton, 1995.

Nogee, Joseph L., and Robert H. Donaldson. *Soviet Foreign Policy Since World War II*. New York: Macmillan, 1992.

Powaski, Ronald E. *The Cold War: The United States and the Soviet Union, 1917–1991*. Oxford, UK: Oxford University Press, 1997.

Read, Christopher. *The Making and Breaking of the Soviet System: An Interpretation*. New York: Palgrave, 2001.

Roeder, Philip G. *Red Sunset: The Failure of Soviet Politics*. Princeton, NJ: Princeton University Press, 1993.

Rubinstein, Alvin Z. *Moscow's Third World Strategy*. Princeton, NJ: Princeton University Press, 1989.

Service, Robert. *A History of Twentieth-Century Russia*. Cambridge: Harvard University Press, 1999.

Streissguth, Tom, ed. *The Rise of the Soviet Union*. San Diego: Greenhaven, 2002.

Thompson, John M. *A Vision Unfulfilled: Russia and the Soviet Union in the Twentieth Century*. Lexington, MA: D. C. Heath, 1996.

Treadgold, Donald W. *Twentieth Century Russia*. Boulder: Westview, 2000.

Zubok, Vladislav, and Constantine Pleshakov. *Inside the Kremlin's Cold War: From Stalin to Khrushchev*. Cambridge: Harvard University Press, 1997.

United States

Acheson, Dean. *Present at the Creation: My Years at the State Department*. New York: W. W. Norton, 1969.

Ambrose, Stephen E. *Rise to Globalism: American Foreign Policy Since 1938*. New York: Penguin Books, 1991.

Bagby, Wesley M. *America's International Relations Since World War I*. Oxford, UK: Oxford University Press, 1999.

Ball, George. *The Past Has Another Pattern*. New York: W. W. Norton, 1982.

Brands, Henry W. *The Specter of Neutralism: The United States and the Emergence of the Third World, 1947–1960*. New York: Columbia University Press, 1990.

———. *The Devil We Knew: Americans and the Cold War*. Oxford, UK: Oxford University Press, 1993.

———. *The United States in the World: A History of American Foreign Policy*. Boston: Houghton and Mifflin, 1994.

Brown, Seyom. *The Faces of Power: Constancy and Change in United States Foreign Policy from Truman to Reagan*. New York: Columbia University Press, 1983.

Builder, Carl H. *The Masks of War: American Military Styles in Strategy and Analysis*. Baltimore: Johns Hopkins University Press, 1989.

Bundy, McGeorge. *Danger and Survival: Choices About the Bomb in the First Fifty Years*. New York: Random House, 1988.

Cohen, Warren I., and Walter Lafeber, eds. *The Cambridge History of American Foreign Relations: America in the Age of Soviet Power, 1945–1991*. New York: Cambridge University Press, 1993.

Freedman, Lawrence. *Kennedy's Wars: Berlin, Cuba, Laos, and Vietnam*. Oxford, UK: Oxford University Press, 2000.

Friedberg, Aaron L. *In the Shadow of the Garrison State*. Princeton, NJ: Princeton University Press, 2000.

Gaddis, John L. *The United States and the Origins of the Cold War, 1941–1947*. New York: Columbia University Press, 1972.

———. *Strategies of Containment: A Critical Appraisal of Postwar American National Security Policy*. New York: Oxford University Press, 1982.

———. *We Now Know: Rethinking Cold War History*. New York: Oxford University Press, 1997.

Garthoff, Raymond L. *A Journey Through the Cold War: A Memoir of Containment and Coexistence*. Washington, DC: Brookings Institution, 2001.

George, Alexander, and Richard Smoke. *Deterrence in American Foreign Policy: Theory and Practice*. New York: Columbia University Press, 1974.

Grose, Peter. *Operation Rollback: America's Secret War Behind the Iron Curtain*. Boston: Houghton and Mifflin, 2000.

Hastedt, Glen P. *American Foreign Policy: Past, Present, Future*. Upper Saddle River, NJ: Prentice Hall, 1999.

Hogan, Michael. *A Cross of Iron: Harry S. Truman and the Origins of the National Security State*. New York: Cambridge University Press, 1998.

Hoopes, Townsend, and Douglas Brinkley. *FDR and the Creation of the U.N.* New Haven: Yale University Press, 1997.

Hunt, Michael. *Crisis in U.S. Foreign Policy: An International History Reader*. New Haven: Yale University Press, 1995.

Immermann, Richard H. *John Foster Dulles and the Diplomacy of the Cold War*. Princeton, NJ: Princeton University Press, 1990.

Johnson, Robert. *Improbable Dangers: U.S. Conceptions of Threat in the Cold War and After*. New York: Palgrave Macmillan, 1994.

Kennan, George F. *Memoirs, 1925–1950*. New York: Pantheon Books, 1967.

———. *American Diplomacy*. Chicago: University of Chicago Press, 1984.

Kissinger, Henry. *White House Years*. Boston: Little Brown, 1979.

———. *Years of Upheaval*. Boston: Little Brown, 1982.

———. *Years of Renewal*. New York: Simon and Schuster, 1999.

Kunz, Diane. *The Diplomacy of the Crucial Decade*. New York: Columbia University Press, 1994.

———. *Butter and Guns: America's Cold War Economic Diplomacy*. New York: Free Press, 1996.

Lafeber, Walter. *America, Russia, and the Cold War, 1945–1996*. New York: McGraw-Hill, 1997.

Leffler, Melvyn. *A Preponderance of Power: National Security, the Truman Administration, and the Cold War*. Stanford: Stanford University Press, 1991.

Lindsay, James M. *Congress and the Politics of U.S. Foreign Policy*. Baltimore: Johns Hopkins University Press, 1994.

May, Ernest R., and Philip D. Zelikow, eds. *The Kennedy Tapes: Inside the White House During the Cuban Missile Crisis*. Cambridge: Harvard University Press, 1997.

Mayer, Michael S. *The Eisenhower Presidency and the 1950s*. Lexington, MA: D. C. Heath, 1998.

Miscamble, Wilson D. *George F. Kennan and the Making of American Foreign Policy, 1947–1950*. Princeton, NJ: Princeton University Press, 1992.

Mitrovich, Gregory. *Undermining the Kremlin: America's Strategy to Subvert the Soviet Bloc*. Ithaca: Cornell University Press, 2000.

Ninkovich, Frank. *Modernity and Power: A History of the Domino Theory in the Twentieth Century*. Chicago: University of Chicago Press, 1994.

Schrecker, Ellen. *Many Are the Crimes: McCarthyism in America*. Princeton, NJ: Princeton University Press, 1999.

Smith, Tony. *America's Mission: The United States and the Worldwide Struggle for Democracy in the Twentieth Century*. Princeton, NJ: Princeton University Press, 1995.

Snow, Donald M. *National Security: A USA Perspective*. Basingstoke, UK: Macmillan, 1998.

Trachtenberg, Marc. *History and Strategy*. Princeton, NJ: Princeton University Press, 1991.

Wenger, Andreas. *Living With Peril: Eisenhower, Kennedy, and Nuclear Weapons.* Lanham, MD: Rowman and Littlefield, 1998.

Vietnam

Anderson, David L., ed. *Shadow on the White House: Presidents and the Vietnam War, 1945–1975.* Lawrence: University Press of Kansas, 1993.

Frey, Marc. *Geschichte des Vietnamkriegs: Die Tagödie in Asien und das Ende des amerikanischen Traums* (History of the Vietnam War: The Tragedy of Asia and the End of the American Dream). Munich, Germany: C. H. Beck, 1998.

Halberstam, David. *The Best and the Brightest.* New York: Random House, 1972.

Herring, George C. *America's Longest War: The United States and Vietnam, 1950–1975.* Boston: McGraw-Hill, 2002.

Kaiser, David E. *American Tragedy: Kennedy, Johnson, and the Origins of the Vietnam War.* Cambridge: Harvard University Press, 2000.

Karnow, Stanley. *Vietnam: A History.* New York: Penguin Books, 1983.

Lind, M. *Vietnam, the Necessary War: A Reinterpretation of America's Most Disastrous Military Conflict.* New York: Free Press, 1999.

Logevall, Frederik. *Choosing War: The Lost Chance for Peace and the Escalation of War in Vietnam.* Berkeley: University of California Press, 1999.

———. *The Origins of the Vietnam War.* New York: Longman, 2001.

McMaster, H. R. *Dereliction of Duty: Johnson, McNamara, the Joint Chiefs of Staff, and the Lies That Led to Vietnam.* New York: Harper Perennial Library, 1998.

McNamara, Robert S. *In Retrospect: The Tragedy and Lessons of Vietnam.* New York: Vintage, 1996.

Moss, George. *Vietnam: An American Ordeal.* Upper Saddle River, NJ: Prentice Hall, 2002.

Schulzinger, Robert D. *A Time for War: The United States and Vietnam, 1941–1975.* Oxford, UK: Oxford University Press, 1998.

Võ, Nguyên Giáp. *Unforgettable Days.* Hanoi: Foreign Languages Publishing House, 1975.

INTERNET RESOURCES

Key Documents

Atlantic Charter
http://www.let.leidenuniv.nl/history/rtg/res1/atlantic.htm

Brezhnev Doctrine
http://oll.temple.edu/hist249/course/Documents/brezhnev_doctrine.htm

George H.W. Bush's State of the Union Address, 1991 ("New World Order")
http://odur.let.rug.nl/~usa/P/gb41/speeches/su91ghwb.htm

Camp David Accords
http://www.ibiblio.org/sullivan/docs/CampDavidAccords.html

Dayton Accords
http://dosfan.lib.uic.edu/ERC/bureaus/eur/dayton/01DaytonContents.html

Gulf of Tonkin Resolution
http://webusers.anet-stl.com/~civil/docs-tonkinresolution1964.htm

Kennedy-Khrushchev Exchanges, 1961–1963
http://www.state.gov/www/about_state/history/volume_vi/exchanges.html

The "Long Telegram" by George F. Kennan
http://www.mtholyoke.edu/acad/intrel/longtel.html

NATO Double-Track Decision
http://www.nato.int/docu/basictxt/b791212a.htm

North Atlantic Treaty
http://www.nara.gov/exhall/featured-document/nato/nato.html

NSC-68
http://sun00781.dn.net/irp/offdocs/nsc-hst/nsc-68.htm

Potsdam Agreement
http://www.cnn.com/SPECIALS/cold.war/episodes/01/documents/potsdam.html

Ronald Reagan's "Evil Empire" Speech, 1983
http://odur.let.rug.nl/~usa/P/rr40/speeches/empire.htm

START I
http://www.defenselink.mil/acq/acic/treaties/start1/startoc.htm

The Antiballistic Missile Treaty
http://www.defenselink.mil/acq/acic/treaties/abm/abmtoc.htm

The Helsinki Final Act, 1975
http://www.seerecon.org/RegionalInitiatives/StabilityPact/helfa75e.pdf

Treaty of Maastricht
http://europa.eu.int/en/record/mt/top.html

Treaty of Rome
http://www.hri.org/docs/Rome57/

Truman Doctrine
http://www.whistlestop.org/study_collections/doctrine/large/doctrine.htm

UN Resolution 819
http://hq.nato.int/ifor/un/u930416a.htm

UN Security Council Resolution 242
http://memri.org/docs/UN242.html

Washington Declaration
http://www.nato.int/docu/pr/1999/p99–063e.htm

Document Collections

George Washington University
Source: The National Security Archive at George Washington University,
http://www.gwu.edu/~nsarchiv/. Extensive and thoroughly researched collection of
    documents.

Records Administration
Source: National Archives and Records Administration,
http://www.nara.gov/. Large collection of declassified U.S. governmental
    documents.

Modern History Sourcebook
Source: The Cold War Internet Modern History Sourcebook,
http://www.fordham.edu/halsall/mod/modsbook46.html. Historical documents,
    speeches, and treaties.

Leiden University
Source: Leiden University,
http://www.let.leidenuniv.nl/history/rtg/res1/histdoc.htm. Well-chosen collection of
    historical documents.

Other Resources

The Armonk Institute: Germany
Source: The Armonk Institute
http://www.armonkinstitute.org/resourcecenter/
Well-researched background papers on twentieth-century German history.

Asian Studies Search Engine
Source: Asian Studies WWW Virtual Library
http://coombs.anu.edu.au/WWWVL-AsianStudies.html
Search engine specializing in the Far East.

The Avalon Project
Source: The Avalon Project at the Yale Law School
http://www.yale.edu/lawweb/avalon/avalon.htm
Large and detailed collection of historical documents on twentieth-century
    history.

Britannica
Source: Britannica.com
http://www.britannica.com
Online encyclopedia providing introductory articles and further reference.

Canadian Forces College: Korea
Source: Information Resource Center, Canadian Forces College
http://wps.cfc.dnd.ca/links/milhist/korea.html
U.S.-Chinese relations, 1960–1998, illustrated with various documents.

Canadian Forces College: Vietnam
Source: Information Resource Center, Canadian Forces College
http://www.cfcsc.dnd.ca/links/milhist/viet.html
Extensive and diverse account of the Vietnam War.

CNN
Source: Cable News Network Interactive (CNN Perspectives series)
http://www.cnn.com/SPECIALS/cold.war/episodes/01/
Comprehensive and detailed overview of Cold War history and culture, including
    interviews and multimedia files.

Cold War International History Project
Source: Woodrow Wilson International Center for Scholars
http://cwihp.si.edu/
The Cold War International History Project provides historical documents and spe-
    cial publications.

Columbia University Middle East Studies
Source: Columbia University Middle East Studies
http://www.columbia.edu/cu/libraries/indiv/area/MiddleEast/index.html
Concise information on political violence, religion, and minorities.

Encyclopedia of the Orient
Source: Encyclopedia of the Orient
http://i-cias.com/e.o/index.htm
Detailed information on countries of the Middle East and North Africa, including
    history, economic data, and maps.

Federation of American Scientists
Source: Federation of American Scientists, Intelligence Resource Program
http://www.fas.org/irp/threat/terror.htm
Information on terrorist groups, with extensive background information on political
    violence.

International Relations and Security Network (ISN)
Source: Center for Security Studies at the ETH Zurich
http://www.isn.ethz.ch
The ISN is an initiative designed to promote the free flow of unclassified informa-
    tion and to facilitate cooperation through training and education using modern
    information technology. The ISN consists of a range of high-quality services
    for people involved in international relations and security policy.

Israel Ministry of Foreign Affairs
Source: Israel Ministry of Foreign Affairs
http://www.mfa.gov.il
Collection of policy statements and press releases, as well as links to recent news
    stories and to further information about Israel.

The Latin American Studies Program
Source: The Latin American Studies Program
http://www.rose-hulman.edu/~delacova/home2.htm
Many links to background articles on contemporary Latin America, U.S.–Latin
    America relations, the ancient history of Latin American civilizations, and
    related fields.

National Security Archive: U.S.-China
Source: National Security Archive Electronic Briefing Books
http://www.gwu.edu/~nsarchiv/NSAEBB/NSAEBB19/
Briefing book No. 19 describes U.S.-Chinese relations, 1960–1998, and is illustrat-
    ed with various documents.

The Non-Aligned Movement
Source: The Non-Aligned Movement
http://www.nam.gov.za/
Homepage of the Non-Aligned Movement, with information on its history, mem-
    bers, and activities.

Parallel History Project (PHP)
Source: Center for Security Studies at the ETH Zurich
http://www.isn.ethz.ch/php/
In response to the progressing declassification of NATO documents and the grow-
    ing availability of documents from the archives of the former Soviet bloc, the
    Parallel History Project on NATO and the Warsaw Pact seeks to collect, ana-
    lyze, and interpret these premier sources for the study of contemporary interna-
    tional history. By relating the documents to current security issues, the PHP
    enhances understanding by highlighting how the documents differ from the
    recent past. It explores how the different alliance experiences have influenced
    the attitudes and behavior of the present members of the enlarged NATO and
    the Partnership for Peace.

Political Resources
Source: Political Resources on the Net
http://www.politicalresources.net/
Lists international political websites by country, with links to parties, organizations,
    governments, media, and more.

Smitha
Source: Noncommercial page by Frank E. Smitha
http://fsmitha.com/h2/index.html

A detailed history of the twentieth century, giving a good overview.

Stanford University: Africa
Source: Stanford University Libraries and Academic Information Resources
http://www-sul.stanford.edu/depts/ssrg/africa/history.html
Large collection of links to information on the history of sub-Saharan Africa, including economic, military, and social history.

U.S. Government Printing Office: U.S.-China
Source: U.S. Government Printing Office
http://www.state.gov/www/about_state/history/vol_xxx/index.html
Detailed account of U.S.-Chinese relations, 1964–1968 (declassified material).

INDEX

387

ABOUT THE BOOK

TRACING THE EVOLUTION OF INTERNATIONAL RELATIONS SINCE THE ONSET OF THE Cold War, the authors of this innovative new textbook draw on recently available archival resources to vividly narrate world affairs from 1945 to the present.

Events are addressed chronologically, with attention to both their motivations and their significance. The focus is on issues of security in the very broadest sense, ranging from politics and economics to ecological and social problems. A distinctive feature of the text is the clear, concise explanation of the key theories and concepts of international relations, supplemented by an extensive glossary. In tying events to international relations theory, the authors succeed in making that theory accessible.

From the Cold War rivalry between the superpowers to the current concerns with global terrorism—including throughout the perspectives of the global south—this is a comprehensive and illuminating analysis designed for students of international relations, security studies, and world history.

Andreas Wenger is professor of international security policy and director of the Center for Security Studies at ETH Zurich (Swiss Federal Institute of Technology Zurich). His publications include *Russia's Place in Europe: A Security Debate* and *Nuclear Weapons into the 21st Century*. **Doron Zimmermann** has conducted research on British political, diplomatic, and military history at the Faculty of History, Cambridge University. He is the head of the Political Violence Movements Project at the Center for Security Studies at ETH Zurich.

405